CHARLES DARWIN AND VICTORIAN VISUAL CULTURE

D1323572

Although *The Origin of Species* contained just a single visual illustration, Charles Darwin's other books, from his monograph on barnacles in the early 1850s to his volume on earthworms in 1881, were copiously illustrated by well-known artists and engravers. Jonathan Smith explains how Darwin managed to illustrate the unillustratable – his theories of natural selection – by manipulating and modifying the visual conventions of natural history, using images to support the claims made in his texts. Moreover, Smith looks outward to analyze the relationships between Darwin's illustrations and Victorian visual culture, especially the late Victorian debates about aesthetics, and shows how Darwin's evolutionary explanation of beauty, based on his observations of color and the visual in nature, were a direct challenge to the aesthetics of John Ruskin. The many illustrations reproduced here enhance this fascinating study of a little known aspect of Darwin's lasting influence on literature, art, and culture.

JONATHAN SMITH is Professor of English at the University of Michigan-Dearborn. He has published widely on nineteenth-century literature and science, and is the author of *Fact and Feeling: Baconian Science and the Nineteenth-Century Literary Imagination* (1994).

CAMBRIDGE STUDIES IN NINETEENTH-CENTURY
LITERATURE AND CULTURE

General editor
Gillian Beer, *University of Cambridge*

Nineteenth-century British literature and culture have been rich fields for interdisciplinary studies. Since the turn of the twentieth century, scholars and critics have tracked the intersections and tensions between Victorian literature and the visual arts, politics, social organisation, economic life, technical innovations, scientific thought – in short, culture in its broadest sense. In recent years, theoretical challenges and historiographical shifts have unsettled the assumptions of previous scholarly synthesis and called into question the terms of older debates. Whereas the tendency in much past literary critical interpretation was to use the metaphor of culture as 'background', feminist, Foucauldian, and other analyses have employed more dynamic models that raise questions of power and of circulation. Such developments have reanimated the field. This series aims to accommodate and promote the most interesting work being undertaken on the frontiers of the field of nineteenth-century literary studies: work which intersects fruitfully with other fields of study such as history, or literary theory, or the history of science. Comparative as well as interdisciplinary approaches are welcomed.

A complete list of titles published will be found at the end of the book.

CHARLES DARWIN AND VICTORIAN VISUAL CULTURE

JONATHAN SMITH

CAMBRIDGE
UNIVERSITY PRESS

CAMBRIDGE UNIVERSITY PRESS

Cambridge, New York, Melbourne, Madrid, Cape Town, Singapore, São Paulo, Delhi

Cambridge University Press
The Edinburgh Building, Cambridge CB2 2RU, UK

Published in the United States of America by Cambridge University Press, New York

www.cambridge.org
Information on this title: www.cambridge.org/9780521135795

© Jonathan Smith 2006

First published 2006
First paperback edition 2009

Printed in the United Kingdom at the University Press, Cambridge

A catalogue record for this book is available from the British Library

ISBN 978-0-521-85690-4 hardback
ISBN 978-0-521-13579-5 paperback

Contents

Illustrations

Acknowledgments

While this book cannot claim to be of Darwinian importance, it was certainly written at a Darwinian pace, and over the course of more than a decade I have accumulated what sometimes feels like a Darwinian-sized set of debts of gratitude. Lee Sterrenburg and George Levine have not only read the entire manuscript but watched and encouraged its development. Susan Erickson, Barbara Gates, David Knight, Rosemary Jann, Bernie Lightman, Robert Patten, Richard Stein, and Rebecca Stott have graciously read and commented on individual chapters. I have benefited from conversations with Dame Gillian Beer and am particularly grateful for her desire to include this book as part of Cambridge's series on Nineteenth-Century Literature and Culture. I have benefited as well from conversations with John Brooke, Ann Datta, Gowan Dawson, Jim Endersby, Jim Helyar, Richard Kaye, Marsha Richmond, Martin Rudwick, Jim Secord, Rusty Shteir, Jonathan Topham, and Paul White. My work on John Gould is deeply indebted to the work and wisdom of the late Gordon Sauer. I've received help with specific questions from Graeme Gooday, Paul Barlow, Peter Morton, Bob Peck, and, like so many Victorianists, from the members of the VICTORIA listserv. From Geoffrey Cantor, Sally Shuttleworth, Harriet Ritvo, and Laura Walls I have received general assistance and support that has helped this book come to be. At Cambridge University Press, Linda Bree has been a patient and encouraging editor.

This project would not have been possible without the helpful assistance of many librarians, curators, and archivists. I'm especially grateful to the staff at the University of Michigan libraries, in particular Franki Hand in Special Collections, Charlene Stachnik at the Museums Library, and Chris Anderson at the Herbarium Library; the Darwin Correspondence Project, particularly Sheila Dean; the Manuscripts Room at the Cambridge University Library, particularly Adam Perkins and Godfrey Waller. At the Natural History Museum in London I owe thanks to Paul Cooper, at the Horniman Museum to David Allen, at the University of Kansas's Spencer Research

Library to Jim Helyar, at Case Western Reserve University's Kelvin Smith Library to Sue Hanson, at the Kalamazoo College Library to Paul Smithson, at the University of Chicago Library to Barbara Gilbert, at the Missouri Botanical Gardens Library to Linda Oestry, at the Royal Academy Library to Andrew Potter, at the Wedgwood Museum to Lynn Miller, at the Michigan State University Library to Peter Berg, and at the Ashmolean Museum to Rupert Shepherd. The interlibrary loan staff at both the University of Michigan-Dearborn's Mardigian Library and Eastern New Mexico University's Golden Library processed many requests for me.

I am extremely grateful for financial support from the National Endowment for the Humanities, the Horace R. Rackham School of Graduate Studies and the Office of the Vice President for Research at the University of Michigan-Ann Arbor, and the Office of Research and Sponsored Programs (particularly Drew Buchanan) at the University of Michigan-Dearborn. This book would not have been researched, written, or illustrated without the generous assistance of each. I also express my deep thanks to Dan Little at Dearborn and Lee Bollinger, Nancy Cantor, and Paul Courant at Ann Arbor for their personal and professional kindnesses.

For a semester largely spent thinking and writing about Darwin at Eastern New Mexico University, I cannot adequately express my gratitude to the extraordinary Jack Williamson, or to my friends and colleagues there, especially Mary Ayala, Nina Bjornsson, Colin Ramsey, and Jerry Spotswood. Words are even more inadequate for thanking my friends and colleagues at Dearborn, in particular Elias Baumgarten, Suzanne Bergeron, Larry Berkove, Scott DeGregorio, Susan Erickson, Jim Gruber, Elton Higgs, Paul Hughes, Maureen Linker, Jim Knight, Sheryl Pearson, Bruce Pietrykowski, Pat Smith, Jackie Vansant, and Kathy Wider.

Finally, Bree Loverich and Marcie Holowicki provided research assistance on the project, Belinda Soliz made sure the manuscript looked good and helped obtain the illustrations, Charlie Myers digitized most of the images, and Christian McDavid kept track of the funds. I am grateful to each.

Earlier versions of parts of Chapters 2, 3, and 4 have appeared in *Reshaping Christianity: Innovation and Pluralization in the Nineteenth Century* (Ashgate, 2001), *The Book Collector*, and *Science Serialized: Representations of the Sciences in Nineteenth-Century Periodicals* (MIT Press, 2004).

Finally, I am thankful for my wife, Michelle, whose love reminds me daily of the power of things unseen.

Note on the texts

Unless otherwise noted, references to Charles Darwin's published works are taken from *The Works of Charles Darwin*, edited by Paul H. Barrett and R. B. Freeman, 29 vols. (New York: New York University Press, 1986–89) and are cited parenthetically in the text. All references to John Ruskin's works are from *The Works of John Ruskin*, Library Edition, edited by E. T. Cook and Alexander Wedderburn, 39 vols. (London: George Allen, 1903–1912) and are noted parenthetically in the text.

CHAPTER I

Seeing things: Charles Darwin and Victorian visual culture

Charles Darwin and Victorian Visual Culture examines the illustrations in Darwin's books from his *Monograph* on barnacles in the early 1850s to his volume on earthworms in 1881, and their relationships to Victorian visual culture and aesthetics. I begin with the barnacle book, his last major work before *The Origin of Species*, because even though it does not mention natural selection, Darwin had already developed his theory and privately found confirmation of his evolutionary views in his surprising barnacle discoveries. In my focus on the publications that followed the *Origin*, I treat not just those that extended the *Origin*'s theoretical project (*The Descent of Man* and *The Expression of the Emotions*), but also the under-studied books on plants and earthworms that both reflect Darwin's experimental interests and overtly sought to expand and buttress the *Origin*'s arguments. Although the *Origin* itself contains just a single illustration, all these other works are copiously illustrated in a range of media, from wood engraving to lithography to photography, by some of the best-known artists and engravers of the period. Despite both considerable recent scholarly interest in the visual, and a body of scholarship on Darwin so extensive as to be deemed an "industry," literary and cultural critics of Darwin on the one hand, sociologists of science, historians of science, and art historians on the other, have paid limited attention to the visual component of his work. This is all the more surprising when we consider that Darwin faced a very basic visual problem: how could natural selection, a concept almost by definition impossible to illustrate directly, be illustrated, especially when the existing visual conventions of the natural sciences were associated in varying degrees with conceptions of species fixity?

In focusing on how illustrations are constructed and their meanings determined, sociologists and historians have tended to rely on the notion that the meaning of images is determined largely by the accompanying text. Literary and cultural studies scholars, on the other hand, while aware that the ambiguities and instabilities of language make control over meaning and audience more problematic, have tended to give short shrift to the original scientific context that so interests historians and sociologists. Instead, these scholars have focused on the way scientific images "travel" in a culture, doing different ideological work in different ideological contexts. In this study I attempt to synthesize these two approaches by looking at the interface between them. I approach Darwin's works as what W. J. T. Mitchell calls "imagetexts." In *Picture Theory*, Mitchell argues that "all media are mixed media," and thus that an illustrated text is better conceived not as a juxtaposition of two media but as a composite, synthetic work combining image and text. Imagetexts, however, are not seamless. When gaps or ruptures emerge between textual and visual representation, the imagetext becomes an "image/text." At such moments representation itself becomes an issue, and the migration of the image into the broader culture is facilitated.[1] These concepts are useful for analyzing the work of Darwin and his opponents. The obstacles to illustrating natural selection made Darwin especially dependent on the symbiosis of visual and textual languages, and they led him to work largely within existing visual conventions rather than inventing new ones more amenable to his theory and his purposes. I thus examine the ways Darwin avoids, manipulates, and modifies these existing conventions in particular works, and I focus on the interplay between his images and texts. As a counterpoint, I also provide similar analyses of the imagetexts of several of Darwin's opponents and of the ways both sides attempted to expose and exploit the instability of their opponents' visual and textual languages. I analyze not just the construction of imagetexts but also their destabilization and breakdown, and the ideological stakes involved both before and after their migration into the broader culture.

My project here thus also connects the illustrations of Darwin and his opponents to Victorian visual culture, to issues of religion and morals, class and nation, gender and sexuality, race and empire. But the most prominent focus, the one that will weave its way throughout this study, is the impact of Darwin on Victorian aesthetic debates, particularly the central role his evolutionary accounts of beauty and color had for the development of a materialist aesthetics that differed fundamentally from the enormously influential views of John Ruskin, the great Victorian critic of art and society. While Ruskin's hostility to Darwinism is well known and has become much more thoroughly understood over the last two decades, I hope to provide here an important and overlooked or at least under-appreciated reason for that hostility. I argue that Darwin's work provided a direct and fundamental challenge to Ruskinian aesthetics, and that Ruskin understood this and sought to counter it. Darwin naturalized the human aesthetic sense in *The Descent of Man*, making our notion of beauty an evolutionary inheritance from animals. In several of his botanical books, Darwin similarly naturalized the existence of color in flowers, arguing that color was an evolutionary adaptation for attracting insects to ensure cross-pollination. Beauty for Darwin was neither a Divine gift to brighten our days nor a sign of moral and spiritual health, as it was for natural theologians and Ruskin, but a utilitarian trait generated by and for evolutionary survival. Coupled with other contemporary work on the physiology of the senses (particularly sight and hearing) and physiological approaches to psychology, these elements of Darwin's theories were central to a new "physiological" (or "evolutionary," or sometimes "empiricist" – the terms varied) aesthetics popularized aggressively in the 1870s and 80s, particularly by Grant Allen, that often positioned itself against Ruskin. Ruskin fought back, and he did so with increasing virulence as the threat posed by physiological aesthetics to his own positions became clearer and more forceful. My point, it should be stressed, is not that Ruskin's *real* objection to Darwinism was aesthetic, but that for Darwin and his followers as well as for Ruskin, the aesthetic, the scientific, and the ideological were inextricably connected. And needless to say, much more was at stake for the Darwinists and the Ruskinians than the philosophical understanding of beauty. At stake was Victorian artistic and visual culture, and Victorian culture generally – the nature of its politics, its social relations, its wealth, its beliefs, its families, its environments.

In the remainder of this introduction, I will develop more fully the arguments and contexts I have just sketched: the importance and functions of Darwin's illustrations; their relation to Victorian visual culture and aesthetics, especially the conflict between physiological and Ruskinian aesthetics; and the lessons that Darwin's imagetexts have for our understanding of scientific illustration and the interplay of word and image in science.

DARWIN'S ILLUSTRATIONS

Opening the final chapter of *The Origin of Species*, Darwin described his book as "one long argument." It was sufficiently long, he felt, that before concluding with ruminations upon his argument's implications for natural history, for the origin and future of organic life, and even for religion, a recapitulation of its major points was required. Forced to publish prematurely when Alfred Russel Wallace sought his assistance with a paper outlining remarkably similar views, Darwin regretted from the outset that this "Abstract," as he called the *Origin*, lacked the references and detailed evidence contained in his "big book" on natural selection, still incomplete after some twenty years. "I can here give only the general conclusions at which I have arrived," he lamented in the Introduction to the *Origin*, "with a few facts in illustration."

But the *Origin* offers limited "illustration" in another and more obvious sense: it contains just a single visual illustration. While Darwin often speaks vividly to the mind's eye, most memorably in the closing paragraph's evocation of a "tangled bank," he has little to offer the reader's physical eye. This may well seem unsurprising, and it certainly is not much noticed. The *Origin* is, after all, as Darwin said, an argument. Insistently textual, it does its work with words, not pictures. A great deal of modern scholarship, by literary critics, historians of science, and rhetoricians, has demonstrated the subtleties and complexities of that textual work. From the influence of *Paradise Lost*, to the definition of "progress," to the function of the elaborate analogy between natural and artificial selection, the *Origin* is arguably science's most closely-parsed text.[2]

Although historians of science have recently begun to devote sustained and serious study to the role of visual material in science, almost no attention has been paid to the visual component of Darwin's work. Martin Rudwick, in his innovative article on the "visual language" of nineteenth-century geology, comments that Darwin "seems to have been exceptionally 'non-visual' as far as the *communication* of his observations and theories was concerned."[3] Rudwick's claim is clearly right in the case of the *Origin*, and it is accurate as an assessment of Darwin's own "artistic competence" in relation to the drawing ability not only of the nineteenth-century geologists with whom he most closely identified himself at least until the mid-1840s, but also of most of the zoologists and botanists among his contemporaries. Geology, zoology, and botany required some competence in draftsmanship, both for observational sketches and more finished drawings, but Darwin's private writings are hardly rich in such visual material, and those that exist are rather crude. In developing illustrations for his books, he had to rely heavily on others and frequently borrowed images that had already been published elsewhere. Compared to the illustrations in other works of natural history, whether aimed at popular, elite, or professional audiences, Darwin's can appear eclectic, derivative, even at times simplistic.

Yet the lack of illustrations in the *Origin* is more striking when we look at the rest of Darwin's work. Unlike his notebooks and letters, his books are rich in illustrations. The five-part *Zoology* of the *Beagle* voyage contains 166 plates, including fifty colored lithographs of birds by John and Elizabeth

Gould and forty-nine uncolored lithographs of fish and reptiles by Benjamin Waterhouse Hawkins. The illustrations for the three parts of the *Geology* of the voyage are not nearly as lavish, but forty-four in-text wood engravings are supplemented in one part by three endpapers and in another by five endpapers (four of them drawn by G. B. Sowerby, Jr.) and a foldout map of the southern part of the continent at the beginning. His *Monograph* on barnacles (1851, 1854) contains forty plates of living species by G. B. Sowerby and seven of fossil species taken from G. B. and James de Carle Sowerby's *Mineral Conchology*. Most of his botanical books of the 1860s and 70s are dominated by wood-engraved in-text figures rather than separate plates: *Orchids* (1862; 2nd edition 1877) has thirty-three, *Climbing Plants* (1865; 2nd edition 1875) has thirteen, *Insectivorous Plants* (1875) has thirty, *Different Forms of Flowers* (1877) has fifteen, and *The Power of Movement in Plants* (1880) has 196. *Different Forms of Flowers* and *Cross and Self Fertilisation* (1876; 2nd edition 1878), on the other hand, are illustrated primarily with tables (thirty-eight and 106, respectively). Wood-engraved text figures also predominate in the non-botanical, post-*Origin* publications: *The Variation of Animals and Plants Under Domestication* (1868; 2nd edition 1875) has forty-three, *The Descent of Man, and Selection in Relation to Sex* (1871; 2nd edition 1874) has seventy-six, and *The Formation of Vegetable Mould Through the Action of Worms* (1881) has fifteen. *The Expression of the Emotions in Man and Animals* (1872) contains twenty-one wood engravings and seven heliotype plates of photographs.[4]

The visual fortunes of Darwin's first book, his *Journal of Researches* of the *Beagle* voyage, are also revealing. It initially appeared in 1839 as one of the four volumes of Captain Robert Fitzroy's *Narrative of the Surveying Voyages of HMS Adventure and Beagle Between the Years 1826 and 1836*. Although it was issued separately just a few months later, Darwin had less initial control over his "first literary child" than he did with his subsequent books. Two large fold-out maps accompanied it, but the text itself was sparsely illustrated with only a few figures. In 1845, when Darwin negotiated a revised, stand-alone edition with John Murray, he was able to secure some additional text figures, but to Darwin's disappointment, the maps were omitted.[5] Even in 1860, when Murray reprinted the *Journal*, presumably capitalizing on demand created by the furor over the *Origin*, Darwin was unable to convince him to restore the maps.[6] Much later, after Darwin's death, Murray brought out an illustrated edition that not only included the maps but added twelve plates and drastically increased the number of figures to ninety-three. Both author and publisher appreciated the value of illustrations and understood their readers would expect a work full of them.

The nature and quality of the visual materials in Darwin's books varied. He used tables, maps, schematic and abstract diagrams, naturalistic illustrations of plants and animals, and photographs of humans. These were reproduced using a variety of techniques in different media: wood engraving, copper engraving, lithography, photoengraving, heliotypy. Some illustrations were copied from other sources; some were commissioned; others were produced by his sons. Well-connected both scientifically and socially, Darwin was able to secure enough external financial support to ensure that even his early publications were well illustrated. A Government grant of £1000 funded the publication of both the *Zoology* and *Geology* of the *Beagle* voyage. The Ray and Palaeontographical Societies, which financed publications from their members' annual subscription fees, brought out the parts of his barnacle *Monograph* devoted to living and fossil species, respectively. Later in his career, Darwin had the money and leverage to guarantee that even with commercial publication his books were illustrated as he desired, and his correspondence is littered with letters dealing in whole or part with visual matters. He sought out some of the best artists and illustrators: Joseph Wolf, W. H. Fitch, G. B. Sowerby, Briton Riviere, T. W. Wood. In several cases, as in his recruiting of John Gould to produce the lithographs for the *Zoology* of the *Beagle* voyage and his use of numerous photographs for *The Expression of the Emotions*, he proved himself to be innovative or at least sensitive to visual trends. As Phillip Prodger confirms in his extensive work on the illustrations for the *Expression*, Darwin oversaw his visual materials with great attention and care.[7]

The illustrations in Darwin's books played important roles in his arguments, and he could deploy them with great skill. The single illustration in the *Origin* is a case in point (fig. 1.1). It is a diagram, introduced in the chapter on natural selection. Offered as an aid in understanding the effects of natural selection on the descendants of a common ancestor, and in particular the principle of divergence, the diagram was, Darwin told Murray, *"indispensable."*[8] Like many of the *Origin*'s textual illustrations, it begins as an idealized, hypothetical case – a thought-experiment. A to L represent the species of a large genus inhabiting a particular geographical region. Each horizontal line represents a thousand or more generations. The dotted lines emanating from A and I – the two most common, widely-diffused, and widely-varying species – represent slightly varying offspring. When a dotted line reaches one of the horizontal lines, a small numbered letter indicates that sufficient variation has occurred to form a well-marked variety. (On the principle that the most divergent variations are preserved and accumulated

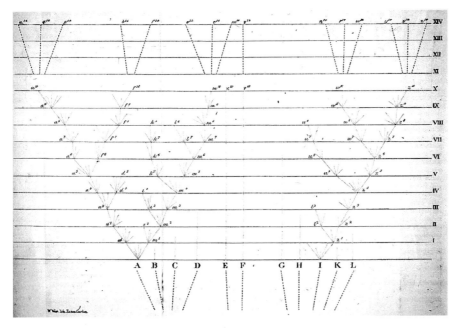

Figure 1.1   Diagram from Charles Darwin, *On the Origin of Species* (London: Murray, 1859), between pages 116 and 117.

by natural selection, the outer dotted lines are the ones that lead to varieties.) This process continues with the varieties up to horizontal line X, after which Darwin presents a simplified and condensed version of it. By the ten-thousandth generation, species A has evolved into three different species (a10, f10, m10); by the fourteen-thousandth generation, it has evolved into eight species (a14 to m14). The original species A, as well as intermediate varieties and species, have become extinct. So, too, have species B, C, and D, which survived for a time but were eventually displaced by the descendants of A. Only one of the original species, F, the most distinct from A and I, survives to the fourteen-thousandth generation. From eleven species, then, fifteen emerge, their relationships to each other and their ancestors different and generally more distinct than in previous generations. So distinct, says Darwin, that we are to imagine the ultimate descendants of A and I to constitute two separate genera, or at least sub-genera.

The diagram, then, is a remarkably economic representation of the effects of natural selection, even incorporating several specific Darwinian principles related to divergence of character and extinction. It is also flexible. Allow each horizontal line to represent a million generations, Darwin says, and the diagram can depict the formation of two families or orders. Or, visualize the horizontal lines as a section of the strata of the earth's crust and the diagram becomes a representation of the fossil record. Darwin uses the diagram in precisely this way much later in the *Origin*, near the end of his two chapters on geology. He demonstrates visually that the imperfection of the fossil record, far from being a problem for his theory, is actually predicted by it. He shows why the oldest fossils generally differ most from existing ones, while some are virtually identical, and how it is that distinct species from consecutive geological formations can be so closely related.

The diagram does not occur in a vacuum; it utilizes and modifies visual conventions of geology and natural history, conventions themselves shaped in part by artistic and literary precursors. As a rendering of natural selection's effects on a group of species, the diagram is a visual corollary of Darwin's evolutionary version of the "Tree of Life." "The affinities of all the beings of the same class have sometimes been represented by a great tree," Darwin writes, and "I believe this simile largely speaks the truth." But he gives this common taxonomic icon, with its Biblical echoes, a more truly organic gloss:

The green and budding twigs may represent existing species; and those produced during each former year may represent the long succession of extinct species. At each period of growth all the growing twigs have tried to branch out on all sides, and to overtop and kill the surrounding twigs and branches, in the same manner as species and groups of species have tried to overmaster other species in the great battle for life. The limbs divided into great branches, and these into lesser and lesser branches, were themselves once, when the tree was small, budding twigs; and this connexion of the former and present buds by ramifying branches may well represent the classification of all extinct and living species in groups subordinate to groups. Of the many twigs which flourished when the tree was a mere bush, only two or three, now grown into great branches, yet survive and bear other branches; so with the species which lived during long-past geological periods, very few of which have left living and modified descendants.[9]

Species are not specially created, suddenly introduced, and then withdrawn according to divine plan, but evolve from other species, and survive and modify or become extinct, in a natural and contingent manner. As Gillian Beer remarks, for Darwin, tree imagery generally is "a condensation of real events, rather than a metaphor."[10]

Similarly, when read downward on the page and backward in time, the diagram evokes the visual conventions of geological sections.[11] While roughly similar in various ways to both traverse and columnar sections, the diagram is even more idealized. Traverse sections, which imagined the strata beneath a section of landscape sliced vertically as they would appear in a quarry or a cliff, attempted to capture the basic contours of the beds and the surface topography, complete with faults and folds and angles of orientation. Columnar sections, on the other hand, depicted strata as they were thought to have been originally laid down, eliminating disturbances to present an essentially horizontal view of the order and relative thickness of the layers. These sections had become highly schematized by the time Darwin took up geology in the early 1830s, but his diagram, with its flat "top" and equidistant horizontal lines, gestures even less at an actual landscape and its strata. For Darwin of course depicts not a particular locale, but a generalized section that can stand, at least in theory, for any spot on earth. In essence he makes the diagram palimpsestic by inviting his readers to superimpose his "tree of life" onto a geological section, thereby creating an evolutionary view of paleontology.

Not all of the illustrations in Darwin's books are as rich and as important as this diagram. But many are. And virtually every one serves more than a merely "illustrative" purpose. Each is there because Darwin wanted it to be. Most, in fact, are the result of a whole series of choices – about what was to be depicted; how it was to be obtained; who was to draw it; in what medium it was to be reproduced and by whom; whether it was to be colored; where it was to be located in the text and whether it was to be grouped with other figures; how it was to be sized, oriented, cropped, and captioned. Like his prose, Darwin's illustrations were assembled in an often laborious, painstaking manner. He clearly saw them as significant components in the communication of his observations and theories. I will thus be providing in this book many readings of Darwin's illustrations, elucidating their contributions to his arguments, and explaining how he utilizes, manipulates, and sometimes departs from existing conventions in scientific illustration to achieve his desired ends.

Understanding the function of Darwin's illustrations is important, because Darwin faced a major illustrative difficulty: how was natural selection to be depicted *visually*? How could something that acts at such a leisurely pace on such tiny variations be captured directly? Gillian Beer, George Levine, and James Krasner have all demonstrated the representational obstacles faced by Darwin in the *Origin* in rendering his theory textually, and Krasner has shown how the new physiological understanding of vision and the eye as limited and imperfect, embraced by Darwin and incorporated into his argument, made the literal act of seeing as well as the textual depiction of the seen deeply problematic. That visual depiction of the unseen posed a comparable problem for him is thus not surprising and may have contributed to the paucity of illustrations in the *Origin*. Geologists, paleontologists, and comparative anatomists had already conjured up what Martin Rudwick calls "scenes from deep time," illustrations of life in primeval seas and prehistoric landscapes, but natural selection was not a phenomenon, an event, or a thing, but a *process*. Darwin was asking his readers to visualize how one scene modified into another via a mechanism that, unlike geological forces, could not be directly observed in the present.

Moreover, many of the conventions of scientific illustration and the assumptions underlying them, including the concept of species itself, were not congenial, and even downright hostile, to Darwin's evolutionary views. According to Ann Shelby Blum, by 1850 professional zoological publications, concerned primarily with taxonomy and usually under cost constraints, tended to depict "several species resting on a single plane, or floating in a space of indeterminate depth" (fig. 1.2). The stylistic hallmark of these plates was what Blum calls "graphic fluency": an emphasis on detail and symmetry with an implied light source beyond the upper-left-hand corner that gave the plate "classical overtones." While such composite plates facilitated the comparative methods then dominating zoology, the goal of comparison was to clarify rather than to blur the boundaries between species, or between species and varieties.[12] The absence from the plates of any environmental background or context also clearly posed a problem for Darwin. Yet as we have already seen in the case of the *Origin*'s diagram, and as we will see in the case of the barnacle *Monograph* (the work of Darwin's that most closely follows the visual conventions of professional, taxonomic natural history), Darwin was both fully aware of the underlying assumptions and traditional uses of these conventions, and adept at manipulating them for his own purposes.

The zoological illustrations in more popular works of natural history at least offered Darwin images of the animal in nature. Such images did not have a particularly long history. Through most of the eighteenth century, animals were usually depicted without a background; when one appeared, it had more to do with providing perspectival orientation than displaying habitat. This became the common mode of representation in works based on the Linnaean system, with its morphological focus. Illustrations indebted to those of Linnaeus's contemporary, the great French naturalist Georges-Louis Leclerc, Comte de Buffon, who stressed the taxonomic importance of an animal's habits, life cycle, and habitat as well, finally made some gesture towards providing an appropriate landscape background.[13] This Buffonian mode was more common in popular works in the early nineteenth century, but it of course emphasized stability and

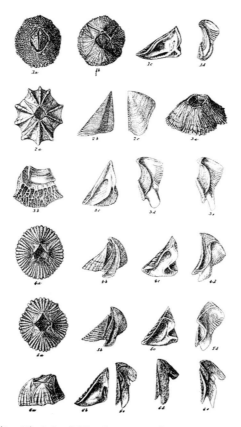

Figure 1.2 "Tetraclita: Elminius." Wood engraving by G. B. Sowerby, Jr. Plate XI from Charles Darwin, *A Monograph of the Sub-Class Cirripedia; The Lepadidae; or, Pedunculated Cirripedes* (London: Ray Society, 1851).

symbiosis rather than competition between animal and environment, and species were no less immutable for Buffon than they were for Linnaeus. In England, William Paley's functionalist natural theology had ensured that depictions of animals in nature were seen as confirmations of Providential wisdom, goodness, and power – animals and their various anatomical features were divinely designed to occupy particular niches in the natural economy.

The problems faced by Darwin are clearly evident in the specific case of ornithology. In the eighteenth century, birds were most frequently depicted in ornithological publications with only the barest of props – gripping a bit of a branch or standing atop a stump. Multiple figures were often arranged on the same plate, with little effort to convey three-dimensionality and

Figure 1.3 "The Bearded Titmouse." Wood engraving by Thomas Bewick, *A History of British Birds*, vol. 1 (Newcastle, 1797), 246.

sometimes with no consistency in scale. This "bird-and-branch" mode remained influential into the nineteenth century. Even Thomas Bewick's magnificent wood engravings for *A History of British Birds* (1797, 1804), while providing a sense of both habitat and depth, did not so much locate the bird *in* a landscape as to position a landscape *behind* a "bird-and-branch" (fig. 1.3). Some thirty years later, when John Gould issued the first of his imperial folio bird books, the colored lithographic plates were very much in the "bird-and-branch" mode. Only gradually were Gould's birds pictured more dynamically and in the kind of lavish habitats found in J. J. Audubon's *Birds of America* (see figs. 1.4 and 3.4). Bewick and Gould were the most influential bird illustrators in nineteenth-century Britain, their images frequently copied in professional and popular ornithological publications. Gould was also arguably Victorian Britain's leading ornithologist, and while his folios were produced for a subscriber list dominated by aristocrats and affluent members of the upper-middle classes, he also intended his books to be used as reference tools by a professional audience. Darwin recruited Gould to examine his bird specimens when he returned from the *Beagle* voyage, owned several of the separately published introductions to Gould's books (some of them presentation copies from Gould), and frequently drew on

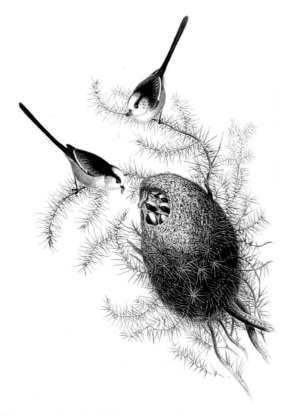

Figure 1.4 "Mecistura Caudata." Hand-colored lithograph of the long-tailed tit by John Gould and H. C. Richter from John Gould, *The Birds of Great Britain* (London, 1862–73), vol. II, plate 28.

Gould's work in the *Origin* and the *Descent*. Yet Gould, like Bewick, cast his work in explicitly natural theological terms, and his own book on British birds, begun not long after the appearance of the *Origin*, seems in many ways clearly a visual riposte to Darwin's theory.

Botanical illustration offered even less to work with.[14] Botanical treatises, like their zoological counterparts, were primarily interested in morphology as a basis for taxonomy. Different taxonomic commitments thus led to differences in how plants were depicted. With the rise of the Linnaean system in the eighteenth century, the flower and its sexual organs (the latter additionally represented in smaller dissection drawings on the same plate), the basis for classification, became prominent (fig. 1.5a). As the "natural system" of Jussieu and de Candolle, which relied on the totality of the plant's organs

Figure 1.5a "Orchis mascula." Hand-colored engraving from William Curtis, *Flora Londinensis* (1777–98), vol. 1, fasc. 2, plate 62.

ORDER LII. ORCHIDACEÆ.—ORCHIDS.

Orchides, *Juss. Gen.* 64. (1789).—Orchideæ, *R. Brown Prodr.* 309. (1810) ; *Rich. in Mém. Mus.* 4. 23.
(1818) ; *Bauer, Francis, and Lindley, Illustrations of Orchidaceous Plants ; Id. Genera and Species
of Orch.* (1830) . *R. Brown Observations on the Sexual Organs, &c. of Orchideæ and Asclepiadeæ*
(1831) ; *Endl. Gen.* lxvi.; *Meisner, Gen.* p. 367.—Vanillaceæ, *Ed. pr.* cexliv.

DIAGNOSIS.—*Orchidal Endogens, with irregular gynandrous flowers and parietal placentæ.*

Herbaceous plants or shrubs, always perennial, occurring all over the world, except in
the very coldest regions, or those where everlasting dryness reigns; in temperate countries
terrestrial, in warmer latitudes growing
on trees (epiphytes), or fixing themselves
to stones. Their roots are fibrous and
fasciculated, fleshy or resembling tubers,
and these filled with starch, or horny
nodules of bassorin. Stem none, or long
and annual, or perennial and woody,
forming a rhizome, or jointed branches.
Leaves flat, terete or equitant, generally
sheathing, membranous, coriaceous, or
hard, never lobed, occasionally bordered
by cartilaginous teeth, their veins parallel,
almost never slightly reticulated. Flowers
☿, irregular, extremely variable in form,
solitary, clustered, spiked, racemose, or
panicled, always supported by a solitary
bract ; very often most gratefully fragrant,

Fig. CXVII.

sometimes fetid, and not un-
frequently scentless. Peri-
anth adherent, variable, herbaceous or coloured, mem-
branous or fleshy, permanent
and withering, or deciduous ;
its parts arranged in two rows,
rarely in 3, free or adhering
in various ways ; very often
resupinate in consequence of
a twist in the ovary. Se-
pals (which, morphologically
speaking, are petals) 3, equal
at the base, or variously-ex-
tended or expanded there ;   Fig. CXVIII.
the two lateral standing in front when the ovary is twisted, and the third then dorsal, or

Fig. CXVII.—Herminium monorchis.
Fig. CXVIII.—Accidental manner of producing a jointed stem in Aspasia epidendroides.

Figure 1.5b Opening page of discussion of orchids from John Lindley, *The Vegetable
Kingdom*, 3rd edn. (London: Bradbury and Evans, 1853), 173. The two wood engravings of
orchid species depict the full plant, including the roots.

for classification, displaced the Linnaean in the nineteenth century, botanical illustrations shifted back to the whole plant (although with dissections often retained), reducing the flower to one aspect among many (fig. 1.5b). As Gill Saunders notes, however, with the exception of the seventeenth-century florilegia (flower books which focused on flowers from a decorative rather than a practical, medicinal, or scientific perspective), botanical illustrations invariably had one thing in common: the depiction of the plant in isolation, without reference to its habitat. The most conspicuous exception, Robert Thornton's *Temple of Flora* (1799–1807), an illustration of Linnaeus's sexual system that purported to render flowers in their natural settings, depicted many of the flowers inaccurately and in landscapes that had more to do with the aesthetics of the sublime, the beautiful, and the picturesque than with the plants' actual habitats.[15]

Darwin dealt with these obstacles not by abandoning the conventions and inventing a new visual language for the various components of natural history. Rather, he did mostly what we have seen him do in the case of the *Origin*'s diagram: he worked with the conventions where he could, modifying them in subtle but significant ways. But also as with the *Origin*'s diagram, his pictures could only be worth a thousand words through his spending thousands more in elucidating them. Darwin's Tree of Life looks different from that of his predecessors not because of anything in the illustration itself, but because of the text that surrounds it and directs us to see each part of each branch not as a separate creative act but as a process of descent with modification. When it came to picturing natural selection, Darwin had to rely heavily on the symbiosis of word and image.

To say that the meanings of Darwin's illustrations were determined and controlled by the text that accompanied them seems like common sense. But as Gillian Beer and George Levine have demonstrated, Darwin found language a slippery commodity. He was trying to deny the existence of a supervising agent in the evolution of species, yet agency is built into the structure of grammatical form. He was trying to refuse human beings a privileged spot in the natural order, yet human language is necessarily anthropomorphic. He was trying to replace cultural narratives about the origins and development of life with an account based solely on natural laws, but language is itself cultural, and for the nineteenth-century English gentleman, unavoidably infused with echoes of Genesis and Milton's *Paradise Lost*. And so the appropriation of Darwin's theory for a wide variety of different and even incompatible purposes, from atheism to Christian theism, from socialism to laissez-faire capitalism, was not merely inevitable but actually facilitated by Darwin's language. To take the most obvious example,

Darwin's analogy between natural selection and the artificial selection practiced by humans on domesticated animals seemed to imply that Nature was
doing the selecting. In that case, many readers argued, natural selection was
not replacing the teleology of the design argument but merely substituting
an abstract concept for the Deity. Darwin complained in subsequent editions of the *Origin* that he used natural selection metaphorically, that nature
no more "selects" than one body gravitationally "attracts" another, but to
little effect.

All of this suggests that in reading Darwin's illustrations we should attend
not just to the meanings he seems to intend for them, but to the potential
instabilities in those meanings and to the ways his illustrations are received
and appropriated. Such sensitivity to Darwin's difficulties in depicting natural selection also respects a paradox about the cultural response to Darwin
as a see-er: although praised even by his critics as a marvelous observer, he
was frequently accused of seeing what wasn't there. This is especially evident in reviews of the post-*Origin* works. By the time the *Origin* appeared,
Darwin had established his credentials through the various *Beagle* publications and the barnacle *Monograph* as a reliable, even gifted, observer. His
careful, judicious, thorough investigations led to surprising discoveries that
others had overlooked. His vista ranged from the microscopic in the case
of barnacles to the continental and global in the case of the geology of
South America, coral reefs, and volcanic islands. Working before the full
codification of what Lorraine Daston and Peter Galison call "mechanical
objectivity," in which the reliability of data was established wherever possible by reliance on self-recording devices rather than human observation,
Darwin earned a reasonably fair hearing for the *Origin* in considerable
degree because his earlier work had confirmed his status as a trustworthy
"gentleman of science" capable of treating even his own ideas and hypothe-
ses with skepticism, detachment, and critical distance, setting them aside
or modifying them as the evidence demanded.[16] But natural selection was
often decried as speculative or fanciful, a product of a wild imagination
rather than sober induction. In responding to Darwin's books of the 1860s
and 70s, most of which were loaded with the kind of original experiments and first-hand observations lacking in the *Origin*, many reviewers
lauded the data but denied the interpretation. Commenting on Darwin's
Orchids in the *Edinburgh Review*, the Duke of Argyll commended Darwin's
"inimitable powers of observation and description," but he utterly rejected
Darwin's recourse to natural selection as an explanation for orchids' strange
structures and fantastic color patterns, which for the Duke were clearly
the result of divine design.[17] As part of *The Unseen Universe* (1875), their

widely-read effort to demonstrate the compatibility between natural science, properly interpreted, and Christian doctrine, the Scottish physicists Balfour Stewart and P. G. Tait praised Darwin's work on pigeons but denied the validity of his analogy between artificial and natural selection.[18] Reviewing Darwin's *Expression of the Emotions* in 1873, T. S. Baynes admitted that "[o]f course the work contains a number of the careful observations . . . with which Mr. Darwin's writings abound," but he complained that Darwin's "zeal for his favourite theory" was undermining his scientific strengths: his "one-sided devotion to an a priori scheme of interpretation seems thus steadily tending to impair the author's hitherto unrivalled powers as an observer." The "disturbing element of speculative conjecture" in Darwin's theory, Baynes continued, had helped to bring about an alarming change "in the very conception of what is scientific . . . Instead of designating what is most rigorous, exact, and assured in human knowledge, natural science is fast becoming identified with what is most fluctuating, hypothetical, and uncertain in current opinion and belief." Far from chasing philosophy and religion from the Temple of Science, Darwinism had restored them, along with the worst vices of metaphysics and theology. Darwin deploys natural selection, Baynes joked, "with all the confidence of a theological disputant applying some dogmatic assumption, such as universal depravity or satanic influence, or defending some sectarian symbol, such as Sacramental Efficacy or an Effectual Call."[19]

Punch, amidst its various comic responses to the *Expression*, offered a variation on Baynes's complaint in a poetic "duet" between Science and Superstition.[20] Science complains of Superstition's credulous belief in table-turning, spirit-rapping, and the like. Hardly cowed, Superstition turns the accusation of irrationality and self-deceit back on Science. "Ancestral apes" are as much imaginative creations as the "airy shapes" of the spiritualists, and to "believe in without seeing" is surely an apt description of evolutionists when they trace every living being back to some hypothetical primeval "monad." Your "speculations" rest not on facts, Superstition shrewdly complains to Science, but on "materialist foundations / Now so dear to common sense." Like Baynes, Superstition objects not just to the equation of science with materialism, but to the positioning of speculative materialism as Huxleyan "common sense."

All parties in the Darwinian debates agreed that seeing is believing, but their confidence in ocular proof was no naive realism, for they argued vigorously about what counted as seeing and what it meant to believe. My title for this introduction, "Seeing things," is borrowed from Seamus Heaney's 1989 collection of poems because this ambiguous phrase captures the complex response to Darwin. Heaney plays on poetry's simultaneous concern with the quotidian and the mystical. In its attention to the details of the everyday world, poetry is an act of seeing *things*. But poetry often invests those everyday details with significance that transcends their physical existence, reading in them the signs of spiritual, moral, intellectual, or emotional truths. It is a poetics that melds the views of two Romantic poets Darwin read as a young man: Wordsworth and Shelley, the poet-philosopher of common life and the poet-prophet. As mystic, philosopher, or prophet, however, the poet is often accused of *seeing* things. He can be depicted as a self-deluded madman, more committed to the creations of his own brain than to reality itself. Science clearly reflects a similar desire both to describe things and to account for them in some larger scheme, even if that scheme is conceived as more directly concerned with physical rather than metaphysical matters. And scientists are clearly also vulnerable to being accused of seeing what is not there, or of seeing what they want to see.

That was certainly true (and remains so today) for Darwin and his opponents. Each condemned the other less for what was seen, than for how — although questioning the how was often a means for circling back to challenge the what. Darwin's supporters, particularly T. H. Huxley, sought to expose and expunge what Huxley called "ecclesiasticism" from natural science. People like the Duke of Argyll or the brilliant comparative anatomist Richard Owen, they complained, look at nature and see the hand, or at least the mind, of God. But the other side could respond, with considerable justification, as T. S. Baynes did, by turning the tables on the Darwinians and painting them as dogmatists on behalf of natural selection, a concept Darwin's critics often regarded as a piece of secular metaphysics. Even without responding in kind, those critical or skeptical of Darwin's theory could, and frequently did, express their discomfort with the speculative, inferential quality of the physical evidence in its favor. That the structures of orchids made their nectar accessible only to certain types of insects, and that this ensured cross-fertilization, was indisputable; that orchids and insects had evolved in tandem, and that cross-fertilization was itself a product of natural selection, was another matter entirely.

The picturing of natural selection, then, was a complicated, controversial, sometimes contradictory affair. Darwin needed and wanted to illustrate his work, but he had no new visual language with which to depict his new theory, and the nature of the material in any case militated against it. So he worked with existing conventions, and he relied on the interaction of his visual and textual languages to clarify each of them. Darwin's imagetexts are often remarkable in the subtle and original ways he sought to overcome both visual and textual obstacles to representing natural selection, and he was adept at exploiting the weaknesses in the imagetexts of his predecessors and opponents. But his own imagetexts were also often fragile and unstable, capable of challenge or counter-appropriation.

DARWIN, RUSKIN, AND VICTORIAN VISUAL CULTURE

The context and impact of Darwin's work were of course not simply scientific. Much of the historical scholarship on Darwin has traced the various sociocultural forces influencing his thinking as well as the various sociocultural uses to which his theories were put, religion and political economy being the most widely investigated. It should come as no surprise, then, that Darwin and his books were also part of Victorian *visual* culture, his ideas often enmeshed in aesthetic debates, his illustrations frequently refracting ways of seeing and modes of representation common to the worlds of both academic art and popular culture, his plates and figures sometimes circulating in new contexts. Stephen Jay Gould has traced back to Darwin's day the visual representation of evolution, particularly human evolution, as a linear, progressive process. Recent studies and biographies of Darwin have made us comfortable with the idea that he was sufficiently famous to be widely caricatured in Victorian illustrated periodicals, and that his controversial theories were sufficiently well known to be poked fun at in cartoons.[21] But visual jokes about human descent from apes are only the tip, even if a prominent tip, of a visual iceberg.

Just to stick for the moment to cartoons, consider that, in the three months following the appearance of Darwin's *Expression of the Emotions in Man and Animals* late in 1872, the Victorian humor magazine *Fun*, a competitor with the more popular *Punch*, published six cartoons devoted in whole or in part to the book.[22] The array of subjects and modes of treatment, as well as the variety of social issues touched upon, begins to suggest the broad visual impact of the *Expression*. Two of the cartoons exploit specific arguments from the book – Darwin's account of blushing and his general view of human emotional expressions as similar to those in animals. The first pictures Darwin as a monkey, taking the pulse of an elegantly-dressed young woman (fig. 1.6), while the second uses the birth of a baby hippopotamus at the Zoological Gardens as its scene. A third cartoon (fig. 1.7), in which a young man asks a young woman if she has read the book and is surprised to receive a very sophisticated characterization of it,

FUN.—November 16, 1872.

THAT TROUBLES OUR MONKEY AGAIN.

Female descendant of Marine Ascidian:—"REALLY, MR. DARWIN, SAY WHAT YOU LIKE ABOUT MAN; BUT I WISH YOU WOULD LEAVE MY EMOTIONS ALONE!"

Figure 1.6 "That Troubles Our Monkey Again." *Fun*, 16 November 1872.

EXACTLY SO !

Our friend Charley :—"Have you read Darwin's book, Miss Gib-
bons?"

Miss G. :—"Oh, yes."

Charley :—"And—ah—what do you think of it?"

Miss G. (who may have been asked the same question before) :—"I think it a
very exhaustive treatise upon the indeterminate modifications in
which the sensibilities of human nature are involved!"

[*Charley is rather sorry he spoke.*

Figure 1.7 "Exactly So!" *Fun*, 26 January 1873.

uses Darwin's work as a prop for an exploration of the relationship between
the sexes and a dig at both intellectual women and vapid men. Another
employs the title of the book for a contrast between Christmas Day drinking
and Boxing Day hangover. Two Valentine's Day cartoons are more direct:
one contains an unseen figure thumbing his nose at the *Expression*, while
the other parodies the book's illustrations by providing one "accidentally
omitted."

Figure 1.8   Heliotype reproduction of a photograph by Oscar Rejlander from Charles Darwin, *The Expression of the Emotions in Man and Animals* (London: Murray, 1872), plate 1, fig. 1. This photograph became known as "Ginx's Baby" after the title character in Edward Jenkins's 1870 novel.

The *Expression*'s importance for Victorian visual culture was not limited to cartoons, however. One of the photographs reproduced in the book, that of a crying child by the London photographer Oscar Rejlander (fig. 1.8), proved to be enormously popular. A reviewer christened it "Ginx's Baby," after the Radical writer Edward Jenkins's popular novel satirizing religious and social attitudes toward poor urban children, and the name stuck. Rejlander apparently objected to the appellation, but it didn't prevent him from selling thousands, possibly hundreds of thousands, of prints of the image.[23] While the *Expression*'s photographs drew the most attention from reviewers, its illustrations of animal expression were also noted, and many commented on the implications of Darwin's discussions for artists. Some felt Darwin had made a significant advance on Charles Bell's *Anatomy and Philosophy of Expression as Connected with the Fine Arts* (1844), while others bemoaned his apparent lack of aesthetic sophistication. One of the latter, T. S. Baynes, was especially blunt, seeing in Darwin's rejection of Bell a threat to the very structure of high culture: "Sir Charles Bell was not more decisively Mr. Darwin's superior as an anatomist and physiologist than as a man of taste and of literary and philosophical culture . . . Mr. Darwin apparently knows nothing of art, and certainly has no perception of its intimate relation to the subject he undertakes to expound."[24] Even the *Art Journal* weighed in. While refusing to comment on the evolutionary link between human and animal expression, it called the *Expression* a work of "undeniable utility" for painters and sculptors and opined that Edwin Landseer's superiority as an animal painter was rooted in his being, like Darwin, "a diligent student of facial expression."[25]

The *Expression*, by virtue of its topic and its illustrations, prompted more direct commentary about visual and aesthetic matters than Darwin's other works. But these other works and their illustrations were also tied to the broader visual and aesthetic culture. Darwin's barnacle *Monograph*, for example, appeared amidst the flood of illustrated books on seaside natural history issued from the late 1840s into the 1860s. As the extension of railways made coastal areas increasingly accessible, the seaside occupied a prominent place in the Victorian visual imagination, and whether in the pages of *Punch* or on the walls of the Royal Academy, its depiction often exposed cultural anxieties about class, sexuality, and religion. Similarly, the illustrations of livestock and pigeons for *The Variation of Animals and Plants Under Domestication* could not help but be seen against the very different social contexts of animal painting, traditionally associated with the aristocratic agricultural improver, and breeders' manuals, with their more urban, middle-class audiences. Many of Darwin's botanical books of the 1860s and 70s, often coupled with his discussion of sexual selection in birds from *The Descent of Man*, were appropriated for popularizations of physiological aesthetics. The illustrations of Darwin's last book, *The Formation of Vegetable Mould, Through the Action of Worms* (1881), especially the depictions of the role played by worms in the burial of ancient buildings and of worm castings themselves, could be viewed in relation to the visual conventions of the picturesque and the grotesque.

The contemporary who perhaps best understood and most strenuously resisted the implications of Darwin's work for visual culture and aesthetics was John Ruskin. Ruskin's acerbic comments about Darwinism in the 1870s and 80s are notorious, yet the awareness they reveal of Darwin's work, particularly of those books rarely read by modern scholars, and of the rival aesthetics that Darwin's theories developed and that was deployed by others against Ruskin's cultural authority on aesthetic issues, has not been appreciated.

Characterizing Ruskin's aesthetics is a complicated matter. He published prolifically for roughly half a century, and over that time he variously reaffirmed, modified, repudiated, and contradicted his earlier positions. When he published the fifth and final volume of *Modern Painters* in 1860, he asserted that none of his aesthetic principles had changed in essentials during the seventeen years that had elapsed since the appearance of the first volume, and yet that assertion was clearly necessitated by his wider exposure to art and the cooling of his evangelicalism. In the works of his later years, even as he referred back to his early books, he also continually revised them for new editions. That Ruskin's own comments on the history of his opinions are not always reliable only adds to the difficulty.

Whatever the developments, tensions, and inconsistencies in Ruskin's aesthetics, however, he adhered throughout his career to the basic positions articulated in the early volumes of *Modern Painters*, positions with which he was closely associated in the public mind: fidelity to nature, and the morality of art.[26] *Modern Painters* began as a defense of the work of J. M. W. Turner, then widely criticized for the seemingly fantastic landscapes of his late career. Defending Turner as the supreme landscapist not merely of the present time but of all time, Ruskin argued that it was Turner, not venerated seventeenth-century masters such as Claude Lorrain and Nicolas and Gaspar Poussin, who represented nature truthfully. Great art, Ruskin agreed, required careful observation and accurate reproduction, but Claude and the Poussins rarely depicted any natural form correctly, whether the leaves of trees, the colors of skies, the reflections in water, or the topography of mountains. They altered and manipulated for the sake of composition and effect, blithely fudging details. Their followers had then reified these inaccuracies into conventions, with the result, in Ruskin's view, that European landscape painting had virtually ceased to care about nature at all. In painstaking detail, Ruskin attempted to demonstrate that Turner, in faithfully painting what he saw rather than following conventions, actually achieved far greater truth to nature than his predecessors had.

Particularly in the second volume of *Modern Painters*, however, Ruskin makes clear that such objectivity is not a sufficient condition for the production of great art. He decries mere imitation or copying, and he criticizes the "ditch-water" realism of Dutch genre painting as sharply as the idealizations of Claude. For great art requires great (although not necessarily elevated) subjects, and great subjects are beautiful subjects, those in which higher truths – spiritual, moral truths – are to be found. Great artists are those rare figures of healthy and vigorous imaginations who can both see and depict these truths. They may thus, as Turner did, depart from strict adherence to what they see in nature, but the grounding of their "subjective" vision in physical truth is what enables them to elucidate the higher ones. Since for Ruskin nature is the creation of God, such faithful art is simultaneously an act of praise, a confirmation of divine attributes, and an uncovering of divine lessons for humankind. While both the depiction and experience of beauty bring pleasure, great art provides more than that. Pleasure is not the end of art, for art is not merely sensual but spiritual. Indeed, Ruskin rejects the term "aesthetic," arguing that to characterize the perception of beauty solely according to pleasure is "degrading it to a mere operation of sense."[27] The perception of beauty is, rather, a function of the moral faculty that Ruskin called, after Aristotle, "theoria," and the study of beauty should thus be called "theoretics" as opposed to aesthetics. While denying a simplistic equation of the beautiful with the true and the good, Ruskin insisted on their connection as a way of countering the utilitarian denigration of art without embracing what he saw as the sensuous amorality of "art for art's sake."

The importance of nature in Ruskin's life and aesthetics also fueled a lifelong interest in science. Like Darwin and so many other Victorians, Ruskin was a patient, careful, amazingly keen-sighted observer of the natural world. The sections of *Modern Painters* devoted to depictions of light and color, trees, water, atmospheric effects, and mountains often read more like disquisitions on optics, botany, meteorology, and geology than on art. A frequent commentator on science throughout his career, Ruskin later wrote books on ornithology (*Love's Meinie* [1873–81]), botany (*Proserpina* [1875–86]), and geology (*Deucalion* [1875–83]). For Ruskin, the study of nature for scientific purposes, properly pursued, was complementary to the properly-pursued study of nature for artistic purposes. His phenomenological visual program, characterized by Elizabeth Helsinger as "the art of the beholder," integrated art and science by stressing the moral health of the relationship between the observer, whether artist or scientist, and nature.[28] By faithfully representing what he sees rather than what he knows or thinks is there, the scientist, like the artist, is opened to the spiritual, moral, religious truths that nature reveals. The "objectivity" of scientists who investigate nature by focusing only on physical facts and physical causes is wrong-headed and barren, and often not objective at all. Like artists, scientists must aim higher than a merely material understanding of nature.

Ruskin's comments on the science of many of his famous contemporaries were caustic, however, and his own science seems strangely, even deliberately, anti-scientific. Some of his most sensitive and sympathetic critics have found them bewildering or embarrassing. Gradually, however, they have come to be seen as directed against the scientific naturalism of Darwin, John Tyndall, and T. H. Huxley.[29] There was much in the work and the pronouncements of these men, especially of Tyndall and Huxley, for Ruskin to loathe. Human descent from apes, protoplasm as the physical basis of life, thermodynamic analyses of the human body, consciousness as a molecular phenomenon – all of these were anathema to Ruskin. But fundamentally, it was the materialism of these explanations that galled him. Darwin, Huxley, and Tyndall tried to remove the soul from nature and man alike, and they explained every conceivable natural phenomenon, human beings and their attributes not excepted, as the result of physical causes. And Ruskin, like Thomas Carlyle before him, saw quite clearly the connection between scientific/philosophical materialism and the economic materialism that in his view was rending the Victorian social fabric as it soiled Victorian skies.

Although Ruskin's view of Victorian science is now seen more clearly, and his opposition to scientific naturalism is regarded as overdetermined, the degree to which Darwin's science challenged the very basis of Ruskin's aesthetics, and the pointedness with which it did so, has not been recognized as a major factor in that opposition. We tend to think of scientific naturalism as excluding the imagination, even as being anti-imaginative, but that was not so in Ruskin's day. In fact, part of the threat posed by scientific naturalism for figures like Ruskin was that it claimed the imaginative, aesthetic realm as its own. According to Tyndall, the scientific imagination was more amazing than the most fantastic flights of the poetic mind, but it had the additional advantage of providing empirical truths. More specifically and ominously for Ruskin, however, scientific naturalism claimed to account for aesthetics itself.

Modern readers of Darwin's *Descent of Man* have tended to concentrate on the first part of the book, in which Darwin argues for humanity's physical, mental, and moral descent from animals. While increasing attention has been paid to the second part of the *Descent*, in which Darwin developed his controversial theory of sexual selection to account for differences in secondary sexual characteristics between males and females throughout the animal world (most famously, the brilliant plumage and ornaments of many male birds), this work has focused largely on the theory's gender politics, a move that has tended to obscure the fact that Darwin is adding the human aesthetic sense, our notion of beauty, to his account of humanity's evolutionary inheritance from its non-human ancestors. Much of what we regard as beautiful among animals is, Darwin argued, the product of sexual selection by, and thus of an aesthetic sense in, females. Similarly, much of what we regard as beautiful among plants – the color and ornaments of flowers, and the colors of seeds and fruit – were, Darwin contended in his botanical books, evolutionary adaptations that attracted insects for cross-pollination and birds and other animals for seed dispersal. Flowers and fruit were not provided by a beneficent Creator for our pleasure and sustenance; they resulted from natural selection and the need of both plants

and animals to survive and reproduce. Meshing with both the new understanding of vision and hearing promulgated by Hermann von Helmholtz
and his followers, and the empiricist psychology of Alexander Bain, G. H.
Lewes, Herbert Spencer, and James Sully, Darwin's work in the *Descent* and
the botany books became a crucial part of a full-scale physiological aesthetics
that was being even more widely disseminated by popularizers like Grant
Allen.[30]

Ruskin saw, correctly, that physiological aesthetics posed a direct and virtually complete challenge to his own positions. However tempting to reduce
the source of his resistance either to the Victorian horror of human descent
from apes or to his well-documented personal queasiness about sexuality, we
ought to acknowledge that for Ruskin natural selection was also a rival. His
resistance was thus perfectly understandable, and the form it took had much
in common with the work of the many scientists and popularizers who continued to promulgate natural theology and to counter scientific naturalism
well after the appearance of the *Origin*. The story of late nineteenth-century
Victorian science was told largely by its Darwinian victors, and it has taken
time for historians to replace those biased, partial accounts with fuller, fairer
ones. Prominent among those stories was the notion that the *Origin* dealt a
death-blow to natural theology, and that only fundamentalist obscurantists
resisted the obvious truth in Darwin's work; in fact, many figures, scientists
and lay people alike, had no difficulty incorporating evolution into their
theology, while Darwin initially convinced very few people, even among his
closest allies, of the efficacy of natural and sexual selection. Literary scholars
in particular, however, still tend to read only the likes of Darwin, Huxley,
and Tyndall, and thus to assume that scientific naturalism is synonymous
with science. Viewed from such a perspective, Ruskin's science looks will-
fully perverse, hopelessly out of step. But Ruskin was not alone, and he was
unusual only in the specific forms his resistance took, not in the fact of his
resistance, nor in the substance of his critiques.

To say that Ruskin's opposition to Darwin was in large measure about
aesthetics is not to say that it was not ideological – the aesthetic is and was
ideological, most certainly so for Ruskin. Closing his chapter on flowers for
Proserpina, Ruskin takes note of "the speculations of modern science" on
"the relation of colour in flowers, to insects – to selective development,"
and acknowledges that there *is* such a relation. But it is only part, and a
comparatively unimportant part, of what we need to know about color and
flowers. The blush of a young girl on her lover's approach may be closely
related to the state of her stomach, he argues, but that doesn't mean that
love and chastity are functions of digestion. So it is with explanations of

the color of flowers, of the ornamental feathers of the Argus pheasant and the peacock, of the blue noses of mandrills. These examples are not casually chosen: they come directly from Darwin's recent work, from his botanical publications and *The Descent of Man*. Even the example of the blushing girl alludes to Darwin's extended discussion of blushing in *The Expression of the Emotions*. Lamenting Darwin's "ignorance of good art," Ruskin wishes he could have him in Oxford for a week, "and could force him to try to copy a feather of Bewick, or to draw for himself a boy's thumbed marble," for then "his notions of feathers, and balls, would be changed for the rest of his life." As it is, Darwin thinks that "mandrills' noses [are] the result of the admiration of blue noses in well-bred baboons. But it never occurs to him to ask why the admiration of blue noses is healthy in baboons, so that it develops their race properly, while similar maidenly admiration either of blue noses or red noses in men would be improper, and develop the race improperly" (xxv:263–64). And the proper development of the race is a matter of physical and moral health, with both of these dependent on the sky and earth and waters being free of poison and pestilence. At stake in the scientific question is an aesthetic question that is, for Ruskin, inevitably and inextricably a matter of morals, of industrialism, of race and gender. Natural selection's account of aesthetics and morals was wrong-headed, and it stemmed from Darwin's ignorance of art and inability to draw.

Darwin's own visual education was admittedly rather limited, and it made him vulnerable to attacks like those from Ruskin and Baynes. He grew up in Shrewsbury, near the Welsh border, far removed from major cultural centers. As a student at Edinburgh and Cambridge, he spent the bulk of his free time hunting and pursuing natural history. Unlike many young men of his social background, Darwin never took the Grand Tour of the European Continent that supplied the English gentleman with much of his cultural education and a first-hand encounter with western art and architecture. He made his only trip across the Channel at age eighteen, spending just a few weeks in Paris. His own Grand Tour aboard the *Beagle*, while far more grand in the geographical sense and at least as important as an exercise in character-building and preparation for life, included South America, South Africa, and Australia, but not Paris, Florence, and Rome. When, living in London after his return, he itemized the reasons to "Marry or Not Marry," Darwin listed seeing the Continent as one of the pleasures he would have to forego if he became a married man (xxix: 220). Whatever the logic involved in this conclusion, it proved accurate. He never visited the Louvre as an adult, never viewed the monuments of classical and renaissance Italy. Although interested in art, his letters as a young man freely express his need for aesthetic mentoring. The prints he purchased to decorate his Cambridge rooms were the result, he wrote to his brother, Erasmus, of "having imbibed your tastes about prints." From South America he asked his friend Charles Whitley to "take me in hand with respect to the fine arts" when he returned to England.[31] But Darwin proved to be no denizen of museums and galleries when back on home soil. He was furiously busy during those five years in London, working on his *Beagle* publications, reading on the species question, marrying, and starting a family. Despite a fairly active social life and connections to the literary and intellectual set in which Erasmus and their cousin, Hensleigh Wedgwood, were immersed, Darwin turned far more to the Zoological Society's Gardens, not the National Gallery or the Royal Academy Exhibitions, when he wanted a break. From the time he and wife Emma moved to Down in Kent in 1842, Darwin lived a life of relative seclusion, traveling to London infrequently, primarily for professional purposes.

Even so, Darwin was no visual illiterate. He became interested in art during his Cambridge years, frequently visiting the Fitzwilliam collection and even looking forward from the *Beagle* to seeing Titian's *Venus and Cupid with a Luteplayer* there once again.[32] In his *Autobiography*, he recalled of his trips to the Fitzwilliam that "my taste must have been fairly good, for I certainly admired the best pictures, which I discussed with the old curator." During this same period he read Reynolds's *Discourses* and took pleasure in many of the works at the National Gallery (xxix:102–03). In his *Journal of Researches* he casually refers to the sight of four soldiers playing cards around a campfire on the Argentine Pampas as "a Salvator Rosa scene" (ii:101–02). Later in life, as his earlier enthusiasms for poetry, Shakespeare, and music disappeared, he also "almost lost any taste for pictures," although he retained some love for fine scenery (xxix:158). Despite this "lamentable loss of the higher aesthetic tastes," Darwin remained attuned to Victorian visual culture. He corresponded with the Pre-Raphaelite sculptor Thomas Woolner (who had executed a bust of Darwin in 1868) about the rudimentary projections in the human ear that link us to our ape-like progenitors and reproduced a drawing by Woolner in the *Descent*. He read the illustrated papers. He scoured London's print and photographic shops in the late 1860s and early 1870s for reproductions of art works containing examples of human facial expression, and several of the books he owned on the subject contained extended analyses of such famous works. In 1871 he received an invitation to the Royal Academy's Anniversary Dinner.

Indeed, Darwin could not help but be visually alert, for he lived in a century and a culture that were relentlessly, explosively visual. William

Ivins has estimated that the number of prints produced in the nineteenth century was greater than the total number produced prior to that time, and that prints reached more people, in all social classes, and did so more frequently and pervasively, than ever before.[33] Multiple factors, technological and social, contributed to this. Among the most direct were the development and refinement of new reproductive media, particularly wood engraving, lithography, and photography. Late in the previous century, Thomas Bewick began to engrave on the end of blocks of boxwood and found that working against the grain of this finely-grained wood made possible a much sharper and narrower line. Wood engraving suddenly produced images whose details and tonalities were roughly comparable to those of copper engraving, but at a considerably reduced cost. More important, since wood blocks could be incorporated with text on a printing press, mass reproduction of image and text was feasible for the first time. As a result, illustrated books and periodicals issued forth in a seemingly ever-increasing torrent. Lithography, also developed during the early decades of the century, enabled artists to draw directly on the reproductive medium rather than making a sketch and then transferring it (or, more typically, having a skilled etcher or engraver transfer it) to wood or metal. Photography, which came on the scene in the 1840s, quickly established itself as far more than a novelty. Although the introduction of photographic prints into books was, owing to a variety of technical hurdles, a slow process, photography's cultural exposure became widespread with the introduction of the carte-de-visite in the 1850s. Coupled with these developments were the broader social and technological ones that made the reproduction and dissemination of images easier and cheaper, and created a wider audience to consume them. The industrialization of printing and papermaking, reductions in the paper tax, the creation of a railroad network, a rising literacy rate and expanded access to education, the ideologies of self-help and rational recreation – these are just some of the forces that, acting in various ways at various times, enabled the Victorians to take the visual turn.

At a more everyday but equally important level, it was a period of optical gadgetry and visual spectacle. The camera, camera lucida, stereoscope, kaleidoscope, phenakistiscope, and a host of other -scopes were all invented in the nineteenth century. In Ireland, the Earl of Rosse built a series of enormous telescopes, the largest of the large, six feet in diameter, christened "the Leviathan of Parsonstown." Drawings *of* these telescopes – including ones of men standing upright in the tube of the Leviathan – circulated at least as widely as the drawings of objects seen *through* them. Panoramas and dioramas were tremendously popular. Theaters proliferated. Printsellers flourished. Within a decade of its invention around 1850, the aquarium had become both a small-scale drawing-room amusement and a large-scale tourist attraction. All of this and much beside – from battles and revolutions to industrial and technological marvels to occasions of state – could be seen in the pages of illustrated papers such as the *Illustrated London News*, while the various "penny" publications provided the working classes with a steady visual diet. Whether we see this as marking the apex of a realistic visual culture stretching back to the renaissance or, with Jonathan Crary, as the launch of modernity and its focus on the subjectivity of the observer, it is clear that nineteenth-century Britain was a time when there was much to see, and a plethora of ways in which to see it.[34]

Both Darwin's account of aesthetics and the illustrations in his books were, in fact, generally if carefully aligned with this vibrant visual culture rather than the high art of the Royal Academy and National Gallery. For figures like Ruskin and T. S. Baynes, a physiological and evolutionary view of beauty was not only dangerous in itself but led to a coarsening of culture, while for disciples of Darwin like Grant Allen, a truly scientific aesthetics democratized taste and spelled an end to the authority of those Huxley would term, in his debate with Matthew Arnold, the "Levites of culture." This opposition was neither absolute nor always straightforward, and it was not the only area of aesthetic debate in decades also marked by the theories of Pater, Swinburne, and Whistler. But over and over in the later work of Darwin and Ruskin, we find the one using what the other condemns or rejects. "Good art" is entirely absent from the illustrations to the *Expression* even though treatises on expression prior to Darwin's invariably contained it, while portrait photography, which Ruskin disliked, is utilized for the first time in a work of English science. Where Darwin does evoke "good art" – as in an illustration of a dead pigeon rendered as a still-life for the *Variation* – it is almost always in a form or a medium that Ruskin loathed. For his own part, in his works on flowers and birds, Ruskin frequently challenges, in pictures as well as words, Darwin's most visually important representations, whether of orchids or primroses or peacock feathers. Although Ruskin left no record of his reaction to Darwin's final book on earthworms, it is easy to imagine his dismay at seeing on the one hand the grotesque display of worm castings, and on the other the conversion of England's most picturesque ruins – including Stonehenge, once powerfully rendered by Turner – into geological sections. But this would have merely reaffirmed for Ruskin what he already felt he knew well: that Darwin's imagetexts were intellectually, spiritually, morally, and aesthetically impoverished.

WORD AND IMAGE IN SCIENCE

For many years, scientific illustrations were studied almost exclusively by art historians rather than historians of science. Contributors to *Picturing Knowledge*, the collection of essays on art and science edited by Brian Baigrie, are in almost unanimous agreement that the positivist/empiricist approaches dominating the history and philosophy of science through the 1960s elevated the textual as the repository of scientific logic and rationality, relegating the visual to a secondary, ancillary, illustrative role.[35] The study of scientific illustrations during this period thus fell to art historians. But if historians of science tended to ignore the visual, art historians tended to pay little attention to the textual. Their work usually charted the evolution of iconography and illustrative techniques in a particular field of science, sometimes investigating the oeuvre of a major figure like Audubon. Illustrations were lifted out of their contexts, often with no attention to the science they were illustrating. Classic examples of this approach, such as Jean Anker's *Bird Books and Bird Art* and Wilfrid Blunt's *Art of Botanical Illustration*, treated scientific illustrators as artists and analyzed scientific illustrations primarily on their aesthetic merits.[36] While in one sense clearly elevating the visual, this work in another sense tacitly endorsed the historians' devaluation of the visual in its original context: scientific illustrations were merely illustrative, becoming visually interesting and important only when subjected to technical and aesthetic evaluation as separate artifacts. Recent studies such as those of Gill Saunders on botany, Ann Shelby Blum on nineteenth-century zoology, and Christine Jackson and Maureen Lambourne on ornithology give greater attention to the social and scientific context of illustrated science texts and less to aesthetic evaluation, but they nonetheless operate in this tradition.[37] Such work has been enormously valuable – for its bibliographic research, iconographic and compositional analyses, and sensitivity to technical and material issues – but it has less to offer when it comes to examining what we have seen to be so important to Darwin's work, and which is important to the examination of any illustrated piece of science: the relation of the visual and the textual.

As historians, sociologists, and rhetoricians of science began to look seriously at scientific illustration, they soon discovered that illustrations are not merely decorative. Visual materials have important roles to play in scientific argument, so scientists often go to great lengths, and must often overcome considerable difficulties, to produce and then reproduce illustrations. And because illustrations don't speak for themselves, they must be manipulated (both technically and textually) and utilized with great care. These difficulties and manipulations, however, are not only rarely mentioned, but usually obscured, for the scientist of course wants the reader/viewer's focus on the content of the image, not its making. Before the development of astrophotography in the latter part of the nineteenth century, for example, many published astronomical drawings were presented as illustrations of a particular object on a particular night even though they were almost invariably composites, developed from separate observations in varying atmospheric conditions over an extended period, by an astronomer sketching in near darkness. To complicate matters further, the object was moving, albeit slowly, across the telescopic field; the accuracy of the drawing depended on the astronomer's own visual acuity and draftsmanship; and the drawing still had to be transferred to another medium for publication. Yet in many cases, particularly representations of nebulae, the most basic aspects of the drawing – the form and brightness of the object – were precisely what was at stake.

As science studies scholars have looked more closely at illustrations, at the complex purposes images serve, and the ways in which images can constitute knowledge rather than merely re-packaging textual statements, they have produced sophisticated accounts of the construction of images. They read illustrations through the eyes of the scientists producing them, seeking a stable meaning or meanings, and thus they treat the relationship between image and text in terms of reinforcement, reciprocity, and symbiosis. This approach, and the characterization of the image–text relationship that follows from it, makes obvious sense. But it also has its limitations, particularly when we are interested not merely in what a scientist intends an illustration to mean, but in what the illustration means to others, and in how it is appropriated. This approach tends to fix and stabilize an illustration's meaning when that meaning is, as in Darwin's case, malleable and unstable. This limitation, which has gone almost unremarked, is present in the two most influential recent approaches to scientific illustration, those of Martin Rudwick and Bruno Latour, and they stem from a common source: the art historian and curator William Ivins.

Rudwick was the first historian of science to conduct an extended case study of scientific illustration, and his concept of a "visual language" for geology has shaped much subsequent work. Rudwick's approach owes a great deal to art history. Surveying geological publications of the late eighteenth and early nineteenth centuries, he catalogues the different kinds of illustrations in geology's visual language, traces the various visual influences on them (including such sources as landscape art, topographical illustration, and mining surveys), and delineates the visual conventions that emerged. But Rudwick also analyzes the role of this visual language in the practice and disciplinary formation of geology. He argues that representational conventions in science, while subject to change, reflect a tacit consensus of the community using them and, more specifically, that the emergence of a stable visual language is part of a scientific discipline's larger process of emergence, complete with clearly-defined intellectual goals and methods and institutional structures. In his subsequent work, Rudwick has applied and extended these ideas. In *The Great Devonian Controversy* he demonstrated how this visual language was put to use in both published and unpublished writings by participants in an important geological controversy. In *Scenes From Deep Time*, his study of early illustrations of prehistoric life, Rudwick aligned his treatment of visuals with constructivist and rhetorical approaches to scientific knowledge by borrowing Steven Shapin and Simon Schaffer's concept of "virtual witnessing." For Shapin and Schaffer, a scientist deploys a "literary technology" of rhetorical strategies designed to make readers the witnesses of experiments they have not themselves observed. Rudwick argued that illustrations of the prehistoric world could be seen in the same terms, with the reader/viewer positioned by the scientist to be an accepting witness of a controversial, theory-laden reconstruction of the past.[38]

In his original article, Rudwick acknowledges his debt to William Ivins's *Prints and Visual Communication* (1953). Ivins, defending the importance of the graphic arts, argues for the importance to our culture generally, and to science and technology specifically, of the "exactly repeatable pictorial statement." As his title implies, Ivins treats prints as repositories of information rather than aesthetic objects. He is interested not in the production of original works of art but in the reproduction of various kinds of "visual statements." More precisely, he is concerned with the processes by which a visual statement (whether an oil painting or a drawing for an anatomy manual) is "translated" into a new medium (e.g. an etching, an engraving, a lithograph) from which multiple and "exactly repeatable" prints can be taken. Since the new medium is a different medium with its own techniques and conventions, the draftsperson must translate the original visual statement into the "syntax" of the new medium. The engraver, for example, manipulates his lines in particular ways to represent the various effects of shading, color, tone, etc. in the original. In Ivins's reading, the history of prints is the increasingly faithful translation of the original, with photographic techniques eventually eliminating the need for a draftsperson–translator, thus providing a comparatively unmediated rendering of the object. Subsequent scholars such as Estelle Jussim, while successfully challenging Ivins's account of the objectivity of photographic and certain pre-photographic technologies, have continued to accept his basic ideas and assumptions, particularly about the communicative function of prints.[39]

To treat scientific illustration as a form of "visual communication," however, necessarily leads to a focus on the intended message of the sender, and thus to a conception of text as a key to understanding that intention. And it's important to note that Ivins's ideas were formulated and articulated in the period, the 1930s through the mid-1950s, during which information theory was developed, primarily by researchers working in or for the American telecommunications industry. The suite of practical issues these researchers were attempting to understand all essentially revolved around how to transmit electronic signals, especially telephone transmissions, in such a way as to maximize speed while maintaining clarity, to ensure that as little "noise" as possible interfered with the reception of the message content. Although Ivins's ideas cannot be explicitly connected to the thinkers and works associated with information theory, the similarity in concepts and terminology is evident.

Rudwick's early work largely puts aside the question of the image–text relationship, simply asserting that the two forms of representation comprise "an integrated visual-and-verbal mode of communication" and that this visual communication "was (and is) broadly *complementary* to verbal communication."[40] *Scenes From Deep Time*, by invoking "virtual witnessing," makes the textual, rhetorical function of images explicit: whether the scientist describes textually or depicts visually, the effort is to "recruit virtual witnesses as the author's allies in building up the authority of the claims embodied in the textual or visual representation."[41] As Blum, following Rudwick, puts it rather less subtly: "natural history illustrations took their meaning from adjacent written descriptions."[42]

The other major approach to the study of scientific images is Bruno Latour's. For Latour, scientific illustrations are part of the process of "inscription" in which the scientist transforms matter into documents. "Nature" must first be converted into forms that are manageable, comparable, measurable – strings of numbers, computer printouts, photographs, machine readings, etc. – that can then be manipulated directly or further transformed (into charts and graphs, for example), ultimately becoming part of a written report or paper. "Scientists start seeing something once they stop looking at nature," Latour remarks, "and look exclusively and obsessively at prints and flat inscriptions." An inscription is an "immutable mobile" – a (usually) two-dimensional representation of nature that can be moved, reproduced, modified in scale, recombined, superimposed, and incorporated into a written text without fundamentally altering its character.[43]

Introducing their collection of essays on *Representation in Scientific Practice*, in which Latour's essay appears, Michael Lynch and Steve Woolgar complain that the "communications" model, while "very powerful," offers "a severely limited and *asocial* view of practical and communicative actions"; approaches like Latour's, on the other hand, restore a sense of the "complex activities" in which scientific representations are produced and in which they acquire their "meaning" and "logical force."[44] In contrast to the view of scientific illustrations as communicators of messages, this sociological approach, they argue, emphasizes the social processes and contexts through which scientific images are developed. This, however, overstates the differences between Latour's approach and Rudwick's. Rudwick's later work clearly offers a social view of the production and function of scientific illustrations, and Latour is, like Rudwick, heavily indebted to Ivins. Although Latour gives less prominence to *Prints and Visual Communication* and more to Ivins's earlier *On the Rationalization of Sight*, with its argument that the scientific revolution was made possible by the revolution in seeing brought about by the development of linear perspective, he rewrites Ivins's work as a history of immutable mobiles. Note, too, that Lynch, Woolgar, and Latour are all in fundamental agreement with Ivins that the purpose of illustrations is the communication of a message with a particular meaning. Latour is not so naive as to think that the rejection or questioning of an image's message is impossible or even unlikely, but he does argue that inscriptions are mobilized so as to impel consent and thereby recruit allies. "Although *in principle* any interpretation can be opposed to any text and image," writes Latour, "*in practice* this is far from being the case; the cost of dissenting increases with each new collection, each new labeling, each new redrawing." Sociological approaches to scientific illustrations thus concentrate on how visual materials are rendered compelling, their meanings stabilized, and as with Rudwick, the visual and the textual are seen as working in tandem, integrated and inseparable. The ability of inscriptions to be incorporated into texts is for Latour one of their chief advantages, the result being that the text is "not simply 'illustrated' [but] carries all there is to see in what it writes about."[45]

A more genuinely distinctive approach to scientific illustration has emerged with cultural studies. This approach is epitomized by Barbara Stafford, Ludmilla Jordanova, Sander Gilman, and W. J. T. Mitchell. These scholars are interested in the cultural work done by scientific images, in the ideological factors shaping the production, but especially the appropriation, of scientific illustrations. Their attention to the narrow scientific context and communicative function of illustrations, the central concern of historians and sociologists, has been for the most part limited. Instead, they have charted the way scientific representations travel into the wider culture, becoming part of discourses about sexuality and the body, gender and race, class and capitalism.[46] This work should not be regarded, of course, as wholly separate – it forms a part of the multidisciplinary matrix now called "science studies" and has much in common methodologically with constructivist history and the sociology of knowledge – but it rarely invokes Ivins and is concerned precisely with the instability, rather than the stability, of scientific illustrations. Its understanding, or at least its practical conception, of the image–text relationship is thus more sophisticated, treating a text as unable to control how readers interpret and appropriate an illustration even when the scientist's intended meaning and ideological stance are clearly marked. But this understanding operates more as an assumption where the original scientific context is concerned: the entry of a scientific image into the wider culture is taken as a given rather than as a phenomenon that itself requires analysis.

In this book I attempt to synthesize these approaches by examining not just scientific contexts and cultural appropriations but the interface between them, by treating the text–image relationship as one just as likely to be characterized by instability, tension, and even contradiction as by stasis and symbiosis. When scientific illustrations migrate into the wider culture, it is rarely a matter of their being wrenched from a context that is "objective" and non-ideological. Rather, as historians of science have repeatedly shown, the scientific context is itself already saturated with ideological assumptions and often with overt ideological claims. In re-envisioning the Tree of Life, Darwin was not replacing a religious image with a secular, scientific one. He was, instead, attempting to provide a new gloss to an image already simultaneously religious and scientific, implicitly interpreting the Tree not as the fulfillment of a divine blueprint but as the working out of a natural process. He couldn't stop readers of the *Origin* from seeing natural selection as divinely inaugurated and delimited – and his text, with its references to the Creator and its claim that natural selection should not upset anyone's religious feelings, even invited them to do so if they chose. But he also couldn't stop readers from either rejecting this olive branch wholesale or extending it further and seeing in natural selection a new teleology, with Providence still to be found in the fall of a sparrow.

In seeking to synthesize the approaches to scientific images taken by science studies and cultural studies, my work here complements recent, similarly motivated collections edited by Timothy Lenoir and Caroline Jones and Peter Galison.[47] Both these collections focus on what Lenoir christens "the materiality of communication" as a way of moving beyond the sterile debates about the relationship between art and science, about realism and relativism, and about the "science wars" and "culture wars" generally. By examining how the communication of scientific knowledge is shaped by material factors, common ground can be located. Whatever our view of scientific epistemology and the ontological status of nature, we can agree that science is a set of material practices whose products, both textual and visual, and the means used to generate them, are themselves material; hence, not only what we can know and how we know it, but even *that* we can know in the first place, is a technological, and a cultural, matter. By "emphasizing the materiality of literary and scientific inscriptions – graphic traces as well as the media for producing signs," writes Lenoir, we can see that this is "a precondition for and constraint upon other forms of literal and literary sense-making."[48] Paradoxically, to insist on the materiality of the visual and the textual leads not to technological determinism but to semiotic multiplicity.

While this book attends to these materialities and their consequences, it argues that common ground between detailed case studies and broader cultural accounts of science can be found without treating the visual and the textual as primarily technological processes and products. As such, its approach to scientific images is very similar to that taken in Simon Schaffer's essay on Rosse's "Leviathan" telescopes, which critiques the extension of his and Shapin's concept of "literary technology" to the visual. The authority of scientific reports, generated in part through the use of literary technologies to create "virtual witnesses," was, Schaffer emphasizes, "always fragile and never unquestioned." Visual representations were local products, their authority equally problematic. Latourian immutable mobiles were "always embedded in rather complex technologies that were not easy to translate, and their evident meaning relied on interpretative conventions that were by no means robust." Schaffer thus traces not just the difficulties faced by Rosse and his allies in producing images of the Great Nebula in Orion and assigning astronomical and social meanings to them, but the various ways in which these meanings were themselves interpreted. "The extension of the account of literary to visual technologies is troubled," Schaffer argues, "and demands new analytical tools drawn from iconography and cultural history."[49]

One such tool – largely overlooked thus far by science studies scholars – is W. J. T. Mitchell's concept of the "imagetext." Mitchell declares that "the interaction of pictures and texts is constitutive of representation as such: all media are mixed media." When pictures and text interact symbiotically, the result is a composite imagetext. When they do not, when gaps or ruptures between pictures and text emerge, we have, in Mitchell's terminology, an "image/text." In both cases, however, these interactions require not simply formal but historical analysis. Their "linkages to issues of power, value, and human interest" must be traced.[50] Applied to scientific works and concepts, Mitchell's approach marks the most significant attempt by a cultural critic to combine readings of images' production with their cultural migrations and meanings. If Mitchell's *The Last Dinosaur Book*, which treats dinosaurs as imagetexts, is more interested in mapping the history of these migrations and meanings from the cultural "birth" of dinosaurs in the 1830s and 40s to the present, it also connects the cultural and the scientific throughout this history. In this book, I will give greater attention to the original scientific context, and I will not attempt to follow the evolution of images of evolution beyond the late nineteenth century, but I will treat the works of Darwin and Ruskin as both imagetexts and image/texts. If dinosaurs are images invariably accompanied by words, natural selection may be regarded as text invariably accompanied by images. Thus I elucidate the efforts of Darwin and Ruskin to create symbiotic, mutually reinforcing relationships between their texts and illustrations, but I also give special attention to the moments where those efforts become strained or even fail, and I link these relationships and their appropriations, both within the scientific community and in Victorian culture more broadly, to "issues of power, value, and human interest" – of religion and morals, class and nation, gender and sexuality, race and empire, and art and aesthetics.

I open the body of this study in Chapter 2 with Darwin's barnacle *Monograph*, which was illustrated according to the conventions of transcendental morphology even though Darwin was already thinking of the "archetype" (an idealized organism representing the Divine blueprint with which actual species were in accord) as an evolutionary common ancestor. I start prior to the *Origin* to show that Darwin's works were already implicated in visual and cultural issues, and to provide a sense both of the difficulties he faced in illustrating his own works, and of the difficulties that he in turn created for others. I reconstruct the typologically based visual natural theology of P. H. Gosse's popular and beautifully illustrated seaside natural history books, charting his use of Darwin's barnacle *Monograph* before and after the publication of the *Origin*, linking his shifting reaction to Darwin's discoveries of the odd life cycle and sexual arrangements in barnacles to mid-Victorian anxieties about seaside resorts as sites for sexual display and the mixing of social classes, invoking William Frith's *Ramsgate Sands* (1854), William Dyce's *Pegwell Bay* (1858), cartoons from *Punch* and *Fun*, and the Barnacle family of Dickens's *Little Dorrit* (1855–57). Ruskin is absent from this chapter, for he was still immersed in his own early writings on art and architecture in *Modern Painters* and *The Stones of Venice* during this decade, and the aesthetic threat posed by Darwin would not begin to become clear until the late 1860s.

Chapter 3 discusses John Gould's illustrated bird books, especially *Humming-birds* (1849–61) and *The Birds of Great Britain* (1862–73), Ruskin's *Love's Meinie* (1873–81), and Darwin's *Descent of Man* (1871). Although Gould had identified Darwin's Galapagos finches and provided illustrations for Darwin's *Zoology* of the *Beagle* voyage, he was not a supporter of natural selection, and I argue that he modified existing conventions of bird illustration to challenge Darwinian views of nature for the benefit of his aristocratic subscribers and conservative scientific colleagues. Gould's nature is ordered and largely tranquil, reflective of the artificial world of landed estates and traditional gender politics, neither the site of a Darwinian struggle for existence nor a staging ground for sexual display. Nonetheless, Darwin successfully exploited the eruptions of violence in Gould's work, and he turned Gould's treatment of the plumage of male birds on its head in his articulation of sexual selection in the *Descent*. Gould claimed that the tail of the peacock and the bright colors of hummingbirds were purely ornamental, serving no useful purpose, but Darwin argued that they helped procure the male a mate, and had in fact been developed over time through the aesthetic preferences of females. Ruskin, in turn, horrified by Darwin's account of the beautiful and of the origin of the human perception of it, appropriated Gould for his own anti-Darwinian bird book.

Chapter 4 contrasts Darwin's six botanical books of the 1860s and 70s with Ruskin's *Proserpina* (1875–86). I examine Darwin's various visual strategies in these works in relation both to the conventions of botanical and horticultural illustration and to Victorian still life and flower painting, charting in particular his modifications of existing conventions to capture plant fertilization and movement. It is in this chapter that I trace most fully the development and popularization of physiological aesthetics, focusing on Grant Allen's use of Darwin's work to promulgate a new theory of beauty openly subversive of Ruskin's writings. In *Proserpina*, I argue, Ruskin responds to this threat by challenging Darwin both textually and visually.

Chapters 5 and 6 discuss *The Expression of the Emotions*. In Chapter 5 I examine Darwin's efforts to undermine Charles Bell's influential natural theological theory of expression, *Anatomy and Philosophy of Expression*, and to distance himself from the visual conventions of works of physiognomy and phrenology. In Chapter 6 I take up the relations between the *Expression* and contemporary visual culture, especially portrait photography and the stage. By relying on photographs of human facial expression for his illustrations rather than "the great masters in painting and sculpture," Darwin clearly wished to distance himself from the tradition in expression studies of using and assessing the works of Renaissance painting and classical sculpture, and he was much more willing to have the *Expression* linked with the contested aesthetic domains of photography and melodrama than with high aesthetic culture. Indeed, Darwin frequently found his work associated with the world of popular visual culture and in some cases seen as a deliberate rejection of the fine arts. While Ruskin's response to the *Expression* was less direct than his pointed rebuttals to the *Descent* and the botanical books, he saw the *Expression* – rightly – as having aesthetic and visual elements sharply at odds with his own. However, Darwin was also cautious about aligning his imagetext too closely with aesthetic and political radicalism, seeking to avoid such connections in the case of physiognomy and phrenology and to mute them in the cases of photography and melodrama. By identifying examples of these connections in Victorian satire and especially caricature, where Darwin's theories were parodied and his own face manipulated, I try to show why Darwin was concerned even as he joined in the laugh. Although Ruskin saw the new evolutionary anthropology and cheap wood engraving as a toxic combination, potentially fatal to both caricature and science, Darwin and his allies worried about the power of caricatures of Darwin to promote misunderstandings and erroneous applications of his theories.

Chapter 7 analyzes the illustrations from Darwin's last book, *The Formation of Vegetable Mould, through the Action of Worms*. It is here that I address the relationship of Darwinism to the grotesque and to Victorian landscape, for the book's illustrations are of worm castings (feces) on the one hand, ruined buildings on the other. While the *Origin* clearly influenced the visual perception of landscape, it was not until his final work that Darwin's illustrations reflected that directly. I argue that Darwin's illustrations subvert the visual conventions of the picturesque – still prominent in the illustrations of antiquarian and archaeological texts – converting them into geological sections. Indeed, Darwin is not really interested in the buildings at all, but in the layers of soil above and surrounding them. The ruins and monuments of Britain's past, from newly-unearthed Roman villas to well-known icons such as Stonehenge and Beaulieu Abbey, are buried – visually, textually, and literally – by worm castings. And the castings are themselves represented as the buildings are not: elevated into "monuments" and "towers" and pictured in full realistic detail. Quietly but in visually direct terms, *Worms*, too, rejects high aesthetic culture, Darwin's imagetext endorsing and embodying what Ruskin called the ignoble grotesque and the low picturesque.

CHAPTER 2

Darwin's barnacles

Any mapping of Darwin's effort to depict natural selection and of its impact on Victorian visual culture must begin not with the *Origin* but with his massive *Monograph* on barnacles (*Cirripedia*). This nearly 1100-page study of living barnacles was published in two parts, the first in 1851 devoted to pedunculated (stalked) species and the second in 1854 to sessile forms (the more familiar "acorn" barnacles cemented as adults to hard surfaces). The corresponding parts of Darwin's much slimmer book on fossil species appeared in the same years. The product of eight years of painstaking dissections, Darwin's *Monograph* has sometimes been regarded as a way for him to divert himself from the species theory he had already sketched out, and the publication of which he had arranged in the event of his death. Whatever the psychology of the matter, Darwin's barnacle work played an important role in the refinement of his theory and increased his certainty of its truth. Yet a taxonomic monograph was certainly not the place to announce a radically new understanding of speciation, so Darwin presented his results, both textually and visually, in the prevailing modes of the day. Thinking of the barnacles in one way while writing of and illustrating them in another may well have influenced Darwin's repeated decision in the post-*Origin* books to work largely within existing visual conventions, constructing image-texts that relied in Darwinian fashion on subtle modifications of such conventions.

By locating Darwin's barnacle *Monograph* in the context of the explosion of interest in seaside life and seaside natural history during the 1850s, we can also appreciate both the visual competition Darwin faced and the cultural meanings with which the barnacles were intertwined. Strange as it may seem, even before the *Origin*, and even with a taxonomic tome of predominantly descriptive rather than theoretical science, Darwin was already producing work that not only fascinated but also unsettled the Victorian reading public. The dramatic increase in seaside visitors fueled by railroad development in the preceding decades had in turn created a demand for popular books on seaside natural history. Generally aimed at a middle-class audience, these books were steeped in bourgeois religious and social views. The study of marine creatures put idle hands to work in reverential contemplation of the Creation. Yet in offering seaside studies – and often the lessons gleaned from the example of individual species – as a spiritually and physically healthy alternative to frivolity and flirtation, idleness and novel-reading, seaside writers also highlighted the intertwined cultural anxieties raised by the shore. In their books as on the beach, questions about gender and sexuality, government and empire, class and classification, faith and religion were crowded together; so, too, in Victorian visual culture, where, whether on the canvases at the Royal Academy or in the cartoons of *Punch*, these tensions and anxieties were put on display. Although many of the seaside writers sought to appropriate Darwin's barnacle research into this bourgeois world, the unusual life cycle and sexual anatomy of barnacles had meanings that were difficult to contain. Even Philip Gosse, who had originally absorbed Darwin's barnacle research into his powerful visual natural theology, struggled to prevent the disruption of his imagetexts when, after 1859, it became possible to understand barnacles in evolutionary terms.

THINK DEVELOPMENTALLY, ILLUSTRATE TRANSCENDENTALLY

Darwin began his barnacle work on the same day he mailed off the proofs from his final *Beagle* publication. He was not, however, turning to a new project, and he certainly wasn't setting out to write a monographic study. In fact, he thought he was simply tying up one last scientific loose end from the *Beagle* voyage by finally describing a strange barnacle he had collected along the Chilean coast. But he soon came to realize that understanding this single specimen would require examining and possibly reclassifying the entire group.[1] Darwin and his confidantes quickly recognized the value in such an investment of time and energy. Naturalists agreed that *Cirripedia* needed to be overhauled, and if Darwin was to write about species he needed to strengthen his reputation for careful empirical work and establish his credentials as a reliable systematist. The condemnations that greeted the evolutionary arguments of Robert Chambers's anonymous *Vestiges of the Natural History of Creation* in 1844, coming from the very scientific authorities whom Darwin hoped to convince, made him keenly aware of the shortcomings in his own theory and his inability to overcome similar objections.[2] Dissecting and classifying barnacles was a way for Darwin to work in the mainstream of natural history and comparative anatomy while thinking heretical thoughts and determining how best to defend them.

The recent discovery that barnacles were closely allied with crustaceans had made a thorough re-assessment of *Cirripedia* necessary. Enlightenment naturalists had classified barnacles as mollusks on the basis of their external resemblance to mussels and clams. That classification was radically altered in the 1830s, however, after the researches of John Vaughan Thompson. Thompson first discovered that crustaceans of the genus *Zoea* were in fact the larval form of crabs, which led him to suspect that metamorphosis was a general characteristic of the *Crustacea*. When he observed another odd marine creature metamorphose into an acorn barnacle, Thompson declared that young barnacles were free-swimming, becoming stationary only as adults, and that barnacles must thus also be crustaceans, not mollusks. While agreement among naturalists was virtually unanimous that barnacles could no longer be regarded as mollusks, many awaited further evidence before deciding whether to place them within the *Crustacea* or to make them a separate but closely related class. When Darwin began working on barnacles in 1846, several major authorities, including Richard Owen, Britain's leading comparative anatomist and one of its best-known scientists, had not accepted Thompson's proposal. Owen was unwilling to place such emphasis on the larval form, especially since adult barnacles, unlike adult crustaceans, were hermaphroditic and immobile. In definitively making cirripedes a sub-class within *Crustacea*, Darwin was not being non-controversial – in spite of his claim in the first part of the *Monograph* that such a grouping was already a matter of "almost universal consent" (XI:I). Henri Milne-Edwards and J. D. Dana did not publish their independent conclusions until 1852, and neither William Bell in 1853 nor Owen in 1855 completely concurred with Darwin.

Although he did not fully accept Darwin's classification, Owen was partly responsible for Darwin's undertaking the study and pursuing it in the way that he did. When Darwin consulted Owen about the paper he had drafted on his Chilean specimen, Owen urged Darwin to compare his aberrant species both with more typical ones and with a typical crustacean. Darwin was already knowledgeable about "transcendental anatomy" and Owen's theory of archetypes. Originally developed by Continental anatomists, transcendental anatomy postulated a Divine skeletal blueprint for different forms of life, with actual organisms varying in greater or lesser degrees from it.[3] If barnacles were crustaceans, it should be possible to demonstrate not only that the two groups share a basic anatomical plan, but also that Darwin's Chilean specimen, however unusual, shared it as well. On the Continent, transcendental anatomy was not incompatible with a belief in the transmutation of species, but when members of London's radical medical

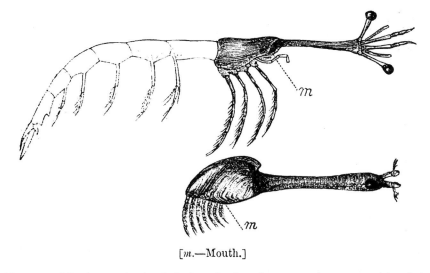

[*m.*—Mouth.]

Figure 2.1   Wood engraving by G. B. Sowerby, Jr., of a stomapod crustacean (above), its abdomen rendered in outline, and a mature pedunculated barnacle (below), the eyes and antennae retained and supposed to have continued growing from the larval stage. From Charles Darwin, *A Monograph of the Sub-Class Cirripedia; The Lepadidae; or, Pedunculated Cirripedes* (London: Ray Society, 1851), 28.

community began to promulgate a materialist, transmutationist version in the 1830s, Owen countered with a revised transcendental program that played up the Divine blueprint and played down any evolutionary implications. In this new natural theology, God was in the general plan rather than the details. The functionalist natural theology of William Paley, with creatures created expressly for their particular environmental niches, fell out of favor among elite naturalists, replaced by a formalist natural theology in which creatures varied from a general anatomical type adaptable to different conditions.

Darwin presented his barnacle work very much in this transcendental framework. The *Monograph*'s initial illustration depicted a typical crustacean and the archetypal barnacle, just as recommended by Owen (fig 2.1). Both forms were manipulated to make their homologies clearer. The abdomenal segments of the crustacean were rendered only in outline, Darwin explained, because "the abdomen . . . becomes in cirripedes, after the metamorphosis, rudimentary, and therefore does not fairly enter into the comparison." The antennae and eyes of the mature barnacle were "retained and supposed to have gone on growing" even though these features exist only in the larval stage (XI:23). This illustration – reproduced by Owen with slight modifications in the second edition of his *Lectures on the*

Comparative Anatomy and Physiology of the Invertebrate Animals – stands over the remainder of the *Monograph*, a visual encapsulation of Darwin's taxonomic argument and a point of reference for the discussion of actual species.[4] Yet Darwin was already thinking of the archetype not as an idealized abstraction existing only in the mind of the Creator, but as an evolutionary common ancestor. The archetypal barnacle, or something very like it, had once swum in primordial seas. Living species had descended from it, modified and diversified over time through natural selection. The shift in conceptualization, in many respects subtle or even simple, was also obviously radical. But for the time being, Darwin kept it to himself and his closest scientific friends.

The plates in Darwin's *Monograph* were also consistent with the visual conventions of taxonomic studies. They contained numerous individual figures floating without background on the plane of the plate. For the most part these figures were arranged in an orderly and if possible symmetrical fashion, guided by what Ann Shelby Blum has called a desire for "graphic fluency."[5] In many instances they were laid out in rows designed to be "read" from left to right and top to bottom. Darwin's plate containing members of the genera *Tetraclita* and *Elminius* (fig. 1.2) demonstrates this particularly clearly. Although the arrangement is not rigidly symmetrical – the bottom row contains five figures whereas the others contain four, and the third species begins at the end of the second row whereas the others begin in the first position of their respective rows – each of the plate's six species is figured in a single row, with similar views of each species aligned vertically. In this case, the symmetrical arrangement facilitates comparisons among related genera and species. Graphic fluency could also be exploited to draw attention to similar parts of different species, as in Darwin's plate comparing the various body parts of species of pedunculated barnacles. Once again, the arrangement is not rigid – a particular body part may take up more or less than a complete row, and the species depicted and the order in which they appear differ from row to row. As with figure 1.2, however, the plate reads left to right down the page, a sequence of mandibles giving way to sequences of other mouth parts. Plates like these were mainly used by Darwin in his discussions of particular genera and species, but his opening description of the entire family of pedunculated barnacles combines references to both types of plates.

By the time Darwin published his *Monograph*, this type of presentation was well established, and it would remain so straight through the evolutionary debates and beyond. Blum argues both that this layout worked well with the dominant comparative methodology that prevailed prior to the *Origin* and that its continued use after the *Origin* is a sign of its being divorced from particular theoretical positions on speciation. While it is true that the visual conventions of taxonomic illustration were not altered in the wake of the *Origin*, clearly Blum's first point shows that these conventions were not atheoretical but rather rooted in widely accepted theoretical positions. And since Darwin's subsequent conversion of Owen's archetype into a common ancestor was an attempt to overthrow the transcendental view about the origin and development of species, his decision to retain these visual conventions – especially while interpreting them very differently in his own mind – is not an obvious one.

If Darwin agonized over this visual dilemma, he left no record of it. But many factors would have influenced a conscious decision to stick with prevailing visual conventions. He was not yet prepared to publish his ideas about natural selection, and altering representational techniques to accommodate his theory better would have required an explanation. Furthermore, establishing his credentials as a taxonomist meant meeting monographic standards and expectations, not departing from them. After all, the distinguished Ray and Paleontographical Societies, which published the parts of the *Monograph* on living and fossil species, respectively, were footing the bill for an expensive project they expected to be the definitive descriptive work on barnacles. And even if Darwin had desired a more congenial visual format, what would that format have been? Was there a way to depict barnacle evolution visually?

Whether Darwin's ability to illustrate barnacles in transcendental terms while thinking of them in evolutionary terms was a matter of choice or necessity, whether it was something he ruminated about or simply did without much thought, it established a pattern for his approach to illustrating his books when he did go public. Generally speaking, Darwin adhered to established visual conventions in natural history. However, he often tweaked or modified those conventions in subtle but significant ways. On some occasions, his decision *not* to include certain visual formats – for example, the absence from his *Expression of the Emotions in Man and Animals* of the types of illustrations found in works of the contested fields of phrenology and physiognomy – relayed important signals about the positioning of his theories. Similarly, decisions to adopt other formats and conventions – such as portrait photography in the *Expression* or the illustrations from breeders' manuals in *The Variation of Animals and Plants Under Domestication* – implicitly aligned him with particular cultural forces and ideological positions he sought in some cases to exploit and in others to resist. Most of all, however, Darwin pursued a strategy of using his textual language to guide his readers' interpretation and understanding of his illustrations. He sought to construct imagetexts, with words and pictures working symbiotically. At a certain level, this may sound obvious, and dangerously close to the notion that Darwin's illustrations were "merely" illustrative, that they simply repackaged his theories in visual form. But my point is that Darwin's illustrations virtually by definition *could not* merely illustrate his texts, because in working within an established visual framework Darwin was providing illustrations that his readers would automatically be inclined to understand from the very perspectives he was laboring to supersede. How would he get his readers literally to see in evolutionary terms what they had been trained to regard very differently? This question could be avoided in the barnacle *Monograph*, but it would have to be faced from the *Origin* on.

THE SCIENTIFIC AND CULTURAL LIFE OF DARWIN'S BARNACLES

Darwin's barnacles were absorbed into the debates and controversies surrounding natural selection with the publication of the *Origin*, in which Darwin used them to buttress a variety of arguments – about cross fertilization and the emergence of sexual dimorphism, the modification of organs, the imperfection of the fossil record, and embryology. Indeed, as Rebecca Stott has shown, marine invertebrates were central to transmutationist thought in the eighteenth and nineteenth centuries, and narratives of human evolution from simple marine forms were as common as those that made humans the descendants of apes.[6] So for most of the 1850s, Darwin's barnacles enjoyed both a significant scientific life and a significant cultural life. The *Monograph* garnered accolades within the scientific community and was put to a variety of cultural uses in a range of works aimed at broader audiences.

Darwin quickly became aware of the importance of his barnacle research for his species theory. In letters to close scientific friends like J. D. Hooker and Charles Lyell, he virtually crowed that barnacles convinced him fully and finally of the truth of natural selection. In particular, barnacles revealed the ubiquity and importance of variation as well as the evolutionary emergence and advantages of sexual dimorphism – their astonishing array of sexual arrangements displayed a series in which species with separate males and females were evolving from an original hermaphroditic ancestor. Yet however easy it is to read natural selection between the lines of the published

Monograph, Darwin's contemporary audience could not see it in these terms until 1858–59, and many of the appropriations of his work during the decade argued explicitly against the "development theory." His scientific readers were impressed nonetheless, for Darwin offered much to amaze even without his private theoretical speculations. His thorough study of the entire group led him to propose a new classification for them. He also provided the first comprehensive description of barnacle metamorphosis and the anatomical processes accompanying it. And his discovery of the bizarre sexual arrangements in several species was completely new. The Royal Society, after considering the merits of Darwin's three volumes on the *Geology* of the *Beagle* voyage, decided in 1853 to award him its Royal Medal on the strength of the first part of the barnacle *Monograph* alone.

The *Monograph* also considerably altered Darwin's public identity as a scientist. Prior to its appearance, Darwin was associated in both public and professional circles with the *Beagle* voyage, from which all of his publications had stemmed. More specifically, his reputation was that of a geologist whose forte was sweeping theories about large-scale phenomena in distant locales – the geological history of southern South America and the coral reefs and volcanic islands of the South Pacific.[7] Although he had worked on marine invertebrates in Edinburgh and on the *Beagle*, Darwin did not have the same specialized knowledge of zoology that he had of geology. Most of the work on the zoological specimens from the voyage had been farmed out to experts, with Darwin serving as a collator and editor. The barnacles thus established his zoological and taxonomic credentials. But they can also be seen as representing his first extended foray into what would become a trademark of Darwin's science: a close examination of the small, the domestic, and the familiar that leads to the revelation not just of their strangeness but of their importance to basic understandings of the natural world. Corals were tiny creatures that worked large-scale wonders, but Darwin had been primarily concerned with the role of geological forces in the development of reefs and atolls rather than with the corals themselves, and he had developed his theory before he ever laid eyes on either reef or atoll. With barnacles, Darwin was discussing an animal with which many if not most of the residents in his island nation were intimately familiar. Barnacles were ubiquitous at the seaside, attached to ships' bottoms and pieces of driftwood, dotting every jetty and pier. They were a nuisance for bathers and a permanent hazard for maritime interests.

Barnacles also had a rich history. They were closely associated, not coincidentally, with stories of transformation. From classical antiquity into the Enlightenment and even beyond, particular species of ducks or geese were thought to develop from barnacles.[8] A variety of factors – including the similarity between the feathers of birds and the cirri of barnacles, the presence of barnacles on driftwood, and ignorance about the mating and nesting habits of some shore birds – contributed to these accounts. In some versions, the barnacles themselves developed when the fruit or leaves of certain trees fell into the sea. In others, the barnacles simply grew directly on wood until they fell into the sea and became ducks or geese. In the Middle Ages, as Lorraine Daston and Katharine Park have shown, barnacle-geese were prominent examples of "wonderful species," the rare or exotic creatures nonetheless viewed as the product of natural causes and part of the order of nature, and thus as candidates for allegorical interpretations of moral or theological truths. During the Enlightenment, however, such wonders came to be regarded not as part of the natural order but as violations of it. This shift, Daston and Park argue, did not represent the triumph of empiricism and rationality as much as a change in intellectual and aesthetic assumptions about nature in European high culture: wonderful species had become "simply vulgar," breaches in the decorum of a natural world characterized by order and regularity. Indeed, the story of barnacle-geese survived longer than the tales of many wonderful species precisely because of their medieval associations with natural causes and natural order.[9]

Thompson alluded to these stories in announcing his discoveries, declaring that the "extraordinary" process of barnacle metamorphosis was "scarcely less wonderful" than "the old and vulgar fable of their being the young or embryo state of the wild-geese which teem over the northern regions of Europe and America."[10] Thompson's characterization both confirms Daston and Park's view and enacts a common trope of Enlightenment and especially Victorian science: that science offers accounts of the natural world that are not just more truthful than "old and vulgar fable[s]" but nearly or equally as imaginative and "wonderful." Crucially, however, Thompson's discovery altered rather than obliterated the association of barnacles with transformation. If tales of barnacle-geese merged two species into one, Thompson's discovery did the same, for the larvae of crustaceans had originally been thought to be a wholly separate organism. But now the mysterious *process* of transformation was charted and made natural, understood as a mechanism evident elsewhere in nature (most familiarly, among insects). Nonetheless, Thompson, like his medieval precursors, drew a theological moral from this new understanding of barnacles: "we recognize the operations of Superior Intelligence . . . in the peculiar structure of these curious and interesting animals."[11]

An army surgeon and medical inspector who spent just three years in England between 1800 and his death in 1847, Thompson was virtually unknown outside the zoological community and only tenuously connected to major English scientific societies and London's scientific elites.[12] His major work, *Zoological Researches and Illustrations*, based on research primarily conducted during his posting in Cork from 1816 to 1835, was self-published. Originally envisioned as a series of regular papers on marine zoology, the installments in fact appeared intermittently from 1828 to 1834. Thompson's income was inadequate to fund the series, and his public pleas – to members of the Zoological Society in particular – did not generate enough subscriptions to maintain it. Although this work received some favorable notices and one of his barnacle papers was published in the Royal Society's *Philosophical Transactions* in 1835, Thompson's account of barnacle metamorphosis did not gain the exposure and acceptance that would have been accorded to a better-connected figure, and his transfer to Sydney that same year removed him even further from the centers of scientific activity. Darwin, of course, did not suffer from these restrictions. As a result, his *Monograph* provided a more accessible and more widely disseminated description of barnacle metamorphosis. Since he had also extended and corrected Thompson's work, Darwin's description was also much more thorough and detailed. Barnacle larvae, Darwin showed, pass through three distinct stages, each free-swimming, the last equipped with antennae and a pair of compound eyes. At the end of the third stage, the barnacle attaches itself upside-down to a stationary surface, molts its eyes, and secretes the cement that glues it down and forms its shell. The feathery cirri, used for locomotion in the larval stage, now sweep outward from the opening at the top of the shell, drawing in seawater full of microscopic animals. As T. H. Huxley succinctly put it to his audience at the Government School of Mines in 1857, "a Barnacle is, in reality, a Crustacean fixed by its head, and kicking the food into its mouth with its legs."[13]

Thompson used two plates to depict barnacle metamorphosis as a simple if surprising transformation. In the first (fig. 2.2a), he illustrates the larva and some of its parts in the upper half of the plate, while the lower half is devoted to the sessile animal after its metamorphosis. The second plate (fig. 2.2b), focuses on the old skin sloughed off by the newly attached barnacle. Both plates, however, contain an illustration of the sessile barnacle in the process of molting. This juxtaposition of larva and adult creates a "before and after" effect that reflects Thompson's emphasis on the oddity of such apparently different creatures being stages in the life of a single

(a)   (b)

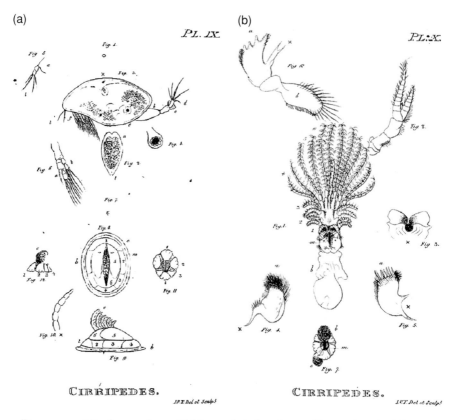

Figure 2.2a Wood engravings of (a) barnacle in larval stage (figs. 1–7) and adult stage (figs. 8–12). and (b) various parts of molt from barnacle in larval stage (figs. 1–6) and of sessile barnacle in process of molting (fig. 7). Plates IX and X from John V. Thompson, *Zoological Researches and Illustrations* (Cork: King and Ridings, 1828–34).

individual. As Gillian Beer has noted, metamorphosis, whether in myth or natural science, is about change rather than death, "the essential self transposed but not obliterated by transformation."[14] So it is for Thompson with the metamorphosis of barnacles. His discovery reveals the "real nature" of barnacles. Penetrating "the complete disguise under which they usually present themselves," Thompson finds not two species but one. Moreover, the purpose of the free-swimming larvae is the selection of appropriate resting places: equipped with "perfect freedom" as well as vision and locomotive power, they have "the means of making that election which is best suited to their respective habits as impressed upon them by Omnipotence."[15] Like Milton's Adam and Eve, Thompson's barnacles are created with free will, literally sufficient to stand.

(a)   (b)

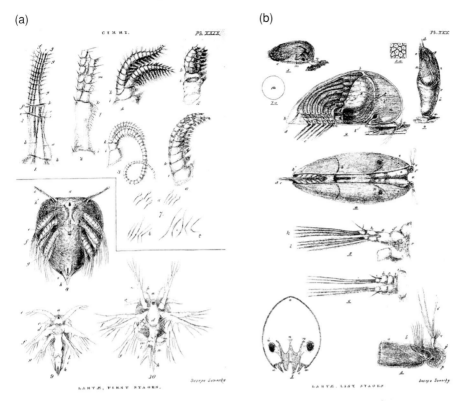

Figure 2.3   (a) "Larva. First Stages" and (b) "Larva. Last Stages." Wood engravings
by G. B. Sowerby, Jr., depicting first stages of barnacle larva of species from several
genera and final stages of barnacle larva of species from *Lepas*. Plates XXIX and XXX from
Charles Darwin, *A Monograph of the Sub-Class Cirripedia; The Balanidae* (London:
Ray Society, 1854).

Darwin's illustrations of barnacle metamorphosis, while broadly similar
to Thompson's, not only reflect his more detailed understanding of the
process but also highlight his somewhat different emphases. He, too, provides depictions of the different larval stages. Part of one plate (fig. 2.3a) is
devoted to drawings of the first stage of the larva of species in three very
different genera. Another plate (fig. 2.3b) contains figures of larvae of the
second and third stages in species of a fourth genera. Unlike Thompson,
however, Darwin does not include on these plates an illustration of the
stationary adult. For Darwin, it is not the end points of metamorphosis
that are of central interest, but the process itself. This is reinforced by a
plate devoted to depictions of the cementing apparatus, by means of which
the larva in the final stage attaches itself to another object. In Darwin's
Monograph, the adult does not represent the essential barnacle self, and the

larva is important to the barnacle's classification. Nor is "the larva" a unitary being – each of the several larval stages is taken on its own terms.

If Darwin confirmed Thompson's claims and added detail to Thompson's account, his discovery of the extraordinary variations in the sex lives of barnacles was all his own. In 1848, while working with the genera *Ibla* and *Scalpellum*, Darwin discovered species with separate sexes, whereas all other known barnacles at the time were hermaphroditic. Even more strangely, he found that some hermaphroditic species also possessed tiny additional or "complemental" males living parasitically within the female's shell. Shortly after this discovery, Darwin wrote to Charles Lyell:

> the other day I got the curious case of a unisexual, instead of hermaphrodite, cirripede, in which the female had the common cirripedial character, & in two of the valves of her shell had two little pockets, in *each* of which she kept a little husband; I do not know of any other case where a female invariably has two husbands. – I have one still odder fact, common to several species, namely, that though they are hermaphrodite, they have small additional or as I shall call them Complemental males: one specimen itself hermaphrodite had no less than *seven* of these complemental males attached to it.[16]

Returning to his strange Chilean specimen in 1853, Darwin realized that it, too, had separate sexes of completely different size and form, the tiny male, lacking most organs but equipped with an enormous penis, living inside the shell of the female. In his *Monograph*, Darwin used language as colorful as he had deployed with Lyell to describe these oddities. He marveled at the diversity and bizarreness of these sexual arrangements and the extraordinary differences between the sexes. The "short-lived" males, he noted, attach themselves in "successive crops" to the females. Lacking a mouth and stomach but equipped with a fully formed reproductive apparatus, these "rudimentary" males are in essence "mere bags of spermatozoa." In his Chilean species, the "wonderfully developed" penis, "when fully extended . . . must equal between eight and nine times the entire length of the animal!" (XII:21, 23). Privately, Darwin saw an evolutionary sequence: an ancestral hermaphrodite evolving into a hermaphrodite with separate, "complemental" males and finally into separate sexes. In the *Monograph*, he contented himself with noting that "in the series of facts now given, we have one curious illustration more to the many already known, how gradually nature changes from one condition to the other – in this case from bisexuality to unisexuality" (XII:26). By leaving unspecified how he understood this process of gradual change, Darwin created the impression that he was merely describing a static picture of nature's profusion.

(a)   (b)

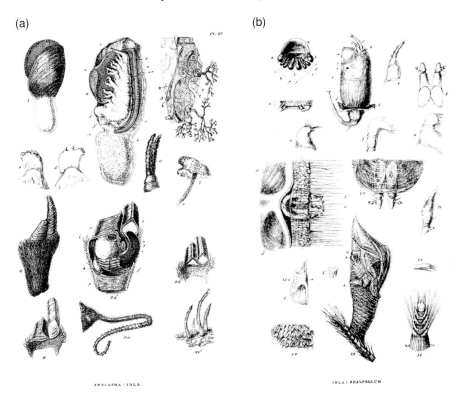

Figure 2.4 (a) "Anelasma: Ibla." Wood engraving by G. B. Sowerby, Jr., of barnacles of
the genera *Anelasma* and *Ibla*. 8a′ depicts the female *Ibla cumingii* with a small male inside
her shell; 9a is the penis of *Ibla quadrivalvus*. Note the way the orderly numbering system
of the figures on the plate is disrupted in the final row. (b) "Ibla: Scalpellum." Wood
engraving by G. B. Sowerby, Jr., of male barnacles of *Ibla cumingii* and complemental
males of *Scalpellum vulgare*. Note the disruption of regular numbering. Plates IV and V
from Charles Darwin, *A Monograph of the Sub-Class Cirripedia; The Lepadidae; or,*
Pedunculated Cirripedes (London: Ray Society, 1851).

These species' unusual sexual arrangements also disrupted the *Mono-*
graph's visual presentation. In the plates for the first volume, all is orderly
and symmetrical until just after the depiction of *Ibla cumingii*, the first
non-hermaphroditic species to be presented (fig. 2.4a). Item 8a′ in this plate
depicts a female of *I. cumingii* with a small male living inside the lower
left-hand part of her shell. This plate "reads" left to right down the page
through this row, but the final row begins with item 9, part of the related
species *I. quadrivalvus*, in which we first encounter "complemental males,"
rather than 8c′, the final illustration of *I. cumingii*, which appears at the
end of the row. Item 9a is the "singular" penis, "surprisingly elongated" in

its unarticulated portion, of the hermaphroditic *I. quadrivalvus* (XI:171). In the plate that follows (fig. 2.4b), almost entirely devoted to the tiny male of *I. cumingii* and the complemental males of *Scalpellum vulgare*, order and symmetry are further disrupted. To a considerable extent, Darwin induces in the reader important components of his own visual experience: the unsettling of expectations based on existing patterns, the need to attend closely to detail, the gradual appreciation of the remarkable sexual arrangements in these species. Having absorbed these lessons, the reader is returned in the next plate to a high degree of order and symmetry, even though it depicts additional and equally bizarre species of *Scalpellum*.

Disruption in the plates of the second volume is more subtle but again occurs with the introduction of sexually complex species. Order and symmetry are mostly retained, but suddenly visual information proliferates in such a way that it spills over from one plate to another, the boundaries of individual plates becoming, as it were, porous. The illustrations of *Alcippe lampas*, the species in which the female keeps two males in her "pockets," cannot be contained on a single plate (fig. 2.5). This in itself is not unusual, but what *is* unusual is the fact that the numbering system on the second plate does not resume at 1 until a new genus, *Cryptophialus*, is introduced. The only prior instance of this continuous numbering occurs in the case of two genera so closely allied (*Pyrgoma* and *Creusia*) that Darwin makes the latter a subgenus of the former and says he would not have separated them at all had several earlier classifiers not already done so. The situation in figure 2.5 is more extreme, however. *Alcippe lampas* is a pedunculated barnacle. It should have been presented, Darwin admits, in his earlier volume on those forms. But it is so different from other members of the family that he did not at the time suspect the resemblance and even now is not sure that he shouldn't create a new family exclusively for it. The similarity in its sexual arrangements to *Ibla* and *Scalpellum*, however, plays a major role in his decision to group it with the pedunculated species and, indeed, to position it as an intermediate genus between the true hermaphroditic forms and those with complemental males. To make matters more complicated, Darwin *does* create an entirely new order for *Cryptophialus minutus*, the odd, sexually dimorphic Chilean specimen with which he began. We might think the solid line – unique in the *Monograph's* forty plates of living species – separating the illustrations of *A. lampas* from those of *C. minutus* is meant to indicate this separation of orders, but the plate that follows, on which the illustrations of *C. minutus* continue until giving way to another new order with a single species, *Proteolepas bivincta*, lacks it. If the structure of the plates cannot be rendered completely coherent, Darwin

(a)   (b)

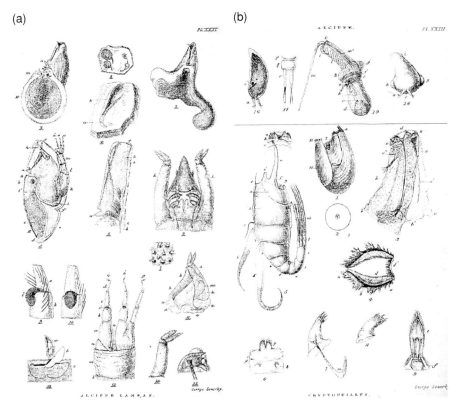

Figure 2.5   (a) "Alcippe Lampas." Wood engraving by G. B. Sowerby, Jr., of *Alcippe lampas*. Although a pedunculated barnacle, *A. lampas* is depicted with the sessile species. (b) "Cryptophialus." Wood engraving by G. B. Sowerby, Jr., of *Cryptophialus minutus*, the odd Chilean species with which Darwin began his barnacle investigations. Note the way the illustrations for *Alcippe lampas* continue at the beginning of the plate, and the solid line separating them from the illustrations of *C. minutus*. Plates XXII and XXIII from Charles Darwin, *A Monograph of the Sub-Class Cirripedia; The Balanidae* (London: Ray Society, 1854).

nonetheless exploits the otherwise anomalous presence of the pedunculated *A. lampas* by stressing how closely its males resemble those of *C. minutus*, both being little more than sperm sacs attached to an elephantine penis.

Tellingly, Darwin had an easier time controlling in print his excitement about the evolutionary implications of barnacle sexuality than he did his amazement at the fact of that sexuality. The language of the *Monograph* on the latter score is barely more clinical and detached than in the letters – barnacle sexuality is insistently rendered in human terms. Janet Browne has suggested that the barnacles reminded Darwin of his own domestic situation as a semi-permanent invalid whose primary role in the household seemed to be keeping his wife pregnant.[17] But his references to "husbands" kept in female "pockets" and to short-lived males with enormous penises whose sole purpose was reproductive also betray broader anxieties about female polyandry and males simultaneously potent and parasitic. Large and fully-formed females with multiple, diminutive male sexual partners, whether these partners were figured metaphorically as husbands or as lovers, raised potentially threatening implications for the political and sexual economies of Victorian Britain.

While the circulation of Darwin's *Monograph* itself was extremely limited, reviews and popularizations of Darwin's work brought barnacle metamorphosis and sexuality into the public domain, generally as part of the explosion of interest in seaside natural history in the 1850s.[18] With the advent of railways, coastal areas became increasingly accessible to all classes for daytrips and holiday excursions.[19] Numerous books – including W. H. Harvey's *The Sea-Side Book* (1849), Ann Pratt's *Common Things of the Sea-Side* (1850), David Landsborough's *A Popular History of British Sea-Weeds* (1851) and *A Popular History of British Zoophytes and Corallines* (1852), Charles Kingsley's *Glaucus; or, The Wonders of the Shore* (1855), J. G. Wood's *Common Objects of the Sea-Shore* (1857), G. H. Lewes's *Sea-Side Studies* (1858), and Philip Gosse's various publications – offered guidance on how to locate, observe, collect, and study the wonders of marine life. Gosse, a respected naturalist, was arguably the most successful and prolific of the seaside writers. As one of the independent developers and most prominent popularizers of the salt-water aquarium, he helped make the aquarium a common sight in middle-class drawing rooms and, on a much larger scale, a major tourist attraction.[20] The flood of often beautifully illustrated books that issued from his pen extolled both the aesthetic pleasure and the scientific and religious knowledge to be gained from the observation of coastal marine life. In the 1850s alone, his popular works on seaside subjects included *A Naturalist's Rambles on the Devonshire Coast* (1853), *The Aquarium* (1854; 2nd edn 1856), *Tenby: A Sea-Side Holiday* (1856), and *Evenings at the Microscope* (1859), while *A Manual of Marine Zoology for the British Isles* (1855–56) and *Actinologia Britannica: A History of the British Sea-Anemones and Corals* (1860) were intended as reference tools for both student and established naturalist. Gosse was also probably most responsible for making Darwin's work more widely known, accompanying his description of barnacle metamorphosis with effusive praise for Darwin's

Monograph. As an anonymous reviewer noted in the *British Quarterly* in 1856, Gosse's books were so popular that "You expect even ladies to come out strong in science, and to talk imposingly about . . . the metamorphosis of cirripeds."[21]

Darwin's work was not simply communicated but appropriated, with barnacle metamorphosis and sexual relations incorporated into various forms of cultural commentary. Much more than mere field guides, the seaside books generally advanced the religious and social values of the middle classes. Most seaside books, including Gosse's, were overtly cast as what Barbara Gates and Ann Shteir call "narratives of natural theology": following William Paley's functionalist arguments, they dwelled on the evidence of divine benevolence and wisdom provided by marine life.[22] Knowingly or not, Gosse echoed Thompson's claim that barnacles reveal "the operations of Superior Intelligence" when he argued in *Tenby* that the "wonderful process" of barnacle metamorphosis is obviously "ordained" by the "wisdom of God."[23]

The seaside books of the 1850s could not defend the virtues of marine zoology, however, without calling attention to the various sins it was said to cure. And in the case of seaside natural history, the temptations of the flesh were as great a concern as those of the spirit – and were intertwined, inevitably, with class concerns. Middle-class visitors to the shore, a site almost by definition for bodily and social display, abjured the aristocratic idleness and debauchery traditionally associated with inland watering places such as Bath and older coastal resorts such as Regency Brighton. Seaside books were meant to provide idle middle-class hands in particular with what Peter Bailey has called "rational recreation," a morally and intellectually uplifting leisure activity. "Few, very few," wrote Gosse in *A Naturalist's Rambles*, "are at all aware of the many stirring, beautiful, or wondrous objects that are to be found by searching on those shores that every season are crowded by idle pleasure-seekers."[24] The *British Quarterly* reviewer affirmed the importance of Gosse's "sermons in the sands," declaring them "a great moral service to society." But in praising Gosse's efforts the reviewer also acknowledged that the middle-class holiday naturalist was more likely to be regarded as an absurd and degraded figure: "Too often it has been supposed," the reviewer admitted, "that a hunter of cirripeds and annelids is a rather ridiculous personage," that "a passion for polypes" is "coarse and inelegant."[25]

While Gosse's program met with some success among the middle classes, working- and lower middle-class shoregoers, whose presence raised similar anxieties, had even less interest in discovering God at the beach. Cheap excursion railway fares made nearby coastal resorts accessible for daytrips and weekend visits by urban laborers and clerks, particularly to seaside towns not far from London. In middle-class eyes, workers on such outings were too often loud and boisterous. They invaded middle- and upper-class spaces, appropriating them for their own uses and driving their social betters out of sight. As the *Illustrated London News* noted of Brighton in August and September, "every Saturday the cheap train disgorges multitudes who can only go 'out of town' with a return ticket, and who . . . swarm over the Esplanade, and fill all the flies till Monday."[26] Samuel Warren, a lawyer and Tory MP, writing anonymously of his summer holiday for *Blackwood's* in 1855, congratulated himself for selecting a French coastal town beyond the reach of "Cockney ken," avoiding "Cockney-crowded sands with a wretched row of 'bathing-machines.'"[27] Working-class visitors to the seaside, oblivious of prohibitions against mixed bathing and unable to afford a swimming costume or hire a bathing machine, further shocked the bourgeoisie by sometimes swimming together in various states of undress.

However, barnacles seemed invariably to be drawn into moral parables written by and for the middle classes. To the *British Quarterly* reviewer, barnacles were emblems of greedy, grasping capitalism: the acorn barnacle's use of its cirri to capture prey is a "cunning piece of mechanism" likened to "many-fingered hands about to gather up the utmost possible quantity of gold."[28] For Charles Kingsley, friend to both Darwin and Gosse, seaside natural history was also about morals and money. It was part of "muscular Christianity," in which Protestantism and social activism were pursued in the context of a vigorous, healthy lifestyle. "Let no one think that . . . Natural History is a pursuit fitted only for effeminate or pedantic men," wrote Kingsley in *Glaucus*. "We should say, rather, that the qualifications required for a perfect naturalist are as many and as lofty as were required, by old chivalrous writers, for the perfect knight-errant of the middle ages" – strong, brave, courteous, gentle, unselfish, reverent, clear-headed, and perseverant. Kingsley was worried less about middle-class businessmen than about their idle – and presumably shore-going – sons. A "frightful majority of our middle-class young men are growing up effeminate," he complained; lacking the "sturdy and manful hill-side or sea-side training" of their fathers, the sons of urban businessmen in particular were spending their free time in "frivolity" and even "secret profligacy."[29] Given such concerns, the sexual arrangements of barnacles were best left unmentioned – and usually were. While Kingsley declared that "the marvels which meet us at every step in the anatomy and the reproduction" of marine animals lead readers "to more solemn and lofty trains of thought, which can find their full satisfaction only in self-forgetful worship" (35), his larger purposes were better served, as Gosse's were, by barnacle metamorphosis. The transformation from the mobile larva to stationary adult proved irresistible. For Kingsley, barnacle metamorphosis provided, not surprisingly, a parable for bourgeois life. Speaking of a species of *Pyrgoma*, Kingsley explains that the free-swimming larva, "having sown its wild oats . . . settled down in life, built itself a good stone house, and became a landowner" (87).[30] Converting Darwin's story of a hermaphrodite's progress into a seaside tale of an aquatic prodigal son, Kingsley makes no reference to those unusual species in which barnacle "wives" do the settling down and keep multiple, parasitic "husbands" solely for the sake of their reproductive capacities.

Glaucus also provided Kingsley with a venue for advocating sanitary reform. The cholera outbreak in London in the summer of 1854 had underscored the reformers' calls for prompt action. In another crustacean, the spider crab, and the polyps parasitic upon it, Kingsley saw the antithesis of Parliamentary delay and the ineffective regulations of the Board of Health. This scavenger, Kingsley noted, "needed not to discover the limits of his authority, to consult any lengthy Nuisances Removal Act, with its clauses, and counter-clauses, and exceptions, and explanations of interpretations, and interpretations of explanations" (134). Having been granted by Nature "those very summary powers of entrance and removal in the watery realms, for which common sense, public opinion, and private philanthropy, are still entreating vainly in the terrestrial realms," the spider crab and its parasites immediately set about eating any dead creatures whose putrefying flesh endangered the purity of the surrounding waters (135). As with the parable legible in the metamorphosis of barnacles, Kingsley argues that the story of the spider crab provides the text of a sermon for those who can read the signs.

Darwin's barnacle work could just as easily be incorporated into reactionary attacks on social reform, however. In his novel, *What Will He Do With It?*, Edward Bulwer-Lytton parodied Darwin as Professor Long, author of the tedious, two-volume *Researches into the Natural History of Limpets*. Bulwer-Lytton's lampoon is predictable – a classificatory study of limpets is pedantic and irrelevant – but it is also nested within a satire directed against Mechanics' Institutes and the liberal intentions behind them. Professor Long is invited to deliver a lecture at the Gatesboro' Athenaeum. The Athenaeum began its existence as a Mechanics' Institute, but the workers showed little interest in the "useful knowledge" the organization's middle-class patrons wished to impart to them. While still clinging to the notion that their Athenaeum "bring[s] classes together in friendly union," these patrons are forced to admit that the workers are too tired to attend Professor Long's lecture and will undoubtedly borrow the latest novel rather than his *History of Limpets* from the Institute's library.[31]

A more extensive and sympathetic exploitation of Darwin's barnacles for social and cultural commentary was pursued by Charles Dickens in his portrait of the Barnacle family in *Little Dorrit* (1855–57). One of the novel's central features is its attack on governmental corruption and mismanagement, which had recently been displayed so spectacularly during the Crimean War. The focus of this attack is the fictional Circumlocution Office, which the Barnacles, refiners of the bureaucratic art of How Not To Do It, have long administered.[32] Dickens was almost certainly familiar with Darwin's barnacle work through the various popularizations of it in books and articles on seaside natural history. Indeed, Dickens's own weekly periodical, *Household Words*, participated in the seaside craze during the 1850s. Numerous articles on the subject appeared in its pages, one containing an extended discussion of barnacles that explicitly credited Darwin's researches. Although this article, which appeared in the midst of *Little Dorrit's* serial run, expressed skepticism about some of the details of barnacle metamorphosis and regarded "the mysteries of their reproduction" as still shrouded in "[d]eep darkness," both of these key aspects of Darwin's work were discussed.[33] In *Little Dorrit* itself, Dickens, unlike his seaside contemporaries, including the reform-minded Kingsley, exploited the more subversive potential of Darwin's discoveries, using his own depiction of the Barnacles less to advance a middle-class agenda than to assault aristocratic privilege.

Much of Dickens's satirical use of the barnacle name admittedly required only a general awareness of the annoyance and danger posed by barnacles for bathers and ships, their ability to attach themselves tenaciously to solid objects and to reproduce rapidly, especially where they were not wanted. The narrator explains, for example, that

what the Barnacles had to do, was to stick on to the national ship as long as they could. That to trim the ship, lighten the ship, clean the ship, would be to knock them off; that they could but be knocked off once; and that if the ship went down with them yet sticking to it, that was the ship's look out, and not theirs. (115; bk. 1, ch. 10)

The national ship being an imperial one, Barnacle sinecures multiply throughout the world, not merely at home:

... wherever there was a square yard of ground in British occupation under the sun or moon, with a public post upon it, sticking to that post was a Barnacle. No intrepid navigator could plant a flag-staff upon any spot of earth, and take possession of it in the British name, but to that spot of earth, so soon as the discovery was known, the Circumlocution Office sent out a Barnacle and a despatch box. (390; bk. 1, ch. 34)

Whereas Kingsley and Bulwer-Lytton drew on barnacles for domestic cultural and political commentary, Dickens also connects his Barnacles to a critique of empire and the British imperial project. Empire itself, of course, is not challenged – the entrepreneurial and nationalistic spirit of the "intrepid navigator" who "take[s] possession" of distant lands "in the British name" is valorized as heroic here – but the administration of empire is. The governing class represented by the Barnacles, its power rooted in privilege rather than merit, is simply not up to the task.

However, the narrator's recurring commentary on how Barnacles obtain their "places" suggests that Dickens was specifically exploiting the physical anatomy and metamorphosis of cirripedes. The novel lays out elaborate genealogies of the various "branches" (103; bk. 1, ch. 10) and "ramification[s]" (201; bk. 1, ch. 17) of the Barnacle family, and it is especially concerned with the differences between older, established members and those younger Barnacles waiting to secure their own permanent positions. The aptly-named Tite Barnacle, the administrative head of the Circumlocution Office, already has his own "snug" place (103; bk. 1, ch. 10). Repeatedly characterized as "buttoned-up" in manner as well as dress, Tite Barnacle wears a coat "always buttoned-up to his white cravat" (548; bk. 2, ch. 12), with the folds of the cravat "wound and wound . . . round his neck" (106; bk. 1, ch. 10), much like an acorn barnacle with its cirri protruding from the top of its shell. He even lives in a cramped, airless house, the door of which is opened, perhaps not insignificantly, by a footman. Tite Barnacle's son, Clarence, more frequently referred to as Young Barnacle or Barnacle Junior, while also well placed in the Circumlocution Office, is more recently settled. As a younger member of the species, Clarence is, appropriately, beginning to display his cirri and lose his vision. His two most prominent features are "the fluffiest little whisker, perhaps, that ever was seen," and a large eyeglass that keeps falling out of an eye in which he is "evidently going blind" (104; bk. 1, ch. 10). Beneath Clarence are those "less distinguished Parliamentary Barnacles, who had not as yet got anything snug, and were going through their probation" (396; bk. 1, ch. 34). Like their larval namesakes, they are locomotive, moving in and out of Parliament, voting this way and that, as directed by their elders. These Barnacles without snug positions will happily accept a permanent place anywhere in the empire: a list of "hungry and adhesive Barnacles," the narrator tells us, already exists for every post that might come vacant, at home or abroad, for the next fifty years (396; bk. 1, ch. 34). Like Kingsley, Dickens exploited the satiric potential of marine organisms, but unlike Kingsley, he figured barnacle metamorphosis as an anti-bildungsroman, a tale of bureaucratic nepotism and inefficiency.

Dickens's interest in Barnacle sexuality also suggests some level of famil-iarity with the results of Darwin's researches as popularized by others in books, articles, and public lectures. If in Kingsley's rendering of barnacle metamorphosis the middle-class prodigal larva sows its wild oats and then settles down, Dickens's portrait of the Barnacles is much closer to Darwin's complex response to those species in which males are both potent and par-asitic. On the one hand, the Barnacles are not virile and productive. Their conversation is not direct and straightforward but obfuscatory and mislead-ing. The Circumlocution Office generates much talk and much paper, but little or nothing of substance. It ultimately frustrates and defeats even the most indefatigable seekers of information and knowledge. Both the activity of the family's younger members and the gouty torpor of their elders serve the purpose of not "doing it" sexually as well as bureaucratically.[34] Young Barnacle keeps his eye-glass "dangling round his neck," for "it wouldn't stick when he put it up" thanks to his "limp little eyelids" and "flat orbits" (104; bk. 1, ch. 10). The inbreeding between one branch of the Barnacles and the Stiltstalkings – both families "better endowed in a sanguineous point of view than with real or personal property" (103; bk. 1, ch. 10) – has rendered Young Clarence, Tite Barnacle's only son and "the born idiot of the family" (302; bk. 1, ch. 26), even more "enfeebled in intellect" (203; bk. 1, ch. 17).

On the other hand, and as we might expect from James Eli Adams's account of the complexities of mid-Victorian masculinity in such writers as Dickens and Kingsley, some prominent Barnacles are energetic and potent. Ferdinand Barnacle, from the "sprightly side of the family," is the "viva-cious, well-looking, well-dressed" young man likely to become the next great Barnacle statesman (110; bk. 1, ch. 10). Henry Gowan, who comes from the same branch, is similarly described as "well dressed, of a sprightly . . . appear-ance, a well-knit figure, and a rich dark complexion" (197; bk. 1, ch. 17). Like Kingsley's *Pyrgoma*, Gowan, having applied himself in early manhood "to the cultivation of wild oats" (201; bk. 1, ch. 17), easily wins the hand of the young woman also desired by the novel's hero. And yet this potency is itself problematic, for Gowan is little more than the parasitic "bags of sper-matozoa" that Darwin found in his most interesting species. Undertaken for mercenary reasons, his marriage hardly constitutes a transformation into happy bourgeois domesticity. The birth of a son is relevant to him only insofar as he benefits from the increased generosity of his in-laws to his wife and child. While Kingsley was certain that the effeminate sons of London businessmen could be steered from profligacy to domesticity through beach-combing, and Gosse was as confident as his *British Quarterly* reviewer that books like *The Aquarium* and *Tenby* would reduce the numbers of "weary men [who] attempt to break the monotony of sea-side exile by plunging into casual flirtations," Dickens was much more skeptical.[35]

Dickens's satirical portrait of the Barnacles was enormously popular with his readers, and his yoking of the Barnacles' sexuality with their corruption and inefficiency was not lost on his contemporaries. As a result, it also drew scathing attacks – some of them launched even before the novel had completed its serial run. The one that most annoyed Dickens came anonymously from James Fitzjames Stephen in the *Edinburgh Review*. While praising Dickens's sensitive depictions of the lower classes, Stephen complained that the characterization of the Barnacles was a dangerous caricature:

We wish . . . he had more liberally portrayed those manly, disinterested, and energetic qualities which make up the character of an English gentleman. Acute observer as he is, it is regretted that he should have mistaken a Lord Decimus [Barnacle] for the type of an English statesman, or Mr. Tite Barnacle for a fair specimen of a public servant. . . . His injustice to the institutions of English society is, however, even more flagrant than his animosity to particular classes in that society . . . the institutions of the country, the laws, the administration, in a word the government under which we live, are regarded and described by Mr. Dickens as all that is most odious and absurd in despotism or in oligarchy.[36]

In making individual Barnacles the "type" and "specimen" of the statesman and public servant, Dickens has failed to portray the "manly, disinterested, and energetic qualities" that comprise the English gentleman. And indeed, Dickens's Barnacles are not "manly," in all the Victorian senses of that term. They are not, as the *OED* has it, courageous, independent in spirit, frank, and upright. The Circumlocution Office may be a "school for gentlemen" (303; bk. 1, ch. 26), but it is a reactionary school, one cheerfully characterized by a Barnacle as "a politico diplomatico hocus pocus piece of machinery" for preserving the power of the aristocratic Barnacles against the inroads of the middle classes (111; bk. 1, ch, 10). Stephen's complaint that the novel depicts the government as despotic and oligarchic is thus accurate, but so, too, is his awareness of Dickens's depiction of the Barnacles' problematic

Figure 2.6 Hablot K. Browne ("Phiz"), detail from cover illustration of monthly parts of
Charles Dickens's *Little Dorrit* (London: Bradbury and Evans, 1855–57).
Wood engraving by J. Swain.

sexual manliness. This is most evident when Stephen later argues that the
cover of the novel's monthly parts (fig. 2.6) offers a visual representation of
the attack on the manliness of Britain's political elite. Across the top of the
cover, says Stephen, we have "Britannia in a Bath-chair, drawn by a set of
effete idiots . . . and a supercilious young dandy" and pushed from behind
"by six men in foolscaps." His patriotic liberalism thoroughly affronted by
this portrait of the nation in the hands of effeminate, inbred idiots, dandies,
and fools, Stephen registers again the anxieties about gender and sexuality
that discussions of barnacles almost invariably generated.[37]

DEPICTIONS OF THE SEASIDE IN THE 1850S

With the seaside's new popularity came different visual representations of it.
Traditional depictions of the lonely wreck or a group of fishermen displaying
their catch or mending their nets made room for bustling canvases of holiday
visitors on the sands. In the illustrated papers and comic weeklies, the seaside
suddenly became an especially popular subject for capturing and satirizing
Victorian life. While Darwin's barnacles did not find their way directly into
these representations, many of the same issues and anxieties that animated
both Darwin's discoveries and the seaside writings popularizing them were
visible here as well. I thus want to read such pieces of visual culture against
the backdrop I have just traced of the craze for seaside natural history and the
dissemination of Darwin's barnacle work, partly for the new insights this
approach can provide and partly to show that relationships of Darwin's work
to Victorian visual culture can be discerned even when they are indirect or
diffused through intermediary imagetexts.

The most famous seaside painting from the 1850s was William Frith's *Life at the Seaside* (*Ramsgate Sands*), exhibited at the Royal Academy in 1854 (fig. 2.7). As Christopher Wood notes, *Ramsgate Sands* established the iconography of seaside pictures, with most of its elements – "crinolines and parasols, children paddling and building sand-castles, donkey-rides and other entertainments, musicians and bathing-machines" – becoming staples of subsequent works. Although its popularity led to Frith's even more ambitious and better-known panoramas, *Derby Day* (1858) and *The Railway Station* (1862), his friends and fellow artists were initially uncertain, as was Frith himself, about such an everyday modern-life subject. Some, like John Leech and Augustus Egg, were encouraging, but others tried to dissuade him from painting seaside life at all. One of them called the painting "a piece of vulgar Cockney business," while a collector who saw an early sketch of the painting reportedly described it to another artist as "a tissue of vulgarity." Frith was vindicated, however, when the painting created a sensation at the Royal Academy Exhibition and was purchased by Queen Victoria, whose artistic tastes, while sentimental, could hardly be described as "vulgar" or "Cockney." The royal purchase confirmed not merely the propriety of the subject matter but its mode of treatment.[38]

Ramsgate Sands simultaneously depicts and erases anxieties about class frictions, sexual display, and irreligious pleasures. Like the Great Exhibition of a few years earlier, which Frith had visited while working up his original sketch for *Ramsgate Sands*, the seaside was a space where usually segregated social groups could encounter each other at close quarters. In packing together people of different sexes, ages, classes, and occupations, Frith's crowded scene threatens to undermine important Victorian distinctions. The presence of telescopes – two in use, at least two others visible – suggests the possibilities of voyeurism, of women becoming the objects of a surreptitious male gaze. Diversions of the sort condemned by the seaside naturalists as frivolous – strolling minstrels, animal acts, a Punch and Judy show – are prominent. Yet Frith clearly seeks to neutralize the potential threat posed by these elements and to incorporate them as much as possible into a harmonious whole. Ramsgate itself was a resort dominated by middle- rather than working-class visitors, and the painting maintains class distinctions. The figures enjoying life at the seaside are all middle class, while those who provide entertainment are not. The lower-class proprietors and vendors are for the most part respectful and deferential. The man with the white mice at the center of the canvas kneels before the group of young women to whom he displays his little pets. While the stout woman at the left is less pleased with the sales efforts of the man at her feet, he, too, is

Figure 2.7   William Powell Frith, *Life at the Seaside (Ramsgate Sands)* (1854). Oil on canvas.

kneeling, presenting his wares almost as an offering. Behind the groups at the water's edge, children are held up by adults to see the shows or select a treat. Only at the right rear is disruption brewing, a respectable couple being either in a dispute with, or aggressively importuned by, the donkey-ride proprietor and his boy. Unlike the depictions of crime and conflict in *The Derby Day* or *The Railway Station*, however, this incident is not central and does not threaten to disrupt or undermine, or even comment upon, the decorous and surprisingly domestic social world of the rest of the painting.[39] Indeed, the most prominent entertainment of *Ramsgate Sands*, positioned at its very center, is a "happy family," an animal act consisting of creatures normally at odds (cat and bird, dog and rabbit) but here interacting without rancor.

Although this is not exactly a world of "rational recreation," and no one is engaged in shell-hunting, many of the figures are reading, and at least seven of the women have books. We cannot tell whether these are novels or volumes of Gosse or Harvey or Pratt, but the readers seem serious rather than frivolous. Only the lounging man to the right has the air of an idler, and only the man in the middle ground center, sitting in a chair with his back to us, leaning forward and looking into the face of the young woman seated next to him, seems to be flirting. Such muting of sexuality is one of the painting's most consistent characteristics. Despite the presence of bathing machines, we see no bathers, no bodies on view. The only flesh to which our eyes are directed is admittedly the central incident on the canvas, but it is merely the legs of the little girl being gently dipped by her mother into the edge of the waves. While one of the figures looking through a telescope is a middle-aged man, the other, standing just in front of him and looking in roughly the same direction, is a fashionably dressed young girl. Voyeurism here is not prurient, but innocent and curious. By depicting the scene from the water rather than, as in the other seaside pictures, from the beach itself (a fact noted by both the *Athenaeum* and the *Times*), Frith locates the artist and spectator in the sea, observing but not seeing what is forbidden.[40]

The writers and illustrators at magazines like *Punch*, however, delighted in exploiting the absurdities of the seaside naturalist and in drawing attention to the inadvertent role of seaside books in promoting rather than salving such sexual and class anxieties. A frequent theme in cartoons was the extent to which the beachcombing activities of women actually increased the voyeuristic opportunities for men. In "Common Objects at the Seaside" (fig. 2.8), the title echoing both Wood's *Common Objects of the Sea-Shore* and Pratt's *Common Things of the Sea-Side*, John Leech captures all of

COMMON OBJECTS AT THE SEA-SIDE—GENERALLY FOUND UPON THE ROCKS AT LOW WATER.

Figure 2.8   John Leech, "Common Objects at the Seaside – Generally Found Upon the Rocks at Low Water." Wood engraving for *Punch* 35 (21 August 1858): 76.

these elements simultaneously. The middle-class women, bent over better to observe the creatures of the tidal pools, their skirts and petticoats upended and exposed, are clearly ridiculous. They even *look* like sea anemones (fig. 2.13b), Gosse's trademark animal, plain and nondescript when its brilliantly-colored tentacles are retracted but an underwater flower when tentacles are extended and waving gently. Women in such a position are "common" objects, however: the popularity of seaside collecting makes this a frequent sight, but the display of their skirts and the turning of their bottoms to passersby is, even if unintended, "coarse" and vulgar. By making a public spectacle of their nether regions, these middle-class women become dangerously similar to prostitutes. Their search for "common objects at the seaside" converts *them* into objects of an implicitly male gaze. But the moment of titillation, the forbidden scopic pleasure to which the idle male shoregoer and the male reader of *Punch* are both treated, is all the sweeter for being a moment of power in which the women are unaware of their position.

"Seaside Sirens" (fig. 2.9) positions the male viewer within the image and trades on a somewhat different set of sexual anxieties. The women are young and fashionably dressed. The one in the center, her long blonde hair

CARTOONS OF THE SEASON.

No. 7.—SEASIDE SIRENS.

Figure 2.9 "Cartoons of the Season. No. 7.—Seaside Sirens." Wood engraving, 1855.

THE SEA SIDE.—DRAWN BY H. K. BROWN ("PHIZ.")

Figure 2.10   Hablot K. Browne ("Phiz"), "The Sea Side." Wood engraving for *The Illustrated London News* 29 (2 August 1856): 131.

hanging loose, resembles Fanny Cornforth, the voluptuous model who from 1856 appeared in so many of Dante Rossetti's canvases. While engaged in a variety of pursuits that include beachcombing, these women are far from being ridiculous. Their absorption in what they are doing is serious and attentive. Unlike their namesakes, they are not luring men to their deaths and seem unaware of the male eyes upon them. Yet the woman in the left foreground, who is about to dislodge the rock for the benefit of her companion with the long-handled net, is bending over, her crinolines lifted up. The men in the background, who seem to have stumbled upon the scene, are taken up short by this vision of loveliness, but their eyes appear to be directed in particular towards the bent-over woman with her skirts in the air. As in "Common Objects at the Seaside," we have a moment of voyeuristic male pleasure, a pleasure that is here even purer because of the beauty of the women and the absence of men from amongst them. But the title of the picture also signals male unease. Is the obliviousness of these "seaside sirens" to their male audience merely an act, their attitudes staged to display them to advantage to strolling males? Even if not, even if they are wholly innocent of the temptation they present, to name them as sirens suggests that the two men who gaze upon them are now trapped, in thrall to their beauty.

A similar motif appears in Hablot K. Browne's "The Sea Side" (fig. 2.10) for the *Illustrated London News*.[41] Browne's cartoon could be Frith's *Life at the Seaside* rotated 90°, the man in the center with the telescope closely resembling the corresponding figure on the left side of Frith's painting. The two men on the left of Browne's cartoon, like their counterparts in "Seaside Sirens," appear to be looking intently at the woman in the left foreground with her back to them. This time, however, the joke is more clearly aimed at the voyeuristic men. The woman is not displaying herself unwittingly to them and is obviously not the beauty they perhaps think her to be.

In contrast to these crowded images, one of the decade's other great seaside paintings, William Dyce's *Pegwell Bay* (fig. 2.11), offers a much starker view. The human figures are scattered about the canvas, many barely distinguishable. Even the three women and the boy in the foreground are isolated from each other, their attention focused in different directions. The tone of the painting is serious, even solemn. Missing is the bustle of pleasurable idling and frivolous entertainment. Commentators on the painting have tended to argue that humans and human life are rendered as insignificant, especially in comparison to the vastness of time (as represented by the geological strata of the cliffs) and space (as represented by Donati's Comet, visible in the sky above the cliffs). Marcia Pointon, for example, emphasizes that the painting's full title, *A Recollection of October 5th, 1858*, draws attention to this temporal element. For Pointon, *Pegwell Bay* is a painting *about* time, and especially about the contrast between human time and deep or cosmic time. The figures in the painting, she notes, with the exception of the artist in the right middle ground, are oblivious to the comet and the cliffs. Astronomy and geology "deny the validity of a single human life and, even more, of a single human day. Nevertheless, sea-shell gathering is the only reality for these people in this place on this day."[42]

If we consider *Pegwell Bay* in light of the seaside natural history of the 1850s, however, the shell collecting activities of the humans in the foreground (and the adult–child pair who seem to be looking amongst the rock pools in the left middle distance) are not to be seen in contrast with the lessons of geology and astronomy but as associated with them. Donati's Comet appears in the center of the canvas, aligned vertically with part of the cliffs and the two women in the middle foreground who are looking down at the sand. Yet their failure to attend to comet and cliffs is not the result of engagement with something frivolous, but with something important. As Gosse and the other seaside writers had emphasized, the study of shells and marine creatures was the study of the handiwork of the Creator. Cosmic lessons of hope, of Divine benevolence, even of the promise of the second coming, could be read from them. To the extent that astronomy and geology rendered humans insignificant, seaside studies offered reassurance

Figure 2.12 "The Plumose Anemone &c." Chromolithograph from a drawing by Philip
Henry Gosse. Plate v from Philip Henry Gosse, *The Aquarium*, 2nd edn. (London: Van
Voorst, 1856).

drawings but also the lithographic "pattern" plates. Gosse's illustrations, as
Herbert Sussman has noted, had much in common with the contemporary
paintings of the early Pre-Raphaelites. Both were shaped by the belief that
careful observation of the natural world could reveal spiritual truths, and
both were characterized stylistically by closely rendered detail, clearly illuminated individual figures with hard-edged outlines on a flattened picture
plane, and definition by (often brilliant) color rather than chiaroscuro.[43]
Indeed, the color in Gosse's illustrations, like that in the Pre-Raphaelites'
canvases, provoked astonishment and even disbelief. In his biography of
his father, Edmund Gosse recalled that several reviewers questioned the
accuracy of the plates of sea anemones in *A Naturalist's Rambles*, and that
the even more spectacular illustrations in *The Aquarium* (fig. 2.12) "made
a positive sensation, and marked an epoch in the annals of English book
illustration."[44] Despite the confirmation of the stylistic affinities between

Philip and the Pre-Raphaelites afforded by Edmund's account in *Father and Son* of their reaction to Holman Hunt's *The Finding of the Saviour in the Temple*, Gosse nonetheless relied on the conventions of popular natural history illustration to provide his readers with a distinctive visual natural theology.[45] And while Gosse successfully incorporated Darwin's barnacle work into his natural theological imagetexts during the 1850s, the publication of the *Origin* at the end of the decade not only made it difficult for him to maintain his earlier attitude towards Darwin's barnacles but also threatened to rupture his imagetexts by undermining their assumptions and exposing their constructedness.

Gosse has had the misfortune to be known to twentieth-century, and now twenty-first-century, audiences primarily through *Father and Son* (1907), his son Edmund's account of their relationship during Edmund's childhood. In *Father and Son*, Philip Henry exemplifies the wrong-headed Victorian Protestant fundamentalism that futilely resisted the advancing tide of scientific naturalism epitomized by Darwin's theory.[46] The relationship between religion and natural science in Gosse's publications, however, was more complex. At one level, Gosse was, as we have seen, a typical if important exponent of British natural theology. He believed that the careful study of the habits and anatomy of even the lowest forms of marine life would lead the idle pleasure-seeker to God. Such study "will not fail to reward us with increased knowledge of His works and ways," compelling us "to say with the Psalmist, 'I will praise Thee; for all is fearfully and wonderfully made.'"[47] Certainly he was not reluctant to echo William Paley's emphasis on the skillfully designed anatomical "contrivances" of his specimens, and like the authors of the Bridgewater Treatises, the eight books "On the Power, Wisdom, and Goodness of God, as Manifested in the Creation" published in the 1830s as a result of a bequest by the eighth Earl of Bridgewater, he frequently praised the evidence of Divine power, wisdom, and goodness.[48] "[T]he contrivances of [marine creatures'] organization," he wrote in *A Naturalist's Rambles*, "are the fruit of his infinite Wisdom" and thus elicit "adoring wonder and praise." *Evenings at the Microscope* is especially fulsome in its praise of Paley's watchmaker-God, whose "wondrous skill" and "Divine mechanics" are evident in the "perfect adaptation of organ to function, of structure to habit" that marks all His works. In the case of the gorgeous coloration of these marine creatures, where no such adaptive fit was evident, the Creator had worked for *our* pleasure and delight. To admire them represents not prurient ogling but "the gratification of our sense of beauty," which has been "implanted in our nature by the beneficent Creator, expressly for our satisfaction."[49]

But the natural theology in Gosse's books nonetheless differed from that in most works of popular natural history. Despite the frequent invocations of Paley's arguments, many Victorians feared the unintended implications of natural theology. As Frank Turner has emphasized, its utilitarian readings of nature meant that the existence of suffering and death in the natural economy had to be minimized or justified by an appeal to some larger (and often unknown) Divine purpose, strategies that contributed to the very secularization of nature that so offended its supporters.[50] Furthermore, the evidence of design in nature could be read as pointing to a designer, but not necessarily to the Christian God immanent in the world. Worse, atheists and evolutionists could deny the inference to a God at all, asserting instead that life continually created itself. While both Paley and the Bridgewater authors were careful to stress natural theology's limitations and its inferiority to revealed religion, such qualifications could be obscured in works that did not repeatedly connect the evidence of nature to that of Scripture. As a result, Gosse often offered frank and forceful critiques of natural theology. In a chapter on "The Right Use of Natural History" in *The Aquarium*, while acknowledging that "some of the attributes of the Creator . . . may be deduced from his works," he insists that "a man may be a most learned and complete expounder of natural theology, and yet be pitiably blind on the all-important subject of a sinner's justification with God." In a fallen universe, nature is not divine, and traditional natural theology cannot possibly teach us the path to salvation. After Darwin's publication of the *Origin*, Gosse was even more emphatic. He closed *A Year at the Shore* (1865), which he announced would be his last work for the public, with an attack on the natural theology of popular scientific writing. While decrying the open assaults on religion in many scientific works, Gosse argued that most popular natural theology was "equally dangerous and more insidious" for ignoring "the awful truths of God's revelation." Natural theology, he wrote, is valuable to someone who is already a Christian, but "to attempt to scale heaven with the ladder of natural history, is nothing else than Cain's religion; it is the presentation of the fruit of the earth, instead of the blood of the Lamb." To avoid this pitfall, Gosse articulated a natural theology in which nature, if read correctly, pointed beyond a kindly Creator to the promises and prophecies of the Christian revelation.[51]

As John Brooke has emphasized, natural theology is better understood in terms of natural theologies, with different versions reflecting various religious cultures.[52] In Gosse's case, his natural theology was shaped by the beliefs and exegetical practices of evangelicalism and especially of the Plymouth Brethren, whom he had joined in 1847. The Brethren believed in the inerrancy of Scripture, rejected ritual and hierarchy, encouraged public testimonials of faith as a tool for proselytization, and scrutinized Biblical prophecy for guidance on the conduct of believers in what they believed were the rapidly approaching final days of divine judgment and the subsequent return of Christ.[53] While living in London, Gosse preached extempore sermons to a congregation at Hackney; moving in 1857 to Marychurch, just outside Torquay in Devon, he quickly became the main preacher and administrator of the small community of Brethren there. Gosse's books were thus an effort to "testify" to Christ's redemptive powers and to provide glimpses in the marine life of England's southwestern coast of the "new earth" of Christ's triumphal reign. Central to Gosse's approach was his application of typological interpretation to the natural world. Evangelicals in particular frequently employed typology to interpret Old Testament stories and figures, which were read as symbols of the New Testament events that fulfilled them. For example, Abraham's willingness to sacrifice Isaac, his only son, and God's provision of a ram as a substitute, were seen as a type of God's gift of Christ, whose death atoned for humanity's sins.[54] Gosse argued that the Scriptures often used natural objects as symbols or types of truths that might be rejected if articulated directly, and thus that we are free to utilize the same process with the actual objects of nature. "All earthly things are types of the heavenlies; the visible, shadows and outlines of the invisible," he wrote. Thus it is "not too much to presume that the order and fashion of material things were planned expressly" to reflect "ideas of heavenly and unseen things" – not merely the attributes of the Creator, but "the God of revelation, the God of Grace, the God and Father of our Lord Jesus Christ."[55] According to Gosse, nature, like the New Testament, teaches salvation through faith and speaks to what will occur in the final days.

Examples of such readings of nature appear throughout Gosse's books but are most prominent, prior to *A Year at the Shore*, in *A Naturalist's Rambles on the Devonshire Coast* and *The Aquarium*. A seaweed that is dull when removed from the water but brilliant when re-submerged "may be compared to some Christians, who are dull and profitless in prosperity, but whose graces shine out gloriously when they are plunged into the deep floods of affliction." The mode of eating of the broad-claw crab, whose hairy claws sweep food to its mouth, reminds Gosse of "the Gospel net, mentioned by our Lord," which is itself used as an image both of the church and of the subsequent separation of nominal from true believers.[56] But the

most common and most extensively developed typological interpretations
of nature emerge from Gosse's discussions of coastal rock pools.

The extraordinary concentration of marine life in these pools made them
the focus of Gosse's field observations and the textual and visual centerpieces
of his books. His narratives frequently move from one pool to another, his
illustrations frequently attempt to represent species in this natural environment, and his descriptions frequently end with a typological reading of their
significance. Gosse recurrently figures the pools as gardens that can either
be "harvested" of their specimens or metaphorically strolled through for the
pleasure they afford. Edenic allusions abound, but the pools are a prelapsar-
ian Eden. In *Tenby*, anemones hang from the walls of one pool "like some
ripe pulpy fruit, tempting the eye and the mouth." In *A Naturalist's Rambles*,
Gosse drops to his knees at the side of a rock pool at Oddicombe, bringing
his face close to the surface of the water in a position that recalls Milton's
Eve. But instead of gazing at his own reflection, or even seeing through a
glass, darkly, Gosse asserts that when the naturalist who worships God peers
through the surface, "the whole interior" of the pool becomes "distinctly
visible."[57]

Indeed, Gosse is himself a sort of Miltonic Adam, for the glories of the
future are revealed to him in these unfallen nooks of Creation. The pools
look forward as well as backward in time, providing a glimpse of the coming reign of Christ on earth and of the heavenly Jerusalem. In *A Naturalist's
Rambles*, describing the amount and variety of marine life contained on a
small piece of stone chiseled from the side of a rock pool, Gosse is most
struck by the "vast amount of happiness we here get . . . a glimpse of!"
Not one of these tiny creatures, Gosse claims, is lacking in health or food,
and hence each is experiencing, relative to its capacities, full and continuous pleasure. Although Adam's sin is borne by the whole creation, "yet
we may suppose that at least the invertebrate portions of the animal creation suffer their share of the fall rather corporately than individually, rather
nominally, in dignity, than consciously, in pain or want." This fairly typical
Paleyan optimism regarding the distribution of pleasure and pain in nature
is couched in characteristically Gossean terms, however. The rock pools are
as close as we can come to a vision of the utter profusion and perfect happiness in nature prior to the fall. As a result, they also suggest what nature
will be like when Christ returns and establishes, with his saints, his reign on
earth, when "creation shall be more than reinstated in primal honour" and
"even these low-born atoms . . . shall . . . get an augmentation of happiness, and thus take their humble share in the blessing of the redeemed

inheritance." Similarly, in *The Aquarium*, Gosse argues that corallines, "a City . . . of myriad individuals" sharing "a common life," reflects that heavenly Jerusalem where "happy spirits in resurrection bodies" collectively form "the Church of the living God, the Bride of Christ."[58] The pleasure we take in the rock pools, which seem to be almost immune from the consequences of the fall, and even in "poor Polype[s]," is a type of the pleasure we shall some day take in all of nature.

Gosse's illustrations were intimately connected to the visuality of the text, the culmination of a series of scopic acts. First, the collecting narratives invited the reader to see vicariously the contents of each rock pool, jetty crevice, or marine cavern. Then these specimens were brought home for observation in one of Gosse's aquariums and/or through a microscope. Finally, Gosse's illustrations generally attempted to represent the specimen as it appeared in its natural environment. While representations of coastal marine life in Gosse's books were thus designed to illustrate the Paleyan vision of organisms designed for their environments, they also reinforced and generally elevated Gosse's own typological readings. The first step in this process was to stress that his drawings illustrated *living* creatures. As Edmund later noted, his father had long complained that natural history had become "a science of dead things," a study not of living organisms in their natural environments but of dried, stuffed, preserved – and consequently deformed and distorted – specimens (*Life*, 228). Clearly the existence of a living God, actively caring for his creation and leaving signs of its fate, could be better seen in living creatures, and the aquarium made that possible. But the interests of Paleyan natural theology were served in Gosse's illustrations primarily by aesthetic beauty. To see creatures "in their proper haunts" was to see them "with their beauty of form and brilliance of colour" – and to know how beneficent God had been in providing us with such pleasure even among the lowest creatures in the most unlikely places.[59] The emphasis on the Creator's wisdom and goodness in designing species with anatomical contrivances relevant to their particular environmental niches, on the other hand – something frequently demonstrated through dissection – tended to be confined by Gosse to his textual descriptions of microscopical investigations. Although Gosse's depiction of representatives of a variety of species in some "proper haunt" implicitly reinforced the connection between species and environment, this was not and could not be his focus, given his view of the limitations of most forms of natural theology. In Gosse's typological readings of the rock pools, the visual emphasis is on the relationship *among* individuals in an environment. His illustrations present a sort of aquatic peaceable kingdom – a submarine "happy family" – with different species coexisting in a benign setting, each with adequate resources. For Gosse, nature is full of almost unlimited joy and happiness, untainted by competition or suffering. The rock pools are pictured as having the same qualities as the unfallen Garden of Eden and the redeemed nature that Gosse's texts claim they represent. It is the visual glimpse of the millennial kingdom that awaits the true believer and will be shared in common with all other believers.

The mediating function of the aquarium in this process cannot be underestimated. As Martin Rudwick has noted in his study of nineteenth-century pictorial representations of the prehistoric world, until the development of the aquarium made the aquarium-view part of Victorian culture's iconography, scientists were reluctant to depict underwater scenes for fear of being labeled fanciful or speculative.[60] By describing his specimens as seen both in nature and in the aquarium, Gosse made the latter a stand-in for the former. His illustrations, although based on aquarium and even microscopical observations, thus could be used to represent "natural" scenes. And by providing his readers with extensive instructions on building and maintaining an aquarium, obtaining specimens, and conducting experiments and observations, Gosse made it possible for them to replicate these visual acts and to connect this artificial, domesticated environment with its wild counterpart.

Gosse's millennial vision faced a special challenge after Darwin published the *Origin*, however. In the first part of his *Manual of Marine Zoology*, Gosse calls Darwin the "paramount authority" on barnacles. In *Tenby*, Darwin's monograph is a "monument of research and acumen" whose startling demonstration of barnacle metamorphosis Gosse has "the pleasure of confirming." He even provides, as I noted earlier, a Paleyan gloss on the phenomenon, declaring it obviously to have been ordained by the wisdom of God. With the appearance of the *Origin*, Gosse apparently realized that in putting Darwin's barnacles to work in support of the argument from design, he had made himself vulnerable in similar ways to the popular expositions of natural theology he despised. Barnacle metamorphosis could be just as easily ascribed to natural selection as to the wisdom of God, so Gosse sought to neutralize the danger. In *A Year at the Shore*, Gosse damns Darwin with the faintly-praising epithet of "a perfectly dependable naturalist" and is content merely to describe his researches.[61] Celebrations both of Darwin's achievement and of the Creator's wisdom vanish. At the same time, Gosse turned increasingly to Darwin's *Beagle* narrative for evidence that he either incorporated into anti-evolutionary arguments or employed in his own typological readings of nature. Gosse uses the Darwin of the South American rain forests or South Pacific islands to demonstrate that the rock pools of the English coast are not the only sites that testify to the Christian's inheritance. In *The Romance of Natural History*, Gosse follows one of Darwin's descriptions of Tahiti with a vision of the earth after Christ's return:

I have delighted to believe, that . . . when, in the millennial kingdom of Jesus, and, still more, in the remoter future . . . the earth – the "new earth", – shall be endowed with a more than paradisiacal glory, there will be given to redeemed man a greatly increased power and capacity for drinking in and enjoying the augmented loveliness.[62]

Tahiti may seem a paradise to Darwin, but for Gosse it, too, is best interpreted typologically as a sign of the "more than paradisiacal glory" of the redeemed earth.

Gosse's drawings show him making a similar visual move, but the comparison of drawings and text often exposes the tenuousness of his representations. Despite his insistence that the aquarium permits us "to bring a portion of the sea . . . to the side of our study-table," Gosse drew individual organisms in isolation, often under a microscope, and almost invariably without the slightest hint of surroundings.[63] He did not, in other words, draw aquarium scenes. Rather, as Edmund pointed out in his father's *Life*, he constructed them:

in late years he was accustomed to make a kind of patchwork quilt of each full-page illustration, collecting as many individual forms as he wished to present, each separately coloured and cut out, and then gummed into its place on the general plate, upon which a background . . . was then washed in. (*Life*, 341)

While this "patchwork" approach had technical advantages and was governed in part by material constraints, it also fitted nicely with Gosse's parallel shift in textual emphasis to a natural theology heavily informed by typological readings of nature. An examination of Gosse's drawings at the Horniman Museum in London, moreover, suggests that this method was used as early as *A Naturalist's Rambles* and began to become common in *Actinologia Britannica*, which originally appeared in parts in 1858–59 and thus bracketed the announcement of Darwin's theory. In figure 2.13, we see that Gosse originally drew *Aiptasia couchii* in isolation on the front of an envelope before copying it onto a proof plate for *Actinologia Britannica*. Although this was designed as a reference work for both beginners and advanced zoologists, Gosse rejects the visual conventions of taxonomic monographs, instead

(a)   (b)

Figure 2.13   (a) Pen and watercolor sketch by Philip Henry Gosse of *Aiptasia couchii* for
Actinologia Britannica, drawn on the front of an envelope. (b) Lithographic proof plate
for plate v of Philip Henry Gosse's *Actinologia Britannica*. *Aiptasia couchii* (item 3) has
been copied from the sketch in (a). From "British Sea-Anemones and Corals: Original
Sketches and Drawings in Colour by Philip Henry Gosse and his Correspondents,
1839–1861," items 44 and 56 on folio pages 25 and 34.

positioning the individual species on his plates in a natural environment,
the rock pools and caverns in which they could be found. Figure 2.14 shows
that two lithographic drawings of *Actinia thallia* have literally been cut out
and pasted onto the proof plate.[64] Gosse thus removed specimens from their
various natural settings, mixed them together in his aquarium, drew them
in isolation, and then re-assembled the individual drawings into a scene presented as a single location in nature where these various specimens lived in
harmonious profusion in the peaceable kingdom that prefigured the world
of the second coming.

   As Christopher Hamlin has noted, however, the aquarium's harmonious
profusion was in practice notoriously difficult to establish and maintain.
An imbalance of plants and animals, the mixing of predators and prey,
fluctuations in light or temperature – any of these could turn an aquarium

(a)

(b)

Figure 2.14   Lithographic proofs of individual figures (a) and the lithographic proof plate itself (b) for plate IV of Philip Henry Gosse's *Actinologia Britannica*. The two figures of *Actinia thallia* in an open and closed state (items 5 and 6) in (b) have been cut and pasted from (a). From "British Sea-Anemones and Corals: Original Sketches and Drawings in Colour by Philip Henry Gosse and his Correspondents, 1839–1861," items 28 and 55 on folio pages 15 and 33.

into a site of death and destruction. As a result, most aquarium writers initially reflected a tension between what Hamlin calls "the harmonious aquarium" and "the evangelical aquarium," with the former increasingly de-emphasized in favor of the latter. From replicating in miniature "the Creator's wisdom and goodness in establishing a beautiful, bountiful, healthful, and self-sustaining world," the aquarium became "a stage for endless moral dramas" involving individual creatures, a place for observing moral conditions, drawing moral lessons, and imposing moral improvements on the inhabitants.[65] Gosse, while exemplifying this tension in his earliest books, resolved it in a somewhat different way. He retained a vision of the "harmonious aquarium," but it symbolized the Creation's past and future states as much as mirroring its present one.

With the advent of Darwinism, however, Gosse's version of the harmonious aquarium and his natural theological imagetexts became vulnerable to fracturing and reinterpretation. This can be exemplified by two plates from *A Year at the Shore*. In the first, Gosse's plate (fig. 2.15a) contains a species of sea cucumber with a dotted siponcle. Although the drawing of the sea cucumber at the Horniman Museum (fig. 2.15b) contains no background, the plate conveys a sense of the location from which Gosse's text says he obtained it. The dotted siponcle, however, is very different in appearance from the sea cucumber and is not mentioned as having been present in the same environment. Its presence in the plate can nonetheless be accounted for by Gosse's explanation that siponcles are the species that connect sea cucumbers with worms, despite their very different appearance from both. The plate is thus the visual rendering of what he calls in *Actinologia Britannica* "radiations of relation," the matrix of complex affinities within and among species.[66] It provides the visual depiction of the fecundity of the Creator's world, of the related but distinct forms that fill every niche of the natural economy. But it does so only by creating an illusion: the juxtaposition, though presented as existing in nature, is not confirmed by Gosse's narrative. And in its attempt to stand as a silent alternative to Darwinian accounts of species relation, it seems almost to invite the Darwinian explanation that these "radiations of relation" are the result of natural selection operating over time on a common ancestor.

In the second plate, Gosse depicts the green opelet and the orange-disk anemone in a scene suggestive of the isolated "rocky channels" that his text gushes over for the beauty and profusion of their inhabitants (fig. 2.16).[67] Yet Gosse's narrative reveals that he obtained the green opelet not in the rocky channels but in a heap of seaweed dredged up in open water a half-hour's row away. As with the first plate, Gosse's cut-and-paste patchwork is used to support his reading of nature, but Gosse's text also potentially undermines the visual statement of his plates – and thus of the typological readings based on them – by revealing that they are not "natural," and in some senses not even accurate, at all. And with the Darwinian view of nature making the peaceable kingdom look increasingly violent and competitive, Gosse's "patchwork" plates came to seem increasingly forced both to the

PLATE 3.

(a)

P. H. GOSSE, *del.*   LEIGHTON, BROS,

DOTTED SIPONCLE.   SEA-CUCUMBER.

(b)

Figure 2.15   (a) "Dotted Siponcle. Sea-Cucumber." Chromolithograph by Leighton Brothers from a drawing by Philip Henry Gosse. Plate 3 from *A Year at the Shore* (London: Strahan, 1865), facing page 28. (b) Pen and watercolor sketch by Philip Henry Gosse of a sea cucumber. From "British Sea-Anemones and Corals: Original Sketches and Drawings in Colour by Philip Henry Gosse and his Correspondents, 1839–1861," item 69+.

PLATE 9.

P. H. GOSSE, *ld*.   LEIGHTON, BROS.

GREEN OPELET.   ORANGE-DISK ANEMONE.

Figure 2.16 "Green Opelet. Orange-Disk Anemone." Chromolithograph by Leighton
Brothers from a drawing by Philip Henry Gosse. Plate 9 from *A Year at the Shore*
(London: Strahan, 1865), facing page 78.

public and to Gosse himself. Edmund asserts that the plates of *A Year at the
Shore* "were a source of acute disappointment" to his father; that while the
individual specimens were produced with great accuracy, the overall "effect"
was less harmonious and provided less pleasure (*Life*, 341).

A humorous anecdote related by Edmund in his father's *Life* captures
the instability of Gosse's imagetexts. Edmund recalls a childhood collecting
expedition with his father during which they encountered a group of similarly engaged women excited by the discovery of a rare specimen. Overcome
with curiosity, Philip asked to examine their specimen, and after doing so,
pronounced it a far more common species. The women, however, refused
to believe him: they "drew themselves up with dignity, and sarcastically
remarked that . . . it *was* the rarity, and that 'Gosse is our authority'" (*Life*,
288, original emphasis). Such was Gosse's dilemma. Although regarded as
an "authority," he saw his work applied in erroneous, unexpected, and often
unwelcome ways. Desirous of making his science a form of worship and his
books a testimonial for Christ, he found himself increasingly at odds with
both natural theology and scientific naturalism. In encouraging the study
of the Devonshire rock pools, he unwittingly contributed to the destruction of the very sites on which his typological readings depended. If Gosse's

imagetexts provide an example of the challenge Darwin had to overcome to establish visual authority for his own way of seeing, their disruption also demonstrates the pressure Darwin's theory exerted on perspectives long assumed to be natural. It wasn't until the 1870s, however, with the publication of *The Descent of Man*, that the aesthetic threat posed by Darwinism truly burst into public view.

CHAPTER 3

Darwin's birds

Darwin was never the expert on birds that he was on marine invertebrates, but he took a keen interest in them, and they were crucial to the arguments of the *Origin*, *The Variation of Animals and Plants Under Domestication*, and *The Descent of Man*. The Galapagos finches, despite the mythic trappings that have come to surround them, really were vital to his conversion to evolutionary thinking in the late 1830s. His interest in pigeon breeding helped him formulate the analogy between artificial selection and natural selection. Birds of various types, but especially those with brilliantly colored or elaborately ornamented plumage, were at the heart of his discussion of sexual selection.

In nineteenth-century England, pictures of birds were everywhere. Thomas Bewick's highly regarded wood engravings for his *History of British Birds* (1797, 1804) were widely reproduced in other books on ornithology and natural history, including some of the later editions of such popular eighteenth-century works as Gilbert White's *Natural History and Antiquities of Selbourne* (1789) and Oliver Goldsmith's *History of the Earth, and Animated Nature* (1779). By the 1830s, a flood of illustrated bird books was appearing, in formats ranging from the small and cheap to the large and sumptuous, many of the latter employing the relatively new medium of lithography. Writing from London in 1835, John James Audubon complained that "Here there are at present three Works publishing on the Birds of Europe – one by Mr. Gould and the others by No one Knows who – at least I do not Know – Works on the Birds of *all the World* are innumerable – Cheap as dirt and more dirty than dirt."[1] Whatever the merits of the notoriously critical Audubon's assessment of the quality of these books, his comment on their quantity seems only slightly exaggerated. John Gould, in addition to his *Birds of Europe* (1832–37), had completed his *Century of Birds Hitherto Unfigured from the Himalaya Mountains* (1830–32) and was in the process of finishing an illustrated monograph on toucans and launching one on trogons. He was assisted by Edward Lear, whose volume on parrots earlier in the decade had received lavish praise. Prideaux John Selby had just closed his splendid *Illustrations of British Ornithology* (1821–34) and was in the midst of his collaborations with William Jardine on *Illustrations of Ornithology* (1825–43) and with Jardine and William Swainson on the fourteen volumes of birds for *The Naturalist's Library* (1833–43), the first inexpensive illustrated work of ornithology for middle-class readers. Swainson, meanwhile, was also authoring the ornithological volumes for the *Cabinet Cyclopaedia* and a few years later would produce *A Selection of the Birds of Brazil and Mexico* (1841). Henry Leonard Meyer had just begun his four-volume *Illustrations of British Birds* (1835–41), while Thomas Campbell Eyton's *Rarer British Birds* would appear in 1836. In 1837, ornithologists William Yarrell and William Macgillivray both began a multi-volume *History of British Birds*. Although the ornithological content of Macgillivray's book was regarded as superior (Darwin used it in the *Descent* as his primary source on British species), its poor illustrations hindered sales; Yarrell's work quickly became the standard illustrated textbook, appearing in new editions in 1845, 1856, and 1871–85. In the second half of the century, this flood only increased. Widely read scientific popularizers such as Jane Loudon (1807–1858) and the Revs. F. O. Morris (1810–1893), C. A. Johns (1811–1874), and J. G. Wood (1827–1889) increasingly provided pictures for children and readers seeking more informal introductions to ornithology in both illustrated bird books and illustrated natural histories.[2]

By the time Darwin began his career as a scientific author, audiences for bird books – whether popular, scientific, or mixed – expected illustrations, and London contained a number of artists, illustrators, lithographers, and engravers with the experience and skill to provide them. For the volume of his *Zoology* of the *Beagle* voyage devoted to birds, Darwin recruited Gould and his wife, Elizabeth, to produce the colored lithographs. But when it came time to decide on illustrations for the *Descent* some thirty years later, Darwin faced a dilemma. Birds were central to the explanation of his theory of sexual selection, his account of the origin of the differences in secondary sexual characteristics between males and females so common throughout the animal kingdom. Sexual selection in birds occurs in a number of ways, but the two most prominent, Darwin argued, were violent competition among males and, especially, female selection of mates with the most brilliantly colored or ornamented plumage or the most pleasing songs. The conventions of bird illustration, however, took little or no account of such behavior. In some cases, Darwin was able to commission illustrations for the *Descent*, especially its second edition, that better reflected his theories, but in general he contented himself with working within existing conventions of ornithological illustration, relying on textual language to control the way his readers viewed the accompanying illustrations. In many instances, attempting to construct his own seamless imagetext required him to expose and exploit the weakness in the imagetexts of others, but particularly those of the ornithologist on whom he had so much depended, John Gould.

Like Philip Gosse's works of seaside natural history, John Gould's bird books provided his subscribers with a form of visual natural theology. But Gould did not share Gosse's radical evangelicalism, and his audience differed in important respects from Gosse's. Gould's subscriber list, which reached 1000 in 1866, was dominated by the wealthy. It included twelve monarchs (headed by Victoria) and numerous members of the aristocracy and landed gentry, those whose parks and forests provided haven for many of the British birds as well as for Gould's researches.[3] Although a self-made man, Gould depended heavily throughout his life, from his early apprenticeship as a royal gardener to his unofficial positions as George IV's taxidermist and Victoria and Albert's bird artist of choice, on the patronage of the royal family and the aristocracy. Similarly, as a scientist, Gould's sympathies clearly lay with those among the conservative elite who rejected scientific naturalism and regarded its sociopolitical implications with suspicion. Audubon had early noted that Gould's connections at the gentlemanly Zoological Society and his correspondence with "the Scientific Gentry" gave him great advantages.[4] Gould provided his subscribers with a fairly aggressive visual response to Darwin's views, particularly in *The Birds of Great Britain* (1862–73), his most successful book and the first to be launched after the publication of the *Origin*. *The Birds of Great Britain* offers this audience a reassuring look at a natural world that is not in flux but fixed, not unstable but stable, not wantonly violent but purposefully designed. The Cambridge ornithologist Alfred Newton, who knew Gould well, declared to his brother in 1864 that Gould "does not care a rap whether [Darwin's theory] is true or not – but he is dreadfully afraid that by prematurely espousing it he might lose some subscribers."[5] Most of all, Gould's British birds are presented in family portraits, with nurturing parents, especially females, caring for their young. This approach, virtually unprecedented in the annals of ornithological illustration, was deliberate and distinctive, a leitmotif that offered a very different view of the natural world from the one painted by Darwin in his accounts of natural and sexual selection. And despite the expense of Gould's books and his limited subscriber list, his birds migrated surprisingly widely in Victorian culture.

John Ruskin was one of Gould's subscribers. His condemnations of Darwinism were directed at a much broader audience, and they were not, like Gould's, indirect and subtle. But he appropriated Gould's books, particularly *The Birds of Great Britain*, for his own book on birds, *Love's Meinie*. Although Ruskin sometimes criticized Gould's imagetexts, he clearly saw in them much with which he was in sympathy. They were thus a vehicle for exposing what was dangerous and wrong with the Darwinian vision of nature, and for Ruskin as for so many of his contemporaries, that had as much to do with social and spiritual concerns as it did with scientific ones. However, for Ruskin, even more than for Gould, those social and spiritual concerns were intertwined with artistic and aesthetic ones. By the 1860s Ruskin had labored for some twenty years to educate the nation about his own moral vision of art and aesthetics, and he had begun more directly to spell out its social, political, and economic implications. He recognized in Darwin's *Descent* a powerful undermining of that project, not merely or even primarily in the account of humanity's physical inheritance, but in its evolutionary explanation for the origin of our moral and rational abilities via natural selection, and of our aesthetic sense via sexual selection. Birds were at the heart of Darwin's argument for the latter, so Ruskin, using Gould, had to respond.

DARWIN AND GOULD

When the *Beagle* left England in December, 1831, John Gould, then the Zoological Society's curator and taxidermist, was nearing completion of his first illustrated bird book.[6] By the time the *Beagle* returned nearly five years later, Gould had three new ones finished or underway. The most successful, *The Birds of Europe*, was already drawing rave reviews. A rising ornithologist and entrepreneur, Gould lost no time when, in January, 1837, Darwin sent the Society his bird specimens from the voyage. By March Gould had classified and displayed the majority of them at the Society's meetings, and he agreed to write up and illustrate the birds for Darwin's *Zoology* of the voyage. His departure on a collecting trip to Australia in 1838 compelled Darwin to obtain other assistance in finishing the work, but Gould had already completed many of the descriptions, and Elizabeth Gould had executed the fifty colored lithographs. Most significantly, however, it was Gould who had correctly identified Darwin's Galapagos finches and mockingbirds as separate but closely related species, and who provided the crucial observation that specific differences seemed to obtain among specimens from different islands in the archipelago.[7]

By the time the *Origin* appeared, Gould's fame had only grown. He had long since resigned his post at the Zoological Society to devote more time to his bird books. His trip to Australia resulted in the identification of numerous species new to science and the publication of three illustrated books. *The Birds of Australia* (1840–48), with its 600 plates, was Gould's largest and most ambitious to date, but it was no sooner completed than he embarked on two equally spectacular works, *A Monograph of the Trochilidae, or Family of Humming-birds* (1849–61) and *The Birds of Asia* (1850–83). Taking advantage of the influx of visitors to the Crystal Palace in 1851, Gould arranged to display his collection of stuffed hummers in a specially built house at the Zoological Society's Gardens. Its popularity and profitability were so considerable – some 80,000 people, including the Royal Family, visited during the six months of the Great Exhibition – that Gould and the Society's Council agreed to keep it open for an additional year.[8] Gould's birds flew off the page to become part of the visual spectacle of London, accessible to thousands who could not afford his prints.

Humming-birds was well along when Darwin and Wallace presented their papers on evolution at the Linnean Society. In the *Introduction* – which, as was his practice, he published separately in 1861 upon the work's completion – Gould claimed to offer no opinion about Darwin's theory. "What we designate a species," he wrote, "has really distinctive and constant characters . . . I have never observed an instance of variation which would lead me to suppose that it was the result of a union of two species. I write this without bias, one way or the other, as to the question of the origin of species."[9] Despite his disclaimer, however, Gould was clearly challenging the very basis of Darwin's views. To assert that the characteristics of a species are "distinctive and constant" – and Gould noted that he had no trouble distinguishing the many different species of hummingbirds – was hardly a neutral stance. Even putting aside his misunderstanding of Darwin (Gould seems to have interpreted Darwin as saying that variation and speciation are the result of hybridization), his assertion that in his experience variation does not lead to new species similarly denies what Darwin is most at pains to show.[10] Gould's *Humming-birds* catalogued in spectacular visual terms what earlier authors had already claimed: the extraordinary beauty of hummingbirds was a sign of divine craftsmanship and a gift from God to man. In his *Introduction*, Gould articulated this view most directly in a quotation from Audubon: "where is the person, I ask, who, observing this glittering fragment of the rainbow, would not pause, admire, and turn his mind with reverence towards the Almighty Creator, the wonders of whose hand we at every step discover?"[11]

Gould's contemporaries had no trouble recognizing that his bird books were shaped by a natural theological perspective, and that their content was meant to reinforce notions of species fixity. Charles Richard Weld, longtime librarian to the Royal Society, reviewing Gould's *Humming-birds* for *Fraser's*, noted approvingly the "strong antagonistic bearing to the Darwinian theory" of Gould's comments.[12] Gould's good friend Richard Owen acknowledged his presentation copy of Gould's *Introduction* by enrolling Gould on the side of the angels. "I don't remember," he wrote, "being more impressed by the unsearchable riches of Creative power – by the vastness of the field in which the various adaptations are manifested . . . the evidence which your daily practical experience enables you to give on the great problem of species is most valuable."[13] For Owen, as for Gould himself, the *Monograph* triumphantly confirmed that the many species of hummingbirds occupied particular niches in nature and varied only within narrow limits. "Adaptations" were the result of design, not natural selection. Gould's "practical experience" with hummingbirds – the exhibition of his collection had displayed him as the expert on them, and his *Monograph* had confirmed it – was far more valuable than Darwin's armchair theorizing.

Gould's hummingbirds were indeed soon appropriated for one of the most popular public rebuttals of Darwin, the Duke of Argyll's *Reign of Law* (1867). Argyll pursued a different strategy from Owen, however. Gould had argued in his *Introduction* that the "gorgeous colouring" of hummingbirds "has been given for the mere purpose of ornament, and for no other purpose of special adaptation in their mode of life – in other words, that ornament and beauty merely as such was the end proposed."[14] Implicit in this comment was a criticism of natural selection that Argyll turned into an explicit attack. If natural selection produces only useful, beneficial modifications, what is useful about the plumage of hummingbirds? Nothing, answered Argyll: "A crest of topaz is no better in the struggle for existence than a crest of sapphire. A frill ending in spangles of the emerald is no better in the battle of life than a frill ending in the spangles of the ruby." Color and ornament served no utilitarian purpose and thus could not be the result of natural selection. Beauty exists for beauty's sake, Argyll asserted, and its source is Divine: "Mere ornament and variety of form, and these for their own sake, is the only principle or rule with reference to which Creative Power seems to have worked in these wonderful and beautiful Birds."[15] And if natural selection cannot account for these ornaments, why should it be regarded as an account of species themselves?

Argyll brushed aside Darwin's claim in the *Origin* that the brilliant plumage of male birds *did* serve a utilitarian function by making males attractive to females. Indeed, Darwin had argued that a whole host of differences in secondary sexual characteristics throughout the animal kingdom were derived from the battle for a mate. Brilliant colors, elaborate markings, vocal capabilities, weaponry of various sorts – all enable the male to achieve reproductive success. In the case of antlers and horns and pincers and spurs, males fight amongst themselves for privileged access to females. In the other cases, especially amongst birds, the competition is mostly or wholly non-violent, with males displaying before the females, and the females selecting the most pleasing males as their mates. This theory of sexual selection was sketched in just a few pages of the *Origin*. Argyll in response denied that Darwin was right at any level. To say that females are attracted to brilliant males ignores the fact that female sparrows are not attracted to peacocks. Siding with Wallace, Argyll argued that it was the dull plumage of females, not the plumage of males, that required an explanation, and that the answer lay in the female's need to be inconspicuous during incubation. So, yes, he admitted, plumage does serve various purposes, but this is utility "conceived as operating by way of motive in a Creative Mind," not "as a physical cause in the production of a mechanical result."[16]

Darwin also received a presentation copy of Gould's *Introduction*. Unlike Gould, Audubon, and Argyll, however, he contemplated hummingbirds without his mind turning in reverence towards the Creator. His letter of thanks confirms that he, too, saw Gould as offering a challenge to natural selection, but even more strikingly, Darwin announces to Gould that he intends to appropriate Gould's work for his own purposes. After gently correcting Gould's misunderstanding of natural selection, Darwin tells him that "One of the points which has interested me most (which you will not approve of) is the number of 'races' or doubtful species. I think I shall extract all their cases; as it will show . . . that the determination of species is not a simple affair."[17] Indeed, Darwin's annotations to his copy of Gould's *Introduction* suggest that Darwin read the work with an eye toward those passages that could be used not only in subsequent editions of the *Origin* but for his work on sexual selection.[18] Hummingbirds came to occupy a prominent place in *The Descent of Man*, and Darwin carefully invoked Gould's expertise before yoking it to his own theories. The extraordinary beauty of male hummingbirds will be admitted by "everyone . . . who has seen Mr Gould's splendid volumes or his rich collection," he wrote. Their ornamentation is remarkably varied, the result of modification in almost every part of the plumage, modifications sometimes carried, "as Mr Gould showed me, to a wonderful extreme." The human breeding of fancy pigeons is similar to what happens in hummingbirds, says Darwin, the "sole difference" between them being "that in the one, the result is due to man's selection, whilst in the other . . . it is due to the selection by the females of the more beautiful males" (XXII:402–03). By the end of the paragraph, Gould's work, and Gould himself, have been co-opted into support of sexual selection. If Gould insisted on putting his birds to work against Darwin, then the illustrator of geese and ganders would be served with a bit of his own sauce.

THE BIRDS OF GREAT BRITAIN AS A VISUAL RESPONSE TO DARWINISM

With *Humming-birds* complete, Gould embarked on *The Birds of Great Britain* as his next project. The choice was in some ways an unusual one, for apart from *The Birds of Europe* a generation earlier, Gould had made his reputation illustrating foreign, exotic species. Moreover, many of the British birds had already been figured in *The Birds of Europe*. But these were also the birds Gould and his subscribers knew best, and in this case familiarity bred sentiment and national pride rather than contempt. In his *Introduction*, Gould explained that he had taken up the British birds "at the solicitation of a large number of private friends and others."[19] For Britain's leading bird illustrator to offer his version of the nation's birds was almost obligatory, and to do so at the height of his fame made great sense, but it also put Gould in implicit competition with both predecessors and contemporaries. Books on British birds were legion, and some, like Thomas Bewick's, were legendary. So Gould attempted both to align his work with Bewick's and to develop the visual traditions associated with Bewick in new directions. At the same time, he sought to offer a picture of the natural world very different from the one offered by Darwin.

The opening words of the introduction to the first volume of Bewick's *History of British Birds* (1797) declare the work's natural theological assumptions: "In no part of the animal creation are the wisdom, the goodness, and the bounty of Providence displayed in a more lively manner than in . . . the feathered tribes."[20] The vignette that appears immediately above these words depicts a rural, agrarian scene, the harmonious intermingling of human beings at work with a veritable barnyard of animals, most of them birds paired two-by-two in Noah's ark fashion (fig. 3.1). Bewick's wood engravings of individual bird species, hailed for their liveliness and detail, typically placed the bird against a detailed background designed to provide a sense of its natural habitat, but without integrating the bird into that habitat, and with no other animals or birds, even of the same species, present

Figure 3.1 Introductory vignette. Wood engraving by Thomas Bewick for *A History of British Birds*, vol. 1 (Newcastle, 1797), p. v.

(see fig. 1.3). This is in keeping with Ann Shelby Blum's demonstration that by 1800 most popular natural history illustrations in Europe and America, and especially those of birds, combined such a profile depiction of the animal in the foreground with some gesture towards landscape in the background. With birds, this primary emphasis on external appearance, on structure and plumage, reflected the concerns of Linnaean taxonomy, while the inclusion of landscape in preference to the background-free bird-on-a-branch reflected the insistence of the French naturalist Buffon on the classificatory importance of an animal's surroundings. As a general rule, both sexes were depicted only when their plumage or ornamentation differed, and even in such cases it was often only the male who was delineated.[21] Gould praises Bewick in the *Introduction to the Birds of Great Britain* and echoes his predecessor's natural theology: the naturalist, says Gould, sees "evidences of a power and skill immeasureably superior to those ever originated by man" and is "deeply impress[ed] . . . with a sense of the wisdom, power, and the beneficence of his Creator."[22] In the earlier *Birds of Europe* Gould generally depicted the male and female of a single species in a static pose; the accompanying flora attempted to associate the birds with a particular tree but did not attempt to conjure up a habitat (fig. 3.2). Over the years, Gould's plates had grown increasingly elaborate, although even the tropical

Figure 3.2 Golden Oriole. Hand-colored lithograph by Elizabeth Gould for John Gould,
The Birds of Europe (London, 1832–37), vol. II, plate 71.

or mountainous backgrounds for the recent hummingbird volumes were
fairly generalized and indistinct.[23] Gould's British birds, however, are often
located in elaborate and detailed contexts (see figs. 1.4 and 3.3). And as the
plates of the robin and long-tailed tit suggest, Gould's major innovation
for *The Birds of Great Britain*, the novelty that set his work apart, was his
focus on young birds. As he explained in the *Introduction*, "I . . . felt there
was an opportunity of greatly enriching the work by giving figures of the
young of many of the species of various genera – a thing hitherto almost
entirely neglected by authors; and I feel assured that this infantile age of bird-
life will be of much interest for science, to my subscribers, and to readers
generally."[24]

   This emphasis on young birds helps make *The Birds of Great Britain* a
celebration of avian family values, of domesticity and parental nurturing.
Numerous plates depict nestlings being fed. Others show parent birds protecting, incubating, or simply hovering over their offspring. The depiction of
a male and female on each plate here creates a nuclear family, usually with
an ornithological equivalent of "separate spheres" – the female attending
directly to the young while the male, having obtained the food, stands

Figure 3.3 "Erythacus Rubecula." Hand-colored lithograph of the European robin by
John Gould and H. C. Richter from John Gould, *The Birds of Great Britain*
(London, 1862–73), vol. II, plate 48.

by. Gould had already pictured numerous nests and nest-scenes in *Hum-ming-birds*, but there the concern was to provide an illustration of the nest, not the young. Except for the plates of the birds of prey, which contained starker and more sublime landscapes, Gould's British birds inhabit a world that is tranquil and ordered, an unspoiled rural world made possible by beneficent aristocrats, the noble proprietors of the great landed estates to which Gould's text repeatedly refers. The sole disturbing forces – and they appear only in the text – are overzealous gamekeepers, who in protecting their lordships' grouse and pheasants destroy too many avian predators, and those landowners more concerned with the introduction of foreign species than the preservation of native ones.[25] It is a place where human beings and human life, and especially the encroachments of an increasingly urban and industrialized society in a decade of political reform, do not appear, not even in the background. Gould lived and worked in London, and its markets were an important source of specimens for him, but the metropolis appears only in passing references in Gould's descriptive text. Moreover, the natural world of the plates is very different from the Darwinian world of violence and competition, of the "law of battle" and "struggle for existence," of male sexual display and female selection in courtship.

As in *Humming-birds*, Gould does not attack Darwin in direct, extended polemic, but his text is peppered with comments that make his allegiances clear. If it were not for "the constancy of species," says Gould, "ornithology would no longer be a science."[26] Discussing the relationship between two closely allied species of crossbills, Gould complains that "to go into the origin of species would be entering the region of speculation, without obtaining any satisfactory proofs," a declaration that does not prevent him from also proclaiming that it requires "little philosophy" to see that the bill of this bird "has been *designed* for some special object."[27] As he had done in *Humming-birds*, Gould claims to remain aloof from the theoretical controversy fueled by the *Origin* even as he makes anti-Darwinian assertions. But because almost all of the hummingbird plates had been executed prior to the announcement of Darwin's theory, Gould's ability to press the plates into service against Darwin was limited. He could do so only retrospectively, and from the separately published *Introduction*. But *The Birds of Great Britain* afforded the opportunity to construct a true imagetext, with words and pictures working together to rebut the Darwinian vision of nature.

In the *Origin*, when Darwin drew his readers' attention to the violence and destruction lurking beneath "the face of nature bright with gladness," he used birds to do so: "we do not see or we forget, that the birds which are idly singing round us mostly live on insects or seeds, and are thus constantly destroying life; or we forget how largely these songsters, or their eggs, or their nestlings, are destroyed by birds and beasts of prey."[28] Gould's plates do contain violence, but it is domesticated, almost invariably presented in the form of parents feeding their young. Audubon's drawings for *The Birds of America* (1827–38) had frequently depicted violent scenes, but these focused on competition and the hunt. In a famous plate, a male and female redtailed hawk fight over a hare, whose blood drips down the female's talons (fig. 3.4). Even Audubon's small birds, however, are frequently captured on the verge of seizing prey, and depictions of acts of destruction aimed at other birds, as in blue jays marauding the eggs of another species or a sparrow-hawk clutching a dead sparrow, are not uncommon. The seemingly endemic and possibly random violence of the natural worlds of Audubon or Darwin occurs off-stage in a Gould plate: we see only its results, repositioned in a domestic context. The contrast between Edward Lear's illustration of the eagle owl for *The Birds of Europe* and the depiction of the same species in *The Birds of Great Britain* some thirty years later makes this clear (fig. 3.5). The figure of the solitary adult in the earlier work is pushed

Figure 3.4 "Red-tailed Buzzard." Lithograph from John James Audubon, *The Birds of America* (New York, 1840–44) 1:50, plate 7.

to the background of a family portrait in the later one; the still-conscious hare that for Audubon was the cause of strife between adult red-tailed hawks is transformed by Gould into food for baby owls. Violence between birds is even rarer in *The Birds of Great Britain*, but it, too, is domesticated: a parent kills a bird of another species only to feed it to its young (fig. 3.6).

Violent behavior that could not be contextualized in this manner raised special anxieties and posed particular representational problems for Gould. His plate of the red-backed shrike (fig. 3.7a), a bird that impales its prey on the thorns of bushes, depicts a female with her "food reserve," about to add the beetle in her beak to her "larder" of insects. Gould's text, however, struggles unsuccessfully to come to terms with the shrike's violent behavior, particularly towards other birds. Despite his nostalgic opening – "It is not until the Hawthorn is in flower, and the grassy meadow bespangled with buttercups, that the Butcher Bird, or Red-backed Shrike . . . makes its appearance in England; before the merry month of May, therefore, it must not be looked for" – Gould must quickly acknowledge this species' "tyrannical and cruel" disposition. It asserts its mastery of the hedgerow by driving away other birds, and even after comparative peace is established,

Figure 3.5 (a) Great Horned or Eagle Owl. Hand-colored lithograph by Edward Lear for John Gould, *The Birds of Europe* (London, 1832–37), vol. 1, plate 37. (b) "Bubo Maximus." Hand-colored lithograph of the eagle owl by Joseph Wolf and H. C. Richter for John Gould, *The Birds of Great Britain* (London, 1862–73), vol. 1, plate 30.

neighboring birds must be wary. Nestlings, Gould says, can prove too great a temptation for the shrike, which "may resume its bad character, seize the nestling by the neck . . . and tear it to pieces with its powerful bill." But just how typical is this trait of killing young birds and small mammals like mice and shrews? "Exceptional," Gould at first assures his readers, the "staple food" of shrikes "doubtless" being insects. This is presumably the basis for the plate containing nothing but insects. Yet impaling the food is common, and Gould's list of the morsels "frequently" to be found on country hawthorn bushes is dominated by the items the plate omits: "the head of a little bird, the mangled remains of a Shrew, a frog's leg, snails, beetles, and other insects, particularly humble-bees." Gould's anxieties show especially clearly in the vacillations of the sentence that follows: "Such an exhibition, however, is not always to be met with; still, now and then it may be; I have seen it myself more than once, and I am sure that most country-people have also."[29] A preliminary drawing for the plate contains no food larder and no beetle in the female's mouth (fig. 3.7b).

The purpose of the impaling is also at issue. In presenting the impaled insects whole and referring to them collectively as a food reserve, Gould

Figure 3.6 "Falco Aesalon." Hand-colored lithograph of the merlin by Joseph Wolf and H. C. Richter for John Gould, *The Birds of Great Britain* (London, 1862–73), vol. I, plate 19.

clearly suggests that this is merely a sort of avian pantry. He explicitly rejects the notion that the shrike places the prey on the thorn and then does the "tearing to pieces." In fact, he says, "it is only the useless and rejected portions" of the prey that are impaled. But if so, this is not a food reserve, and the plate is fundamentally misleading and even inaccurate. Gould's domestic analogy, which had softened the shrike's violent and cruel behavior, begins to come unraveled. He is "unable to say" why the bird does this, ultimately denying that there is any "end and object" to it at all: "the practice would seem to be a habit rather than to answer any special purpose in the bird's economy." Gould is particularly at pains to absolve the shrike from the charge that it attacks such a useful and industrious insect as the bee. The impaled bees that he and others have often seen close to the ground on the windy side of low hedges could not possibly have been placed there by shrikes, he argues, so they must have been blown there by gusts of wind! Gould's language is extreme – the death in such a fashion of both hive and bumble bees is a "calamity" and a "catastrophe" – but the absence of impaled bees from the plate reflects his view that shrikes are not responsible.

The plate of the red-backed shrike was among the earliest Gould produced for *The Birds of Great Britain*. Six years later, in 1868, he faced these

Figure 3.7 (a) "Enneoctonus Collurio." Hand-colored lithograph of the red-backed shrike by John Gould and H. C. Richter from John Gould, *The Birds of Great Britain* (London, 1862–73), vol. II, plate 15. (b) Partially-colored sketch of the red-backed shrike that was the basis for the finished plate. The food larder and beetle in the female's mouth are missing from this sketch.

issues again when he depicted the great gray shrike (fig. 3.8). This plate also contains impaled prey, but this time both a small bird and a shrew are among the victims. Since Gould's text describes the gray shrike's violent propensities without the anxiety-ridden vacillation present in the discussion of its red-backed cousin, it might appear that Gould was no longer troubled by this behavior. Several other differences, however, suggest Gould was simply pursuing strategies that would enable him to avoid a direct explanation for the shrike's apparent cruelty. Whereas the earlier plate shows a female stocking the family larder with insects, the illustration of the gray shrike lacks a female, making the male responsible for this slaughter of small mammals. And the very brief discussion of the plate calls attention not to the impaled bird, but to the shrew. This eruption of what Gould and his sources openly regard as excessive violence, in which fledglings are not the beneficiaries but the prey, is here partly neutralized by being gendered male and focused on a more acceptable victim.

An even more telling example, because not involving a bird commonly known for its violence, is Gould's treatment of the moorhen. This is a classic

Figure 3.8 "Lanius Excubitor." Hand-colored lithograph of the great gray shrike by John
Gould and H. C. Richter from John Gould, *The Birds of Great Britain* (London,
1862–73), vol. ɪɪ, plate 13.

case in which Gould wanted to focus attention on the beautifully colored but
rarely seen young birds. The various preliminary sketches of the scene and
its details indicate that this plate was worked up with considerable care (figs.
3.9a and b).[30] The published version (fig. 3.9c) presents a domestic idyll:
"as night approaches, [the chicks'] sensitiveness to cold prompts them to
seek shelter under the wings of the careful mother: the clucking male is now
assiduously attentive, and protects both her and her progeny from danger,
flits his white tail, and exhibits evident signs of pleasure." Since depicting the
chicks beneath the female's wing would obscure them, the water lily serves

Figure 3.9   Moorhen. Pencil and watercolor sketch, with annotations, of the moorhen (a) and a moorhen chick (b).

(c)

Figure 3.9   (c) The finished hand-colored lithographic plate of the moorhen by Joseph Wolf and H. C. Richter for John Gould, *The Birds of Great Britain* (London, 1862–73), vol. IV, plate 85. Gould Drawings 266 and 262, Kenneth Spencer Research Library, University of Kansas. Moorhen plate courtesy of the University of Michigan Special Collections Library.

this sheltering function. While the preliminary sketch showed the female feeding one of the chicks, in the finished plate Gould opted to omit this, concentrating instead on the parents' joint protectiveness, on warmth rather than food. The female swims close to her brood, eyeing them attentively; the male stands guard over both mother and offspring but is able to direct his gaze at the domestic tableau and take pleasure in it.

Gould's discussion of the plate, however, occurs only after he has offered a very different view of the moorhen's character. "Boldness and pugnacity" are so much a part of its nature that "its quarrelsome disposition renders it an unpleasant neighbour to any peaceful bird that may live in close contiguity." Indeed, says Gould, it has a trait that "will not redound to its credit" but that he feels obliged to disclose, and of which he provides several accounts: the moorhen suddenly and violently kills chicks of other birds with blows of its bill. Such a fact stands in virtually complete antithesis to the scene presented in the plate. Gould is too thorough an ornithologist not to acknowledge the moorhen's murderous propensities, and the decision to illustrate the chicks is an obvious one for a variety of reasons. But against the backdrop of Darwinism (this plate was published in 1862), Gould's choice – not to

(a)   (b)

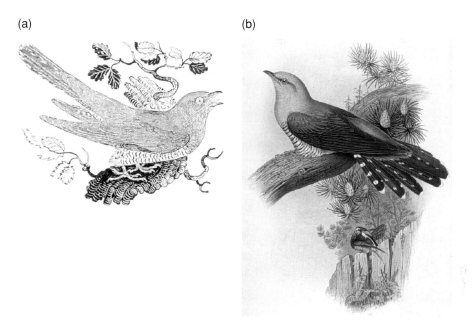

Figure 3.10   (a)"The Cuckoo." Wood engraving by Thomas Bewick for *A History of British Birds*, vol. 1 (Newcastle, 1797), p. 104. (b) "Cuculus Canorus." Hand-colored lithograph of the cuckoo by John Gould and H. C. Richter from John Gould, *The Birds of Great Britain* (London, 1862–73), vol. III, plate 67. The much larger young cuckoo is fed by its foster parent in the background.

mention the visual and textual heightening of the scene's anthropomorphic qualities – carries special weight. The slaughter of the innocents is pushed aside in favor of the more "pleasing" and reassuring vision of a "careful" mother and "assiduously attentive" father with their cute and aesthetically pleasing young.[31]

Perhaps the most fascinating example of Gould's efforts to exclude or control violence without creating a rupture between image and text, however, appears in his treatment of the cuckoo. The cuckoo conjured up complex associations, as Gould's text acknowledges. On the one hand it raised "joyous emotions" as a harbinger of summer. In "To the Cuckoo" (1807) Wordsworth had welcomed the "darling of the Spring" as a "blessed bird" whose call spoke of both present sunshine and flowers and of "visionary hours."[32] On the other hand, it was notoriously parasitical, laying its eggs in the nests of other birds, whose unhatched eggs and fledglings were later ejected by the young cuckoo. Like Bewick's wood engraving of the cuckoo, Gould's original plate of the bird avoids depiction of nest ejection entirely (fig. 3.10). In the background, however, Gould depicts a scene in keeping

with his domestic emphases – the much larger young cuckoo being fed by its
foster parent. His textual description of the bird explicitly dissents from the
view that the young cuckoo ejects its foster siblings, arguing instead that
this is accomplished by the foster parents in their inexplicable but fierce
protection of the cuckoo rather than their own young. Even here, in other
words, what Gould calls "the unseemly cruelty" of ejecting "the rightful
possessors" is ascribed to an excess of nurturing and love.[33]

By the time *The Birds of Great Britain* was completed, however, Gould had
received from the Duke of Argyll a vivid description and a sketch of a young
cuckoo's "unseemly" act executed by Jemima Blackburn, a successful artist
and illustrator married to the Scottish mathematician Hugh Blackburn.[34]
To Gould's credit, he worked this sketch into a plate (fig. 3.11), which he
included in the final installment of the work, and in the *Introduction* to the
finished volume he issued a retraction, providing two verbatim accounts
of nest-ejection. Discomfort is registered in the language of Gould's correspondents, who describe the young cuckoo as a "blind little monster" and a
"serpent" whose "gruesome" behavior produces a feeling of "horror."[35] The
act, in other words, is controlled by exclusion: it is simply unnatural. Gould's
strategy in the plate is somewhat different. Whereas the sketch from which
he worked focused on the nest and the act of ejection, Gould widens the
scene to include the helpless bodies of two ejected nestlings and a cracked
egg, an apparent expansion of the scene's violence and anti-domesticity.
But Gould also makes a significant addition that seeks to retain his earlier
speculation: the scene is presided over by the foster parent, implying that
this violence, like the violence of the scenes in which parents feed their offspring, is both necessary and planned, superintended by a beneficent, caring
parent and, ultimately, by a beneficent God. The stability of his imagetext
threatened, Gould attempts to limit and even avoid the potential damage.
Order and design emerge from chaos just as in Gould's books themselves,
when, at the end of publication, Gould provided a table of contents inform-
ing subscribers how the serial parts, with their miscellaneous groupings of
birds, should be dismantled and reassembled for binding.

Gould's treatment of the cuckoo went neither unremarked nor unex-
ploited. Jemima Blackburn, whose sketch also appeared in *Nature*, wrote
that while she was flattered to have provided the basis for Gould's plate, she
wished not to be regarded as the authority for its details, and especially not
for the presence of the foster parent.[36] For his part, Darwin quickly seized
the opportunity presented by Gould's retraction. In order to accommodate
the cuckoo's actions into a natural theological perspective, Gould and others
had argued that the wonderful instinctive power of both the parent cuckoo

Figure 3.11   "Cuculus Canorus. Young [cuckoo] ejecting its nestling companions."
Hand-colored lithograph by John Gould and William Hart from John Gould, *The Birds
of Great Britain* (London, 1862–73), vol. III, plate 68. Gould retains the foster parent in
the background, even though the drawing from which he worked did not contain it.

and the young bird could only have been provided by a Creator. They suggested that this arrangement was beneficent in that it ensured the survival of the young cuckoo while mercifully bringing death to the foster siblings before they were old enough to have acquired much feeling.[37] One of Darwin's judiciously placed exclamation points in the *Origin* conveys his sense of the tenuousness of such an explanation. For Darwin, the cuckoo provided a central example in his argument that "instinct" is in fact a product of natural selection. "I can see no special difficulty," he wrote, "in [the cuckoo] having gradually acquired, during successive generations, the blind desire, the strength, and structure necessary for the work of ejection; for those young cuckoos which had such habits and structure best developed would be the most securely reared."[38] Having previously acknowledged Gould's dissent from the view that the young cuckoo was responsible, Darwin immediately incorporated Gould's admission into the 1872 edition of the *Origin*. In this case, the rupture in Gould's imagetext was easily exploited, the gap between visual and textual representation exposing the ideological stakes embedded in the scientific controversy over the cuckoo's behavior. Gould's attempt to restore the seamless reinforcement of word and image was simply too subtle on the one hand, too strained on the other, to compete with the drama of the behavior and the rhetorical force of his own retraction.

DEPICTING SEXUAL SELECTION

Visually and aesthetically, *The Descent of Man* is far more important than the *Origin*, both in its copious illustrations and its subject matter. The bulk of the *Descent* deals not with human descent from apes, but with sexual selection. While Darwin surveys sexual selection throughout the animal kingdom, he gives by far the most attention to birds, where male "antics" and display are much more important than violent combat. Of the thirteen chapters on sexual selection, Darwin devotes four to birds but only two each to mammals and humans. In terms of pages, the discussion of birds takes up a third more space than that of mammals and humans combined. Darwin justifies this attention on the grounds that secondary sexual characteristics in birds take a greater variety of forms and are more conspicuous, but he also notes that birds are ideal for considering the source, development, and character of the human aesthetic sense. "On the whole, birds appear to be the most aesthetic of all animals, excepting of course man," Darwin writes in the opening of the first bird chapter, "and they have nearly the same taste for the beautiful as we have" (XXII:373).

Darwin's treatment of sexual selection is saturated with culturally-bound notions, particularly about gender and sexuality. One of his strongest grounds for regarding avian and human taste as similar, for example, is that "our women, both civilized and savage, deck their heads with borrowed plumes, and us[e] gems which are hardly more brilliantly coloured than the naked skin and wattles of certain birds" (xxii:374). As feminist critics have pointed out, Darwin's comments about women and about sexual selection in humans are to a considerable extent the result of reading birds through Victorian eyes. Middle- and upper-class European women wear bird feathers in their hair and gems on their breasts to make themselves attractive to men, so their taste is similar in both form and origin to the peahen or the female hummingbird. Built into such arguments are assumptions about female vanity and superficiality, their limited capacity for rational thought, the domestic as their proper sphere. When Darwin turns back to humans, these assumptions are then rediscovered and reconfirmed, but as facts of nature rather than constructions of culture.[39]

Much truth inheres in this feminist critique of sexual selection. But in arguing that Darwin projects Victorian patriarchy onto the natural world, it fails to acknowledge that Darwin was spectacularly unsuccessful at convincing his contemporaries – including, as I mentioned earlier, Wallace – that sexual selection really occurred.[40] If Darwin treated the mating process among birds as a Victorian courtship novel, if he regarded nature as if it were a drawing room, why did Victorian readers dismiss sexual selection with virtual unanimity?

The answer lies in the fact that Darwin's theory disrupted bourgeois views of gender and sexuality in several important ways. Most significantly, as Helena Cronin has shown, Darwin ascribed considerable choice and an aesthetic sensibility to female animals. This view was strenuously resisted. In the decades following the publication of the *Descent*, the prevailing view of sexual selection – Wallace's – sought to do away with almost any notion of female choice. The male's color and ornament were the norm, with the female's drabness conferred by natural selection for protection during incubation. Male coloration and "antics" were the result of "surplus vitality." Writing on hummingbirds in *Fraser's* in 1877, Wallace asserted that the brilliant plumage of the males of three South American species, stemmed from "the superior energy and vitality in the male . . . the special tint being determined either by local conditions or by inherited tendencies in the race" – with no reference at all to female selection.[41] Two decades later, G. N. Douglass predicted that "gestures and gambollings of all denominations throughout . . . nature – from the usual antics and gyrations of worms up

to the contortions performed by the gilded youth in modern ball-rooms –
will ultimately be found to be only the outcome of . . . 'surplus vitality.'"
At about the same time, Karl Groos contended that "seldom or never does
the female exert any choice. She is not the awarder of the prize, but rather a
hunted creature."[42] The female response to male ornament and finery and
beauty is passive and programmed, physiological rather than active and
rational. Female animals, even female birds, simply do not have an aesthetic
sense, and even if they did, it would not be sufficiently precise to appreciate
subtle differences in color and shading. And to the extent that females do
choose, Wallace and his followers argued, they read the males' vitality as a
sign of health and vigor.

In giving so much attention to males with the gaudiest colors and most
elaborate rituals of display, Darwin depicted sexual selection as driven by
the eyes of the female rather than by either her head or her reproductive
organs. In many species, females choose the posturing, self-absorbed dandy,
the exotic, rather than the sober, industrious provider. "Whilst preening
their feathers," Darwin writes in the *Descent*, male birds "have frequent
opportunities for admiring themselves, and of studying how best to exhibit
their beauty" (XXII:416). The need to satisfy female preferences can lead
males into absurd behavior such as the "indescribably odd attitudes" of the
English bustard (XXII:395). In some cases like the peacock it can shackle them
with unwieldy physical attributes. And the "surplus vitality" of male birds is
often shown by Darwin to be a cocktail of violence and sexual passion, with
male-on-male combat immediately preceding the forcible appropriation of
a female. While Darwin's depiction of courtship amongst birds frequently
presents a "civilized" picture of coy females having their sexuality aroused
by ardent but restrained males, the gender plots of the *Descent* are multiple
and frequently disruptive. Gould's world, by contrast, is, as we have seen,
both visually and textually one of happy monogamous domesticity.

The importance of illustration to the *Descent*'s exposition of sexual selection can be measured by the fact that only two of the first edition's seventy-
four wood engravings appear in the section on human evolution. Of the
remaining seventy-two engravings in the part on sexual selection, bird illustrations are the largest single category – one-third of the total and roughly
50 percent more than the next-largest categories, insects and mammals.
About half of the images depict birds against a landscape background. With
one exception, Darwin's birds were engraved in fairly detailed static profile,
foreground foliage and/or background landscape represented in a much
sketchier fashion, thus following the conventions of popular ornithological illustration as epitomized in England by Bewick and Gould. They also

show some of the birds most closely associated with Gould: humming-birds, bower-birds, birds of paradise, peafowl, and the Argus pheasant. Yet Darwin does not use Gould's illustrations. Instead, he reproduces eleven birds from the popular German naturalist A. E. Brehm's *Illustrirtes Thier-leben* (1864–69).

Why did Darwin prefer Brehm's illustrations to Gould's? While he did not own Gould's folios himself, he could have accessed copies directly from Gould or at the Athenaeum Club.[43] Despite their theoretical disagreements, Gould and Darwin remained friendly through the 1860s, with Darwin con-sulting Gould on several occasions about issues crucial to the *Descent*. And although Gould enticed subscribers in part by emphasizing that his works would appreciate because of the limited number he produced, he sometimes allowed his plates to be copied. However, having already approved the use of other Brehm illustrations for the Russian translation of *The Variation of Animals and Plants Under Domestication*, Darwin was able to obtain Brehm's woodblocks from Brehm's German publisher. It was cheaper and easier to print Brehm's birds directly than to commission wood engravings based on Gould's lithographic plates. Moreover, Brehm was a supporter and popu-larizer of Darwin's theories.[44] While his bird illustrations were no better than Gould's for capturing the violence of natural selection or the courtship behavior of sexual selection, they were also not saturated with the domestic motifs so prevalent in Gould's work of the 1850s and 60s.

In the first edition of the *Descent*, Darwin thus constructed his imagetext from what was available to him in Brehm. Doing so, however, created diffi-culties and in some cases enmeshed him in contradictions. Six of the eleven bird illustrations show a single male. In these, Darwin's text draws attention to the secondary sexual characters – everything from vocal sacs and wing-spurs to ruffs, top-knots, and colorful or ornamented feathers. But because the illustrations themselves do not show these features in use, Darwin must describe them in an expanded, erect, or vibrating state, and with a female audience present. In the case of *Palamedea cornuta*, the only illustration of a single male that focuses on weaponry, Darwin admits that the female also has wing-spurs and that they are just as large as the male's. The lone illustra-tion with a single female, a species of snipe, appears in the section dealing with those cases where the female, not the male, is larger or more brightly colored. Although the text describes various ways in which female snipes differ from the males, the species depicted in the illustration is not discussed, and without a male the illustration provides no basis for comparison.

The success of the illustrations with more than a single male is also mixed. Brehm's two humming-bird drawings are very similar to Gould's.

Figure 3.12 "The Ruff or Machetes pugnax (from Brehm's *Thierleben*)." Wood engraving. Figure 37 from Charles Darwin, *The Descent of Man, and Selection in Relation to Sex*, 2 vols. (London: Murray, 1871) II:42.

Both illustrations depict a male and female perched near each other. In neither instance is the male displaying his plumage for the female's benefit, and the presence of a nest in one of the illustrations confirms that these are not courtship scenes. But Darwin does not focus here on male display, emphasizing merely that the males are elaborately ornamented, and that this is the result of selection by the females. We are implicitly invited to read that selection narrative into the history of the birds before us. In the case of the illustration of *Machetes pugnax* (fig. 3.12), Darwin struggles with a different problem. He contends that the bird's ruff "probably serves in chief part as an ornament," but as "pugnax" would suggest, the male is "notorious for his extreme pugnacity," and Darwin uses it as an example of the battles amongst males (XXII:375). Brehm's illustration shows a group of birds in the background, two males confronting each other, one with the ruff expanded, with two other birds, apparently females, looking on. This is the sole illustration in the first edition of the *Descent* that even gestures at the use of the secondary sexual characteristic under discussion, but it hints only indirectly at the potential for the ruff to be deployed for charming a female. On the other hand, it supplies an illustration of "the law of battle" in sexual selection, and of a species Darwin points out is polygamous.

Yet one of Darwin's illustrations, that of the spotted bower-bird (*Chlamydera maculata*), is, in fact, Gould's. Brehm's drawing is clearly based on Gould's illustration of the bird in *The Birds of Australia* (fig. 3.13) thirty years earlier.[45] Gould's accounts of the bower-birds, which build elaborate and highly decorated structures, were among the most famous discoveries, for both the scientific world and the public, from his Australian sojourn. His extraordinary double plates (each took up two full imperial folio pages)

Figure 3.13 (a) Spotted bower-bird. Hand-colored lithograph from John Gould, *The Birds of Australia* (1840–48), vol. ɪᴠ, plate 8. (b) "Der Kragenvogel (*Chlamydera maculata*)." Wood engraving of the spotted bower-bird from A. E. Brehm, *Illustrirtes Thierleben*, 3 vols. (1864–69) ɪɪ:160. Darwin reproduced this illustration, which had itself been copied from Gould's plate, as Figure 46 in *The Descent of Man, and Selection in Relation to Sex*, 2 vols. (London: Murray, 1871) ɪɪ:70.

of the spotted and satin bower-birds, depicted in the kind of lavish "scenes" that would only later become standard for Gould, were especially striking. The naturalist Hugh Strickland told Gould they were "truly pictorial and *Audubonic*," a comment echoed in the *Annals of Natural History*.[46] Indeed, Gould apparently had oil paintings of these plates to display at the 1841 British Association meeting in Plymouth, and his illustrations and accounts of the bower-birds circulated widely in the works of prolific scientific popularizers such as Jane Loudon and J. G. Wood in the coming decades.[47] Publishing an illustration of a new species of bower-bird in one of the supplemental installments to *The Birds of Australia* many years later, Gould made clear how closely he was associated with these birds: "if any one circumstance . . . would tend to hand down the name of the author of the 'Birds of Australia' to posterity, it would be the discovery and the publication of the singular habits of the Bower-birds."[48]

In both his *Introduction* (1848) and his two-volume *Handbook* (1865) to *The Birds of Australia*, Gould was only slightly more forthcoming about the bowers' role in mating. "It has now been clearly ascertained," he writes in the *Handbook*, "that these curious bowers are merely sporting-places in which

Although originally published well before the *Descent*, these plates show Gould already constructing a domestic tableau out of what he knew to be a courtship site. In his initial description of the birds at the Zoological Society in 1840, Gould stated that the bowers were specifically constructed by the males "to attract the females."[49] In the text for each of these plates, however, Gould is much more equivocal and euphemistic. The bowers are "playing-grounds" and "halls of assembly." The bower of the satin is "certainly not used as a nest, but as a place of resort for many individuals of both sexes, which . . . run through and around the bower in a sportive and playful manner." Near the end of his description, Gould mentions it is "highly probable" that they are used "at the pairing time."[50] Yet he also asserts that the bowers are probably where the female lays and incubates her eggs, and the plates are clearly designed to make the bowers *look* like nests. The plate of the spotted bower-bird is ambiguous because the text tells us that the sexes have similar plumage, but clues in both the image and the text suggest that the female is in the bower. The plate of the satin (fig. 3.14a) is even more nest-like: it contains two young birds as well as the parents, again with the female inside the bower. That this was Gould's intent is evident from an early sketch of a young bird with its parents, one of whom has food in its beak, apparently completed in Australia before Gould obtained a bower and thus never published (fig. 3.14b). Like the later plates in *The Birds of Great Britain*, these are domestic scenes of married life, not courtship.

In both his *Introduction* (1848) and his two-volume *Handbook* (1865) to *The Birds of Australia*, Gould was only slightly more forthcoming about the bowers' role in mating. "It has now been clearly ascertained," he writes in the *Handbook*, "that these curious bowers are merely sporting-places in which

(a)

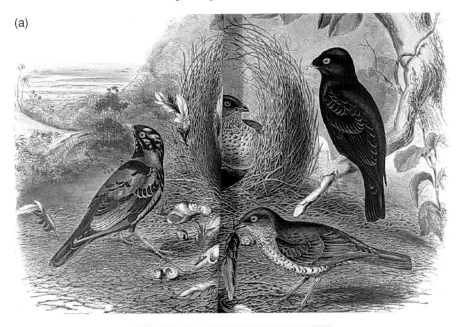

(b)

Figure 3.14   (a) Satin bower-bird. Hand-colored lithograph from John Gould, *The Birds of Australia* (1840–48), vol. IV, plate 10. (b) Satin bower-bird. Pencil and watercolor sketch. This preliminary sketch differs drastically from the finished plate.

the sexes meet, and the males display their finery, and exhibit many remarkable actions." Although Gould now acknowledges the courtship function of
the bowers, he continues to call them "sporting-places," the "merely" curi-
ously reducing them, against the grain of his own text, to insignificance.[51]
He also provides no description of these remarkable male actions. And the
Handbook's account of the spotted bower-bird makes no reference to mating
at all.

Darwin appropriated Gould's bower-birds for the *Descent*, exploiting
these ruptures in his friend's imagetext. Although heavily indebted to information in Gould's *Handbook*, Darwin opens his discussion of bower-birds by
framing it in terms of natural selection. The various species of bower-birds
have inherited their instinct for bower-building from a single progenitor
species. This instinct, the most curious and striking example of male "love
antics," is itself the product of sexual selection, of females preferring the
males who have constructed the most beautifully decorated bowers. Where
Gould minimizes or even suppresses the bower-birds' courtship and mating, Darwin revels in it. Whatever tranquil domesticity or female coyness
in courtship is evident in the plate is shattered by Darwin's text. The bowers are built "for the sole purpose of courtship," he says (XXII:395). These
are not nests, for the nests are constructed in trees. In its Darwinian context, Gould's ambiguous plate can be read quite differently: we see either
the male in the bower, attempting to entice the female, or the female in
the bower having already been enticed. And while Darwin has to rely on
his textual language to emphasize the frenetic sexuality of the male, he
makes this aspect of the male's behavior much more prominent than it is
anywhere in Gould. Quoting another observer's description provided but
passed over without comment by Gould, Darwin writes: "the male will
chase the female all over . . . then go to the bower, pick up a gay feather or
a large leaf, utter a curious kind of note, set all his feathers erect, run round
the bower and become so excited that his eyes appear ready to start from his
head" (XXII:395). This is hardly the language of a Victorian courtship novel.
The male's behavior is neither innocently flirtatious nor vaguely civilized,
but simultaneously ridiculous and menacing. It is perhaps too suggestive
for middle-class Victorians of what lay behind the trappings of courtship,
whether in the wild or in the drawing room, and it confirms why Gould,
not Darwin, is much closer to providing an avian analogue for bourgeois
family values in his depictions of birds.

Bowers were unsettling in another way as well, as the "best evidence" of
a "taste for the beautiful" in birds (XXII:428). Darwin admits it is difficult to
obtain direct evidence that females appreciate the beauty of male plumage

and ornament. But the construction and especially the decoration of bowers are so elaborate and particular, he argues, that it is impossible not to believe that aesthetic taste is involved. Each of the three Australian genera builds a distinctive style of bower and decorates the area around it with particular colored objects and certain kinds of shells and stones, often obtained from a considerable distance. Whereas Gould sees behind these "wonderful instances of bird-architecture" the hand of the Divine architect, Darwin sees the aesthetic sensibility of female progenitors. By focusing on beauty as non-utilitarian, Gould and the Duke of Argyll left themselves open to Darwin's appropriation of their arguments for the *Descent*. Simply dismissing Darwin's assertion of the utility of beauty in the *Origin* was no longer tenable after the lengthy exposition of sexual selection. Aggressive statements about beauty for beauty's sake, the exquisite taste of female birds, and the differing standards of beauty in different species were gleefully endorsed by Darwin and put to his own uses. For if his opponents invoked the human aesthetic sense as different in kind from that of animals, and the aesthetic sense in all creatures as a providentially-implanted instinct ensuring that like pairs with like, he would show that the difference was one only of degree, and that aesthetics itself was a product of natural and sexual selection. But Darwin found it easier to convert Gould's imagetexts into image/texts than to construct and maintain an imagetext of his own.

Even before the first edition of the *Descent* reached booksellers early in 1871, Darwin regretted using Brehm's illustrations. Responding to P. L. Sclater, who apparently disparaged Brehm's work while checking the proofs of the bird chapters in the *Descent* for Darwin, Darwin wrote that "I wish with all my heart I had thought of consulting you about woodcuts . . . but I thought Brehm's drawings fairly good enough for my purpose of popular illustration; & it saved me trouble; but I now much regret I did not get better drawings."[52] Darwin's characterization of his illustrative needs as "popular" presumably reflected his sense that he did not require a high degree of ornithological accuracy in his depictions of secondary sexual characteristics. But his desire for "better drawings" was primarily a desire for a different *kind* of drawing, one showing secondary sexual characteristics *in use*. And the desire was sufficiently intense that the search for better drawings began almost immediately, with the first edition barely in print and the second almost three years away. A few months after his expression of regret to Sclater, Darwin's publisher, John Murray, commissioned the zoological artist T. W. Wood, almost certainly at Darwin's behest but unquestionably with Darwin's approval, to re-draw several of Brehm's birds. Of the four Brehm illustrations replaced by Wood's drawings, three were

Figure 3.15 "Tetrao cuido: male. (T. W. Wood)." Wood engraving from a drawing by
T. W. Wood. Figure 39 in Charles Darwin, *The Descent of Man, and Selection in Relation to
Sex*, 2nd edn. (New York: Burt, 1874), 422. The illustration of this bird for the first edition
did not show the vocal sacs expanded and did not contain females in the background.

fundamentally reconceived, and two of these depicted sexual selection in
action. Wood asked Darwin for a copy of the *Descent* to assist him in his
work, "as I should wish to know what characters were particularly pointed
out in the text." His version of the prairie grouse (fig. 3.15) thus showed the
male with his vocal sacs expanded while two females and a male in the middle
ground looked on, and his rendering of the peacock pheasant (fig. 3.16) contained a male displaying before a (seemingly inattentive) female. In addition,
Darwin paid Wood for a completely new illustration for the second edition:
a male Argus pheasant displaying his wing feathers for an undepicted female
(fig. 3.17).[53]

Commissioning such illustrations, however, did not fully solve Darwin's
difficulties. Depicting male display was not the same thing as depicting
female choice, and it was female choice, and the aesthetic sensibility seemingly implied by it, that made Darwin's contemporaries uneasy. Even Wood
was not convinced: "although I feel convinced of the truth of your theory of
the origin of species," he wrote to Darwin, the perfect ornamentation of the
male Argus "seems to point to (& almost to prove) the existence of a great

Figure 3.16 "Polyplectron chinquis, male. (T. W. Wood)." Wood engraving from a drawing by T. W. Wood. Figure 51 in Charles Darwin, *The Descent of Man, and Selection in Relation to Sex*, 2nd edn. (New York: Burt, 1874), 450. The illustration of this bird for the first edition did not depict the male displaying for females.

artistic power." He continued to feel, as the Duke of Argyll had in *The Reign of Law*, that the Argus pheasant confirmed spectacularly the fundamental convergence of human and divine aesthetics, both the male's aesthetically perfect wing feathers and the female's attraction to them ultimately originating in an external power rather than a natural law.[54] Darwin's illustrations of sexual selection, in other words, required rather than replaced thousands of words, and those words still could not fully control the meaning of the illustrations.

RUSKIN'S *LOVE'S MEINIE* AND THE REJECTION OF THE *DESCENT*

Ruskin was another contemporary who came to see Gould's work as anti-Darwinian or at least useful for anti-Darwinian arguments. A regular subscriber to Gould's books, Ruskin rated them highly, especially for students of art and ornithology. In *Fors Clavigera* he spoke of the "boundless choice for pleasing children in Gould's marvellous plates."[55] He relied extensively on plates from *The Birds of Great Britain* for the Oxford lectures that

Figure 3.17 "Side-view of male Argus pheasant, while displaying before the female. Observed and sketched from nature by Mr. T. W. Wood." Wood engraving from a drawing by T. W. Wood. Figure 52 from Charles Darwin, *The Descent of Man, and Selection in Relation to Sex*, 2nd edn. (New York: Burt, 1874), 452. The first edition contained no illustration of the Argus pheasant displaying.

became *Love's Meinie*, initially placing some of them in the permanent collection of the drawing school there but later donating the entire work, along with many of Gould's other books, to the Museum of the Guild of St. George. In the early 1880s he began giving the unbound parts of Gould's final book, *The Birds of New Guinea*, to Whitelands College in Chelsea, a teacher-training school for girls (xxi:226–27; xxx:264–65). For "the living bird rightly drawn," something he claimed was rarely found in art, Ruskin ranked Gould's work third among all nineteenth-century illustrated ornithologies, and *The Birds of Great Britain* he regarded as the best ever on British birds (xxv:78). He explained after Gould's death that he would have spoken more admiringly of it "had not I known, that the qualified expressions necessary for true estimate of his published plates, would have caused him more pain, than any general praise could have counteracted or soothed." And so, while warning students not to suppose Gould's work "exemplary as art," Ruskin made *The Birds of Great Britain* his primary visual reference and organizational model for *Love's Meinie*.[56]

Like *Proserpina*, its botanical counterpart, *Love's Meinie* is designed for the art education of young people ("meinie" is the old English word for "many," used in the sense of a group of attendants like bridesmaids or courtiers; thus Ruskin's title makes birds the attendants of Love, but love understood quite differently from the physical attraction in sexual selection). As the first Slade Professor of Fine Art at Oxford, Ruskin interpreted his responsibility to be the provision of both University members and "general students who do not intend to become artists" with "such knowledge of art, and such experience in the practice of it, as properly rank among the elements of liberal education."[57] His science was neither anti-science nor science-as-art, but science in relation to art and to liberal education generally. He lectured and wrote about ornithology because, in his view, England lacked a true natural history of birds. Such a work could only be written "by a scholar and gentleman; and no English gentleman in recent times has ever thought of birds except as flying targets, or flavourous dishes." As a result, the job had been left to Bewick, "a card-printer's lad of Newcastle" (25:19). Despite his admiration for Bewick's achievement, Ruskin sees him as the equivalent of a Gothic stone carver rather than a medieval architect or artist.[58] Lacking a liberal education himself, Bewick cannot serve as a visual model for Ruskin's project.

The vulgarity of Bewick and even of the grouse-hunting nobleman cannot compare, however, with the vulgarity of modern science in its "arrogance and materialism" (xxv:20). Ruskin's complaints about modern science are summed up in his caustic characterization of the information provided in most ornithological accounts of a bird: the name and estate of the gentleman whose gamekeeper shot the last one seen alive in England; stories of doubtful origin about the bird, repeated from other sources; an enumeration of the colors of the feathers even though the living bird is never to be observed by English eyes again; a justification of the author's creation of yet another scientific name for the bird despite the dozen or so already in existence. The fouling of land, air, and water has increasingly driven birds to the estates of wealthy landowners, he complains, where they are rendered inaccessible and are more apt to be hunted than left in peace. Ornithologists take so little interest in the life and habit of birds that they rely uncritically on the observations of others and no sooner see a bird than they shoot it for dissection or stuffing. Rare and new species are especially likely to meet this fate, for scientists hungrily compete to establish priority or ownership, with no regard for the confusion of nomenclature this creates for nonspecialists and students.

In contrast, Ruskin will focus on the living bird, its habits and external appearance, rather than its anatomy. "Most English youths would have more pleasure in looking at a locomotive than a swallow," he laments, decrying not only the fascination with mechanism and the inner workings of things, but the fact that "many English philosophers would suppose the pleasure so received to be through a new sense of beauty" (xxv:45). Even more important, he will discuss the human relationship to birds not in terms of sport or gastronomy or fashion, but in terms of myth, of the imaginative response of both ancient peoples and modern writers to the natural world, and the lessons and truths to be gleaned from these encounters. The mythology of a bird, Ruskin contends, is the most important part of its natural history for the liberally-educated student. It is an exercise in understanding rather than mastery, in self-effacement rather than aggrandizement. Comparing the "transformations" of mythology with those of Darwinian science, he writes:

The transformations believed in by the mythologists are at least spiritually true; you cannot too carefully trace or too accurately consider them. But the transformations believed in by the anatomists are as yet proved true in no single instance, spiritual or material; and I cannot too often, or too earnestly, urge you not to waste your time in guessing what animals may once have been, while you remain in nearly total ignorance of what they are. (xxv:57)

Gould's work was not immune to some of these faults. His text frequently identifies the nobleman on whose estate a bird was seen or shot, sometimes by Gould himself. Ruskin on many occasions criticizes him, as he does other ornithologists, for descriptive vagueness, nomenclatural inaccuracy, or the failure to provide information about some crucial aspect of a bird's appearance or habits. The son of a gardener who had worked his way up to a position at Windsor, Gould was closer to Eton than the "card-printer's lad of Newcastle" only in geographic terms. Nonetheless, Gould's books came closer to Ruskin's ideal natural history of birds than anyone else's. Ruskin praises Gould for his careful, lifelong observations of British birds, and he borrows Gould's "practical and natural" arrangement of them (xxv:79). Although he doesn't say so, Ruskin must also have been pleased by the frequent "mythological" references in Gould's text, the quotations from the Bible and English poets. The plates also generally measured up to Ruskin's exacting standards. While Gould was sometimes criticized for exaggerating color in his plates, Ruskin, who had vigorously defended both Turner and the Pre-Raphaelites against a similar charge, invariably applauds the color of Gould's birds and the flora that surrounds and complements them.[59] In several instances he also compliments Gould's rendering of a bird's attitude, the particular way it stands or walks or flies or swims. And Gould's refusal to guess what a particular species must once have been – indeed, his frequent assertion of the constancy of species – was echoed by Ruskin's comment that "the wonder is, not that species should sometimes be confused, but that the greater number of them remain so splendidly, so manifestly, so eternally distinct" (xxv:55–56).

Ruskin understood and appreciated the anti-Darwinian implications of Gould's emphasis on tranquil, domestic scenes featuring female birds nurturing their young, and on color and ornamentation serving little or no purpose in a bird's "well-being and economy."[60] Writing about the Rev. William Houghton's *Country Walks of a Naturalist with His Children* (1869) in the March 1875 letter of *Fors Clavigera*, Ruskin bemoaned that Houghton had chosen to reproduce Gould's great gray shrike (see fig. 3.8) rather than one of his many plates showing a female incubating her eggs or feeding her young, in particular the long-tailed tit (see fig. 1.4) with its exquisitely built and decorated nest. The great gray shrike is "the horriblest creature" in Gould's book, Ruskin complains, "transfixing mice on the spines of the blackthorn, and tearing flesh from them as they hang." Houghton's selection of it is further evidence for Ruskin of the "extraordinary instinct for the horrible, developing at present in the English mind" (xxxiv:291). Ruskin has hunting and vivisection (over which he would later resign the Slade Professorship) most immediately in mind here, but the very language of the comment, as well as its context, suggests that Ruskin is also thinking of Darwinism. The natural history of birds should be an exercise of and about love and beauty, not violence and horror, and love and beauty as conceived in the Ruskinian rather than the Darwinian sense.

This is especially evident at the end of *Love's Meinie*, when Ruskin begins his "rough generalization of results" (xxv:122) by returning to the second volume of *Modern Painters* (1846) and his distinction between aesthesis and theoria. It is one of those late passages in which Ruskin repudiates his earlier Evangelicalism while insisting that the core ideas were, and remain, true. Ruskin tells his students that what others call aesthesis is not perception of beauty but merely a physical, bodily response, which he prefers to call sensation. Theoria, on the other hand, is the true perception of beauty, for while it includes sensation, it involves "the whole moral being in some measure right and healthy" (xxv:124). The perception of beauty in the natural world, however, Ruskin argues, should not be naive. This is a fallen world, a cursed world, and as a result it is full of ugliness and violence and pain. Simple-minded natural theology is untenable: "There is no possibility of explaining the system of life in this world, on any principle of *conqueringly* Divine benevolence" (xxv:125; original emphasis). While it is possible to read moral lessons from nature, the evidence is complex, equivocal, multiform. There are butcher-birds as well as long-tailed tits. The charming moorhen is a devoted parent who also wantonly crushes the skulls of other birds' fledglings. Gould's invocations of the Creator's goodness are not adequate in such cases, as Gould's difficulty even in acknowledging this violent behavior indicates. Although Gould's domestic tableaux are morally valuable, they provide no guidance in these other cases, the ones that raise most insistently the questions Ruskin regarded as most important: how are we to live in this fallen world, and what are we to do to mitigate the effects of the curse under which it lies? In the moral diatribe that closes *Love's Meinie*, Ruskin upbraids with equal vehemence the uncouth, liberty-loving workman; the money-grubbing merchant; and the fox-hunting, horse-racing aristocrat for their collective indulgence in violence, sensuality, and materialism, but he frames this condemnation as an aesthetic – or to speak in Ruskinian terms, theoretic – issue, and he launches it with an analysis of bird drawings.

Ruskin saw clearly that Darwin's theory of sexual selection took the "sensation" school of aesthetics to new levels, and that it posed a direct and fundamental challenge to his own views. The *Descent* appeared early in 1871; two years later Ruskin delivered at Oxford the first lecture of what would become *Love's Meinie*. Using the robin to instruct his audience on his main topic, the structure of feathers, Ruskin offered one of his most flippant parodies of Darwinian thinking. Pausing in the midst of his discussion of the relationship between the form and arrangement of feathers and their use in flight, he commented:

I have no doubt the Darwinian theory on the subject is that the feathers of birds once stuck up all erect, like the bristles of a brush, and have only been blown flat by continual flying.

Nay, we might even sufficiently represent the general manner of conclusion in the Darwinian system by the statement that if you fasten a hair-brush to a mill-wheel, with the handle forward, so as to develop itself into a neck by moving always in the same direction, and within continual hearing of a steam-whistle, after a certain number of revolutions the hair-brush will fall in love with the whistle; they will marry, lay an egg, and the produce will be a nightingale.[61]

While Ruskin's lampoon pokes fun at Darwinian transformations generally, it specifically links bird plumage and song with courtship, love, and beauty. The fantastic generation of a nightingale from the marriage of hair-brush and steam-whistle is clearly a response to the *Descent*'s discussion of sexual

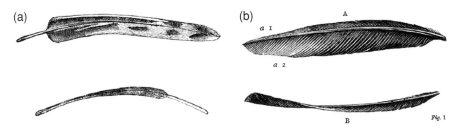

Figure 3.18 (a) "Outer tail-feather of Scolopax frenata" and "Outer tail-feather of Scolopax javensis." Wood engravings. Figures 42 and 43 from Charles Darwin, *The Descent of Man, and Selection in Relation to Sex*, 2 vols. (London: Murray, 1871) II:64. (b) Outline (A) and Profile (B) of wing-feather of a robin. Figure 1 from John Ruskin, *Love's Meinie. The Library Edition of the Works of John Ruskin*, ed. E. T. Cook and Alexander Wedderburn, 39 vols. (London: Allen, 1903–12) XXV:37.

selection in birds, and in particular to Darwin's claims about "instrumental music" in birds.

While male birds from numerous species utilize existing structures (wings, quills, beaks, ruffs, etc.) to produce the sounds that draw or impress potential mates, Darwin argues that in some cases feathers have been specially modified for this purpose. The strange sound made by the feathers of male snipes descending rapidly from great heights during the mating season is caused by the peculiar form of the outer tail feathers. The ornithologist who made this discovery, Darwin reports, "found that . . . by fastening [the feathers] to a long thin stick and waving them rapidly through the air, he could reproduce the drumming noise made by the living bird" (XXII:391). This discussion occupies only a few pages of the *Descent*, but it appears in an important section in which Darwin argues that both "the drumming of the snipe's tail" and "the song of the nightingale" are the product of female taste (XXII:394).

This discussion is also important visually. Roughly half of the bird illustrations in the *Descent* are of feathers or details of feathers, and one of the two groups of feather illustrations (fig. 3.18a) is associated with this particular discussion. Ruskin answers with his own, similar illustrations (fig. 3.18b). But whereas Darwin's illustrations are of these specially modified feathers, Ruskin's depict the "typical" feather from the wing of that "moderate and balanced" bird, the robin (XXV:36). Turning then to a breast feather, Ruskin describes the way its gray feathers separate the red breast from the brown of the rest of the bird, setting the red off to its best advantage and adding to the robin's quiet, decorative charm. No illustration of the breast feather is included, but the editors of the Library Edition insert here a plate of a peacock feather and filaments (fig. 3.19a), drawn by Ruskin in 1873 and apparently used to illustrate the lecture.[62] Why use a peacock feather to illustrate a lecture on robins? Part of the motivation must have been to respond to Darwin's other set of feather drawings, those from birds like the peacock and the Argus pheasant with ocelli (eye-spot markings) in their tail-feathers or wing-feathers.

The *Descent* contains nine illustrations of the ocelli in Darwin's famous and extended account of how these fantastic ornaments could have been produced by sexual selection. *His* illustration of a peacock feather (fig. 3.19b) comes from the tail, not the breast. Even more important, however, was his lengthy discussion of the Argus pheasant's ball-and-socket ocelli. This case is to the *Descent* what his evolutionary explanation of the eye is to the *Origin* – the application of his theories to a seemingly impossible case. "Could such artistically shaded ornaments have been formed by means of Sexual Selection?" Darwin asks (xxii:412). He admits that the notion that these ocelli have been produced by a process that didn't have that end in view "seems as incredible, as that one of Raphael's Madonnas should have been formed by the selection of chance daubs of paint made by a long succession of young artists, not one of whom intended at first to draw the human figure" (xxii:450). In a tour-de-force of reasoning, Darwin shows that the Argus pheasant's feathers contain a series of markings ranging from irregular spots to the perfect ball-and-socket ocellus, and that the locations of the more perfect ocelli correspond to positions more easily seen by the female when the male displays his plumage for her. So perfect are the most developed ocelli that "though occupying very different positions with respect to the light, all appear as if illuminated from above, just as an artist would have shaded them" (xxii:456).

Darwin seems to have been especially desirous of constructing an integrated textual and visual rebuttal of Argyll on this point, and of linking Gould to it. Initially puzzled by the orientation of the wing-feathers in the specimen at the British Museum, Darwin explains in the first edition of the *Descent* that "Mr. Gould soon made the case clear to me" by showing him a drawing Gould had made of a male in the act of displaying.[63] The illustration of the displaying Argus pheasant (see fig. 3.17) added to the second edition was not taken from Gould's drawing, however, but from T. W. Wood's first-hand sketch. Gould remains responsible for "mak[ing] the case clear" to Darwin in the second edition, but it is Gould's manipulation of the British Museum specimen, not his drawing, that facilitates Darwin's understanding: "he held the feathers erect, in the position in which they would naturally be displayed" (xxii:412). And Darwin is careful to retain

(a)

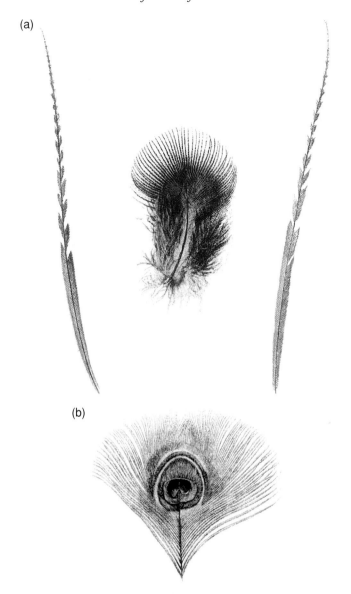

(b)

Figure 3.19   (a) "Peacock's Feather with enlarged filaments." Photogravure from a
drawing by John Ruskin. Plate v from John Ruskin, *Love's Meinie. The Library Edition of
the Works of John Ruskin*, ed. E. T. Cook and Alexander Wedderburn, 39 vols. (London:
Allen, 1903–12) xxv:39. (b) "Feather of Peacock . . ." Wood engraving from a drawing by
G. Ford. Figure 53 from Charles Darwin, *The Descent of Man, and Selection in Relation to
Sex*, 2 vols. (London: Murray, 1871) ii:137.

in the second edition his comment that Gould not only supplied him with some of the feathers he used in his examination but "fully agrees with me in the completeness of the gradation" of the ocelli (XXII:457). The Duke of Argyll rightly argues that natural selection cannot explain this case, Darwin notes, but he wrongly "passes over" the action of sexual selection. Gould, having provided Argyll with many of his most prominent examples, finds himself turned against his aristocratic subscriber and acquaintance, incorporated into a defense not merely of sexual selection, but of its radical aesthetic implications:

Many will declare that it is utterly incredible that a female bird should be able to appreciate fine shading and exquisite patterns. It is undoubtedly a marvelous fact that she should possess this almost human degree of taste. He who thinks that he can safely gauge the discrimination and taste of the lower animals may deny that the female Argus pheasant can appreciate such refined beauty; but he will then be compelled to admit that the extraordinary attitudes assumed by the male during the act of courtship, by which the wonderful beauty of his plumage is fully displayed, are purposeless; and this is a conclusion which I for one will never admit. (XXII:414)

In casting his dispute with Argyll as a contrast between the utility and non-utility of beauty, Darwin partly misrepresents what was actually an argument about the definition of utility. But the passage makes explicit Darwin's larger purpose, the connection of the human aesthetic sense to that of animals. The female Argus pheasant's "almost human degree of taste" and appreciation of "refined beauty" mean that even the human aesthetic sense is shared by and inherited from animals. Human art, human art criticism, and human art critics like Ruskin are all enfolded into an evolutionary genealogy.

Ruskin understood the threat. His lifelong efforts to educate humans in the appreciation and understanding of natural beauty had always hinged on moral rather than physical connections. He thus attacked Darwin's views of the Argus pheasant and the peacock as examples of the "materialism" and "unclean stupidity" of much modern science (XXV:263), although he did so not in *Love's Meinie* but in the second part of *Proserpina*, published in 1875. In his "one-sided intensity," Ruskin complains, Darwin proves himself incapable of seeing, let alone thinking about, color, and his contention that the ocelli of the Argus pheasant are "artistically gradated" merely demonstrates his artistic ignorance. (In the second part of *The Laws of Fésole* [1878], one of his elementary treatises on drawing, Ruskin would attempt to circumvent such artistic ignorance about feathers in his students by including an exercise on the decorative plumage of the peacock [fig. 3.20], a copy of which he rather cheekily sent to Darwin after a meeting with him the

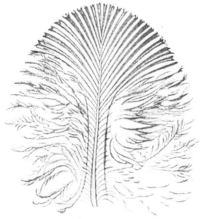

Figure 3.20   "Decorative Plumage. Peacock." Steel engraving by George Allen from a
drawing by John Ruskin. Plate v from John Ruskin, *The Laws of Fésole. The Library
Edition of the Works of John Ruskin*, ed. E. T. Cook and Alexander Wedderburn, 39 vols.
(London: Allen, 1903–12) xv:411. Ruskin sent a copy of this engraving to Darwin.

following summer.)[64] At an even more basic level, however, Darwin fails to
ask, or even consider, why the admiration of blue tails is a sign of health in
peahens. Darwin thinks this is "proper" to peafowl, Ruskin complains, in
the sense merely of it being one of their "properties" rather than in the sense
of it being "becoming." Similarly, "when he imagined the gradation of the
cloudings in feathers to represent successive generation, it never occurred
to him to look at the much finer cloudy gradations in the clouds of the
dawn themselves; and explain the modes of sexual preference and selective

development which had brought *them* to their scarlet glory" (xxv:264; original emphasis). Although his lectures on "The Storm-Cloud of the Nineteenth Century" were nearly a decade off, changing atmospheric conditions in England were already on Ruskin's mind, and with the plumage of birds as with the clouds of the dawn, the issue was ultimately theoretic – which is to say, aesthetic and moral. Darwin never sees the difference between ugliness and beauty, decency and indecency, glory and shame, folly and sense, for "the perception of beauty, and the power of defining physical character, are based on moral instinct, and on the power of defining animal or human character" (xxv:268). Yet it is not simply that Darwin ascribes "discrimination" and "taste" and the ability to "appreciate . . . refined beauty" to the female Argus pheasant and the peahen, not even that he makes the perception of beauty a matter purely of sensation. It is that Darwin goes a step further: by locating the origin of the human aesthetic sense in the physical sensations of animals, he provides a naturalistic basis for the aesthetics of both bourgeois materialism and Art for Art's Sake. If beauty is ultimately about utility rather than truth, then art becomes just another Victorian commodity, produced and consumed, trafficked in and hoarded. If it is ultimately about physical sensation and sexual reproduction rather than morality and character, then it becomes just another form of Victorian escapism, a retreat from commodity culture rather than a confrontation with it. For Ruskin, the stakes could not have been higher. And the awareness that Darwin was making similar arguments about the beauty of flowers only made matters worse.

CHAPTER 4

Darwin's plants

Darwin's botanical writings are today perhaps the most overlooked aspect of his career. Although that is bound to change as the publication of Darwin's Correspondence moves further into the 1860s and on into the 1870s, it is for now necessary to emphasize that plants were his major experimental interest in the decades following the *Origin*. He spent countless hours in the greenhouse he ordered to be built at Down. His children were recruited to observe the visits of bees to wild orchids in the nearby fields, to count and draw pollen grains, even to scream and shout at various sensitive species. He besieged his good friend Joseph Hooker with requests for specimens from Kew Gardens. He counted and measured and weighed and watched. Much of the work seems simplistic and primitive: inserting needles and sharpened pencils into orchids, gluing bits of paper to the tips of climbing plants and charting their motion on a piece of glass with marks of grease pencil, weighing pieces of cooked egg white and raw meat to determine the digestion rate of "carnivorous" species. But between 1862 and 1880, Darwin published the results of his experiments in six botanical books: on orchids, climbing plants, insectivorous plants, plant fertilization, the different forms of flowers in plants of the same species, and plant movement. Several appeared in second editions. If these works didn't receive the level of exposure or provoke quite the level of response as the *Origin* or the *Descent*, they were nonetheless widely reviewed and commented upon, and their significance was not lost on contemporaries. For these were works that attempted to provide empirical evidence for natural selection and to use the theory to solve or reinterpret a number of botanical conundrums.

The conventions of botanical and horticultural illustration, like those of ornithological illustration, were not very congenial for Darwin's purposes. As he would later do in the *Descent*, Darwin in his book on orchids thus worked largely within existing conventions, but modifying and tinkering with them, and relying on the combination of his illustrations and his textual descriptions and explanations to enable readers to see orchids very differently. But the fact that Darwin was attempting to explain the relationship between structure and process in fertilization and movement rather than writing classificatory treatises proved in some ways an advantage, for it allowed him to develop novel forms of illustration.

Darwin's botany was also more directly controversial in its aesthetic implications, however, because it invited Victorians to look at flowers in a new way. Much of what made flowers beautiful – their colors, delicate or elaborate structures, and ornamentation – was, Darwin argued, the evolutionary result of the advantages conferred by cross-fertilization, a process frequently accomplished through the agency of insects. What the *Descent* did for beauty in the animal kingdom, in other words, the botany books did for beauty in the world of plants. By the mid-1870s, Darwin's plant work was being aggressively popularized, often as part of a full-scale naturalized aesthetics – an evolutionary and physiological account of beauty throughout the natural world. Beauty was neither a divine gift nor an expression of divine delight but the utilitarian means by which individuals secured the best breeding partners and species promulgated themselves. John Ruskin, recognizing that the agenda of scientific naturalism included this new aesthetics so philosophically at odds with his own, attacked and countered it in many of his writings, but especially in his own botanical work, *Proserpina*. To do so meant attacking and countering Darwin and his botany, both textually and visually.

THE SIGNIFICANCE OF DARWIN'S BOTANY

Plants had long been a keen interest of Darwin's. In his autobiographical recollections he noted that by the time he was eight he had "tried to make out the names of plants." More fancifully, he told another little boy that he "could produce variously coloured polyanthuses and primroses by watering them with certain coloured fluids." At Cambridge he attended the botany lectures of John Stevens Henslow, who soon became his chief mentor. Darwin accompanied Henslow on his long daily walks, dined frequently with his family, and took part in the botanical excursions he organized. It was through Henslow that Darwin received the offer to sail on the *Beagle*, and while he produced no *Botany* to accompany his *Geology* and *Zoology*, Darwin was attentive to plants throughout the voyage. In 1838–39 his speculations about species led him to investigate the cross-fertilization of flowers, particularly native orchids, by insects, a subject to which he gave some attention in virtually every subsequent summer. In the years before and after the barnacle dissections, Darwin's study filled with potted plants and trays of germinating seeds. He visited nurseries and corresponded with nurserymen, read and published in *The Gardeners' Chronicle*. Hooker supplied the steady stream of botanical advice and exotic specimens that Darwin increasingly demanded. By the first edition of the *Origin*, Darwin had collected so much information on crossing and fertilization that he felt comfortable declaring as "a law of nature" his belief that "no organic being self-fertilises itself for an eternity of generations." In the winter of 1862–63, after the publication of the orchid book and the appearance of an article on primroses in the Linnean Society *Journal*, the greenhouse was built. In 1864 his long paper on climbing plants was published. Much of this botanical work began to find its way into the *Origin*, especially in the heavily revised fourth edition in 1866. While *The Variation of Animals and Plants Under Domestication* (1868) dealt primarily with animals, two chapters were devoted to cereal plants, vegetables, fruit, ornamental trees, and cultivated flowers. In the early 1870s Darwin busied himself with the two editions of the *Descent*, *The Expression of the Emotions*, and the sixth edition of the *Origin*, but the latter half of the decade saw an intense spurt of botanical publications. In 1875 he brought to fruition fifteen years' study of insect-eating species such as the sundew and Venus flytrap with the publication of *Insectivorous Plants*; in 1876 he published a comprehensive study of fertilization in *The Effects of Cross- and Self-Fertilisation in the Vegetable Kingdom*; an expanded edition of *Orchids* appeared the following year, as did the issue in book form (as *The Different Forms of Flowers on Plants of the Same Species*) of the Linnean Society papers of the previous decade on primroses, cowslips, oxslips, flax, and loosestrife. In 1880 came *The Power of Movement in Plants*, which vastly expanded his earlier study of climbing plants, and a new edition of *The Different Forms of Flowers*.[1]

Opening his introduction to *The Different Forms of Flowers*, Darwin apologized that his subject "ought to have been treated by a professed botanist, to which distinction I can lay no claim" (xxvi:1). Yet contemporaries soon came to regard Darwin's botanical work as significant, even as having revolutionized the field. As it had in zoology, natural selection provided a different approach to botanical classification and new explanations of geographical distribution and morphology. Experimental and physiological without smacking of the laboratory, theoretically informed but carefully descriptive – there was nothing quite like Darwin's botany. His work on fertilization in particular opened the botanical floodgates to a host of similar studies. Hooker could complain in 1860 that Darwin's work on the importance of cross-fertilization was "much underrated," but by 1878 William Ogle, the High Church physician and editor of the *British and*

Foreign Medico-Chirurgical Review, was looking back upon Darwin's *Orchids* as a "classical work" that disclosed "a wide and unexplored region to the research of physiological botanists." Just a few years later, the Darwinian botanist Hermann Müller was actually warning that recent investigators had endorsed and extended Darwin's emphasis on the benefits of cross-fertilization too uncritically, raising it to the level of dogma. Darwinians of course had a vested interest in constructing contemporary botany as undergoing fundamental changes in response to Darwin's views, but they were sufficiently successful that even those opposed to Darwinian interpretations of botanical phenomena usually acknowledged the influence of Darwin's work.[2]

Darwin's botany had several layers of significance for evolutionary theory and its applications. At a general level, it broke down rigid distinctions between plants and animals. Insectivorous species captured and digested insect "prey." Climbing plants were capable of what seemed almost voluntary movement. Indeed, Darwin came to argue, movement in response to various environmental stimuli was a phenomenon common to all plant species, and thus plants, while lacking the nervous system of animals, should be seen as operating in closely analogous ways. Ever the boundary-blurrer, Darwin confessed in his *Autobiography* that it "always pleased me to exalt plants in the scale of organized beings" (XXIX:156). Darwin's allies and supporters worked to publicize this exaltation of plants in the periodical press, while opponents resisted it. In "On the Border Territory Between the Animal and the Vegetable Kingdoms" for *Macmillan's Magazine*, T. H. Huxley declared that the old distinctions between these two kingdoms had been completely broken down, with the differences between plants and animals a matter of degree rather than kind. In the *Cornhill*, Andrew Wilson also answered with a Huxleyan negative the question of his title, "Can We Separate Animals from Plants?" Reviewing Darwin's *Power of Movement in Plants* for the *Edinburgh Review*, however, the popular textbook author R. J. Mann complained that analogies between plant movement and animal locomotion, "especially dear to the hearts of evolutionists," should not be allowed to obscure the crucial distinction that the latter is volitional while the former is not.[3]

Darwin's botanical books also built the case for natural selection. A study of orchids might appear (and did appear to some contemporaries) an odd follow-up to the *Origin*, but the work offered the kind of empirical evidence that Darwin had promised to provide, and it did so with a detailed case study of a most unlikely group. For how could natural selection possibly account for the elaborate markings, fanciful structures, and gorgeous color of orchids? Surely here was a classic example of the breathtaking beauty and grotesque drolleries of a non-utilitarian Creator who exercised his powers for our pleasure and his own? No, answered Darwin, orchids were the product of natural selection, of the evolutionary dance between flowers and insects. Their beauty and bizarreness had nothing to do with us, but instead served the purpose of attracting certain insects and in particular of assuring cross- rather than self-fertilization. Writing to his publisher, John Murray, Darwin described the work as "Like a Bridgewater Treatise" in that "the chief object is to show the perfection of the many contrivances in Orchids."[4] The Bridgewater Treatises were the eight works on natural theology published between 1833 and 1836 that had updated the design argument with the latest knowledge of the natural world. While several of the Treatises had sought with varying intensity to move natural theology away from William Paley's still-influential functionalist, utilitarian arguments about organisms being provided by the Creator with anatomical "contrivances" that fit them for their environmental niches, this aspect of natural theological discourse had remained prominent and popular, even with the increasing ascendance of Richard Owen's version of transcendental anatomy among elite naturalists in the 1840s and 50s. As numerous commentators have pointed out, the *Origin* sought to provide an alternative explanation for "contrivances" by making them the product of natural selection rather than an omnipotent, omniscient, and benevolent God. Darwin's use of this rhetorical strategy was both disingenuous and necessary. He knew as well as anyone that Paleyan functionalism was no longer on the theoretical cutting edge, yet the *Origin* was aimed at a broader audience for whom such views were almost a literal article of faith. If Darwin saw the audience for *Orchids* as limited to those with "a strong taste for Natural History" (xvii:1), that would still include the descriptive botanists, orchid enthusiasts, and nurserymen he numbered among his correspondents. And so perhaps even more directly than in the *Origin*, Darwin deployed the language of natural theology – even featuring the word "contrivances" prominently in his title – for the purpose of subverting it. *Orchids* was an anti-Bridgewater Treatise. "This treatise" – for so Darwin characterized his book in the Introduction – "affords me . . . an opportunity of attempting to show that the study of organic beings may be as interesting to an observer who is fully convinced that the structure of each is due to secondary laws, as to one who views every trifling detail of structure as the result of the direct interposition of the Creator" (xvii:1).

The Different Forms of Flowers extended the results of *Orchids* on the role of insects in effecting cross-fertilization, and it did so with another group of familiar but odd species. Why would plants like the oxslip, cowslip, and loosestrife have two or even three distinctly different sexual forms, their stamens and pistils set at different heights? Much to his surprise, Darwin found that the different sexual forms functioned almost as separate sexes. A flower with long stamens and short pistils achieved full fertility only when pollinated by a flower with short stamens rather than with pollen from its own long stamens or even a separate long-stamened individual. Flowers with short stamens similarly produced more seeds and more vigorous offspring when fertilized with pollen from flowers with long stamens. An insect visiting a short-stamened flower would be dusted with pollen in a position on its body from which the pollen was easily transferred only to the pistils of a flower of the other form, and vice versa. These different sexual forms thus functioned not only to minimize self-fertilization but also to facilitate crosses with a different sexual form. As in his earlier work on barnacles, Darwin saw the ubiquity and importance of variation in sexual organs and sexual arrangements. In his book on *Cross- and Self-Fertilisation*, Darwin buttressed these earlier claims about plant fertilization and the evolutionary advantages of crosses by producing the results of eleven years' worth of experiments in his greenhouse on a range of species.

The three books that questioned the plant–animal boundary – *Climbing Plants*, *Insectivorous Plants*, and *The Power of Movement in Plants* – also showed how both typical and unusual forms of plant behavior could be accounted for by natural selection. In *Climbing Plants* Darwin rebutted his mentor Henslow's notion that these species possessed an innate tendency to grow in an upward spiral, arguing instead that the many "beautiful adaptations" of climbing plants "illustrate in a striking manner the principle of the gradual evolution of species" rather than the action of divine design (XVIII:v; XXIX:152). As *Cross- and Self-Fertilisation* showed that the benefits of cross-fertilization were not limited to orchids and primroses, so *The Power of Movement* endeavored to demonstrate that plant movement was not limited to climbing plants – heliotropism, the "sleep" and sensitive responses of leaves in various species, even the inexorably downward motion of the root tip were all for Darwin modifications by natural selection of a common property of circular movement in plants that he called "circumnutation." For its part, *Insectivorous Plants* displayed the surprising variety of structures and movements by which natural selection had enabled these species to thrive in nutrient-poor soils. Darwin's comment to Murray about *Orchids*, that "I think this little volume will do good to the Origin, as it will show that I have worked hard at details, & it will, *perhaps*, serve [to] illustrate how natural History may be worked under the belief of the modification of Species," proved to be accurate in some degree for all his botanical works.[5]

Victorians encountered pictures of plants in a variety of places: botanical works both technical and popular, horticultural publications, flower books, drawing manuals, works of fine art from flower painting and still life to the canvases of the Pre-Raphaelites, and throughout the decorative arts.[6] Images for specialist botanical and horticultural publications often circulated well beyond their original, limited audiences, for they were frequently copied in other, more widely distributed works and appropriated for other purposes. English porcelain manufacturers (including Darwin's relatives, the Wedgwoods) copied illustrations from the same botanical folios and expensive horticultural magazines that Ruskin used as sources of drawing exercises for his students.[7] The most immediate visual influences on the figures in Darwin's plant-fertilization books, not surprisingly, were botanical and, to a lesser extent, horticultural illustration. These provided models for both the naturalistic and the schematic drawings that Darwin utilized. As usual, however, Darwin had to manipulate, revise, and in some cases depart from those conventions to construct his imagetexts, for he was more interested in showing how certain behaviors and structures had been acquired via natural selection, than in using those behaviors and structures to construct taxonomies.

That Darwin did not look to the fine arts for illustrative models is less obvious than it might seem. Flowers were of course long a staple of still life painting, and if the floral still life had faded in both popularity and status from its zenith in seventeenth-century Dutch art, its history had always been intertwined with botanical illustration, and it remained part of the Victorian painter's training. Moreover, one of the illustrations for Darwin's *Variation of Animals and Plants Under Domestication* clearly displayed a visual debt to the still-life featuring wild game (fig. 4.1). Luke Wells, one of the artists employed by W. G. Tegetmeier at *The Field*, provided seven drawings for Darwin's crucial chapters on pigeons; the other six were typical of those that usually appeared in *The Field* and in breeders' manuals such as those by E. S. Dixon and B. P. Brent (fig. 4.2). That Wells drew the bird in this fashion was a function of the fact that he worked from a dead specimen, but it also reflected Darwin's illustrative needs – since Darwin was arguing that all fancy breeds of pigeons were modifications of the wild rock pigeon, he wanted the rock pigeon's characteristic markings to

Figure 4.1 "The rock-pigeon, or *Columba livia*. The parent-form of all domesticated Pigeons." Wood engraving from a drawing by Luke Wells. Figure 17 from Charles Darwin, *The Variation of Animals and Plants Under Domestication* (London: Murray, 1868).

(a)   (b)

Figure 4.2 (a) The English Carrier. Wood engraving from a drawing by E. Whimper for B. P. Brent, *The Pigeon Book*, 3rd edn. (1871), p.25. (b) "English Carrier." Wood engraving from a drawing by Luke Wells. Figure 19 from Charles Darwin, *The Variation of Animals and Plants Under Domestication* (London: Murray, 1868).

appear for comparative purposes. Tegetmeier, having recommended Wells over Harrison Weir, the well-known animal artist whose work also appeared in *The Field*, on the grounds that "accuracy is better than high art," worried that Darwin would "object to a drawing looking like an artistic sketch of 'dead game.'" Willing to accept "high art" as long as it was also accurate, Darwin included Wells's still life in the *Variation*. Perhaps, too, Darwin was more comfortable with illustrations rooted in the masculine worlds of the breeder, the agriculturalist, and – though he had long ceased to take pleasure in killing for sport – the hunter than those from the feminized realm of flowers and flower painting. Although he seems to have felt comparably if less intensely at home in the masculine world of horticulturalists, nurserymen, and collectors, Darwin positioned his more horticultural illustrations in the visual kingdom associated with his friend Hooker at Kew, where scientific botany and horticulture overlapped.[8]

By the middle of the nineteenth century, scientific botany generally employed, often on the same plate, two different styles of illustration: the "illusionistic pictorial" and the "outline schematic," as Gill Saunders calls them in *Picturing Plants* (see figs. 1.5a and 4.3). In the former in particular the main illustration of the plant or flower was often accompanied by smaller images (sometimes actual size, sometimes magnified) of isolated parts or microscopic details. Both styles isolated the specimen on the page, making no effort even to suggest its context in nature. Contemporary horticultural publications generally used three different types of illustration: the specimen portrait of flower, stem, and at least one leaf; the composite portrait with a group of flowers in various colors or forms; and the diagrammatic portrait providing a geometric outline. Considerable overlap existed between botanical and horticultural illustrations – the horticultural specimen portrait was often rendered in the illusionistic pictorial style, while the horticultural diagrammatic portrait relied heavily on the schematic outline – and thus the illustrations for the *Botanical Magazine*, under the control of the Hookers, appealed simultaneously to botanists, nurserymen, and flower enthusiasts.

The displacement of Linnaeus's sexual system of taxonomy in favor of the "natural" system of Jussieu and De Candolle also contributed to the convergence between botanical and horticultural illustration. In the eighteenth century, the increasing acceptance of Linnaeus's sexual system, in which plants were classified according to the number of stamens and pistils in their flowers, meant that botanical illustrations actually provided *less* information about a plant, focusing for the first time on the flower and especially the sexual organs. In Darwin's day, however, scientific botanists

631.
11,05.

Orchis mascula.

Figure 4.3 "Orchis mascula." Partially hand-colored engraving by James Sowerby for
James Edward Smith, *English Botany* (1790–1814), vol. 9, plate 631.

regarded the Linnaean system as too arbitrary, preferring the way in which
the natural system took the whole plant into account. While the flower's
centrality in botanical illustration was reduced under the natural system, it
nonetheless remained of considerable importance. Similarly, while dissections under the natural system were no longer required, as they generally
had been under the Linnaean system, to provide illustrations of the sexual
organs, botanical illustrations frequently continued to include them.

For the illustrations in several of his botany books, Darwin drew heavily on botanical conventions, relying on a combination of pictorial and
schematic illustrations; but because he was not writing classificatory treatises, he was free to mix and match, pick and choose, and even to innovate
as his needs demanded. *Orchids* was filled with illusionistic pictorial illustrations of orchid flowers, most accompanied by detailed smaller figures, with
a number of outline schematic illustrations sprinkled in. Only a handful of

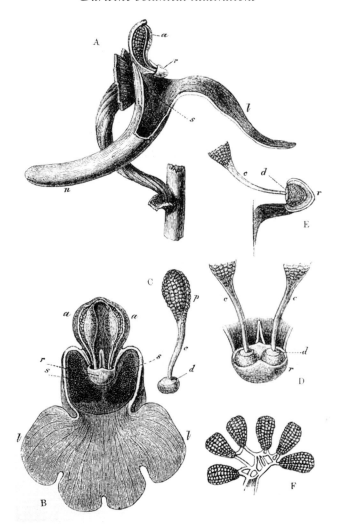

Figure 4.4 "*Orchis mascula*." Wood engraving from a drawing by G. B. Sowerby. Figure 1 from Charles Darwin, *On the Various Contrivances by which British and Foreign Orchids are Fertilised by Insects, and the Good Effects of Intercrossing* (London: Murray, 1862), facing p. 18.

the main illustrations depicted the entire flower, however: in most, petals and sepals were removed to expose the positioning of the sexual organs (fig. 4.4). In *Climbing Plants*, eleven of the thirteen figures, all drawn by George Darwin, were naturalistic renderings of particular species, but in the act of climbing or clasping. The naturalistic illustrations for *Insectivorous Plants* by George and Francis Darwin, are the volume's most numerous and

Figure 4.5 "(*Drosera rotundifolia*) / Old leaf viewed laterally; enlarged about five times."
Wood engraving. Figure 2 from Charles Darwin, *Insectivorous Plants* (London: Murray,
1875), p.4.

striking (fig. 4.5). Yet on only two occasions is so much as a branch of one of these plants depicted. Most others focus on a single leaf or (in the case of water plants) a single bladder, or even a more detailed part of the leaf or bladder. This attention to the leaf or bladder is the result of Darwin's interest in the insectivorous behavior of these plants, the leaf or bladder being the site where insects are captured. On other occasions, however, detail, even microscopic detail, is rendered schematically rather than naturalistically. As would be expected, schematic representations tend to appear when a general point is being illustrated or when detail is not important. The only case in which a leaf with captured prey is depicted in rough or schematic terms also follows this pattern, for Darwin's point is simply that the large, thick leaves of the butterwort are sensitive and capable of curving inwards.

Some of Darwin's botany books either eschewed botanical illustration entirely or developed new forms of illustration. *Cross- and Self-Fertilisation*, with its massive compilation of data about heights, weights, numbers of seeds, etc., simply contained table after table of numbers. This sober and unadorned presentation, however, reinforced both the sheer bulk and statistical significance of Darwin's patiently accumulated evidence, making his sweeping and surprising claim for the advantages of cross-fertilization more compelling. One of the thirteen figures in *Climbing Plants* was an unusual, abstract representation of the motion of a young pea plant over the course of a day (fig. 4.6) that became the basis for the almost two hundred similar diagrams in *The Power of Movement*. Darwin made this representation by placing a hemispherical piece of glass over the plant and marking on the glass with a grease pencil the location of the uppermost internode or stem joint at irregular intervals. The numbered dots were then copied onto paper and the dots connected. In the figure (which Darwin reduced in size by one-half), each numbered dot corresponds to a time listed in the caption. The line from one dot to the next roughly approximates the path traveled by the internode as seen from above, although Darwin notes that if the time

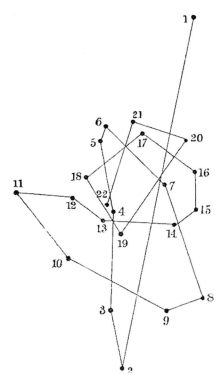

Figure 4.6 "Diagram showing the movement of the upper internode of the common pea, traced on a hemispherical glass, and transferred to paper; reduced one-half in size. (1 Aug.)" Wood engraving. Figure 6 from Charles Darwin, *The Movement and Habits of Climbing Plants*, 2nd edn. (London: Murray, 1875).

intervals had been smaller the straight lines would instead be curved, thus representing the true elliptical path of the movement. Even better, he says, if it were somehow possible to attach a small pencil to the moving plant itself, the plant could trace its own motions directly and continuously on the underside of the glass. Darwin and George subsequently developed methods to approximate such self-tracing for *The Power of Movement*. Attaching a thin glass filament with a small paper triangle affixed to each end to the part of the plant whose movement they wished to chart, they took a data point by lining up the two triangles and marking the glass plate with a grease pencil. With this method, too, Darwin noted, the movement appeared as straight lines rather than ovals and ellipses, and he admitted that the translation of the three-dimensional paths to a two-dimensional surface introduced errors, but the diagrams capture, he insisted, "the general character of the movement" (XXVII:6).

This emphasis on "general character" reflects Darwin's rather different aim in *The Power of Movement*. The purpose of the early diagram in *Climbing Plants* is to demonstrate not merely the pea's spiral motion but the reversal of direction in the spiral. Whereas twining plants generally revolve in one direction, leaf-climbers and tendril-bearers (the pea being an example of the latter) can reverse direction, which enables them to sweep a much wider space in search of something to grasp. In *The Power of Movement*, however, Darwin's argument is that circumnutation is both constant throughout the plant and characteristic of all plants. Thus the diagrams are greater in number and trace the movement of different parts of the plant (root tips, stems, runners, and leaves as well as the uppermost internode) in species across the vegetable kingdom. Like the tables in *Cross- and Self-Fertilisation* that support a similarly broad claim, the diagrams in *The Power of Movement* are worth thousands of words: he had "perhaps introduced a superfluous number of diagrams," Darwin admitted, "but they take up less space than a full description of the movements" (XXVII:5).

These diagrams, it should be noted, were not visually innocent. Spirals in nature, with their pleasing and almost mathematical regularity, were often invoked as indicators of design. Writing just before the *Origin*, Christopher Dresser had incorporated spiral arrangements and movements through-out his copiously illustrated *Unity in Variety, as Deduced from the Vegetable Kingdom* (1859), a frankly transcendental attempt to uncover, as the book's subtitle put it, "that oneness which is discoverable in the habits, mode of growth, and principle of construction of all plants." Darwin's illustration of the irregularities in the spiral movement of plants, not to mention his use of natural selection to account for them, thus quietly challenged another of natural theology's aesthetic arguments. Dresser, Professor of Botany in the Department of Science and Art at the South Kensington Museum, went on to become one of the period's most influential and controversial designers.[9] Darwin's work on plant movement hardly signaled the death-knell for such arguments, however. Historian Theodore Andrea Cook made extensive use of Darwin's work in his *Spirals in Nature and Art* (1903) and *The Curves of Life: Being an Account of Spiral Formations and Their Application to Growth in Nature, to Science and to Art* (1914), but if neither work argued for a natural theological interpretation of spirals, Cook also did not champion Darwin's evolutionary explanations. D'Arcy Wentworth Thompson's *On Growth and Form* (1917) similarly criticized transcendental arguments as well as Darwinian ones, but physiologist J. Bell Pettigrew was more partisan – his three-volume rebuttal of scientific naturalism, *Design in Nature*

(1908), was "Illustrated by Spiral and other Arrangements in the Organic and Inorganic Kingdoms."

As unusual as the movement diagrams were, it was two of Darwin's three fertilization books that had the greatest visual and aesthetic impact. This had less to do with the illustrations themselves than with the fact that Darwin was providing an evolutionary account of the beauty of flowers, but some of the illustrations for these books were widely commented on and recycled. In *Orchids* and *Different Forms of Flowers*, while Darwin adhered fairly closely to the general conventions of botanical illustration, he manipulated those conventions to his own ends, and where he used horticultural illustrations he obscured their source, making them more botanical.

Darwin originally conceived of *Orchids* as a paper he would publish in the Linnean Society's *Transactions*. But upon completing it he realized that the length of the text and the number of illustrations made this impractical, as he explained to Hooker:

When I finished a few days ago my Orchis paper, which turns out 140 folio pages!! & thought of the expence of woodcuts, I said to myself I will offer the Linn. Soc^y to withdraw it & publish it as a pamphlet. It then flashed on me that perhaps Murray would publish it, so I gave him a cautious description & offered to share risks & profits. This morning he writes that he will publish & take all risks & share profit & pay for all illustrations.[10]

Darwin had already engaged G. B. Sowerby, Jr., to execute the drawings for his paper. In fact, Sowerby came to Down for ten days, preparing the drawings under Darwin's direct supervision. In the midst of it, Darwin complained that the work was "the devil's own job" and left him "half-dead." "We found it impossible to draw on wood," Darwin told Murray, "& it was absolutely necessary first to make perfectly shaded drawings on paper." The cost for these drawings was nearly £11, but that did not include transferring them to wood blocks (an expense Darwin also offered to bear) and actually having them cut (which Murray would pay for). Darwin wanted Sowerby not only to transfer the drawings to wood "as he will do it best" but also to oversee the engraving. Although he feared the expense would be "considerable," Darwin stressed that "a *first-rate* cutter *must* be employed." The volume's illustrations were clearly of great importance to Darwin. He had engaged his own artist, was willing to publish at his own expense rather than forego the necessary figures, and desired to maintain as much control over the production of the illustrations as possible even when part of the costs was being absorbed by the publisher. "If not done excellently well," Darwin argued to Murray, "the whole thing will be a failure."[11]

His opening figure, of *Orchis mascula* (see fig. 4.4), which stands over almost all the others, may serve as an example. Although by mid-century the distinction between botanical and horticultural illustration was not firm, this figure announces itself in several ways as primarily botanical rather than horticultural. First, it is a wood engraving rather than a lithograph. Lithography had become the popular medium for horticultural illustration, but it was not good for the kind of fine detail that Darwin needed. Years before, in fact, he had complained to James de Carle Sowerby, engaged by Darwin on drawings of fossil barnacles, that the "muzziness" of lithography had been "highly injurious" to natural history illustration: "I do not care for artistic effect," wrote Darwin at the time, "but only for *hard rigid* accuracy." By "muzziness" and "artistic effect" Darwin also apparently referred to the limitations of lithography's thick line for rendering shading. In essence, he criticized Sowerby for producing undisciplined drawings concerned more with the "artistic effect" of chiaroscuro than the precise delineation of anatomical detail, and thus better suited for transfer to the lithographic stone than the wood block. A couple of Sowerby's drawings, Darwin complained, were "useless, from indistinctness & shading, just like Lithographs."[12]

Second, it is uncolored. While this may seem obvious – Darwin's only works to employ colored illustrations extensively were the Mammalia and Bird volumes of the *Zoology* of the *Beagle* voyage – it would have been perhaps more obvious to contemporaries for a book on orchids to contain at least some colored illustrations, especially when Darwin's arguments were in part about the role of color in guiding insects to the nectary. The orchid-mania of the preceding decades had made orchids a popular subject in horticultural publications, and Darwin had at his disposal the greatest flower illustrator of the day, Walter Hood Fitch, the botanical artist at Kew and sole illustrator for the *Botanical Magazine*.[13] Indeed, Darwin had already engaged Fitch to make the two drawings and woodcuts of *Primula* for his Linnean paper that will be discussed below.[14] But if Darwin was fearful of the cost of quality wood engravings, colored lithographs, even had he desired them, would have been prohibitive, and once the publication was taken on by Murray at his own risk, colored lithographs would have been out of the question.

Third, Darwin did not really employ any of the three styles of illustration common to contemporary horticultural publications: the specimen, composite, or diagrammatic portrait. Instead, the vast majority of the figures for *Orchids* consisted of partial portraits of a flower and detailed renderings of the pollinia or other elements of the reproductive system. While the figures

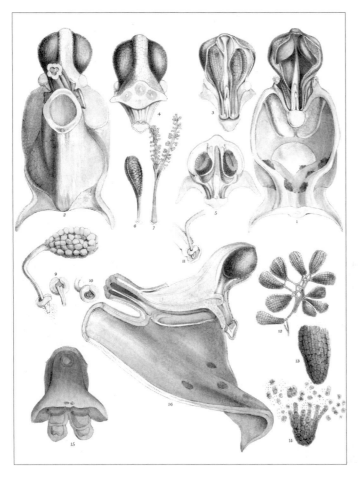

Figure 4.7 "Fructification: The sexual apparatus of Orchis mascula . . ." Hand-colored lithograph by M. Gauci from a drawing by Francis Bauer. Tab. 3 from Francis Bauer, *Illustrations of Orchidaceous Plants* (London: James Ridgway, 1830–38).

were often composites, they were more in keeping with the composite presentations of anatomical details in botanical illustrations, as a comparison of fig. 4.4 with fig. 4.7, Francis Bauer's plate of *Orchis mascula*'s sexual apparatus, indicates. In fig. 4.4, items A and B represent the side and front views, respectively, of the flower, but with petals and most of the sepals removed, while items C through F represent different aspects of the pollinia. Like his Linnaean precursors, Darwin focused on the flower and its sexual organs, but his interests lay more specifically with the mechanisms and structures of fertilization. In the case of *Orchis mascula*, when one of the flower's pollinia attaches itself to an insect's proboscis, the pollinium then drops forward

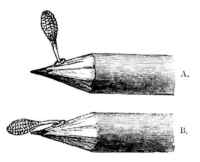

Figure 4.8 "A. Pollen-mass of *O. mascula*, when first attached / B. Pollen-mass of *O. mascula*, after the act of depression." Wood engraving from a drawing by G. B. Sowerby. Figure II from Charles Darwin, *On the Various Contrivances by which British and Foreign Orchids are Fertilised by Insects, and the Good Effects of Intercrossing* (London: Murray, 1862), 15.

about 90° over the course of approximately thirty seconds. By dropping forward, the pollinium is in a position to fertilize another flower's stigmas; the elapsed time, however, ensures cross-fertilization, for the insect has flown on to another plant. This is demonstrated in fig. 4.8, with the pencil used by Darwin to mimic the insect's proboscis. In his next figure in *Orchids*, of *Orchis pyramidalis*, Darwin in essence combines these first two illustrations: a depiction of the flower with petals and sepals removed, and representations of the pollinia at various points in the process of fertilization, two including the end of the needle Darwin used as a stand-in for the proboscis of a moth.

The illustrations for *Different Forms of Flowers*, like those for *Orchids*, focused on sexual organs and fertilization but were generally much simpler, the species under consideration achieving cross-fertilization not through a variety of elaborate "contrivances" but by means of two or three different height relationships between stamens and pistils. The book's opening illustration (fig. 4.9) of the two sexual forms of the common cowslip, *Primula veris*, is thus typical of the bulk of the volume's figures. In most cases, as here, the front petals and part of the calyx are not depicted in order to make the arrangement of the stamens and pistils clearly visible; in a few cases only the sexual organs are depicted. In the long-styled form of the cowslip, the stamen is long, with the stigma at the flower's mouth, while the pistil is short, with the pollen-bearing anthers about halfway down the calyx; in the short-styled form, this arrangement is reversed, with the stamen short and the pistil long, the anthers at the mouth of the flower and the stigma below. An insect dusted with pollen while visiting one form, Darwin found, is more likely to deposit the pollen on the stigma of the other form.

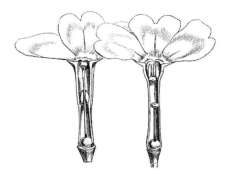

Figure 4.9   *"Primula veris."* Wood engraving. Figure 1 from Charles Darwin, *The Different Forms of Flowers on Plants of the Same Species* (London: Murray, 1877), 15.

Visually, then, all Darwin needed was an illustration that clearly showed the difference between the two forms and enabled the reader to appreciate from his descriptions of insect visitors why cross-fertilization occurs more commonly.

Although Darwin sought to present his figures in a predominantly botanical fashion, his modifications of and departures from the conventions of botanical illustration also signaled that these were not works of taxonomy. The content of the illustrations made little or no sense without the textual explanations describing the process of fertilization in which they were embedded. But by the same token, Darwin understood that this work demanded extensive and detailed illustrations if his readers were to visualize his descriptions. In the case of *Orchids*, he fussed over the illustrations because he needed a seamless imagetext, the structure *and* function of these wonderful contrivances conclusively demonstrated and inextricably linked. At that he largely succeeded, for reviewers overwhelmingly acknowledged the persuasiveness of Darwin's case that the forms, markings, and colors of these bizarre and beautiful flowers facilitated their cross-fertilization by insects. But Darwin's anti-Bridgewater Treatise could not simply replace the Creator with natural selection as the source of these orchid "contrivances." This can be appreciated by the Duke of Argyll's response to another prominent illustration in *Orchids*, Darwin's homological diagram of the orchid flower (fig. 4.10).

At the end of his survey of the eight orchid genera, Darwin offered an extended discussion of the "Homological Nature of the Several Parts of the Flowers of the Orchideae." "No group of organic beings can be well understood until their homologies are made out," he wrote, "that is, until the general pattern, or, as it has often been called, the ideal type, of the several

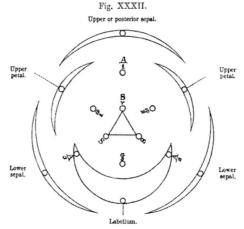

Figure 4.10 "Section of the flower of an orchid." Wood engraving. Figure XXXII from Charles Darwin, *On the Various Contrivances by which British and Foreign Orchids are Fertilized by Insects, and the Good Effects of Intercrossing* (London: Murray, 1862), 292.

members of the group is intelligible" (XVII:163). His diagram renders this general pattern in abstract form: the fifteen small circles represent the fifteen different organs found in every orchid flower, much modified and sometimes confluent, arranged in five alternating "whorls" of three elements each. Darwin did not invent this diagram – it is based on one in John Lindley's *Vegetable Kingdom*.[15] But whereas in his barnacle *Monograph* Darwin was content to discuss the cirripedia in relation to his homological illustration of the "ideal" barnacle as an "ideal" crustacean, in *Orchids* he made explicit what he had kept to himself a decade earlier:

Homology clears away the mist from such terms as the scheme of nature, ideal types, archetypal patterns or ideas, etc.; for these terms come to express real facts. The naturalist, thus guided, sees that all homologous parts or organs, however much they may be diversified, are modifications of one and the same ancestral organ; in tracing existing gradations he gains a clue in tracing . . . the probable course of modification through which beings have passed during a long line of generations. He may feel sure that . . . he is tending towards the knowledge of the actual progenitor of the group, as it once grew and lived. (XVII:164)

Not "ideal types" but "real facts" and an "actual progenitor" – Darwin uses natural selection to literalize transcendental botany. Despite their elaborate and diverse structures, orchids share a common structure that has been modified over time. And Darwin of course proceeds to unpack his diagram in evolutionary terms, focusing on the ways natural selection has tinkered with or overhauled some organs while leaving others untouched. Indeed, the language and structure of this chapter's penultimate paragraph echo quite clearly that of the *Origin*'s famous conclusion, although in *Orchids* Darwin goes on to offer a final paragraph that directly asserts the superiority of natural selection as an explanatory tool rather than merely implying its equivalence with invocations of the Creator:

It is interesting to look at one of the magnificent exotic species, or, indeed, at one of our humblest forms, and observe how profoundly it has been modified, as compared with all ordinary flowers – with its great labellum, formed of one petal and two petaloid stamens – with its singular pollen masses . . . with its column formed of seven cohering organs, of which three alone perform their proper function, namely, one anther and two generally confluent stigmas – with the third stigma modified into the rostellum and incapable of being fertilized – and with three of the anthers no longer functionally active, but serving either to protect the pollen of the fertile anther, or to strengthen the column, or existing as mere rudiments, or entirely suppressed. What an amount of modification, cohesion, abortion, and change of function do we here see! Yet hidden in that column, with its surrounding petals and sepals, we know that there are fifteen groups of vessels, arranged three within three, in alternate order, which probably have been preserved to the present time from being developed at a very early period of growth, before the shape or existence of any part of the flower is of importance for the well-being of the plant.

Can we feel satisfied by saying that each orchid was created, exactly as we now see it, on a certain "ideal type"; that the omnipotent Creator, having fixed on one plan for the whole order, did not depart from this plan; that he, therefore, made the same organ to perform diverse functions – often of trifling importance compared with their proper function – converted other organs into mere purposeless rudiments, and arranged all as if they had to stand separate, and then made them cohere? Is it not a more simple and intelligible view that all the Orchideae owe what they have in common, to descent from some monocotyledonous plant, which, like so many other plants of the same class, possessed fifteen organs, arranged alternately three within three in five whorls; and that the now wonderfully changed structure of the flower is due to a long course of slow modification – each modification having been preserved which was useful to the plant, during the incessant changes to which the organic and inorganic world has been exposed? (XVII:172–73)

Orchids is in a sense Darwin's version of Dante Rossetti's "The Woodspurge" (written in 1856, published in 1870), in which a grieving speaker recounts his healing through an encounter not with the supernatural meanings of the woodspurge's flower, "three cups in one," but its physical structure: "From perfect grief there need not be / Wisdom or even memory; / One thing then learned remains to me – / The woodspurge has a cup of three."

The Duke of Argyll was unconvinced, offering anonymously in the *Edinburgh Review* but then incorporating into his widely read *The Reign of Law*, a considerably different interpretation of Darwin's diagram and its "Threes within Threes." These regular, symmetrical arrangements beneath "all the strange and marvellous forms of the orchids" are "expressions of a numerical idea, as so many other things – perhaps as all things – of beauty are." Darwin's notion that orchids are the product of the evolutionary dance between flowers and insects – between "nectaries and . . . noses," as the Duke jokingly puts it – is at best a very partial understanding of the matter. Numerical relations imply order, and order implies purpose and intention, and since these purposes and intentions are not our own, they must be those of "One whose manifestations are indeed superhuman and supermaterial." Invoking from Tennyson's *In Memoriam* the "Living Will that shall endure," Argyll argues that in nature as in religion this superintending will does not act arbitrarily but instead enacts "Freedom within the bounds of Law."[16] It is a Creator, not natural selection, to which homological regularities and their corresponding beauties point.

Two illustrations from *Different Forms of Flowers* – diagrams illustrating the levels of fertility in different acts of fertilization – proved more popular than any single figure from *Orchids*. Often described and sometimes reproduced in other botanical works, especially those for general audiences, these fertility diagrams tended to be incorporated into natural theological arguments rather than aggressively challenged, Argyll-like. The first (fig. 4.11a) showed the two forms of the cowslip, *Primula veris*, this time without any petals or calyx. The horizontal dotted arrows indicate fertilization of a flower of one form by a flower of the other form; the vertical dotted arrows indicate fertilization of a flower of one form by a flower of the same form (or by the flower's own pollen). The former Darwin termed a "legitimate union" resulting in "complete fertility" while the latter was an "illegitimate union" resulting in "incomplete fertility." This diagram provided a sort of visual summary not only of Darwin's tables of experimental results (comparisons for the different "unions" of the number of flowers fertilized, the number of seed capsules, number of good seeds, and weight of seeds produced) but of his argument about the beneficial results of crossing these different forms. And since these results held for Darwin's experiments on dimorphic species generally, the diagram implicitly encapsulates his findings for all flowers

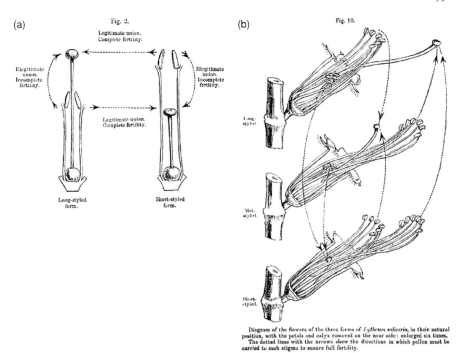

Figure 4.11 (a) Schematic representation of the different "unions" possible in long- and short-styled flowers of the common cowslip, *Primula veris*. (b) Schematic representation of the "unions" among the three forms of loosestrife, *Lythrum salicaria*, that result in "full fertility." Wood engravings. Figures 2 and 10 from Charles Darwin, *The Different Forms of Flowers on Plants of the Same Species* (London: Murray, 1877), 27, 139.

with two distinct sexual forms (and hence, perhaps, the figure does not have a caption specifically mentioning the cowslip).

The second and even more striking fertility diagram depicts the "unions" of loosestrife, *Lythrum salicaria* (fig. 4.11b), which has not two but *three* different sexual forms. In addition to a "long-styled" and "short-styled" form, *Lythrum* has a "mid-styled" form. But to make matters more complicated, each form has *two* sets of stamens – the long-styled form has a set of both short and medium-length stamens, the mid-styled has sets of long and short stamens, and the short-styled has both long and medium-length stamens. Thus, no fewer than eighteen different "unions" are possible. "In their manner of fertilization," Darwin commented, "these plants offer a more remarkable case than can be found in any other plant or animal" (xxvi:98). The dotted lines in the diagram represent the six "legitimate" unions that result in full fertility: crosses that involve the stigma of one form being fertilized with pollen from the sets of anthers of the corresponding height in the other forms. The twelve other possible unions, which do not achieve full fertility, Darwin again terms "illegitimate." These illegitimate unions include fertilization not only by the two sets of anthers in a flower of the same form, but also by the set of anthers not of the corresponding height on each of the other forms. Thus, for example, the long-styled form is fully fertile when pollinated by the long anthers of the mid- and short-styled forms, but it is not fully fertile when pollinated by either the anthers of its own form or the short or mid-length anthers of the other forms. As with the *Primula* diagram, Darwin provides a succinct visual rendering of five tables and many pages of text. While the diagram also captures a number of naturalistic details of the different forms – the heights of the three elements in the three forms closely correspond, longer anthers are also larger in size than shorter ones, the orientation of the anthers varies with their location – it is the "fertility narrative" on which Darwin places the greatest visual and textual emphasis. These fertility narratives, however, are clearly if implicitly presented as further supporting natural selection, particularly in providing additional evidence for the ubiquity and importance of variation, and evolutionary explanations for the emergence of various sexual forms and the advantages of cross-fertilization. Yet if Darwin's *Lythrum* diagram could be reproduced in modified form by his friend Lubbock for his popular *British Wild Flowers Considered in Relation to Insects*, it could just as easily be incorporated into J. E. Taylor's *Flowers: Their Origin, Shapes, Perfumes, and Colours*, which sought to present "a clearer conception of Creational Power and Wisdom."[17]

POPULARIZING DARWIN'S BOTANY: PHYSIOLOGICAL AESTHETICS

As the works of Lubbock and Taylor would suggest, Darwin's botanical work was beginning to be extensively popularized by the mid-1870s – it had even served as the basis for some of the satire in Samuel Butler's novel *Erewhon* in 1872 – and as with the *Origin*, reactions and appropriations varied. Taylor endorsed the "new philosophy of flowers," asserting that flowers were not created for the delight and use of humans but had evolved for their own survival. Nonetheless, he argued, Darwin's work could be easily incorporated into, and would in fact strengthen, a natural theological understanding of nature. "The teachings of modern botanists and naturalists concerning flowers and the insects," Taylor wrote, "are of a higher and more spiritual kind than those they have replaced" and will "excite more reverence

and admiration of Creatorial wisdom than the older teachings could educe."
In the final paragraph of *The Sagacity and Morality of Plants* (1884), Taylor
offered a revision of the *Origin*'s conclusion, arguing that "it does not seem
possible to contemplate this tangle of Vegetable Life and its conditions . . .
without feeling that underneath and behind all are the Untiring purposes of
Divine Wisdom and Love!"[18] M. C. Cooke, on the other hand, kept natural
selection at arm's length in his *Freaks and Marvels of Plant Life*, published by
the Society for Promoting Christian Knowledge in 1882. Although fourteen
of the book's twenty chapters are explicit summaries of Darwin's work,
Cooke contends that he is not concerned with arguing the merits of natural
selection but with ensuring that the just-deceased Darwin be remembered
amongst the general public as a patient observer and collector of facts.
As a result, while accepting Darwin's demonstration of the benefits for
the plant of various structures and behaviors, and sometimes mentioning
Darwin's explanations about natural selection's role in the development of
these structures and behaviors, Cooke certainly does not endorse natural
selection. Indeed, he repeatedly frames Darwin's work in terms of Divine
design, stating that his purpose is to increase his readers' appreciation for
"the power and beneficence of the great Author of all these marvels."[19]

By far the most prolific popularizer of Darwin's botany, however, was
Grant Allen (1848–1900). Keenly interested in natural science, when the
Oxford-educated Allen returned to England from Jamaica in 1876, he sought
to earn his living by popularizing and extending the evolutionary theories
of Darwin, Spencer, Wallace, and Huxley.[20] He turned initially to what
he called, in a book of the same name in 1877, "physiological aesthetics."
Synthesizing Darwin's work on mate-selection in animals and the evolutionary relationship between flowers and insects with the physiological psychology of Spencer and Alexander Bain and the physiology of sight and hearing
most closely associated with Hermann von Helmholtz, Allen argued that
aesthetic feelings have a physical basis, are the product of natural and sexual
selection, and thus are not unique to humans. His 1879 follow-up book, *The
Colour-Sense*, developed the more specific claim that the human color-sense
had in fact been inherited from fruit-eating ancestors whose ability to dis-
criminate color had been developed in the same way and for the same reason
as that of birds and insects. Although neither book sold well, *Physiological
Aesthetics* brought Allen to the notice of the scientific naturalists and opened
doors for him in London's intellectual and journalistic circles. *The Colour-
Sense*, which embroiled him in a controversy with W. E. Gladstone, made
a bigger splash and was more widely and favorably reviewed. By the time it
appeared, Allen was already placing articles on botany and aesthetics in the

periodical press, and over the next decade he would publish a host of pieces in a range of venues. Middle-class monthlies such as *Cornhill*, *Macmillan's*, and *Longman's*; London evening papers such as the *Pall Mall* and *St. James's Gazettes* for gentlemen in their clubs; popular science such as Richard Proctor's *Knowledge* and specialist journals such as *Nature* and *Mind* associated with the scientific naturalists – all published Allen's writings on botany and evolutionary aesthetics. These essays were also frequently collected and/or revised for issue as books, which were then reviewed in many of the same periodicals. Essays from the *Pall Mall* and *St. James's* became *Vignettes from Nature* (1881), *The Evolutionist at Large* (1881), and *Colin Clout's Calendar* (1882). A series on "The Colours of Flowers" for *Nature* in 1882 appeared in book form later that same year, while a group of essays on flowers for various middle-class monthlies was collected as *Flowers and Their Pedigrees* in 1883.

Bernard Lightman characterizes Allen's popular essays as "evolutionary epics" that enact "the secularization of wonder" by grafting evolutionary genealogies onto the conversational stories of personal encounters with nature so common during the latter half of the century.[21] This element of secularization is perhaps even more aptly captured by the Huxleyan term "lay sermon." In several essays Allen refers to the natural object he is examining as the "text" on which he will "preach," and on at least one occasion he explicitly invokes the term. Almost all of the botanical essays follow the Huxleyan pattern of drawing evolutionary lessons from a common plant or flower.[22] And one of their most prominent lessons is the physiological and evolutionary character of aesthetics, almost invariably delivered by way of an examination of flowers and fruits. In an essay on bindweed, for example, Allen notes that "The old school of thinking imagined that beauty was given to flowers and insects for the sake of man alone: it would not, perhaps, be too much to say that, if the new school be right, the beauty is not in the flowers and insects themselves at all, but is read into them by the fancy of the human race." The "whole loveliness of flowers" ultimately depends on "all kinds of accidental causes – causes, that is to say, into which the deliberate design of the production of beautiful effects did not enter."[23] The development of color in nature, and of color contrast, depended on chance variation and the ability of insect eyes to perceive, and at a primitive aesthetic level appreciate, color difference. As Allen put it in an 1884 essay on "Our Debt to Insects," "I believe we owe almost entirely to insects the whole presence of colour in nature, otherwise than green; without them our world would be wanting in more than half the beautiful objects which give it its greatest aesthetic charm in the appreciative eyes of cultivated humanity."

Moreover, according to Allen it is not fanciful to speak of the insects as having particular aesthetic "tastes." While the ability to distinguish colors "is a mere question of the presence or absence of nerve-centres," the association of food with color ultimately associates pleasure with color, even for insects: "creatures which pass all their lives in the search for bright flowers must almost inevitably come to feel pleasure in the perception of brilliant colours."[24] Colored flowers have not been divinely created for human benefit and pleasure, but have been self-generated by the reproductive needs of plants and the nutritional needs of insects.

Allen was no mere passive popularizer or diffuser of Darwin's botanical work.[25] He combined it with that of other thinkers in original ways, and he supplemented, modified, and extended Darwin's observations and experiments with original observations and experiments of his own. Wallace, reviewing *Vignettes from Nature*, declared not only that Allen "stands at the head of living writers as a popular exponent of the evolution theory" but also that Allen had so thoroughly "mastered" it as to be "able to apply it in an intelligent and often original manner." Darwin, writing to Allen in praise of *The Evolutionist at Large*, similarly recognized the dual function of Allen's writing: "Who can tell how many young persons your chapters may bring up to be good working evolutionists! . . . Several of your views are quite new to me, and seem extremely probable."[26] In particular, Allen drew out and aggressively promulgated the implications of Darwin's botany for aesthetics in ways that Darwin himself had not. Darwin had acknowledged in the *Origin* that if structures "have been created for the sake of beauty, to delight man or the Creator," it was "absolutely fatal" to his theory. He declined in the first edition to enter into an extended account of his utilitarian view of beauty, but by the fourth edition in 1866 he felt sufficiently confident in his researches on sexual selection among animals and fertilization in plants to insert a paragraph outlining his position. "Flowers and fruit," he wrote in that paragraph, "have been rendered conspicuous by gaudy colours in contrast with the green foliage, in order that the flowers might be easily seen, visited, and fertilized by insects, and the fruit have their seeds disseminated by birds."[27] Sections on his orchid research and on dimorphic and trimorphic species were added to this edition as well, yet Darwin did not elaborate on the aesthetic implications of this work. Nor did the botanical books themselves stress these implications in the way that the *Descent* did. It was in other venues, and primarily from the pens of Allen and others, that this occurred.

Thanks largely to the work of Allen and those responding, pro or con, to *The Descent of Man* and Darwin's botany, physiological aesthetics was known and accessible across a wide swath of Victorian culture in the 1870s and 80s, and it had secured a place in serious discussions of art and beauty. By the turn of the century, the power of physiological aesthetics to shock was diminished, but acceptance of it was limited. In his 1887 book on *The Development of Taste*, Scottish philosopher Proudfoot Begg examined the work of Darwin and Spencer extensively, and although he allowed that their utilitarian accounts of the function of beauty in the natural world might be true, he insisted that this was not – and could not be – the last word, for to halt at such a materialist explanation would "strike at the root of all morality and religion, and land us in universal skepticism." Begg closed his book with a quotation from *Modern Painters*, noting that he was content to maintain allegiance to men such as Ruskin.[28] In his *History of Aesthetic* (1892), Bernard Bosanquet regarded physiological aesthetics as the most significant but decidedly secondary alternative to the thought of Ruskin and William Morris in England over the second half of the century. Vernon Lee [Violet Paget] and Clementina Anstruther-Thomson's "Beauty and Ugliness" (1897) was aggressively physiological, but by the essay's 1912 reprint Lee was softening her position.[29] In his 1902 *Evolution in Art*, a survey of the "life-histories of designs," zoologist Alfred Haddon of Dublin's Royal College of Science acknowledged the existence of a considerable body of work in physiological aesthetics but also noted its scientific and cultural limitations. "Art has also a physical and physiological aspect," Haddon declared, and "much has been done towards establishing a physical basis" for it. Yet in spite of specifically eschewing the "purely subjective" aesthetic judgments of art critics, Haddon declined to take up art's "physical and physiological aspect" on the grounds that not enough was known about it, pursuing instead his own "biological" approach that involved tracing specific designs back in time as if they were species.[30]

   Art historians and literary critics have tended to focus on the aesthetic battles in the second half of the century between those like Ruskin and Arnold who continued to stress the importance of morality in art, and the supporters of various movements – Aestheticism, Impressionism, Decadence, Art Nouveau – in which moral subject matter treated in a morally appropriate way was subordinated to purely aesthetic issues of color, form, and composition. The self-consciously revolutionary postures of these movements, the cries of "art for art's sake," Pater's claim that the Arnoldian desire to see the object as in itself it really is requires first knowing one's own impression as it really is, Wilde's assertion that "no artist has ethical sympathies," the Whistler–Ruskin trial – all these beg for an interpretation of the Victorian aesthetic battlefield as largely divided into two camps. Yet even as recent scholarship has blurred this neat division, offering a more complex and nuanced sense of the relationships, it has continued to under-estimate the importance of physiological and evolutionary aesthetics in shaping discussions of art and beauty in the 1870s and 80s.[31] This is especially the case with Ruskin, who recognized the threat to his own work in the alternative aesthetics posed by scientific naturalism, and who saw arrayed against him an increasingly aggressive number of competitors for cultural authority, their approaches and agendas both distinctive and overlapping, on matters of art and its relation to social issues.

RUSKIN'S *PROSERPINA* AND THE RESPONSE TO PHYSIOLOGICAL AESTHETICS

Interested in plants and flowers, as he was in most other elements of nature, from his boyhood, Ruskin had undertaken more focused botanical study in the 1840s and 50s for his discussions of "truth of vegetation" in *Modern Painters I* (1843) and "leaf beauty" in *Modern Painters V* (1860). In 1866, however, he turned to botany with renewed vigor, working extensively into 1869, when the duties of the Slade Professorship at Oxford caused him to set his botanical work largely aside until 1874. By late in 1868 he had begun what would become *Proserpina*, his "Studies of wayside flowers while the air was yet pure among the Alps and in the Scotland and England which my father knew." Like *Love's Meinie*, *Proserpina* was published irregularly in parts – two in 1875, two in 1876, one in 1878 and 1879, two in 1882, one in 1885 and 1886 – with the first six parts collected and published separately in volume form in 1882.

Ruskin reminds his readers throughout *Proserpina* that he is not writing a treatise on scientific botany. The work is tentative, provisional, conditional – a book "of studies – not of statements" (xxv:216). His names and classification scheme are meant to be useful for novices. He adopts what we would call an ecological or environmental perspective: he is interested in the living plant in its habitat rather than the dead specimen dissected and studied under a microscope. Without rejecting his earlier distinction in the Preface to the second edition of *Modern Painters I* (1844) between the botanist's study of flowers and the poet's or painter's – the former concerned with classification, the latter with the flower as a "living creature" that can be made "the vehicle of expression and emotion" – he seeks to meld "a science of aspects," of the appearances of things and their significance for humans, with one of essences (iii:36–37; v:387).[32] Classification in his system is to be rooted in aspects, not sexual anatomy or evolutionary genealogy. Young

people, those new to the study of plants, those learning to draw and paint –
these are the readers to whom *Proserpina* is addressed, for *Proserpina* is at
heart an educative work.[33] It seeks to teach the things about plants and
flowers that in Ruskin's view botanical treatises, even most introductory
ones, do not. Before, or at least in addition to, learning a plant's Linnaean
name, and all about its internal structure, the student should encounter
the plant in nature, understand where and how it grows, examine its colors
and external form, and consider its painterly and poetic, mythic and moral,
meanings.

But why did Ruskin feel compelled to turn so attentively to botany in
the late 1860s, and to work so intensively at it in the late 1870s and early
80s? Why was the writing of *Proserpina* so necessary in *those* years? Both
Frederick Kirchhoff and Dinah Birch have shown that *Proserpina* constitutes
a critique and rejection of Darwinism as well as being part of Ruskin's more
general resistance to the rising influence of scientific naturalism. But they see
this rejection of Darwin in very general terms, as discomfort with notions
of the struggle for existence, the instability of species, and the centrality
of sexuality in the process of evolution. Both are also concerned to locate
Proserpina in relation to Ruskin's interest in myth, while Birch also connects
Ruskin's botany to his private obsessions for Rose La Touche, the young Irish
girl with whom Ruskin had been infatuated since 1858, when she was just
thirteen, and who died in the year that the first part of *Proserpina* appeared.
While she argues that "the enduring value of Ruskin's rival venture into
scientific writing lies in its dissent," Birch ultimately focuses more on the
"pervasive effect" of Ruskin's love for Rose on his botanical studies. Ruskin
biographer Tim Hilton follows Birch, acknowledging that the "intellectual
programme" of *Proserpina* was "to oppose Darwinism and to insist on the
eternal value of myth," but arguing that the key to understanding the work
is to see it as one of Ruskin's "memorials" to Rose.[34]

Yet Ruskin's dissent from Darwin in *Proserpina* is specifically botanical,
and it is both precise and comprehensive. Although Ruskin refers explicitly only to Darwin's work on orchids, many of his remarks clearly target
Darwin's botany, and he dwells at length on many of the same plants (such
as the primrose, sundew, cyclamen, and butterwort) featured by Darwin.[35]
He had certainly read some of the digests of Darwin's work on fertilization
by Darwin's allies that appeared in contemporary periodicals, citing John
Lubbock's 1875 *Nature* articles (which made Ruskin "miserable") and Asa
Gray's 1882 article for the *Contemporary Review*. His comment that he has
"nothing whatever to do" with "the recent phrenzy for the investigation
of digestive and reproductive operations in plants" amounts to a sweeping

dismissal of Darwin's work on fertilization and insectivorous plants and the researches both inspired. Ruskin's dig at "the microscopic malice of botanists" characteristically complains about reliance on the microscope rather than the eye and bemoans the tearing to pieces of the living thing, but his delineation of the purposes of botanical microscopy sounds more specifically like a catalogue of Darwin's work in *Orchids, Different Forms,* and *Insectivorous Plants.* Ruskin declares himself "amazed and saddened" by the "ill-taught curiosity" that seeks to explain "every possible spur, spike, jag, sting, rent, blotch, flaw, freckle, filth, or venom, which can be detected in the construction, or distilled from the dissolution, of vegetable organism." By the mid 1880s, Ruskin was even backing away from earlier comments about the spiral movement of roots and stems and climbing plants, and while he does not cite Darwin's *Climbing Plants* or *The Power of Movement,* it is difficult to believe that Ruskin was not familiar with the evolutionary arguments of these books as well, either directly or through the popular accounts of them.[36]

Ruskin was troubled by many of the same things that troubled other commentators on Darwin's plant work. Discussions of plant movement and the "digestion" of "carnivorous" plants misleadingly reified analogies and metaphors, unjustifiably confusing distinctions. Speaking of an unpublished pamphlet sent by an unnamed author, on "every sort of plant that looked or behaved like an animal, and every sort of animal that looked or behaved like a plant," Ruskin makes clear his sense of the pointlessness of such an exercise: "He gave descriptions of walking trees, and rooted beasts; of flesh-eating flowers, and mud-eating worms; of sensitive leaves, and insensitive persons; and concludes triumphantly, that nobody could say either what a plant was, or what a person was." His disgust at Darwinian botany's fascination with "*obscene* processes and *prurient* apparitions" is clearly linked with his own sexual squeamishness and his vision of Rose and of other young girls, for he especially "warn[s] my girl-readers against all study of floral genesis and digestion" and instructs them to avoid such questions as "how far flowers invite, or require, flies to interfere in their family affairs." But the fact that fertilization is connected to the beauty of the flower, roots Ruskin's alarmed response deeply in aesthetic and intellectual issues rather than merely personal ones. To connect plants to animals at the levels of reproduction, digestion, and locomotion was to connect them at their lowest common denominator. To make beauty utilitarian, to put it in the service of deceitfully procuring sex and food, could not be borne. "The final end of the whole flower," Darwin had asserted in the final chapter of *Orchids,* ". . . is the production of seed" (XVII:194). Ruskin's denial was direct: "the flower exists for its own sake, – not for the fruit's sake. The production of the fruit is an added honour to it – it is granted consolation to us for its death. But the flower is the end of the seed, – not the seed of the flower." Flora for flora's sake, but not in the way Darwin thought, and not without reference to us. Flowers are not a vehicle for ensuring reproduction. They express "purity, radiance, [and] serenity," from which we benefit, with the fruit, in a Ruskinian wrinkle on the standard argument, offered to us as a "consolation" for the flower's death (xxv:507–08, 391 [my emphasis], 413–14, 249–50).

Ruskin, was, moreover, aware of the evolutionary gloss that Darwin and his followers supplied to his plant investigations and, like many popularizers and reviewers, could accept the validity of the observations without accepting the gloss. Discussing the relations of herbs and sunflowers, Ruskin notes that Darwin could undoubtedly supply instances of the evolution of one into the other, but that he himself will not contemplate these possible "parental relations." A reference to recent speculations on "the relation of colour in flowers, to insects – to selective development, etc., etc." clearly indicates that Ruskin was aware of the stakes, and he even agrees that "there *are* such relations" between flower color and insects. But that they are the product of "selective development" is both speculative and basely material. "So also," Ruskin writes, "the blush of a girl, when she first perceives the faltering in her lover's step as he draws near, is related essentially to the existing state of her stomach; and to the state of it through all the years of her previous existence. Nevertheless, neither love, nor chastity, nor blushing, are merely exponents of digestion." What is "miraculous," he insists, is "the fact of the *confirmation* of species in plants and animals," that plants, despite their susceptibility to external conditions and their extensive variability, are "restrained within impassable limits . . . from generation to generation" by "constant Omnipotence" (xxv:291, 264 [original emphasis], 361 [original emphasis].

Ruskin saw himself as at war not merely with the botanists' words but with their illustrations, writing towards the end of *Proserpina* that "I feel every hour more and more the necessity of separating the treatment of subjects in *Proserpina* from the microscopic curiosities of recent botanic illustration." Ruskin's plates – mostly steel engravings executed by George Allen from Ruskin's own drawings – thus do not contain dissections or isolated parts of a flower. While they rarely depict the whole plant, they tend to show a large portion of it – flower with stem and a few leaves, for example – the specific content varying with Ruskin's focus. Emphasis is generally on form and arrangement rather than structural detail. This formal emphasis obtains as

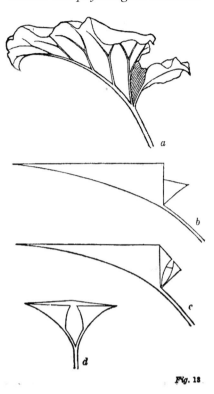

Fig. 13

Figure 4.12 "Outline of a Leaf of Burdock, With Perspectives of the Elementary Form."
Wood engraving by Arthur Burgess from a drawing by John Ruskin. Figure 13 of John
Ruskin, *Proserpina. The Library Edition of the Works of John Ruskin*, ed. E. T. Cook and
Alexander Wedderburn, 39 vols. (London: Allen, 1903–12) xxv:304.

well, although in a different fashion, with the bulk of Arthur Burgess's wood-
engraved figures (many again from Ruskin's drawings) in the text.[37] Most of
these text figures depict a much more limited part of the plant in question –
a leaf, the flower, a petal – but never at the level of detail of Darwin's orchid
pollinia or cowslip stamens. On only one occasion does Ruskin provide a
microscopical illustration, but it is copied from another work, and on only
one other does he employ a lens himself (apparently a hand lens rather than
a microscope) to delineate in cross-section the stem of a young tree. Indeed,
unlike the plates, which almost uniformly depict a particular individual,
the text figures are frequently diagrams, rough outline sketches, and even
abstract geometrical renderings of a "typical" leaf or flower or petal or stem. A
striking set of figures take this formal abstraction to an extreme, illustrating
not the plant itself (or a part of it) but pieces of paper folded in such a way
as to represent it. But as fig. 4.12 makes clear, the realistic representation of

the particular individual and the abstract representation of the typical form were, for Ruskin, closely aligned.

Ruskin's choice of steel engraving over lithography (of which he had a low opinion) also helped differentiate Ruskin's plates from those of contemporary publications. Ruskin repeatedly linked his plates with the early copper engravings of William Curtis's *Botanical Magazine* and especially those for the *Flora Danica* prior to 1820 and the first two volumes of Curtis's *Flora Londinensis* (1777, 1798). Three of his own plates and four of his figures were copied from the *Flora Danica*; the plates of the *Flora Londinensis* he called "miracles of skill, patience, and faithful study," claiming he would not have begun *Proserpina* had he known of their existence (xxv:464).[38] By contrast, Ruskin had almost nothing but criticism for the plates of James Sowerby's *English Botany*, the nineteenth-century standard whose plates are still cited and copied, of which Ruskin owned both the first (1790–1814) and third (1863–72, 1886) editions.[39] Indeed, several of Ruskin's plates and figures (of heather, poppy leaves and petals, and burdock leaves) are offered as explicit corrections of what he deemed Sowerby's carelessness and inaccuracies. And yet, Ruskin does not simply model his plates on the *Flora Londinensis*, as is evident from a glance at its plate of the primrose (fig. 4.13). The entire plant, including the roots, is depicted – a throwback to the herbal tradition that Ruskin does not follow, presumably because we do not encounter the primrose with its roots exposed and free of soil. More important, although the entire plant dominates the plate, it also contains Linnaean details of the sexual organs, including separate representations of the two sexual forms of the flower in longitudinal section with front petals and sepals removed as in Darwin's illustrations for *Different Forms of Flowers*.

Proserpina also provides a visual rebuttal to Darwin. As many of *Love's Meinie's* illustrations responded to those in the bird chapters of the *Descent*, a number of *Proserpina's* illustrations counter those in Darwin's botanical books. Crucially, the first plate illustrating Ruskin's chapter on "Genealogy," in which he offers an extended account of his own classificatory methods, depicts *Orchis maculata*, a native species closely related to *O. mascula*, with which Darwin had begun *Orchids*. Desirous of "fastening the thoughts of the pupil on the special character of the plant, in the place where he is likely to see it; and therefore, in expressing the power of its race and order in the wider world, rather by reference to mythological associations than to botanical structure," Ruskin depicts the stalk of the flower twisted through one and a half revolutions, for the "special character" – indeed, the "one constant character" – of the orchids is "*some* manner of *distortion*." Since *O. maculata's* particularly striking characteristic is its strong purple color,

Primula acaulis.

Figure 4.13 "Primula acaulis." Hand-colored engraving for William Curtis, *Flora Londinensis* (1777–98), vol. ɪɪ, fasc. 6, plate 16. Note the long- and short-styled forms of the flower in the cut-away views to the left and right of the main specimen's roots.

Ruskin re-christens it *Contorta purpurea*, Purple Wreath-wort (fig. 4.14). The contrast with Darwin's figure of the same species (see fig. 4.4) is evident. Whereas Darwin focuses on parts of the flower and particularly those aspects central to the mechanism of fertilization, Ruskin depicts the plant as it is "exhibited to an English child" in its native meadows. Whereas Darwin provides no information about the individual specimen or specimens from

Figure 4.14 "Contorta Purpurea. Purple Wreath-Wort." Steel engraving by George Allen
from a drawing by John Ruskin. Plate xxiii in John Ruskin, *Proserpina. The Library
Edition of the Works of John Ruskin*, ed. E. T. Cook and Alexander Wedderburn, 39 vols.
(London: Allen, 1903–12) xxv: facing page 341.

which his illustration was taken, Ruskin's is typical in a more Wordsworthian
way: his plate represents "an ordinary spring flower in our English mountain
fields," an "average example, – not one of rare size under rare conditions, –
rather smaller than average, indeed, that I might get it on my plate." Whereas
for Darwin color is, compared to structure, a very minor concern in general
with orchids, color for its own sake is central to Ruskin. Having earlier
acknowledged Darwin's proof that orchids depend on insects for their existence, Ruskin is nonetheless silent here about the role of color in attracting
and guiding insects to the flower's nectary. Indeed, it is significant that,
of the three divisions of orchids, Ruskin chooses to illustrate only the one
whose members inhabit English meadows and Alpine pastures, eschewing
not merely those that live on bad soil amongst "swarms of nasty insects"
but those graceful species, which Ruskin also closely associated with insect

546   PROSERPINA

5. CONTORTA PURPUREA

17. The Contorta Purpurea rises out of a group of Arethusan leaves
(see Plate XXIII. p. 341) which are of pale dull green on the outer
surface, but spotted (morbidly) with black on the inner. I had no room in
my plate to draw a full-grown blossom, so the crowded cluster represents
only the earlier stage of the flowers, which presently rises into a purple
spire composed of from twenty to thirty flowers set in close order on their

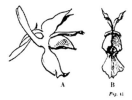

A   B
Fig. 41

virgula, which at the top becomes purple *with* them, as also the twisted
stalks of each separate blossom which we have now to examine. A single
one is drawn in profile at A, in front at B, Fig. 41.

It consists essentially of the twisted stalk, carrying six petals. Of these
six petals, two, *a* and *b* (Fig. 42), form what I shall call the crest of the
flower; one, *c*, its lappet; two, *d* and *e*, its casque (these
being prolonged backwards and upwards into a spur); and
finally one, *f*, its gorget.

In Contorta Maculata, which I find in my upper field,
16th June, the crest leaves diverge on a level on each
side of the lappet (Sowerby says they are reflexed upwards [1]),
and the gorget, divided as he describes into three lobes, is
veined, tiger-like, with purple or white—the whole flower
pale lilac in effect. The two casque-petals, in the Acria
sent me by Miss Beever,[2] are depressed beneath the spur,
which opens into a huge cup above the gorget.

The lappet is laid over the junction of the two pieces
of the casque, exactly as a protective piece of armour might
be (or a roofing tile over the two below), and under the
shelter of the casque rise the grotesque seed-producer-portions
(which Mr. Darwin has sufficiently described [3]), but these
have nothing to do with the effect of the flower, except so far as that the
gorget, underneath them, is pale, and spotted with extremely dark spots of

Fig. 42

[1] [Vol. ix. p. 101: letterpress opposite the plate of Orchis maculata, Spotted
Orchis.]
[2] [See the Introduction, above, p. xxxix.]
[3] [See ch. i. of *The Various Contrivances by which Orchids are fertilised by Insects.*]

Figure 4.15 "Flower of Contorta Purpurea: Profile and in Front" and "'Crest,' 'Lappet,'
'Casque,' and 'Gorget.'" Wood engravings by Arthur Burgess from drawings by John
Ruskin. Figures 41 and 42 of John Ruskin, *Proserpina. The Library Edition of the Works of
John Ruskin*, ed. E. T. Cook and Alexander Wedderburn, 39 vols. (London: Allen,
1903–12) XXV:546.

fertilization, that attach themselves in the air to the trunks and branches of
trees (xxv:340–43 [original emphasis], 224).

Ruskin did not include in *Proserpina* a series of figures of *Contorta purpurea* that are more botanical in nature but that contrast differently but
just as starkly with Darwin's (fig. 4.15). The first consists of side and frontal
views of a single flower; the second is an outline drawing of the flower's
six petals; the third an outline drawing of the lower petal. Unlike Ruskin's
plate of the cluster of flowers on its leaf-stalk, these figures in their general form are similar to those in *Orchids*. But whereas Darwin frequently
removes some or all of the petals and sepals in his illustrations, Ruskin
in his first two figures does not. And when Ruskin isolates a single petal,

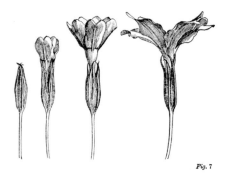

Figure 4.16 "Four Stages in the Young Life of a Primrose." Wood engraving by Arthur Burgess from a drawing by John Ruskin. Figure 7 of John Ruskin, *Proserpina. The Library Edition of the Works of John Ruskin*, ed. E. T. Cook and Alexander Wedderburn, 39 vols. (London: Allen, 1903–12) xxv:261.

as he does in his third figure, he insists that it is impossible to draw it properly. Again, however, what links these figures together against Darwin's is Ruskin's refusal to depict what Darwin focuses on. The petals, Ruskin notes, protect "the grotesque seed-producer portions (which Mr. Darwin has sufficiently described), but these have nothing to do with the effect of the flower." Darwin displays what Ruskin calls the flower's "germinal processes" by stripping away its "armour," but Ruskin in plate and figures keeps the "grotesque seed-producer portions" chastely covered, concerned with the effect of the flower's form and color on a human observer (xxv:546–47).

As the plate and woodcuts of *Contorta purpurea* are to the opening figure of *Orchis mascula* in Darwin's *Orchids*, so is Ruskin's illustration of the primrose (fig. 4.16) to the opening figure of the cowslip in Darwin's *Different Forms of Flowers* (see fig. 4.9). Ruskin's common English primrose (*Primula vulgaris*) is a species discussed extensively by Darwin in *Different Forms* and a close relation of the cowslip (*Primula veris*). That Ruskin has Darwin very much in mind here is evident from the fact that this illustration, which appears in the chapter of *Proserpina* on "The Flower," leads directly into the passages already quoted on the relation of color in flowers to insects and "selective development," and the "unclean stupidity" of Darwin's materialism, particularly on matters of color, ornament, and form. Here again, Ruskin does not strip away petals, as Darwin does, to expose the flower's sexual organs. Indeed, by adopting a line of sight from slightly below the petals, Ruskin ensures that the reproductive parts are not visible at all. Although Ruskin, like Darwin, attempts to depict process, his process is the growth that occurs in an individual flower prior to fertilization – these are "four stages in the young life of a primrose" – rather than fertilization itself (xxv:312–13).

Despite the mental illness that punctuated Ruskin's life in 1870s and 80s, *Proserpina* displays at least as much method as madness. Ruskin recognized the threat that Darwin's botany, especially when coupled with sexual selection, posed to his own life's work. Grant Allen made this threat an open one, frequently opening or closing his writings on both botany and aesthetics with contrasts to Ruskin.[40] In his preface to *Physiological Aesthetics*, Allen argued that his theory sought to answer the very questions Ruskin regarded as unanswerable: "'Why we receive pleasure from some forms and colours and not from others,' says Professor Ruskin, 'is no more to be asked or answered than why we like sugar or dislike wormwood.' The questions thus summarily dismissed by our great living authority on Aesthetics are exactly the ones which this little book asks, and, I hope, answers." And the answers, says Allen, in fact lie with Darwin, "our great teacher." Just as our differing reactions to sugar and wormwood can be explained by their differing physical effects on our bodies, so our differing reactions to forms and colors can be regarded as the "constant subjective counterparts of certain definite nervous states." Our aesthetic responses are themselves "the necessary result of natural selection."[41] Allen pursued a similar strategy in his periodical essays. Opening his essay on "Aesthetic Evolution in Man" in *Mind*, for example, Allen argues that "the construction of a scientific doctrine of aesthetics" must reject the approach of such "professors of fine art" as Ruskin (who, at the time the essay was published, had recently resigned the Slade Professorship). The "psychological aesthetician" cannot concentrate his attention on "the very highest feelings of the most cultivated classes in the most civilised nations" but must instead examine the common, universal feelings on which cultivated aesthetic tastes are based: "It is enough for him," wrote Allen, "that all village children call a daisy or a primrose pretty."[42] In making this proclamation, Allan echoed the blunt statement with which he had closed "Dissecting a Daisy" two years earlier in the *Cornhill*:

Aesthetics is the last of the sciences in which vague declamation is still permitted to usurp the place of ascertained fact. The pretty imaginative theories of Alison, of Jeffrey, and of Professor Ruskin are still allowed to hold the field against scientific research. People think them beautiful and harmless, forgetting that everything is fraught with evil if it "warps us from the living truth." We shall never understand the nature of beauty so long as we attack the problem from the wrong side. As in every other department of knowledge, so in aesthetics, we must be content to begin at the beginning, and then we may perhaps have fair hopes of some day reaching the end.[43]

It is difficult to imagine a more biting assessment of Ruskin's work. His famous prose style is reduced to "vague declamation," his vast oeuvre to "pretty imaginative theories." His repeated claim to have based his criticism in careful, detailed observation of the natural world is stood on its head – he is instead the enemy of "ascertained fact" and "scientific research." His aesthetics, despite his insistence that he transcends the analysis of mere physical beauty and physical pleasure, rising instead to the uncovering of moral and spiritual truths, is in fact "fraught with evil." Indeed, Ruskin's entire program approaches aesthetics "from the wrong side." To "begin at the beginning" in aesthetics is, according to Allen, to begin with physiological aesthetics.

An equally un-Ruskinian assessment of both the present and future state of art, couched in Ruskinian language and invoking both Turner and Titian, the artistic heroes of the first two volumes of *Modern Painters*, closed Allen's "The Origin of Fruits":

What a splendid and a noble prospect for humanity in its future evolutions may we not find in this thought, that from the coarse animal pleasure of beholding food mankind has already developed, through delicate gradations, our modern disinterested love for the glories of sunset and the melting shades of ocean, for the gorgeous pageantry of summer flowers, and the dying beauty of autumn leaves, for the exquisite harmony which reposes on the canvas of Titian, and the golden haze which glimmers over the dreamy visions of Turner! If man, base as he yet is, can nevertheless rise to-day in his highest moments so far above his sensuous self, what may he not hope to achieve hereafter, under the hallowing influence of those chaster and purer aspirations which are welling up within him even now toward the perfect day![44]

This was what Ruskin well understood, and perhaps most feared, in scientific naturalism: not that it rejected the moral, the aesthetic, the imaginative, but that it claimed them for its own, and wove them together in a narrative of social progress. *Proserpina* was the venue in which he chose to respond most fully to Darwinism because it was in botany that Darwinism's most persuasive and popular argument for an evolutionary understanding of aesthetics was to be found.

In his famous letter to the *Times* defending the Pre-Raphaelites in 1851, Ruskin had said of Charles Collins's *Convent Thoughts* (fig. 4.17) that "as a mere botanical study of the water lily and *Alisma* [*plantago*, the water plantain], as well as of the common lily and several other garden flowers, this picture would be invaluable to me, and I heartily wish it were mine" (XII:321). With their careful, loving attention to natural detail and color, the Pre-Raphaelites promised fair to become the first great painters of flowers. In his *Notes* on the 1858 Royal Academy Exhibition, however, Ruskin expressed

Figure 4.17 Charles Allston Collins, *Convent Thoughts* (1851). Oil on canvas. 84 × 59 cm.

surprise and disappointment that they and their followers had not in the intervening years offered a single true painting of the flowers of an English spring (XIV:154). Just two years later, in the final volume of *Modern Painters*, he was happy to note that a number of artists had taken up his challenge and were including in their canvases beautiful and carefully delineated flowers

(VII:120). But then came Darwin, and the representation of plants and trees, leaves and flowers, in all branches of art, suddenly regressed. In his inaugural *Lectures on Art* as Slade Professor at Oxford in 1870, Ruskin lamented that "our artists are so generally convinced of the truth of the Darwinian theory that they do not always think it necessary to show any difference between the foliage of an elm and an oak; and the gift-books of Christmas have every page surrounded with laboriously engraved garlands of rose, shamrock, thistle, and forget-me-not, without its being thought proper by the draughtsman, or desirable by the public . . . to observe the real shape of the petals of any one of them" (XX:101). To blame Darwin for the poor quality of both leaf-painting and the floral ornamentation of Christmas albums might have been unfair, but Ruskin apprehended what would only become worse in the coming decade, as the *Descent* and the remainder of the botany books developed a truly evolutionary aesthetics.

CHAPTER 5

Darwin's faces I

Darwin originally intended *The Expression of the Emotions in Man and Animals* to appear as part of *The Descent of Man*, but the length of his treatment of sexual selection caused him to publish what he called his "essay" on expression in a separate book the following year. Like the *Descent*, the *Expression* is animated by Darwin's desire to connect humans to animals in an area previously thought to distinguish them, as well as to establish the commonalities, and hence the common ancestry, of the various human races. Its running argument is with Sir Charles Bell (1774–1842), distinguished anatomist, surgeon, and Bridgewater author, whose influential work on expression had emphasized a natural theological reading of facial musculature: the Creator has provided humans with a special set of facial muscles that enable us to express emotions that animals do not experience because they result from our unique mental and moral capacities. The *Expression*, then, completes the thoroughgoing naturalization of humans begun in the *Descent*. The case for the physical evolution of the human body – already made by others, predominantly Huxley – was the least ambitious component of Darwin's human project. Taken together, the *Descent* and the *Expression* confronted those aspects of humanity that even those who were willing to accept the physical evolution of *Homo sapiens* often felt could not have been the product of natural selection: intellect, morality, aesthetics, and emotional expression. If all life has a common ancestry, and if humans have evolved from animals, then natural selection should be able to account for everything about us. It was this that made the *Descent* and the *Expression* the boldest and most controversial of Darwin's works since the *Origin*.

   The *Expression* was well and variously illustrated.[1] Three wood engravings of facial muscles were reproduced from other sources, one from Bell's *Essays on the Anatomy of Expression in Painting* (1806) and two from the first volume of Jacob Henle's *Handbuch der Systematischen Anatomie des Menschen* (1858). Six wood engravings of dogs and three of cats were made, one from a photograph by the London photographer Oscar Rejlander and two original drawings each by the artists A. D. May, Briton Riviere, T. W. Wood, and Joseph Wolf. Riviere was, with Edwin Landseer, Britain's leading animal painter, Wolf its leading animal illustrator. Wood also contributed drawings of porcupine quills, a hen, a swan, and a chimpanzee, while Wolf provided two of the Niger macaque. Wood engraved his own drawings, but Darwin hired J. D. Cooper to execute the others. Cooper employed photoengraving (a copy of the image was transferred using photography to the wood block and then engraved) for some of the illustrations, probably the Rejlander dog photograph and three photographs of humans (one from James Crichton Browne, two from photographic plates in G. B. Duchenne de Boulogne's *Méchanisme de la Physionomie Humaine* [1862]).[2] Seven plates of photographs originally taken by Rejlander, Duchenne, A. D. Kinderman, and G. C. Wallich were reproduced using the newly developed heliotype process, making Darwin's book one of the first scientific works to be illustrated with photographs. As a photomechanical process, heliotypy enabled Darwin to mass produce plates of photographs instead of tipping in individual photographs, a more labor-intensive and thus much more expensive procedure. John Murray nonetheless worried about the expense of the heliotype plates (the price of the book was ultimately raised to cover their cost) and tried to persuade Darwin to rely exclusively on wood engraving. The production of the plates also proved to be problematic, for when unexpected interest in the work from booksellers prompted Murray to increase the initial print run from 2000 to 7000, the Heliotype Company had trouble meeting the demand for plates. Darwin's correspondence regarding the illustrations for the *Expression* is particularly extensive, not just with Murray but with photographers and artists – at least ten extant letters between Darwin and Riviere over the course of just two months, for example, are devoted to Riviere's dog drawings.[3]

The subject matter and the eclectic forms of its illustrations made the *Expression* the most closely and broadly tied of Darwin's books to Victorian visual culture. Treatises on human expression had for several centuries been associated in Europe with the fine arts, particularly classical and Renaissance sculpture and Renaissance painting. Some, like Charles Le Brun's widely reprinted 1668 lecture on *L'Expression Générale et Particulière* and Bell's *Essays*, were specifically directed to artists. Facial expression in painting and sculpture was both used as source material for anatomical and physiological theories and evaluated in terms of them. In Darwin's book, however, the fine arts are conspicuous by their comparative absence. So, too, however, are references to works of physiognomy and phrenology, those popular but contested theories that sought to read moral and intellectual character from the features of the face or the shape of the skull. Physiognomic and phrenological texts, widely read in the nineteenth century, were often crammed with illustrations of faces. Yet Darwin, opening his introduction to the *Expression*, invoked physiognomy only to dismiss it, and referred to phrenology not at all. On the other hand, Darwin's use of photography positioned the *Expression* in relation to the visual conventions of portrait photography and implicated the work in contemporary debates over whether photography was itself a fine art or merely a mechanical process. The "staging" of several of Darwin's photographs also linked them to the illustrations in acting manuals and to the spectacle of melodrama, while the depiction of faces displaying extreme or ostensibly pure states of emotion invoked the traditions of English caricature, especially as practiced in popular contemporary humor magazines such as *Punch*.

If the illustrations for the *Descent* and the botany books largely show Darwin tweaking the conventions of zoological and botanical illustration to accommodate natural and sexual selection, the *Expression*'s illustrations suggest that Darwin wanted *this* imagetext to enter more directly, though quietly, into the world of Victorian visual culture and aesthetics. For the illustrations to the *Expression* make clear, as those to the *Descent* and the botany books had not, that Darwin appreciated the ways in which his theories constituted an assault on the cultural authority of the fine art tradition. This was not lost on a number of readers and reviewers of the *Expression*, including Ruskin, who attacked Darwin for his lack of aesthetic refinement and sensitivity. Perhaps in anticipation of such challenges, however, the illustrations of the *Expression* also suggest that Darwin wished to avoid associations with those aspects of visual culture that were too "low," too philosophically or politically radical. The imagetext that is the *Expression* attempts to offer in its integration of pictures and words an aspect of what Adrian Desmond and James Moore have argued Darwin offered with natural selection: a bourgeois version of evolutionary theory subversive of vested cultural interests but differentiable from those of the lower classes and their allies. In this chapter I will trace the fine but often shaky visual line walked by Darwin with regard to the intertwined visual traditions of expression in the fine arts, physiognomy, and phrenology from which he sought to dissociate himself; in the following chapter I will perform a similar analysis on the contemporary visual forms with which he aligned his work, particularly photography and the stage.

THE *EXPRESSION* AND THE FINE ART TRADITION

"I had hoped to derive much aid from the great masters in painting and sculpture," Darwin wrote in his introduction to the *Expression*, ". . . but, with a few exceptions, have not thus profited" (XXIII:10). Unable to venture far from Down, Darwin scanned commercially available photographs (the reproduction of fine art being one of the first uses to which photography was put) and engravings of famous paintings and sculpture for examples of expression.[4] Yet he was disappointed to discover that artists were generally compelled to subordinate truth to beauty in their delineations of the human countenance. They conveyed emotion with "wonderful force and truth," but they did so through "skilfully given accessories" rather than "strongly contracted facial muscles" (XXIII:10). This implied opposition between science and art, however, should not itself be taken at face value.

That Darwin initially turned to reproductions of works of art for illustrations of expression rather than to photographs of living humans was not merely a function of photography's technical limitations in capturing instantaneous expression. It was, quite simply, what writers on expression did. Le Brun was himself a painter and head of the French Academy. But even those writers who were not artists drew on the evidence of the fine arts. Johann Caspar Lavater (1741–1801), the Swiss theologian whose writings on physiognomy in the 1770s were translated and widely popularized in England from 1789, included illustrations taken from famous artists and works of art. In obtaining a copy of Lavater, particularly in some of the expensive early editions, "one acquired . . . a picture gallery executed by some of the leading painters and engravers," but even cheap editions were copiously if less lavishly illustrated.[5] The Dutch anatomist Peter Camper's famous facial angle theory – in which the slant of the face in profile was used to differentiate species and especially the various human races – was originally delivered as a two-part lecture to the Amsterdam Drawing Academy in 1770 and made use of classical sculpture. Camper presented three more lectures on drawing and aesthetics to the Academy in 1774, 1778, and 1782, the first concerned with the depiction of the passions. Although these lectures were not published until 1791 and 1792, Camper's facial angle theory had already become well known, for he publicized it extensively in correspondence and during his travels, including before the Royal Society in 1785 during one of his visits to England. These Amsterdam Drawing Academy lectures were translated into English in 1794, with a second edition in 1821. French physician L.-J. Moreau's ten-volume edition of Lavater, *L'Art de Connaître les Hommes par la Physionomie*, the 1820 edition of which was owned and heavily annotated by Darwin, was more accurately a compendium of physiognomy. In addition to reproducing Lavater's various commentaries on the visual arts, Moreau devoted one volume to his own *Anatomy and Natural History of the Face, Considered in Relation to Physiognomy and the Fine Arts*. Bell's *Essays on the Anatomy of Expression in Painting* was written as part of an unsuccessful campaign to obtain the anatomy chair at the Royal Academy. Although the first edition contained limited references to specific works of art, the much enlarged and significantly re-titled third edition, *The Anatomy and Philosophy of Expression as Connected with the Fine Arts* (1844), the one from which Darwin worked, was written after a trip to the Continent that had finally afforded Bell the opportunity to study in person the works of the old masters. Edinburgh phrenologist George Combe penned a series of articles on phrenology and art in the mid-1840s after a similar Continental visit, revising them for book publication in 1855 as *Phrenology Applied to Painting and Sculpture*. Combe criticized both Bell and physiognomy for the inadequacies and limitations in their respective understandings of expression.[6]

Artistic and aesthetic considerations were also prominent in Duchenne de Boulogne's *Mécanisme de la Physionomie Humaine*, the contemporary work Darwin regarded as having most advanced the study of expression. Duchenne's book is divided into "scientific" and "aesthetic" sections; the final chapter of the former contains a critical examination of several pieces of classical sculpture, including the *Laocoon*, while the latter attempts to demonstrate how artists can achieve both beauty and accuracy. Duchenne dressed and posed one of his female patients for photographs in order to evaluate famous paintings and sculpture, using the galvanic apparatus with which he stimulated individual facial muscles to capture particular expressions. In some cases he created general "scenes" designed to depict the desired emotion – a lady surprised by a man while dressing, a mother whose sick child recovers, a young woman displaying compassion by visiting a poor family – while in others he posed the woman as a specific literary or historical figure – the Madonna, Lady Macbeth, the Medusa. Celestial love in Bernini's *St. Cecilia* at St. Peter's, joy mixed with pain in Poussin's *Resurrection of a Young Japanese Girl* and Rubens's *Birth of Louis XIII* (1622–25), aggression and cruelty in Salvator Rosa's *The Conspiracy of Catiline* (1663) and Paul Delaroche's *Assassination of President Duranti* – all were critiqued by Duchenne. He even cast smaller, remodeled versions of the *Laocoon* and the Uffizi *Niobe* to demonstrate how the facial expressions in these works should have looked. These, of course, were not arbitrary selections – like the writers on expression before him, Duchenne focused on some of the most famous works of western art, ones widely used as exemplars in art education for the depiction of expression.[7]

The example of Darwin's predecessors and contemporaries, and especially of Duchenne, underscores the oddness of Darwin's limited reliance on fine art sources and his refusal to evaluate them. Yet, his opening dismissal notwithstanding, Darwin *did* invoke artistic depictions of the emotions, and he wanted his book brought to the attention of artists. The *Laocoon* and *Arretino*, Fra Angelico's *Descent from the Cross*, da Vinci's *Last Supper*, and Hogarth's *Rake's Progress* are used as examples, and Joshua Reynolds's *Discourses* are quoted (XXIII:140–41, 160n, 185n, 220, 224). Like his predecessors, Darwin also relies on descriptions of the expression of emotions in literary works – Shakespeare especially, but also Homer, Plautus, Chaucer, Milton, Scott, Dickens, and Tennyson. It was Darwin, not his publisher, who suggested that the book be sent to art journals for review.[8] While Darwin did not set out to position the *Expression* in opposition to the fine arts any more than his botanical work was motivated by the desire to naturalize beauty, his work was seen in some quarters as a threat to the status of the fine arts, a threat made worse by the fact of his obviously limited aesthetic sensibilities. The prestigious *Art Journal*, in its brief notice of the *Expression*, was comparatively unconcerned, recommending the book as a work of "undeniable utility" to the artist, although it hastened to add that this did not imply an endorsement of Darwin's evolutionary views about humans. But William Brighty Rands, in a mostly sympathetic review of the book for *Saint Paul's*, suggested Darwin had not found works of art helpful because he lacked "the very special sensitiveness" necessary for their proper examination. Challenging Darwin's account of devotion, Rands relied on photographs of a Raphael *Virgin and Child* and a Girard *Cupid and Psyche*. The reviewer for the *Athenaeum* similarly declared that Darwin had "an imperfect knowledge of what Art has done." In the *Edinburgh*, T. S. Baynes challenged Darwin's aesthetic competence far more aggressively, accusing Darwin of selective evidence-gathering and a lack of taste and refinement so pernicious as to implicitly undermine "higher culture."[9] Darwin's failure to appreciate the evidence of masterpieces in painting and sculpture proved him to be interested only in the lowest, meanest emotions shared by humans and animals. Great art was the best source for knowledge of the higher and more complex emotions, Baynes argued, but Darwin was out to prove his a priori thesis that humans and animals are fundamentally alike. Launching into an extended contrast between Darwin's ignorant, biased narrow-mindedness and Bell's cosmopolitan, judicious sensibility, Baynes finds in the *Expression*'s style as well as its content an essential and encompassing vulgarity:

Sir Charles Bell was not more decisively Mr. Darwin's superior as an anatomist and physiologist than as a man of taste and of literary and philosophical culture. His style is marked by the rarest union of gracefulness and strength, of purity, precision, and admirably co-ordinated scientific and literary power. On the other hand, Mr. Darwin's writing is marked by slang phrases, vulgarisms, and a pervading looseness of structure . . . We only wish there were space at command to exemplify Sir Charles Bell's immense superiority in this respect. But all who are familiar with his essay will remember how happily it illustrates the higher culture that illuminates special knowledge, connects science with history and philosophy, and thus gives to its expositions a distinctively literary character, and a broadly human interest. The author's varied, rich, and refined training as a thinker and critic appears in every part, not only in the style, but in the finished accuracy, fulness, and plastic grouping of the details, in the firm and flexible command of general principles, and in the rare beauty of the illustrations, both literary and artistic.

Bell's book, Baynes argues, is itself a work of art. Its structure, illustrations, and prose all reflect the nobility and refinement of its author's mind. And Bell went to Italy to study the works of the old masters first-hand, Baynes notes triumphantly, while Darwin merely looked over a few photographic reproductions of them. Authentic culture – scientific as well as intellectual and artistic – is to be gleaned from the Continental Grand Tour that Darwin never took.

 Ruskin had a similar reaction. Responding simultaneously to the *Descent* and the *Expression* in *Proserpina*, Ruskin attacked Darwin's almost complete lack of familiarity with good art, his ignorance about color, and his inability to draw. Ruskin did not share Baynes's unbridled enthusiasm for Bell – commissioned by Murray to review the 1844 edition of Bell's *Anatomy and Philosophy of Expression* for the *Quarterly*, Ruskin studied the work closely but ultimately declined to write the review on the grounds that he could not satisfy Murray's desire to gratify Bell's widow with a uniformly favorable assessment. But the second volume of *Modern Painters* (1846) contained a number of complimentary references to Bell, both to *The Anatomy and Philosophy of Expression* and to his Bridgewater Treatise on *The Hand: Its Mechanism and Vital Endowments as Evincing Design* (1833).[10] And Ruskin certainly shared with Baynes an awareness of the potential aesthetic implications of Darwin's rejection of fine art sources and illustrations. Both men understood that Darwin's evolutionary naturalism sought to bring beauty under its explanatory aegis. Both recognized that this aspect of Darwin's program was being carried out on a variety of fronts. And both recoiled from the prospect of a human society in which the civilizing, enculturating effects of art were effaced. Only great artists, Baynes argued, are capable of depicting and interpreting humanity's "ideal aims" as well as its "outward conditions and bodily wants," of providing "a spiritualistic conception of life and labour." Baynes complained that whereas for Bell expression was merely "the material reflex or manifestation" of mind, for Darwin the materiality and animality was all.[11] The *Expression* was a piece of aesthetic vulgarity that could only drag down human culture.

ANSWERING BELL

Baynes and Ruskin also understood that the *Expression*, like *Orchids*, was an anti-Bridgewater Treatise, although its target was not Bell's book on the hand but *The Anatomy and Philosophy of Expression*. The *Anatomy*, as I have noted, was explicitly natural theological, arguing that humans were endowed by their Creator not only with a set of emotions unknown to animals but also with a special set of facial muscles for their expression. While "the mind is dependent on the frame of the body," wrote Bell, this fact should not be regarded as "humiliating," nor as denying the existence of spirit. For the Creator is the source of our "higher intellectual faculties," and "He has laid the foundation of emotions that point to Him, affections by which we are drawn to Him, and which rest in Him as their object." Darwin was explicit in the introductions to both the *Descent* and the *Expression* that he found this view unsatisfactory – indeed, that it could not be reconciled with an evolutionary understanding of humanity – and wished to replace it with an account in which the expression of human emotions was linked to animal expression and had been acquired gradually from our animal progenitors.[12] Yet Bell was in Darwin's eyes nonetheless the true architect of the scientific study of expression. He had not only "laid the foundations of the subject as a branch of science" but had "built up a noble structure" for it; Darwin both agreed with and depended on Bell's "graphic description of the various emotions" and his demonstration of the connection between expression and respiration (XXIII:1–2). In his innovative work on the human nervous system, Bell had shown that different nerves served distinct functions, and that the respiratory nerves, arising from a separate area of the brain, controlled the movements of muscles central to expression (vocal and facial) as well as to breathing.

In challenging Bell's theory of expression, Darwin was not simply taking on a dead classic. The status of Bell and his work, including that of *The Anatomy and Philosophy of Expression*, was higher than ever at the time

Darwin was writing the *Expression*. Henry Bohn issued a new edition of Bell's *Anatomy* in his Artist's Series in 1865, with another following in 1872 and yet another in 1877. The appearance in 1870 of a selection of Bell's letters to his brother, George, led inevitably to years' worth of articles on Bell in various magazines and reviews. Writing in *Fraser's* in 1875, Frederick Arnold, the Anglican divine and editor, declared that "his fame doubtless stands at a higher point now than it did during any period of his lifetime."[13]

Bell's book was also "admirably illustrated" (xxiii:2), as Darwin acknowledged in the *Expression's* opening paragraphs. It thus required a visual as well as a textual rejoinder. As was so often the case for Darwin, then, his problem was how to respond visually to representations whose content he regarded as unobjectionable even if he wished to challenge the theory on which they were based. While there is no evidence to confirm that Darwin consciously positioned the illustrations in the *Expression* as a reply to those in Bell's book, they certainly give the appearance of it. The selection and deployment of Darwin's illustrations, coupled with his appropriation of Bell's language and ideas, exploit the fractures in Bell's imagetext and subtly highlight the differences in their views.

Bell's third edition was much more fully illustrated than the first two, with the illustrations falling broadly into three groupings. The first consists of illustrations of facial musculature, in keeping with his interest in expression rather than physiognomy's and especially phrenology's focus on the permanent form of the skull. The largest and most concentrated grouping of illustrations is of Camperesque skulls and profile faces with lines showing various angles of inclination. These occur in the extended section discussing Camper's theories and reflect Bell's respectful consideration – and ultimate rejection – of his fellow anatomist's views. Depictions of human emotions comprise the other large grouping of illustrations. These were mostly original drawings by Bell himself, although some were copied from famous sculpture such as the *Laocoon* and the *Dying Gladiator*. Appearing in the essays on facial expression, most of these illustrations were of heads.

These images of expressive heads aligned Bell in general ways with his predecessors and contemporaries. But Bell's specific purposes are evident, differentiating his agenda from theirs. His illustration of "Weeping," for example, is not of a human at all, but of a *faun*. He has done this, he explains in a footnote, because the expression of weeping from pain is "inexpressibly mean and ludicrous in the countenance of a man" (148). Yet weeping, along with its opposite, laughter, is the most extreme form of emotional expression and is "peculiarly human" (145). Moreover, weeping and

(a)   (b)

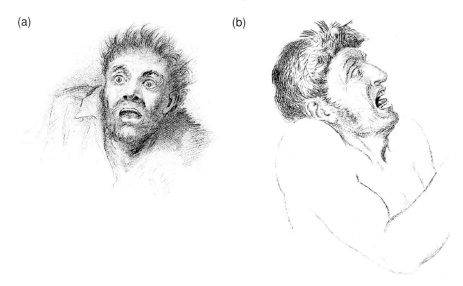

Figure 5.1 Fear. Engravings from sketches by Charles Bell for his *The Anatomy and Philosophy of Expression as Connected with the Fine Arts*, 3rd edn. (London: Murray, 1844), 165, 166. Bell describes (a) as fear "mingled with wonder" and (b) as "more strictly animal" and "common to brutes."

laughter demonstrate conclusively the importance of the respiratory muscles to expression, and the fact that these diametrically opposite emotions are expressed by the same group of muscles is "a proof of *design* . . . that all our emotions are intended to have their appropriate outward characters" (149; original emphasis). Bell's illustrations of facial expression are invariably embedded in detailed discussions of the muscular action that produces them, the expression and muscular action being likened to or differentiated from those in animals depending on whether the emotion is ignoble or noble. Thus, in Bell's paired illustrations of fear (fig. 5.1), the first, "fear mingled with wonder," is demonstrably human (166), while the second verges on the "mere bodily fear" of animals that is "without dignity," being "the mean anticipation of pain" (164). Similarly, rage is "a brutal passion" displayed by the tiger, the wolf, or "the human brute strangling helpless age or infancy" (175), but even the murderer who is beginning to display regret and remorse for his just-completed deed is expressing what tiger or wolf cannot (fig. 5.2). By contrast, devotion (fig. 5.3), in which the eyes – themselves "indicative of the higher and the holier emotions – of all the feelings which distinguish man from the brutes" (101) – are instinctively raised upwards to express the gratitude towards our Maker that is both "the debt of our nature" and "the distinguishing character of our minds" (105).

(a) (b)

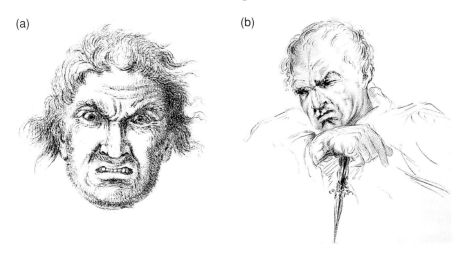

Figure 5.2 Rage. Engravings from sketches by Charles Bell for his *The Anatomy and Philosophy of Expression as Connected with the Fine Arts*, 3rd edn. (London: Murray, 1844), 176, 178. Bell describes (b) as representing "that expression which succeeds the last horrid act of revenge: the storm has subsided, but the gloom is not yet dissipated."

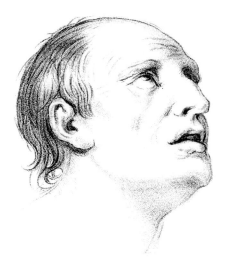

Figure 5.3 Devotion. Engraving from a sketch by Charles Bell for his *The Anatomy and Philosophy of Expression as Connected with the Fine Arts*, 3rd edn. (London: Murray, 1844), 104.

Rather surprising, in light of his discussion of animal expression and the stark distinction he draws between it and its human counterpart, is the limited number of animal illustrations Bell provides. His chief interest is the difference in expression *among* animals, between that of carnivores (represented by the lion) and that of herbivores (represented by the horse). Here again, he treats expression in relation to musculature and especially to muscular action associated with respiration. As a result, two of the four animal illustrations depict the facial musculature of the lion and the horse. The other two are of horses' heads, one copied from Giulio Romano as an example of an idealized head that does not accurately depict expression, the other an "animated sketch" of the facial musculature diagram. This latter head stands directly above the section comparing animal and human facial musculature in which Bell explains "the remarkable difference between the range of expression in man and animals" as being the result of the "special provision" to humanity of its "peculiar set of muscles" for expressing its higher moral and intellectual powers (130–31). Absent from Bell's text are the juxtapositions of human and animal physiognomies made popular by Giambattista della Porta (1535–1615) (fig. 5.4) and Le Brun.

In constructing an imagetext to answer Bell's, Darwin characteristically worked from both directions, using his animal illustrations as well as his human ones to break down rigid distinctions between the two groups. Drawing attention to Bell's claim that animals' faces basically can only express rage and fear, Darwin noted that "man himself cannot express love and humility by external signs so plainly as does a dog, when with drooping ears, hanging lips, flexuous body, and wagging tail, he meets his beloved master. Nor can these movements in the dog be explained by acts of volition or necessary instincts, any more than the beaming eyes and smiling cheeks of a man when he meets an old friend" (xxiii:8). And so Darwin's discussion of general principles of expression in the opening chapters of his book includes both animals and humans, and the illustrations are overwhelmingly of dogs and cats. Whereas Bell must explain away the nobility, courage, and seeming intelligence in a horse's face, Darwin depicts dogs and cats that are attentive and affectionate as well as angry and apprehensive. In his chapter on the "special expressions of animals" (by which he means the specific ways in which particular species express various emotions), he depicts the Niger macaque in a placid and a pleased state, and a chimpanzee that is disappointed and sulky. The content, placement, and meaning of the animal illustrations deny any fundamental difference between humans and animals in emotional expression and present animals as capable of expressing a broad range of emotions.

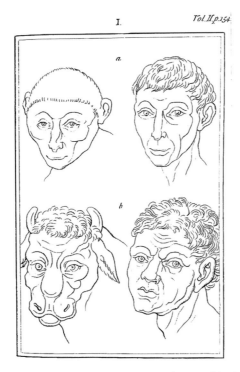

Figure 5.4 Comparison of the face of a monkey (a) and an ox (b) with that of a human of comparable characteristics. Wood engraving copied from Giambattista della Porta's *De Humana Physiognomica*. Plate 1 from Johan Caspar Lavater, *Essays on Physiognomy*, trans. Thomas Holcroft, 2nd edn., 3 vols. (London: Symonds, 1804) II:154.

Darwin's human illustrations in the *Expression* are much more similar to Bell's than his animal illustrations are, but he nonetheless deploys them in such a way as to draw out his theoretical differences with Bell. Despite Bell's emphasis on the uniqueness of human expression, most of his human illustrations are of humans at their most animal-like. A demoniac, a hydrophobe, a madman, the weeping faun, and those gripped by fear or rage – these far outnumber the unambiguously human countenances depicting laughter and devotion. Ironically, then, the overall effect of Bell's illustrations of human expression can be read as undermining his textual arguments. They narrow and blur the distinction between humans and animals by showing humans in brutish rather than noble moments. Whether or not this fracture in Bell's imagetext was exploited consciously by Darwin, it certainly made possible a set of subtle visual contrasts between Darwin's book and Bell's. Although Darwin provides images of many of the same extreme animalistic emotions depicted by Bell – anger, terror – he also provides

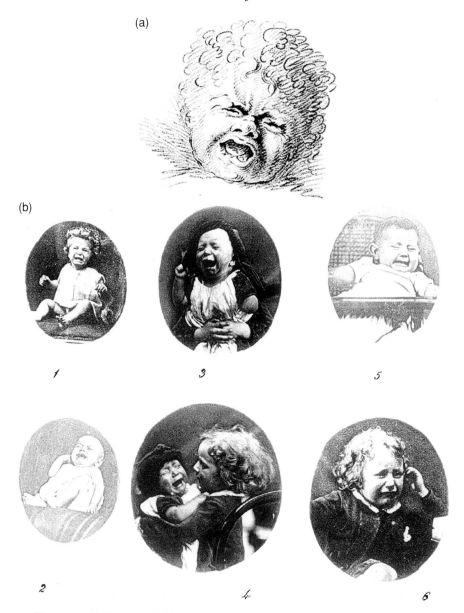

Figure 5.5 (a) Weeping child. Engraving from a sketch by Charles Bell for his *The Anatomy and Philosophy of Expression as Connected with the Fine Arts*, 3rd edn. (London: Murray, 1844), 155. (b) Photographs of crying children. Heliotype reproductions of photographs by Oscar Rejlander (figs. 1, 3, 4, 6) and A. D. Kindermann (figs. 2, 5). Plate 1 from Charles Darwin, *The Expression of the Emotions in Man and Animals* (London: Murray, 1872).

Figure 5.6 Photographs of smiling faces. Heliotype reproductions of photographs by
Oscar Rejlander (figs. 1, 3), G. C. Wallich (fig. 2), and G. B. Duchenne de Boulogne
(figs. 4, 5, 6). Plate III from Charles Darwin, *The Expression of the Emotions in Man and
Animals* (London: Murray, 1872).

far more images than Bell of the emotions Bell himself regarded as characteristically human. Bell's rough sketch of the head of a weeping child
(fig. 5.5a) is expanded in the *Expression* into a whole plate of photographs
of screaming infants (fig. 5.5b); Bell's single laughing man becomes a plate of
smiling, laughing girls and a grinning old man (fig. 5.6). Bell's depiction of
melancholy – presented as "testy, petty, peevish" (172) – is in Darwin a plate
dominated by contrasting pairs of photos of an individual in a placid and
grieving state (fig. 5.7).

Figure 5.7 Photographs of individuals with placid and grieving expressions. Heliotype reproductions of photographs by G. B. Duchenne de Boulogne (figs. 1, 2), Unknown (fig. 3), and Oscar Rejlander (figs. 4, 5, 6, 7). Plate ii from Charles Darwin, *The Expression of the Emotions in Man and Animals* (London: Murray, 1872).

Darwin's explanations of his plates frequently show him incorporating Bell's insights into his own evolutionary arguments. Darwin's extended discussion of weeping, for example, explicitly adopts and extends Bell's contention that violent emotions are connected with violent respiration, that tears result from the contraction of the muscles around the eye, and that this contraction serves to protect the eye. As we have seen, however, Bell regarded this as a proof of divine design, that "all our emotions are intended to have their appropriate outward characters" (149). Not so for Darwin. The children of early humans cried out when hungry or distressed; extended crying caused the blood vessels around the eye to swell; the eye muscles were contracted, "at first consciously and at last habitually" (xxiii:133), to protect the eyes; this contraction induced tears; through repetition, association,

Figure 5.8 "Horror and Agony, copied from a photograph by Dr. Duchenne." Wood engraving from a photograph by G. B. Duchenne de Boulogne. Figure 21 from Charles Darwin, *The Expression of the Emotions in Man and Animals* (London: Murray, 1872), 306.

and inheritance, suffering led to weeping among all humans, even when unaccompanied by extended wailing. Similarly, in his chapter on hatred and anger Darwin depicts not rage and revenge, as Bell had, but indignation and the sneering defiance in which one of the canine teeth is displayed. Bell acknowledges that humans possess the "snarling muscles" (131) that enable carnivorous animals to display their canines, but he argues that we are also endowed with the muscles with which graminivorous animals expose their incisors to graze, and that these latter muscles modulate the action of the former and create "the utmost perfection" in "the motions of the lips" (136). For Darwin on the other hand, the defiant display of the canines is an evolutionary remnant of our ancestors' penchant for using their own much larger canines in fighting.

Darwin, not surprisingly, also exploits the near approach of human and animal expression that Bell's text rejects. In his chapter on "Surprise – Astonishment – Fear – Horror," Darwin's only photographic illustration is of surprise; the illustrations of fear, terror, and horror are wood engravings made from photographs. Here again, Darwin depicts two emotions, terror and horror (fig. 5.8), that Bell had not, even though Bell regards both as unique to humans. Both involve the imagination, horror being "superior" to terror because it is "more full of sympathy with the suffering of others, than engaged with our own" (169). Darwin quotes and endorses Bell's descriptions of terror and horror, including Bell's notion of horror as a product of the sympathetic imagination, but neither of these emotions, nor the means for expressing them, is for Darwin uniquely human. The signs that for Bell are specially provided by the Creator as a tool for human communication are for Darwin inherited vestiges of once-useful behaviors and the physiological effects that accompanied them.

Similar differences are underscored by Darwin's failure to provide an illustration of an emotion that was a prominent concern of Bell's: devotion. As we have seen, devotion is for Bell the quintessentially human emotion of the eye, the upward movement of which is involuntary, implanted in us by the Creator for expressing our gratitude to Him. Darwin, on the other hand, says devotion requires only a brief notice. It is not itself a special expression but a combination of other, common emotions – reverence, affection, and fear. The turning upward of the eyes in prayer is "probably . . . conventional" (XXIII:169), Darwin argues, the product merely of a *belief* that heaven is above us. The kneeling posture with joined palms that so often accompanies devotion seems to be confined to Europeans of the Christian era and thus is neither innate nor universal – this being one of the rare instances when Bell argued for equality and similarity across the races and throughout history while Darwin rejected such a view. Darwin not only denies that these gestures are "truly expressive" but even doubts that devotional feelings themselves existed among our uncivilized ancestors. Indeed, says Darwin, invoking the explanation offered by his cousin, Hensleigh Wedgwood, this devotional attitude probably derives from "the attitude . . . of slavish subjection" of suppliants and conquered enemies, "'the pictorial representation of the Latin *dare manus*" (XXIII:169). Although Darwin does not allude to it directly, this image of "slavish subjection" was also the pictorial representation on the famous Wedgwood medallion for the anti-slavery movement (fig. 5.9). His potentially incendiary naturalizing and historicizing of devotion is muted by the visual association with this Evangelical icon, and a contrast implied with Bell's dismissive reference to "the idolatrous Negro . . . praying for rice and yams," whose instinctively upturned eyes nonetheless confirm "the universal belief that the Supreme Being has His throne above" (103). The *Expression* quietly reverses this formulation: the "idolatrous Negro" and European Christian are brothers, but through an evolutionary genealogy rather than divine creation, and their expressions of devotion point not to "universal belief" but to local culture.

Bell's reputation was such, particularly among the scientific and cultural elite, that Darwin probably could not have ignored *The Anatomy and Philosophy of Expression* even if he had wanted to. But it seems clear he didn't want to ignore it, for the *Anatomy* made a perfect imagetext against which Darwin could position his own. He thus repeatedly invoked Bell's

Figure 5.9 "Am I Not a Man and a Brother?" Black on yellow Wedgwood Jasper slave
medallion. Designed by William Hackwood (1787).

insistence on the uniqueness of human emotions and the divine provision
of a special set of facial muscles for expressing them whenever he wished
to highlight his own investigations and explanations. (By contrast, Darwin
simply ignored Duchenne's similar reliance on the Creator, probably because
Duchenne's work was almost unknown in England.) Yet Darwin could also
accept and pay homage to Bell's anatomical discoveries, an area in which
Darwin, the failed medical student, lacked Bell's status and credentials.
Bell's other advantage over Darwin, his standing as a man of culture who
had studied many of the great works of western art at first hand, is mainly
left unacknowledged in the *Expression*. Darwin at one point uses Bell's figure
of abject terror and at another mentions Bell's discussion of a Hogarth print
(XXIII:211, 220), but Bell's comments on art and sculpture are passed over
even when Darwin refers to specific works or artists also analyzed by Bell.
And Darwin's reliance on photography in preference to painting, drawing,
and sculpture silently stands as an undermining of Bell's cultural advantage.
Whatever the problematics of photographs – and Darwin was certainly
aware of their limitations, or came to be so – they provided a more objective
and reliable record of facial expression than the other visual arts did.[14]

As measured by the responses of reviewers, Darwin's success in creating
an imagetext that counteracted Bell's was mixed. Some saw the *Expression*
as largely extending Bell's work and regarded Darwin's controversial evolutionary explanations as separable from his descriptions and observations of
expressions. Frederick Arnold, for example, in his article on Bell for *Fraser's*,
declared that Darwin's book "includes and supplements" Bell's, even while

he noted that Bell's contrast between human and animal expression represented "the converse of Mr. Darwin's reasoning."[15] Others praised Darwin for successfully demolishing Bell's natural theological explanations. Still others, like Baynes, condemned Darwin for his attempt (in their view, unsuccessful) to overturn Bell, seeing in the *Expression* both natural selection's general threat to morality and social order and its specific threat to high aesthetic culture's reinforcement of that order. And the specific threat was furthered by the association of Darwin's illustrations with more popular forms and venues of visual culture.

PHYSIOGNOMY AND PHRENOLOGY

If Darwin dissociated the *Expression* from the visual traditions of high culture, he seems to have been even more concerned to obscure, deny, or minimize connections, conceptually or visually, between his work and the fields of physiognomy and phrenology. By the time of the *Expression* both physiognomy and phrenology were largely discredited in elite scientific circles, but both remained popular and influential in the wider culture.

Physiognomy regarded facial features as markers of character traits. With a long tradition that could be traced back to the ancients, it had been reinvigorated in the final third of the eighteenth century by the work of Lavater. Twelve English versions were published in the 1790s alone, among them an inexpensive translation by the Radical writer Thomas Holcroft that became the most popular of all, appearing in its fifteenth edition in 1878. While physiognomy was largely supplanted by phrenology in the 1820s and 30s as a "scientific" account of the relationship between anatomy and mental and psychological traits, Lavater continued to be published and read. One hundred and fifty editions existed by the middle of the nineteenth century, with production only beginning to diminish around the time of the *Expression*. As John Graham puts it, Lavater's book "was reprinted, abridged, summarized, pirated, parodied, imitated, and reviewed so often that it is difficult to imagine how a literate person of the time could have failed to have some general knowledge of the man and his theories."[16] As this would imply, physiognomy was interpreted and applied for different ideological purposes. Lavater himself explicitly did not write for the masses – he published his physiognomic ideas in a lavishly illustrated and thus expensive edition aimed at enlightened Protestants who were to use physiognomy to promote knowledge and the love of mankind.[17]

Phrenology treated the size and shape of the skull in a similar way. Phrenologists argued that the brain was the organ of the mind and that every intellectual or psychological "faculty" of the mind had its "seat" in a particular part of the brain, which in turn implied that an individual's most prominent mental faculties were reflected in the large size or distinctive aspect of the corresponding parts of his skull. Thus, the head could be "read" as an index of mental faculties. Inaugurated by the Viennese physician Franz Joseph Gall (1757–1828) in the 1790s and popularized in Britain by his student, Johann Gaspar Spurzheim (1786–1832), and by the Edinburgh lawyer George Combe (1788–1858), phrenology was widely adopted among both the working classes and the liberal intelligentsia through mid-century. Combe's wide-ranging application of phrenology to human life, *The Constitution of Man* (1828), was one of the century's most widely read books, selling 80,000 copies in its various editions by 1847, 100,000 by 1860. Phrenology was also a vital component of two other mid-Victorian scientific sensations, the multi-edition *Vestiges of the Natural History of Creation* (1844), published anonymously by Combe's friend Robert Chambers, and mesmerism. By 1870 its influence had waned substantially in bourgeois and professional circles, but it remained vibrant in working-class culture, thanks to itinerant phrenological lecturers and head-readers and a continuing supply of inexpensive phrenological books.[18]

Darwin knew physiognomy and phrenology well. As a student in Edinburgh he was exposed to the lively debates over phrenology then engaging the city's medical and intellectual communities. A few years later he was nearly rejected for the *Beagle* because Fitzroy, "an ardent disciple of Lavater" and an equally firm believer in phrenology, doubted "whether anyone with my nose could possess sufficient energy and determination for the voyage." "But I think," Darwin commented archly in his *Autobiography*, "he was afterwards well-satisfied that my nose had spoken falsely" (XXIX:110–11). Yet Darwin in the 1830s approached Lavater respectfully if carefully. He read Holcroft's 1804 edition of Lavater in 1838, taking notes and recording his responses primarily in the notebooks on expression he began that year. Admonishing himself to be "very cautious" with Lavater, Darwin nonetheless wondered if physiognomy might provide evidence of evolution: "is there – anything in these absurd ideas. – do they indicate mind & body retrograding to ancestral type of consciousness," he asked himself.[19] Darwin also had access to almost the entirety of the physiognomic tradition via his copy of Moreau's *L'Art de Connaître les Hommes par la Physionomie*. While giving pride of place to Lavater, Moreau also included the work of della Porta and Le Brun, as well as his own writings on physiognomy. Darwin does not seem to have taken a comparable interest in phrenology during his investigation of expression – he apparently did not own a copy of Combe's *Constitution of Man*, for example, and the expression notebooks of 1838–39 contain just two passing references to the subject.[20] But these two references in the notebooks are at least somewhat open-minded, and the continuing popularity of phrenology in the century's third quarter would have been vividly brought home to Darwin, if he needed to be reminded of it, by *Vestiges*. When William Marshall's *A Phrenologist Amongst the Todas* – illustrated with a number of photographs of members of this South Indian tribe – appeared in 1873, the year after the *Expression*, Darwin obtained and read a copy, although he was clearly in search of evidence relevant to the forthcoming second edition of *The Descent of Man* and did not deem Marshall's phrenological chapter and phrenological readings of Toda heads worthy of annotation.[21]

Both physiognomic and phrenological texts were heavily illustrated. Those for the former were often quite varied but usually included several distinctive types. Probably the most common was the individual head or face, which was of course "read" physiognomically. Many of these were copied from busts or portraits of famous figures whose character was well known, but others were of unidentified individuals representative of different nations, races, temperaments, or professions. Such facial illustrations ranged from the careful and detailed to the crude and schematic, frequently in the same work. Lavater also relied heavily on the newly popular silhouette, which made up for loss of detail with a more accurate rendering of the profile. Physiognomists also read and illustrated individual features – Le Brun gave special attention to the slope of the eyes, which for him was the key to character, while Lavater's work contained numerous plates of noses, mouths, and foreheads as well. Facial illustrations sometimes also included lines whose slope differentiated among temperaments, races, or species. Camper's facial angle was the most famous, but both Le Brun and Lavater employed their own systems of lines to distinguish and assess character, and Lavater subsequently utilized Camper's. Such illustrations depicted the gradations from animals to humans or among different human races or nationalities, often establishing or implying hierarchical sequences with Europeans at their apexes.[22] Physiognomists also read animal faces and even compared human and animal physiognomies. Inspired by the juxtaposed human and animal faces in della Porta's *De Humana Physiognomonia* (1586), Le Brun added to the stock of these paired images, which showed how human character could be discerned by comparing an individual's face to its animal counterpart – a gluttonous man and a pig, a stubborn man and an ox (see fig. 5.4). Although these drawings were not included in the editions of Le Brun's lecture published in the seventeenth and eighteenth centuries (including the one owned by Darwin), they were separately engraved by Le

Brun and became well known during his lifetime; after their publication in an 1806 French edition, they were frequently incorporated into physiognomic works, including Moreau's Lavater, where Darwin would have seen them.[23]

Since the emotions were ephemeral, distorted the facial features, and thus interfered with the reading of characteristic traits, most of the illustrations in physiognomic works rendered the face in repose. But a significant subset of facial illustrations depicting strong emotions, or what were often called "the passions," usually appeared in these texts. This was especially the case in works such as those of Le Brun, Camper, and Bell that were aimed specifically, in whole or part, at artists. Le Brun's illustrations of the passions – from astonishment, joy, and veneration to scorn, terror, and rage – were not only the basis for Camper's illustrations but found their way into various editions of Lavater, including Moreau's and Holcroft's.

Heads in repose were also of course the staple visual form of phrenological works. Diagrams of the phrenological head – a rendering, initially naturalistic but quickly stylized, that mapped the various faculties to their cranial regions – served as a "key" for interpreting the numerous illustrations of actual heads, usually taken from portraits and busts (and later photographs) of famous figures whose characteristic mental faculties could be agreed upon.[24] At least some sharing of illustrations occurred across physiognomic and phrenological texts – an 1819 atlas illustrating Gall's theories borrowed heavily from Moreau's edition of Lavater.[25] Because of its focus on the skull rather than the face and its comparative lack of interest in expression, phrenology could rely on a more restricted range of illustrative types than physiognomy and had less need to mine works of art for examples.

Darwin's *Expression*, however, does not mention phrenology, and its opening paragraph essentially dismisses physiognomy. The older physiognomic works, Darwin says, "have been of little or no service to me." Le Brun's contains "some good remarks" but is mostly "surprising nonsense," while Camper's "can hardly be considered as having made any marked advance in the subject" (xxiii:1, 3). Of the work of Lavater and his followers, Darwin says only that he is not concerned with the interpretation of character. Darwin regards Moreau's edition of Lavater as valuable only for Moreau's own descriptions of the movement of facial muscles, yet even Moreau's comments on the meanings and origins of expression are essentially useless.

Why would Darwin deny physiognomy and phrenology even the bare validity he accorded the study of expression in the fine arts? The reasons are probably multiple. First of all, physiognomists and to a lesser extent phrenologists were themselves reliant on the evidence of the fine arts. Moreau's *L'Art de Connaître les Hommes* was indeed a picture gallery. Many of its heads and faces were copied from portraits and busts. In a number of cases, whole works – from the *Laocoon* and other classical sculpture to paintings and drawings by Raphael, Van Dyck, Hogarth, and Fuseli – were reproduced. Half of the thirty plates in the opening, introductory volume were vignettes inspired by various fine art traditions, from the allegorical "Nature Nourishing Her Children," which depicts a many-breasted woman embracing an angel and child; to "Maternal Piety and Tenderness," in which two seated women hold infants on their laps, an image based on representations of Mary and Jesus with Elizabeth and the young John the Baptist; to genre scenes such as "A Child Climbing a Tree" and "Two Old Men Gardening." Darwin's sense that artists and sculptors rarely captured accurately the necessarily fleeting nature of facial expression would have given him further cause to regard physiognomy's foundations as tenuous. Phrenology was more likely to be applied to the making or criticism of such works than to use them as evidence – even Combe's *Phrenology Applied to Painting and Sculpture*, which examined numerous works of art, included no illustrations of them. But phrenology also drew extensively on portraits and busts of famous figures, often the same ones reproduced in physiognomy texts. In the art community, the value of physiognomy and phrenology was a matter for debate – Bell opposed them, while his pupil, the Royal Academician Benjamin Haydon, defended them strenuously in his *Lectures on Painting and Design* (1844, 1846) – but their influence on artists was considerable.[26] Darwin, however, is likely to have found the application of physiognomic and phrenological principles to art a case of circular reasoning.

More important in Darwin's rejection of physiognomy and phrenology, however, were their uncongenial associations and marginal status in elite scientific circles. Bell had rejected both the physiognomic tradition that preceded him and the phrenological frenzy that surrounded him. He labeled della Porta's attempt to derive character traits from facial resemblances between humans and animals "unjust and dangerous" (144). Camper's facial angle received a much fuller and more respectful hearing but was ultimately deemed to be inadequate. This single measure is too reductionistic, Bell argued, for we judge beauty and nobility by the whole set of facial features, especially as they are related to the higher, uniquely human mental qualities and the unique anatomical and physiological mechanisms for their expression. Bell had to be careful about the precise relationship between brain, skull shape, and mind, however. Speaking of Lavater's work, Bell acknowledged its continuing popular influence – which he ascribed to the attraction of its illustrations – but declared that "the study of the physiognomy is now abandoned for that of the cranium" (144). Lest anyone confuse "the study of the cranium" with phrenology, Bell took pains to pronounce the latter dead as well. "All physiologists," he insisted, are "confident in affirming that anatomy affords no foundation for mapping the cranium into minute subdivisions or regions" (53). Brain size and shape do reflect intellectual and moral development and are in turn necessarily reflected in the size and shape of both skull and countenance, but in no direct or simplistic or highly detailed way.

Darwin's sarcasm about Fitzroy's misguided devotion to Lavater in the *Autobiography* – which Darwin wrote for his family rather than for publication, just four years after the *Expression* – indicates he had far less respect for physiognomy in the 1870s than he did in the 1830s. And the conflicting nineteenth-century appropriations of Lavaterian physiognomy by both materialists and anti-materialists provided Darwin with no incentive for linking his own theories with it. On the one hand, rooted in conceptions of the Great Chain of Being and natural theology, the Swiss pastor's physiognomy assumed and reinforced the physical, moral, and spiritual superiority of humans over animals and denied the possibility of transmutation. Lavater's famous plates containing a series of faces from the frog to the Apollo Belvedere, inspired by Camper, depicted the plenitude of the Great Chain, not an evolutionary genealogy. On the other, Lavater's work had been embraced by many radicals and was seen by numerous establishment figures, including Bell, as having dangerous materialist implications. While Bell provided illustrations of the passions and of facial angles for *The Anatomy and Philosophy of Expression*, he did not include physiognomic readings of faces in repose, and, despite his endorsement of racial and species hierarchies, he did not provide visual renderings of them.

Phrenology's working-class popularity and materialist potential were even clearer. Haydon, incorporating physiognomy and phrenology into his *Lectures on Painting and Design*, was careful both to impugn materialism and to deny that physiognomy and phrenology were examples of it, asserting with Bell that human expressions were unique and divinely created. Although phrenology was more easily assimilated than physiognomy into evolutionary thought, its use by Chambers in *Vestiges* connected it to the very radical intellectual and political forces from which Darwin sought to distance his own views. As James Secord has shown, Darwin's ridicule of *Vestiges* as a popular but unreliable work in the opening pages of the *Origin* was a strategy for preventing readers from approaching his work too much on the terms of *Vestiges*.[27]

Yet Darwin's "evolutionary physiognomy," as Rosemary Jann has argued, actually bore a much more complicated relationship to the physiognomic tradition than his opening dismissal in the *Expression* allows. Darwin adopted approaches and language often quite similar to those of earlier physiognomic works. This facilitated the absorption of Darwin's views, for readers were already primed to accept human–animal comparisons in expression, and hierarchical sequences were easily reconceptualized in developmental or evolutionary terms. But the *Expression* was also often read in light of physiognomy, which meant that some of the more subversive implications of Darwin's work were obscured, and even that his work could be interpreted as reinforcing the division between humans and animals and the superiority of the former.[28] As natural selection looked and worked very much like the transcendental anatomy and natural theology it sought to replace, so Darwin's evolutionary physiognomy revised rather than simply rejected this older physiognomic tradition.

For Darwin to associate his book too closely with physiognomic and phrenological texts and their visual conventions would have provided the skeptical readers he most wanted to convince with another reason to reject it. Since the mere presence of illustrations of heads and faces would call to mind such works, Darwin in this instance needed to prevent his readers from making of the *Expression* a physiognomic or phrenological imagetext. But this was a complicated task.

First, it must be noted that, in spite of his evolutionary argument about expression, Darwin does not depict human and animal faces together. Illustrations of animals appear in the book's first six chapters, which are devoted to general principles of expression and to animal expression specifically; illustrations of human faces occur exclusively in the chapters on human expression that comprise the remainder of the book. (The three opening diagrams of human facial musculature do not depict expressions and are employed by Darwin to identify and name the muscles to which he will repeatedly refer.) Phillip Prodger notes that the separation of animal and human subjects (a separation further heightened by Darwin's use of photographs to illustrate human expression) risked casting doubt on his claim for the commonality of expression, but he argues that Darwin's return to engravings at the end of the section on human expression invites readers to connect them with the animal engravings in the early chapters.[29] While Prodger is right about the risk, his speculations reflect his focus on Darwin's use of photography, whereas in this instance it is more enlightening to consider the animal illustrations in relation to their treatment in physiognomic works. Comparing human and animal expressions, whether in one-to-one juxtapositions or as part of a series, would have been not merely the obvious choice for Darwin but one with well-established precedents. That he did not pursue this strategy is thus extremely striking. Since separating humans and animals clearly runs counter to his argument, it seems more likely that Darwin regarded the cost of having his work associated visually with the conventions of physiognomic illustration to be so high as to make him willing to pay the price of adopting a visual strategy that in an important way worked against him. That Darwin was, as we have seen, not only capable but adept at manipulating uncongenial visual conventions in the construction of his imagetexts further underscores the significance of his decision not to attempt that here.

Moreover, of the fourteen engravings devoted to animals, ten depict the whole animal rather than just its face. This enhances the difference between Darwin's behavioral approach to expression and the physiognomic tradition's focus on character. Less obvious – and more significant, in terms of Darwin's distancing efforts – is the fact that although most of the captions for the animal engravings imply a "scene," something happening outside the illustration's frame that is generating the emotion portrayed, that scene is never depicted. Thus we have a dog "approaching another dog with hostile intentions," but no other dog (fig. 5.10a); a cat, "savage, and prepared to fight" an undelineated adversary; a swan "driving away an intruder," but the intruder unseen. Having hired several artists renowned for their ability to produce just such scenes, Darwin then restricted them to individual figures. While Darwin's primary interest is with the animal's expression, the context in which that expression occurs is not omitted from the illustration on the grounds of irrelevance. Darwin and Riviere agreed that Edwin Landseer's *Alexander and Diogenes* (1848; fig. 5.10b) provided a model of how *not* to render a hostile dog (Darwin having already rejected a photograph sent to him by Riviere for its failure to capture such a dog's "eminently characteristic bristlings of the hair"), and Darwin objected to Riviere's initial sketch of an affectionate dog on the grounds that he and his family members "*all* thought . . . that the expression was that of a humble dog coming to be beaten."[30] Darwin's text also stresses a situational context. Although the caption of the illustration of the "hostile" dog has it approaching another dog, Darwin's text describes the dog as walking towards "a strange dog or man" (xxiii:37), with the illustration of the "affectionate" dog then imagined to represent the same dog "suddenly discover[ing] that the man whom he is approaching is not a stranger, but his master" (xxiii:42). In the case of

(a)

(b)

Figure 5.10 (a) "Dog approaching another dog with hostile intentions. By Mr. Riviere."
Wood engraving from a drawing by Briton Riviere. Figure 5 from Charles Darwin, *The
Expression of the Emotions in Man and Animals* (London: Murray, 1872), 52.
(b) Edwin Landseer, *Alexander and Diogenes* (1848). Oil on canvas, 112.5 × 142.6 cm.
Darwin and Riviere agreed that the hair of Alexander, the dog at the center of the canvas,
was inaccurately represented. The painting was well known by the time the *Expression*
appeared. It was exhibited at the Royal Academy in 1848, in Birmingham in 1854,
Manchester in 1857, and London in 1859, when it was bequeathed to the National Gallery.
An engraving appeared in the *Illustrated London News* in 1848 and another was produced
for sale in 1852. Tate Gallery, London.

Figure 5.11 "Chimpanzee disappointed and sulky. Drawn from life by Mr. Wood." Wood engraving from a drawing by T. W. Wood. Figure 18 from Charles Darwin, *The Expression of the Emotions in Man and Animals* (London: Murray, 1872), 141.

Wood's drawing of a "disappointed and sulky" chimpanzee (fig. 5.11), a specific rather than a hypothetical scene is depicted: according to Darwin, the sketch was made after the animal had been offered an orange that was then taken away. The chimp's pouty lips, Darwin notes, drawing attention to the evolutionary connection between chimps and humans, can also be seen in sulky children (XXIII:102–03). Such illustrations, which both invite and constrain associations with the animal painting and illustration of Landseer, Riviere, and Wolf, are also unusual in the physiognomic representation of animals. Interested in expression rather than facial features and character traits, Darwin provides illustrations of hostile, fierce, terrified, affectionate, sulky, and pleased animals that most closely approximate the depictions in the physiognomic tradition of the *human* passions.

Darwin's illustrations of human faces also differ in many respects from those found in physiognomy texts. While such texts would later employ photography, Darwin's use of the medium – and the wood engravings of human faces in the *Expression* were made *from* photographs – provided a degree of separation from the illustrative techniques of most nineteenth-century physiognomic works, especially of cheaper publications. By relying on photographs, Darwin also avoided taking busts or portraits, or engravings of them, as his sources. And while Darwin, like physiognomists, provided illustrations of both single heads and several heads grouped together, his treatment of them reflected his own purposes. Whereas physiognomists usually illustrated a face in repose, reserving depictions of an expressive face for illustrations of particular (and finely graded) emotions, Darwin often juxtaposed photographs of a passive and expressive face of the same individual or provided multiple images of different individuals displaying the same expression. To evaluate facial expression properly, Darwin wrote to James Crichton Browne, "I believe it is quite necessary to study the previous appearance of the countenance."[31] Such contrasts and repetitions reinforced Darwin's immediate illustrative goal: depicting the muscular contractions that accompany particular emotions. These illustrative strategies were also necessary given the shortcomings of photography as evidence, especially in photographs taken from another photograph rather than directly from the negative.[32] But Darwin is ultimately not interested to anything like the same degree as physiognomists in generating a detailed, subtle taxonomy of expression. His chapter on "Surprise – Astonishment – Fear – Horror" is typical. In Darwin's words, it "describe[s] the diversified expressions of fear, in its gradations from mere attention to a start of surprise, into extreme terror and horror" (XXIII:242). This is, at a superficial level, similar to LeBrun's depictions of different forms of a general emotion, something also present in a series of plates inspired by Le Brun in Moreau's *L'Art de Connaître les Hommes*.[33] But not surprisingly, Darwin's emphasis is on the "gradations," the way one emotion shades into another rather than being divided firmly from it. Astonishment is thus for Darwin merely a more extreme form of surprise, terror a case of extreme fear, horror a state of mind that includes terror and in some cases is "almost synonymous" (XXIII:240) with it. And as both the chapter's conclusion and its many references to the expression of these emotions among animals and "savages" make clear, it is the *source* of these facial expressions that Darwin wishes most to account for. While Darwin acknowledges that the immediate causes are physiological ones that may not have conferred an evolutionary advantage and thus were not inherited, at least some expressions are the vestiges of ancestral behavior that did facilitate survival. The wide opening of the eyes in surprise and fear enabled our early progenitors to see more broadly and quickly, and so we have inherited that expression. Our hair stands on end in such situations as it does with many animals, even though we, unlike them, have lost the need to appear larger and more frightening to our enemies.

It's an easy matter to construct rationales for Darwin's visual strategies in the *Expression*. But did his apparent efforts to prevent or minimize the association of the *Expression* with physiognomic imagetexts work? That is more difficult to gauge. If reviews are any guide, Darwin enjoyed considerable but by no means uniform success. Most reviewers were silent about the *Expression*'s relationship to physiognomy and phrenology. Such silence implied acceptance both of Darwin's explicit claim that his work differed fundamentally from physiognomy and of his tacit rejection, through his own silence, of phrenology. Some reviewers not only echoed but reinforced Darwin's dismissal of physiognomy, the *Athenaeum* saying of Lavater's book that it contained "a great deal of twaddle." But some others came to the defense of physiognomy and phrenology, seeking to link Darwin to those traditions. A reviewer for the *Journal of the Anthropological Institute* claimed that Lavater's illustrations of humans and animals "establish[ed] the affinity between the nature of man and that of animals . . . perhaps even further than Mr. Darwin has done." And Rands argued in his pseudonymous review for *St. Paul's* that Darwin's principles of expression were in many respects indistinguishable from the phrenological principles of Spurzheim.[34] Such readings confirm that the *Expression*, despite Darwin's best efforts, could be linked, both textually and visually, to the very works from which Darwin sought to dissociate himself.

Nor could Darwin prevent his own physiognomy from being appropriated. The prolific physiognomic writer and lecturer Joseph Simms (1833–1920) used Darwin to illustrate "Observativeness Large" (fig. 5.12a) in his *Nature's Revelations of Character; or Physiognomy Illustrated*. Originally published privately in Britain in the same year as the *Expression*, Simms's book was issued by a trade publisher later in the decade and quickly became popular; widely and favorably reviewed across the entire English-speaking world, it went through several editions into the early 1890s. Although Simms invokes natural selection at one point, *Nature's Revelations of Character* incorporates physiognomy into a liberal and progressive Protestantism. The "Author of creation," Simms asserts, has designed the Universe for "that ethereal essence, the highest, infinitely the highest, organism of which we can have any conception, the SOUL." Progress is the law of nature and of the human mind, and both individuals and societies have the ability to reduce their defects and move towards perfection. These were precisely the sorts of sentiments that made Darwin uneasy, yet here he would have found his own now-famous face (Simms's engraving was copied from a widely circulated photograph of Darwin) deployed as a physiognomic exemplum – and staring across the page at the faces of unknown individuals and animals (fig. 5.12b).

Ruskin, discussing the study of the human face more than a decade after the *Expression*, adopted a rather different perspective, acknowledging but lamenting the transformation of physiognomy from a moral science to an evolutionary one. In his 1883 Oxford lecture on the work of *Punch* artists

(a)

Observativeness Large—Mr. Charles Darwin, the Author of "The Origin of Species by Means of Natural Selection," and several other valuable works.

(b)

THE FACULTIES, THEIR SIGNS AND PRINCIPLES.   193

safely be considered the certain evidence of remarkable PERSEVERANCE. *This faculty is large in the bull-dog, and small in the fox and wolf.*

Persistenacity very Large—In confirmation of an examination of this gentleman by the Author, he said, "I have lost thousands of dollars by my excessive Persistenacity."

Persistenacity very Small—Johnny, who could not persevere in any undertaking sufficiently to succeed.

The long under jaw indicates tenacity of purpose, inasmuch as the formation shews the presence of great strength

Persistenacity Small—A prairie Wolf, or Coyote.

Persistenacity Large—A Bull-dog.

to hold on with the jaws when once they seize an object,

Figure 5.12 In (a), "Observativeness Large – Mr. Charles Darwin . . ." Darwin is himself used as an example in a physiognomic treatise. On the facing page of that treatise, (b), sets of human and animal faces illustrate "Persistenacity very Large . . . ," "Persistenacity very Small . . . ," "Persistenacity Small – A prairie Wolf, or Coyote," and "Persistenacity Large – A Bull-dog." Wood engravings, Darwin's taken from a photograph, for Joseph Simms, *Nature's Revelations of Character; or Physiognomy Illustrated* (New York, 1879), 192–93.

John Leech, John Tenniel, and George du Maurier for *The Art of England*, Ruskin wrote:

I find myself grievously in want of such a grammar of the laws of harmony in the human form and face as may be consistent with whatever accurate knowledge of elder races may have been obtained by recent anthropology, and at the same time authoritative in its statement of the effect on human expression, of the various mental states and passions. And it seems to me that by arranging in groups capable of easy comparison, the examples of similar expression given by the masters whose work we have been reviewing, we may advance further such a science of physiognomy as will be morally useful, than by any quantity of measuring savage crania.[35]

Although Ruskin does not mention Darwin by name, his statement that he lacks an authoritative "grammar" of the effect of "mental states and passions" on human expression is a clear rejection of Darwin's book, which of course aimed to provide just such a grammar. The science of physiognomy, Ruskin argues, has now become evolutionary and narrowly empirical, concerned only with the measuring of the skull of modern savages and ancient races. Although never a devotee of Lavater, whose name does not appear in his voluminous writings, Ruskin sees that a new physiognomy, unambiguously materialistic, evolutionary, and amoral, is supplanting its predecessor. In such a context, the old way of studying faces becomes worth defending. If he only had the space to do so, Ruskin would arrange the work of the *Punch* artists and their Continental counterparts – "our European masters of physiognomy" – into "a very curious series of illustrations of character" linked to national types. Invoking some of the most common applications of Lavaterian physiognomy, Ruskin further argued that "the difference between the features of a good and a bad servant, of a churl and a gentleman, is a much more useful and interesting subject of inquiry than the gradations of snub nose or flat forehead which became extinct with the Dodo, or the insertions of muscle and articulations of joint which are common to the flesh of all humanity" (XXXIII:363–65).

But Ruskin's lament is also, and more importantly, aesthetic (or again, in his sense, theoretic). His lecture on the *Punch* artists is framed by a discussion of wood engraving and its potentially pernicious effects in popular magazines and books. "The interests of general education compel . . . our consideration of art-methods to which the conditions of cheapness, and rapidity of multiplication, are absolutely essential" (XXXIII:350), he wrote. Because wood is durable yet comparatively easy to engrave, publishers have foisted a mass of vilely designed and poorly executed work on the public. But the mischievous potential of the woodcut is tripled, Ruskin argues, "by its morbid power of expressing ideas of ugliness or terror," its ability to represent "every form of vulgarity and unpleasantness . . . to the life." This is especially the case, he says, in "our popular scientific books," which depict (the pun no doubt intended) "every species of the abominable." For his first example – subsequently placed in his Drawing School's Reference Series for student study – he exhibits a series of woodcuts from an article in the scientific periodical *Knowledge* on "The Evolution of Human Physiognomy" (fig. 5.13).

(a)   (b)   (c)

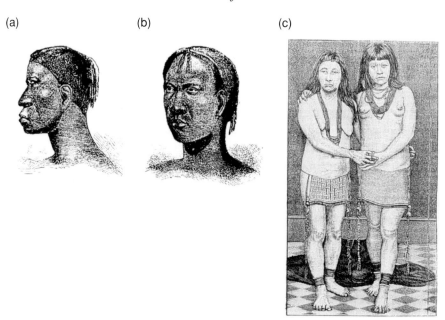

Figure 5.13 (a) "Profile of a Luchatze negro woman, showing deficient bridge of nose and chin, and elongate facial region and prognathism." (b) "Face of another negro, showing flat nose, less prognathism and larger cerebral region. From Serpa Pinto." (c) "Esquibo Indian women, showing the following peculiarities: deficient bridge of nose, prognathism, no waist, and . . . deficiency of stature through short femur. From photographs by Endlich." Wood engravings. Figures 5, 6, and 7 from E. D. Cope, "Evolution of Human Physiognomy," *Knowledge* 4 (1883):168–69. Ruskin regarded these illustrations as so "ignorantly drawn and vilely engraved" that he used them as negative examples for Oxford's art students to study.

Based on a lecture given in Philadelphia by the American E. D. Cope, the article attempts to marry physiognomy and evolution and to demonstrate the inferiority of the Negro and Mongolian races to the Indo-European. The images of the former, "ignorantly drawn and vilely engraved," are typical of the scientific illustration of the human figure, exhibiting "all that is savage, sordid, vicious, or ridiculous in humanity, without so much as one exceptional indication of a graceful form, a true instinct, or a cultivable capacity" (xxxiii:353–54).[36] By contrast, the *Punch* artists, highly skilled and deeply moral, depict humanity's vices only to expose them, setting these against what is graceful, virtuous, and honorable.

Darwin's *Expression of the Emotions* was not a cheap publication, and Ruskin had more in mind here than Darwin. But the portrait of humanity that stared out at Ruskin from the *Expression* and the *Descent* was for him from the outset a morbid one. Many of the illustrations in the *Expression* were quite literally representations of "ugliness and terror." More dangerously, Darwin's was the physiognomy and pathognomy of the vulgar and the unpleasant, in which beauty and its moral meanings were unapprehended, unappreciated, and unwanted. Darwin's ignorance about art, his inability to draw, his insensitivity to color – all of these are bad in themselves, but worse for where they led, to what Ruskin derided as the "unclean stupidity" of a materialism that considers only what is, and never what is "proper" (xxv:264). That many of the faces staring out of the *Expression* did so from photographs only made matters worse for Ruskin.

CHAPTER 6

Darwin's faces II

If illustrating a treatise on emotional expression automatically forced
Darwin to position himself in relation to the visual traditions of the fine arts,
physiognomy, and phrenology, it also immersed him in several prominent
aspects of contemporary visual culture and the debates surrounding them.
This is especially the case with Darwin's use of photography and his heavy
reliance on the work of Oscar Rejlander, a well-known art-photographer
who also operated a commercial photographic portrait studio. Victorian
interest in photography exploded in the 1850s, but this led to considerable
disagreement about photography's aesthetic and epistemic status – could
it claim to be a fine art, or was it merely a chemical/mechanical process?
To what extent did it provide an objective representation of its subjects?
The presence of Rejlander photographs in a work that held painting and
sculpture at arm's length could not help but send signals about Darwin's
view of photography's status. Nor could the presence of Duchenne's photographs or James Crichton Browne's photographs of the insane fail to imply
positions about medical photography and its documentary potential. And
for that matter, depictions of the expressions induced by strong emotions,
especially when these emotions were staged, as they were in many of the
photographs Darwin used, could not be separated from the visual spectacle
of Victorian theater and the manuals that instructed actors how to display
these same emotions. Here, too, aesthetic issues and their cultural associations were unavoidable. Despite its roots in the revolutionary politics of late
eighteenth-century France, melodrama was already being absorbed into the
world of the middle-class stage in Darwin's youth; by the time the *Expression* was published, the bourgeois theater was heavily reliant on adaptations
of contemporary sensation fiction, and classical and melodramatic acting
styles were little different.

Darwin was clearly much more willing to have the *Expression* associated with the contested aesthetic domains of photography and melodrama
than with the traditions of high aesthetic culture. For those commentators

opposed to or skeptical of Darwin's theories, such associations went hand in hand with his efforts in the *Descent* and the botany books to provide an evolutionary account of beauty, confirming his myopic attention to the material over the moral. But as with his efforts to distance himself from physiognomy and phrenology, Darwin was also cautious about aligning his imagetext too closely with aesthetic and political radicalism. How he handles his illustrations of humans in the *Expression* is thus particularly complex and subtle. While often successful, Darwin of course could not fully control the interpretation and circulation of his images – or of his own image, for that matter. And so an important visual form about which the *Expression* is almost entirely silent – caricature – became a prominent cultural medium for responding to Darwin and Darwinism. This chapter closes with an analysis of a series of comic representations of Darwin and his theory in the context of the *Expression*'s appearance. Caricature testified to Darwin's fame, but it could also promulgate what Darwin and his allies regarded as misunderstandings or misapplications of his theories.

DARWIN AND THE PHOTOGRAPHIC IMAGE

Darwin's use of photographs of human subjects necessarily connected the *Expression* with the explosive popularity of mid-Victorian portrait photography, especially as manifested in the carte-de-visite, and the aesthetic debates surrounding this new medium. Photographs of 3.5 by 2.25 inches (90 by 57 mm) printed on slightly larger card stock, cartes-de-visite, despite their name, were used much less as calling cards than as modern-day snapshots and school photos are – for giving to family and friends. But their popularity was such that they also functioned much as trading cards do today – images of famous figures were collected and exchanged by the general public, with many purchased as albums featuring a particular group of celebrities, such as members of the royal family, politicians, or authors. Available from about 1850, cartes became especially popular in England late in that decade thanks to their embrace by members of the rich and fashionable, J. E. Mayall's 1860 album of the royal family providing a particular spur. William Darrah has estimated that from 1860 to 1867 at least three hundred *million* cartes were sold annually in England, with decline setting in only around 1880. At a cost of about sixpence each, the carte-de-visite was not popular among the working classes, but it nonetheless represented an extensive democratizing of portraiture.[1]

The Darwin family shared the new cultural enthusiasm for photography and the carte-de-visite, and as a famous scientist Darwin found his own photographic image circulating in the shop windows and albums of photographic studios. Among the earliest family photos in the Darwin Papers at Cambridge are the often-reproduced 1842 daguerreotype of Charles and his eldest son, William, as well as a number taken of the Darwin children in the late 1840s and early 1850s. Darwin's sons took an interest in photography, and many of the photos of individual family members and family groups in the Cambridge collection were made by them. But the family also utilized the services of well-known photographic studios in London, Cambridge, and various holiday spots. Darwin sat regularly for his photographic portrait at commercial firms from about 1855 on, sending them to friends and in some cases permitting their sale to the public individually or in albums. One such portrait, taken in the studio of Henry Maull in the mid-1850s, appeared in *Literary and Scientific Portrait Club*, but a second Maull photo from 1857 was apparently the first to become widely available when the firm received permission from Darwin to reproduce and sell it late in 1862. "I have long been desirous of obtaining your photograph, but have never seen any for sale," wrote W. G. Tegetmeier to Darwin. "On walking down Chancery Lane to day I saw a 'Carte' of you by Maule [*sic*] . . . The vendor told me that he had not put the name as he was not sure about it – that he had long been wanting to get the Cartes and that he should order some more at once before the sale was stopped." In 1866 Darwin sat for a photo by Ernest Edwards that was used in *Portraits of Men of Eminence* (1863–67). Another, taken by William Darwin around 1864, became the basis for a lithographic portrait of his father that appeared in the *Quarterly Journal of Science* in 1866. In 1868 he sat to Julia Cameron. When he began work on the *Expression* Darwin scoured London's photographic shops for portraits with particular expressions, and his correspondence of the period is full of letters in which he exchanges photographs and commentary upon them.[2]

The vast majority of the thirty photographs in the *Expression* came from two sources: Duchenne's *Mécanisme de la Physionomie Humaine* (six) and the London photographer Oscar Rejlander (nineteen). (Darwin reproduced two additional Duchenne photographs as wood engravings and referred to several others in his text.) Of the Duchenne photographs, two were of "a young man who was a good actor" and the remainder of "an old man" (XXIII:139, 157). This elderly man happened to suffer from a form of facial paralysis, and thus Duchenne could stimulate particular muscles with electrodes while leaving others unaffected, artificially inducing expressions that could be maintained for the lengthy exposure times required by early photography. Rejlander's photographs were of children (ten) and posed expressions (nine), six of the latter featuring Rejlander himself. The *Expression's* photographic illustrations thus fell into three categories: documentary photography, especially for medical purposes; portraiture of children; and the representation of emotion in acting.

Before considering Darwin's use of each of these categories, however, it is again worth noting what Darwin did *not* use: art photography, images of the insane, and images of other races. In stumbling upon Rejlander, Darwin encountered not simply one of London's many commercial photographers, but arguably the best known and most controversial practitioner-advocate of photography as an art form at that time. Trained as a painter, Rejlander approached photography with traditional artistic categories (landscape, portraiture, genre scenes, and expression/character studies) in mind and often used famous works of painting and sculpture as the basis for his photographs. Charting the debates that raged in the 1850s and 60s over photography's aesthetic status and potential, Mary Warner Marien has called art photography "symbolic terrain upon which mid-nineteenth-century progressives and conservatives contested," with figures like Rejlander defending its "promise of moral uplift through the visualization of ennobling scenes and sentiments" against critics who saw only "a parody of cultural attainment."[3] Rejlander gained fame in the mid-1850s with his "combination pictures," allegorical compositions assembled from multiple negatives, particularly *The Two Ways of Life*, which was first displayed at the Manchester Art Treasures Exhibition in 1857, where it created a scandal for its inclusion of nudes but was purchased by Victoria and Albert. In the 1860s Rejlander became better known for his expression studies, advocating photography, despite its technical limitations, as superior to painting and sculpture for capturing emotional expression. It was during this period that he acquired his reputation for being especially skilled in photographing children, whose restlessness and strong emotions posed particular technical challenges. Late in the decade he began producing genre photos of urban working-class and middle-class domestic subjects, many inspired by both traditional and contemporary painters. Although as a portraitist (and like most photographers of the period, Rejlander earned his living with commercial portraits) Rejlander was less innovative, he was nonetheless regarded as painterly in his ability to capture the personality of his sitters despite the serious, generalized expressions that tradition, Victorian bourgeois values, and lengthy exposure times demanded.[4]

Darwin was initially drawn to Rejlander's photographs of "all sorts of chance expressions exhibited on various occasions, especially by children, and taken instantaneously."[5] Impressed by Rejlander's careful observation of expressions and his "passion" for photographing them, Darwin eagerly examined Rejlander's existing work, including his expression studies, and commissioned new photographs from him. Rejlander accepted Darwin's challenges but was forthright about the difficulties of capturing expressions in both "instantaneous" photographs and posed studies. "It is very difficult to get, at will – those expressions you wish," Rejlander wrote to Darwin. "Few have the command or imagination to appear real." In a November letter he told Darwin the season's fading light did not permit him to capture fleeting expressions: "You ask more than I can do – this time of year – at least."[6] That Darwin was satisfied by some of Rejlander's expression studies is evident from his inclusion of a number of them in *Expression*. But what Darwin did *not* include were examples of Rejlander's more self-consciously "artistic" photography, and it is evident from the collection of Rejlander's photographs in the Darwin Papers that Darwin had seen examples of these as well. While drawing a rigid distinction between "artistic" and "scientific" renderings of expression by Rejlander is impossible – and something Rejlander himself would not have sanctioned – it is clear that Darwin more readily appropriated or utilized those photographs with fewer artistic markers. Among the unused Rejlander photographs in Darwin's collection, for example, are a man and woman posed as in a marriage or engagement photo (their heads touch, the man gazing at the woman, arm around her waist, holding her left hand), two portraits of a young woman with long, dark, wavy hair reminiscent of Dante Rossetti's paintings featuring Jane Morris, several of a woman holding a baby, and one similar to Rejlander's genre works of a posed street urchin.[7]

Darwin's effort to avoid close associations with the fine art tradition in his photographic illustrations as well as in his engravings and text is further strengthened by a glance at the photographs in Duchenne's work that he neither utilizes nor refers to. In his aesthetic section, Duchenne provides photographs of elaborately staged scenes to show that aesthetic effect is best achieved through the combination of beauty of form and exactness of expression. In these photographs, he says, he selected more attractive models and took much greater care with lighting, gesture, pose, and focus. His chief model in this section is a young woman of regular features but nearly blind from optic nerve atrophy; as one of Duchenne's patients, she is used to being treated with the electrodes. Duchenne poses her as a nun or a Madonna to capture the expression of devotion, as a coquette interrupted by a man while dressing to capture surprise, as a lady visiting a poor family to capture compassion, and as Lady Macbeth to capture aggression and cruelty. As in the case of Rejlander, it would be erroneous to regard these photographs as "artistic" in contradistinction to Duchenne's "scientific" photographs of the old man. And the mere fact of these photographs being posed clearly was not the issue in Darwin's ignoring of them, for several of the Rejlander photographs in the *Expression* are posed. Rather, Darwin wished to focus on the disposition of the facial muscles or the accompanying bodily gestures without the presence of the "accessory circumstances" that so influence our identification of expression. But by choosing not to include Rejlander's and Duchenne's more artistic efforts, Darwin implicitly minimized the association of the *Expression*'s photographs with art photography.

The absence of images of the insane and people of other races is also striking. In the Introduction to the *Expression*, Darwin listed the six sources on which he had relied for determining whether particular facial movements and bodily gestures are truly expressive of particular emotional states: infants, the insane, Duchenne's photographs, painting and sculpture, members of non-European races, and common animals. As we've seen, the book is rife with illustrations of infants and animals and contains numerous reproductions of Duchenne's photographs. Illustrations taken from the fine arts are absent because Darwin found them of little use. But Darwin relied extensively in his text on evidence taken from the insane and people of other races, so the lack of these illustrations is surprising. And it's not because he didn't have such images. Although Darwin was unable to locate photographs of the insane in his search of London shops, he had access to the extensive collection of photographs of the insane made by and under the direction of James Crichton Browne, the director of the West Riding Lunatic Asylum in Yorkshire.[8] Browne and Darwin corresponded regularly for several years, Browne sending Darwin many of his photographs and Darwin sharing his precious copy of Duchenne's book with Browne. Photographs of racial types were also part of Darwin's stock of photographs: he owned both a folio of racial images from the Collection Anthropologique de Paris and a series of prints of the German actor Ernst Schulz depicting different races and nationalities.[9]

The limitations of such anthropological and pseudo-anthropological photographs of racial and national types for Darwin's needs are obvious. Darwin required strong expressions, and anthropological photography overwhelmingly depicted individuals in a placid state, the focus being on racial features.[10] And indeed, Darwin does not appear to have made the same kind of efforts to locate appropriate photos of other races as he had to locate photos of children and the insane. Moreover, it seems possible that an additional factor might have been Darwin's desire to distance himself from the visual traditions of racial display we have already noted in physiognomy, where racial differences were often positioned, implicitly

(a)   (b)

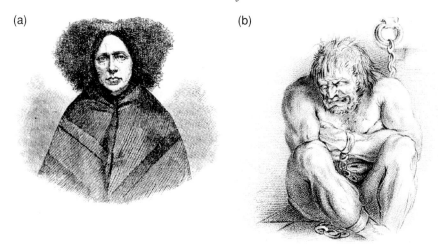

Figure 6.1 (a) "From a photograph of an insane woman, to show the condition of her
hair." Wood engraving from a photograph given to Darwin by James Crichton Browne.
Figure 19 from Charles Darwin, *The Expression of the Emotions in Man and Animals*
(London: Murray, 1872), 141. (b) Madness. Engraving from a sketch by Charles Bell for
his *The Anatomy and Philosophy of Expression as Connected with the Fine Arts*, 3rd edn.
(London: Murray, 1844), 180.

or explicitly, as inherent and hierarchical. The *Expression*, it is worth remem-
bering, was originally to have been part of *The Descent of Man*, a fundamental
argument of which was the monogenist one that all humans are members of
a single species. The fact that many emotions are expressed in uniform ways
across human cultures, Darwin wrote in the *Expression*'s Introduction, is
"evidence of the close similarity in bodily structure and mental disposition
of all the races of mankind" (XXIII:12). Anthropological photographs, on the
other hand, were already steeped in the representation of difference.

Darwin's better-documented decision not to use Browne's photographs
of the insane was more complex, but it, too, came down to the comparative
absence of strong expressions. Although he regarded Browne's photos as
excellent ones, Darwin doubted from the beginning that they would be of
any "special use" to him. As publication of the *Expression* neared, however,
Darwin was asking Browne if he could purchase copies of particular photographs, for there were "one or two," and "possibly others," he would like
to reproduce. But when he met Rejlander shortly thereafter, Darwin told
Browne his photos of the insane were "not expressive enough for my purpose." In the end, Darwin praised Browne's observations and descriptions
but not his photographs, reproducing just one of them, as a wood engraving
(fig. 6.1a). Taken during an interval in an insane woman's violent outbursts,

it illustrates the bristling of the hair during fear and rage, a phenomenon Darwin uses as a link between humans and animals. (Since Darwin privately thought this woman looked like a Papuan, this is also the closest the *Expression* comes to presenting an illustration of a racial type.)[11] The focus of this single image of the insane, then, is not even the face, the expression of which is in any event quite placid, in contrast to many influential representations of the insane, including Bell's, as animalistic and depraved (fig. 6.1b).

Darwin's decision not to include more of Browne's photographs of the insane should not be taken as a rejection of medical photography, or even of psychiatric photography. His enthusiasm for, and reproduction of, Duchenne's photographs of the old man are evidence of his belief that such material was valuable both as illustration and in some cases as evidence. By the same token, his preference for Duchenne's photographs over Browne's shows that Darwin's embrace of photography was fairly cautious and constrained. Sander Gilman has argued that Darwin's enthusiasm for photography's ability to provide an empirical record of expression waned as he came to appreciate the personal and cultural factors that shaped the making and interpretation of such images.[12] It might be more accurate, however, to characterize Darwin's sense of photography's limitations as increasing, for Darwin was skeptical about the utility of Browne's photographs from the outset, and he was already familiar with photography's technical limitations and the subjective elements of photographic production and interpretation. Thus Jennifer Green-Lewis's picture of a rather naive Darwin, unwittingly selecting images whose multiple meanings undermined his claims of photographic objectivity, is even less satisfying. According to Green-Lewis, Darwin "defers to a positivistic model in which total knowledge is defined as scopic and determined, while his chosen illustrations (impressionistic, interpretive) undermine their own testimony in their obvious hermeneutic instability."[13] As Prodger has demonstrated, however, Darwin was an active participant in the manipulation of his chosen illustrations, and he was not working in a context in which rules of photographic objectivity had been fixed. The *Expression* "could not conform to rules about scientific photography," Prodger pithily notes, "because it was part of the creation of those rules." Yet Prodger, too, concludes that in his use of Duchenne's photos Darwin "cultivated an appearance of objectivity that actually misrepresented experimental events."[14] By cropping Duchenne's photographs to further minimize the already limited signs of the galvanic apparatus and the operator's hands and body, and in the case of the engravings eliminating even the presence of the electrodes, Darwin, Prodger argues, attempted to convert these equivocal, manipulated representations into unproblematic illustrations of natural expressions.

Darwin's understanding of the issues surrounding the evidentiary status of photography was quite sophisticated, however, and his use of Duchenne's photographs drew attention to their shortcomings as well as their strengths. Darwin employed photography because he felt it was *better* for capturing emotional expression than other means, not because he thought it was objective in some absolute sense. However, photographs of the kind of strong expressions in which he was interested were available and more clearly captured in the artificially induced expressions of Duchenne and the simulated expressions of Rejlander than in the "natural" expressions of Browne's patients and anthropological subjects. Since Duchenne often photographed the placid countenances and natural expressions of his subjects, his work also contained the "before and after" images that Darwin regarded as so crucial for analyzing expression. ("Though photographs are incomparably better for exhibiting expression than any drawing," Darwin wrote to Browne, "yet I believe it is quite necessary to study the previous appearance of the countenance, its changes, however small, and the living eyes, in order to form any safe judgment [of an expression].")[15] The greater accuracy and clarity of photographs in turn increased the value of evidence derived from asking viewers to identify the emotions depicted in them. Explaining this in the Introduction to the *Expression*, Darwin makes explicit the very different types of value in Duchenne's photographs:

Several of the expressions were instantly recognized by almost every one, though described in not exactly the same terms; and these may, I think, be relied on as truthful, and will hereafter be specified. On the other hand, the most widely different judgements were pronounced in regard to some of them. This exhibition was of use in another way, by convincing me how easily we may be misguided by our imagination; for when I first looked through Dr Duchenne's photographs, reading at the same time the text, and thus learning what was intended, I was struck with admiration at the truthfulness of all, with only a few exceptions. (xxiii:10)

Prodger, quoting this passage, rightly stresses Darwin's emphasis that Duchenne's photographs required interpretation and explanation, and could in fact be seen in different ways by different viewers. He also notes Darwin's attraction to photography's "objective power" in capturing what would normally be invisible or unnoticed.[16] But by omitting the sentences in which Darwin mentions the photographs described in similar terms by almost everyone, Prodger creates the impression that Darwin continued to use Duchenne's photographs even after being disabused of his naïve admiration of their truthfulness and objectivity, merely cultivating an "appearance of objectivity" in them. Offering to lend his copy of Duchenne to Browne in 1869, over a year and a half before he began writing the *Expression*, Darwin told Browne that "the plates are hardly intelligible without reading the text" and thus combined them for Browne in what he thought "the most convenient plan."[17] When Darwin refers to one of Duchenne's photographs in the *Expression*, however, whether he reproduces it or not, he almost always provides a summary of the responses of the people to whom he showed it. In some cases the responses are nearly uniform and thus suggest that Duchenne has captured a "truthful" expression; in others, the difference in responses, or even the presence of a minority of different responses, becomes a basis for Darwin to criticize Duchenne's image or modify Duchenne's analysis.

Indeed, what is perhaps most surprising about Darwin's use of Duchenne's photographs is that he reproduces so *few* of them. Despite their importance to him, Darwin was willing to associate himself with medical photography in only a limited way. Of the six Duchenne photos, four are of natural, not galvanized, expressions. Although Darwin reduces the evidence of the galvanic apparatus in the two that contain it, and eliminates the electrodes and operator's hands from the two Duchenne photos reproduced as engravings, he does show the apparatus in two photos, and he invariably notes in his text that these are galvanized expressions, even in the cases where the electrodes have been removed. Darwin's treatment of the Duchenne photos is thus broadly in keeping with the consensus among contemporary photographers that they should absent themselves from their works but acknowledge any mechanical or chemical manipulations.[18] Duchenne's galvanized faces are valuable for showing the state of facial muscles when contracted, but they cannot be used as evidence of emotional expression unless viewers agree in their identification of the emotion depicted.

Thanks mainly to Rejlander, Darwin also had plenty of photographs of children displaying strong emotions more or less naturally. Those employed in the *Expression* served simultaneously to align and distance Darwin from the photographic portrait generally and that of children in particular.[19] Darwin's use of such photos inevitably suggested the portrait studio, but his focus on facial expression meant that the props and backdrops ubiquitous in studio portraits were reduced or eliminated. We see this clearly in a plate containing two photographs, one of a crying, frowning child and the other of a sneering woman (fig. 6.2a). Kindermann's original photo of the child (fig. 6.2b) shows her with book, chair, and poodle, but Darwin had the poodle cropped out. The sneering woman we see only from the shoulders

(a)   (b)

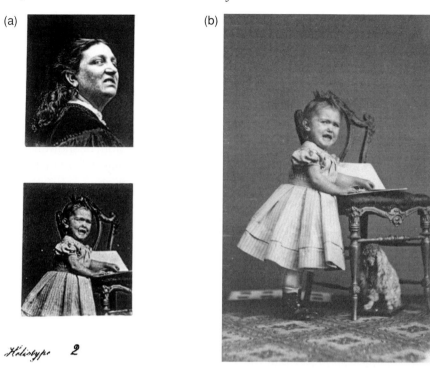

Heliotype **2**

Figure 6.2 (a) Sneering lady and crying, frowning child. Heliotype reproductions of photographs by Oscar Rejlander (fig. 1) and A. D. Kindermann (fig. 2). Plate IV from Charles Darwin, *The Expression of the Emotions in Man and Animals* (London: Murray, 1872). Darwin describes the sneering woman as "a lady, who sometimes unintentionally displays the canine on one side, and who can do so voluntarily with unusual distinctness" (XXIII:190). Of the crying child Darwin says, "If a child frowns much whilst crying, but does not strongly contract in the usual manner the orbicular muscles, a well-marked expression of anger or even of rage, together with misery, is displayed" (XXIII:176). (b) Kindermann's original photograph of the crying, frowning child. Note that Darwin has had the dog and part of the chair cropped out for his reproduction. Darwin Papers, Cambridge University Library, DAR.53.1:C.122.

up. Photographs of crying and frowning children outnumber placid or smiling ones in the *Expression* by two to one, and even children in the latter group are captured with what appear to be extremely natural expressions rather than posed and deliberately sentimental ones, as can be seen by contrasting the exception (the girl on the lower left in fig. 5.6) with the others. Darwin's babies bawl, his children are petulant pouters. There are no dreamy Cameron or Carroll kids here.

Indeed, the most famous and widely circulated of the illustrations in the *Expression* was of a crying baby (see fig. 1.8). The public was captivated by the child's vivid expression, while critics and devotees of photography were amazed by Rejlander's technical achievement in capturing it. Rejlander sold thousands, possibly hundreds of thousands, of prints of the photograph, most of them in carte-de-visite format. It acquired the name "Ginx's Baby," after Edward Jenkins's satirical 1870 novel of the same title, itself a best-seller, and the novel and the photograph quickly became inextricably linked in Victorian popular culture. As Prodger has revealed, however, Rejlander's photograph was in fact a drawing made from a photograph. Rejlander carefully copied his original photograph, making a number of alterations to it as he did so, then photographed the drawing. Darwin was clearly aware that the image had been manipulated but presented it in the *Expression* as an "instantaneous" photograph.[20]

What is striking to me, however, is less the issue of the photograph's evidentiary status than the confirmation "Ginx's Baby" provides of the way Darwin's use of such photographs aligned him with bourgeois and poten-tially even radical culture. Jenkins was a political satirist who in 1874 became the Liberal MP for Dundee. *Ginx's Baby* is the story of the thirteenth child of an impoverished working-class London family. Unable to support this new baby, Ginx intends to throw his son into the Thames but is prevented from doing so. The child is then passed from one charity or reform-minded group to another, none displaying any real concern for the boy's welfare. Ultimately he is taken in at a London social club, but its members exploit him for political purposes while making him a servant and ignoring his needs. Miserable and lonely, he leaves the club at age fourteen and throws *himself* into the Thames. Since Rejlander's photograph became the basis for illustrations of the child in subsequent editions of the novel, the evi-dence commissioned by Darwin for the *Expression* quickly migrated into the world of social and political debate, "Ginx's Baby" becoming an icon of the helpless, working-class child victimized by a Dickensian array of telescopic philanthropists, uncompassionate conservatives, bitter religious zealots, and self-serving reformers. If Darwin had labored to minimize the association of the *Expression*'s photographs with fine art and high culture, he had certainly not courted visual connections with political radicals and the working poor. When a strike by workers at the Heliotype Company, which was producing the photographic plates for the *Expression*, threatened to delay the book's appearance and the quality of its illustrations, Darwin's sympathies lay with the company, his concern with his own reputation. "It is a very bad job about the Heliotypes and will I fear cause us loss," Darwin wrote to his publishers, "but it is obvious that the Co[mpan]y must be almost as anx-ious as we are . . . It will be necessary to have a look at the Plates, to see that they do not palm off poor copies owing to the employment of incompetent workmen; and it would be very bad if customers were to return copies as defective."[21]

As in other cases of the *Expression*'s illustrations, Darwin effectively positions the work in a visual middle ground, attempting to limit the possibilities for his work to be seen in conjunction with visual forms that were either too high or too low. If Darwin does not appear to have wanted his work linked too closely with art photography, he also seems to have been uncomfortable with the physical and metaphysical materialism of documentary realism. Whether intended or not, one of the effects of the presence of Rejlander's work is thus to provide a visual counterweight to Duchenne's physiological experiments on the old man. Indeed, many of the tensions that both Green-Lewis and Prodger rightly identify in the *Expression*'s photographic illustrations were even more evident to Darwin's contemporaries, many of whom had reason to be surprised by a collaboration between England's most famous scientist and a photographer well known for his manipulation of photographs to achieve artistic effects. Implicitly immersing himself in the debates over photography's status, Darwin was willing to defend its superiority over the fine arts for depicting expression but reluctant to embrace its realistic and documentary claims too thoroughly. His visual balancing act was for the most part successful – reviewers of the *Expression* tended to praise the work's illustrations and draw attention to the novelty of the heliotypes. But the images of Duchenne's old man depicting terror and horror (see fig. 5.8) were too stark and striking to be completely offset by Rejlander's crying babies and posed representations of milder expressions. "The photographic illustrations of this volume have suffered greatly from a sort of galvanised look they wear," complained the *Athenaeum*, while T. S. Baynes in the *Edinburgh* railed against "the hideous portraits of the galvanised old man." Indeed, those reviewers most critical of the Duchenne photos were also the ones who regarded Darwin's work as threatening from a high cultural perspective and Darwin's own aesthetic sensibility as sadly underdeveloped. For Baynes, the images of the old man were grotesque anti-portraits, the "repulsively unnatural" product of unnatural manipulations, with "unhuman" expressions that capture only the "harsher," more animalistic aspects of our humanity. Whereas the reviewer for the *Graphic* referred to the "beautiful" heliotype process by which Darwin executed the "vivid" illustrations, for Baynes all three of these processes – Duchenne's galvanic experiments, the photographs that recorded them, and the heliotypy that reproduced them – were grotesque in their materiality.[22]

RUSKIN AND PHOTOGRAPHY

While Ruskin did not comment specifically on Darwin's photographic images, there is no doubt about his rejection of photography as fine art. His initial enthusiasm for the daguerreotype was considerable – writing to his father from Padua in 1845, Ruskin declared it a "blessed invention," the "one antidote" amidst "all the mechanical poison that this terrible 19th century has poured upon men."[23] But as his description of photography as a "mechanical invention" would suggest, from the outset Ruskin regarded it merely as an efficient means for recording visual data rather than as a new artistic medium. Daguerreotypes provided highly detailed renderings of Italy's old buildings much faster and with more accuracy than Ruskin could draw them. They thus permitted Ruskin to see and take away more from his visits – an important consideration, given that the buildings in which Ruskin was interested were either crumbling away from neglect or being "restored" out of existence. Over the years Ruskin also used photographic reproductions of works of art fairly extensively in his teaching, even arranging their separate sale, but either for studying or for copying, never for the photographs' artistic merits (xv:100–03; xvi:151; xxviii:446–47, 459; xxxviii:97–98). As early as 1846, even while singing the daguerreotype's praises, he asserted that "as regards art, I wish it had never been discovered." In the 1850s, as Rejlander and other art photographers increasingly asserted photography's artistic potential, Ruskin argued more vociferously against it. In the Conclusion to the final volume of *The Stones of Venice* (1853), a work for which he had relied on photography's documentary capabilities, Ruskin declared of Fox Talbot's calotype process that "a photograph is not a work of art, though it requires certain delicate manipulations of paper and acid, and subtle calculations of time, in order to bring out a good result . . . It is no more art to use the cornea and retina for the reception of an image, than to use a lens and a piece of silvered paper" (xi:201–02). In his inaugural Slade lectures at Oxford in 1870, published that same year as *Lectures on Art*, he was even more emphatic: "photographs supersede no single quality nor use of fine art" (xx:165).[24]

For Ruskin, art required the active presence of the human intellect, selecting and arranging. Since accurate representation was in Ruskin's eyes merely a starting point for art, not something to be slavishly adhered to and never an end in itself, photography almost by definition could not rise beyond a chemical/mechanical process for recording facts. Why take a photograph of a landscape, Ruskin asked, in preference to drawing from nature? More good is to be got from sketching a single woodland glade, he argued, than from a whole portfolio of photographic panoramas. Ruskin had a similar view of photographs of the human figure. Writing to Julia Cameron in 1868, Ruskin told her that he had long ceased to take an interest in photography, knowing well its capacities and limitations. "Depth of expression" in portraiture, he later asserted in *The Art of England* (1883), is "unattainable by photography" – it can only be captured by the artist's, not the camera's, eye (XXXIII:302). The implications of these views for assessing the photographic illustrations of Darwin's *Expression* from a Ruskinian perspective are clear. The photographs of Duchenne and Rejlander may well provide an accurate register of expression, particularly the effects of the contractions of facial muscles on the features. But this is not the "depth of expression" that discloses the sitter's moral character. Darwin's reliance on a mechanical invention in preference to fine art would thus have been for Ruskin not merely misguided but symptomatic of Darwinism's reductionistic materialism. In his 1872 Oxford lectures on "The Relation of Natural Science to Art," published later that year as *The Eagle's Nest*, Ruskin railed against the "French anatomy" that had led to the production of natural history books full of admirably drawn but ugly creatures – rats, weasels, and apes – and ill-drawn noble ones – horses, lions, and humans. The only science absolutely essential for the understanding and production of art, Ruskin told his listeners, was the science of "how to behave": "You cannot so much as feel the difference, between two casts of drapery, between two tendencies of line, – how much less between dignity and baseness of gesture, – but by your own dignity of character" (XXII:233). Darwin's study of expression was concerned with expression and gesture solely, not with the difference between nobility and baseness, and his illustrations for the book included not only well-drawn apes but humans photographed at some of their most undignified moments. That Darwin examined and illustrated expression in the way that he did stemmed from his complete disinterest – fatal, in Ruskin's mind, to both Darwin's scientific and aesthetic sensibilities – in how to behave.

ACTING AND EXPRESSION

Commenting on Darwin's use of Rejlander's staged photographs of the emotions, the *Athenaeum* reviewer expressed surprise and dismay that "acting can satisfy our author and produce what he considers satisfactory illustrations of the emotions." Rejlander, the writer complained, was neither a good actor nor a talented director of others; his photographic "performances" were "almost sure to mislead any one who puts much faith in them." The fine arts, the reviewer argues, are a much better source for illustrations of

Figure 6.3 Disdain. Heliotype reproduction of a photograph by Oscar Rejlander. Plate v,
figure i from Charles Darwin, *The Expression of the Emotions in Man and Animals*
(London: Murray, 1872). Darwin describes this photograph as a representation of the
form of disdain in which the eyes "seem to declare that the despised person is not worth
looking at, or disagreeable to behold." Specifically, Darwin says that this photograph
"represents a young lady, who is supposed to be tearing up the photograph of a despised
lover" (xxiii:196).

emotional expression. He is troubled, in other words, not by the representational aspect of these photographs, but by Darwin's preference for the
representational modes of photography and acting over those of painting
and sculpture. In fact, the reviewer wants his poses at a *further* representational remove. He accepts that emotions are expressed not just with the face
but through the positioning and gestures of other parts of the body, but he
rejects Darwin's notion that *photographs* of posed expressions are superior
to paintings, drawings, and sculpture of posed expressions. That Darwin
preferred these posed expressions to those found in paintings was a painful
sign of Darwin's "imperfect knowledge of what Art has done."[25] His reliance
on photography and acting – and bad acting at that – exposed his visual
illiteracy, his lack of aesthetic refinement and taste.

The extent of Darwin's reliance on posed expressions was, as we have seen,
considerable. Almost one-third of the *Expression*'s photographic illustrations
contained Rejlander's simulations, six depicting Rejlander himself. Two of
the Duchenne photos were of a young man with a talent for simulating
expressions, and another of uncertain provenance was of a young woman
with an unusual ability to furrow her brow voluntarily. Darwin makes no
effort to hide the fact that these photographs are posed, and as with his
illustrations of animals he sometimes constructs a dramatic "scene."[26] An
illustration by Rejlander of disdain (fig. 6.3) "represents a young lady, who

is supposed to be tearing up the photograph of a despised lover" (XXIII:196). Describing a plate of photographs representing indignation and helplessness Darwin constructs a dramatic dialogue between the individuals in the separate photographs: "we may imagine one of the figures on the left side to have just said, 'What do you mean by insulting me?' and one of the figures on the right side to answer, 'I really could not help it'" (XXIII:213). Darwin urges any reader skeptical of the accuracy of these renderings of an indignant man's erect head, expanded chest, and clenched fists to stand before a mirror and "vividly imagine that he has been insulted and demand an explanation in an angry tone of voice" (XXIII:188). While he does so infrequently, Darwin also draws on examples from actors and acting for evidence of expression.

Darwin was not the first student of expression to invoke actors. Bell occasionally does so in *The Anatomy of Expression*, at one point (in a passage cited by Darwin) contrasting Sarah Siddons's and John Kemble's "remarkable capacity for the expression of the nobler passions" (136) with another actor's ability to express hatred. Darwin also had access, in Moreau's edition of Lavater, to some of the most influential and widely reproduced images of expression for actors, those in Johann Jacob Engel's *Ideen Zu Einer Mimik* (1785). Engel's work was originally translated into French in 1795 and subsequently adapted for the English stage in 1807 as *Practical Illustrations of Rhetorical Gesture and Action* by Henry Siddons (Sarah's son). Moreau reproduced more than half of Engel's illustrations, while Siddons retained all of them, updating some with anglicized costumes. Siddons's work, issued in a second edition in 1822, was widely copied in actors' handbooks through the middle of the century.[27]

Darwin's debt to the visual traditions of the stage can be captured in one of his photographic illustrations of indignation. Fig. 6.4 shows the photograph of Rejlander simulating indignation, the illustration of resistance from Engel, its reproduction in Moreau and, as "Menace," in Siddons. The rigidly suspended arms and clenched fists emphasized by Darwin as often accompanying indignation are clearly present in each. Compressed mouth and furrowed brow, while less obvious in the engravings than in the photograph, are also evident. So, too, is the posture Darwin describes as common to indignation: "an indignant man unconsciously throws himself into an attitude ready for attacking or striking his enemy, whom he will perhaps scan from head to foot in defiance" (XXIII:187). While none of the other naturally simulated expressions in Darwin's book can be matched up quite so directly with figures in Engel, the general connection between Darwin's posed expressions and the theatrical conventions for the acting of various passions is clear. The point, of course, is not that a wide swath of

Figure 6.4 (a) Indignation. Heliotype reproduction of a photograph by Oscar Rejlander. Plate VI, figure 2 from Charles Darwin, *The Expression of the Emotions in Man and Animals* (London: Murray, 1872). Rejlander's pose is clearly rooted in widely-reproduced illustrations for acting manuals to which Darwin had access. (b) Resistance. Engraving. Figure 32 from Johann Jacob Engel, *Ideen Zu Einer Mimik* (1785), *J. J. Engel's Schriften*, vol. VII (Berlin: Mylius, 1804), facing p. 290. (c) Resistance. Engraving. A reproduction of fig. 6.4b in L.-J. Moreau, ed., *L'Art de Connaître les Hommes par la Physionomie* (Paris, 1820), vol. III, plate 120, figure 11. (d) "Menace." Engraving adapted from fig. 6.4b for Henry Siddons, *Practical Illustrations of Rhetorical Gesture and Action* (London: Phillips, 1807), between pages 148 and 149.

Victorian society was reading actors' handbooks, but that the images in the handbooks reflect what Victorians were seeing on the stage and in visual representations of actors at work, whether in paintings, popular prints, promotional materials, illustrated newspapers, or cartes-de-visite.[28]

The figures in Engel's work, especially as they appeared in Henry Siddons's English adaptation, were associated in the early part of the century with the statuesque, declamatory acting style of Sarah Siddons and John Kemble rather than the more emotional, histrionic technique of Edmund Kean, itself connected to the dramatic postures, exaggerated facial expressions, and heightened, bombastic language of popular melodrama. This contrast between an essentially neoclassical and an essentially Romantic aesthetic was also initially highly politicized, for melodrama emerged in late eighteenth-century France around the time of the Revolution as a deliberate and democratic departure from the formality and language-centeredness of the classical theater. By the time of Darwin's youth, however, the acting styles of both melodrama and the classical stage were emotionally and physically emphatic, differing only in degree rather than kind. Despite a slowly growing tendency towards a more naturalistic style over the course of Victoria's reign, the stage remained a site for the exaggerated display of emotions at the time of the *Expression*. Similarly, although the storylines of English melodrama gradually moved away from their early Gothic influences and towards greater domestic realism, the domestic realism was that of the sensation novel. Having contributed to sensation fiction's appearance, melodrama then borrowed heavily from its plots or simply staged adaptations of the latest successful thriller. Melodrama itself enjoyed enormous popularity, and while especially associated with the urban working classes, was performed at all theaters, including the patent theaters of London.[29]

Darwin's willingness to connect his illustrations with the visual world of the theater thus constituted another embrace of bourgeois aesthetics at the expense of high culture. These were figures in modern dress embedded textually in melodramatic scenes – the young woman tearing up the photograph of a despised lover, the sneering woman, the indignant man – straight from the contemporary stage. That Rejlander employed himself and other models who were not professional actors further contributed to the melodramatic associations and perhaps even gave these photographs the air of the amateur theatrical. Despite their genealogy, in other words, these were not images of Siddons or Kemble in classical or Shakespearean tragedy. The *Athenaeum* reviewer both recognized this fact and understood its aesthetic significance.

The association of Darwin's illustrations with acting also had the potential to connect the *Expression* to the Lavaterian physiognomy he had dismissed in the book's opening pages. While Engel's work was designed in part as a riposte to Lavater, an effort to demonstrate the inadequacy of facial expression alone for conveying emotion and character, Moreau had included Engel's plates in his edition of Lavater, and physiognomy sometimes exerted influence on actors' handbooks. *The Actor's Art* (1882) of Gustave Garcia, Director of the Royal Academy of Music and Dramatic Art since 1868, not only devotes a lengthy chapter to physiognomy but also makes it the basis for the poses, facial expressions, and gestures appropriate for acting different emotions. The book is illustrated much as a physiognomic treatise was, and Darwin is not referred to even when the movement of facial muscles is discussed, whereas he is frequently invoked in William Archer's *Masks or Faces? A Study in the Psychology of Acting* (1888), which does not rely on physiognomy.[30]

Using posed expressions linked to the visual traditions of the stage was thus not without risk for Darwin. It increased his vulnerability to criticisms about his lack of taste and refinement, and it made possible the identification of his work with both working-class culture and Lavater's physiognomics. While the *Athenaeum* reviewer was unusual in his denunciation of Rejlander's "performances," that is almost certainly because for him, as for other reviewers, it was Darwin's preference for photography over painting and sculpture that most merited comment. For those who lamented this preference, Darwin's invocations of the stage, and especially the melodramatic stage, would have raised similar concerns; for those untroubled by, or in agreement with, this preference, looking to the stage rather than the fine arts for examples of emotional expression would have made eminent sense.

DARWIN AND VICTORIAN CARICATURE

A book illustrated with images of expressive human faces could not fail to bring to mind in its readers the world of Victorian caricature. This world is absent from the *Expression* for the obvious reason that Darwin wanted as objective and natural renderings of human faces as possible, and caricature is by definition an art of exaggeration and distortion. Moreover, like physiognomy and unlike melodrama, it emphasized the features over expressions. Apart from his two references to works of Hogarth, then, Darwin does not draw on the great tradition of English caricature, nor does he mention the teeming universe of caricature in his own day, epitomized in the pages of *Punch* and its host of competitors and imitators.[31]

SUGGESTED ILLUSTRATION
For "Dr. Darwin's Movements and Habits of Climbing Plants."
(*See Murray's List of Forthcoming Works.*)
₊ We had no notion the Doctor would have been so ready to avow his
connection with his quadrumanous ancestors—the tree-climbing Anthropoids
—as the title of his work seems to imply.

Figure 6.5 "Suggested Illustration for Dr. Darwin's Movements and Habits of Climbing Plants." Wood engraving by Linley Sambourne for *Punch* 69 (11 Dec. 1875): 242. Sambourne uses the common "Darwin as monkey" joke even in a cartoon associated with one of Darwin's botany books.

But if caricature's impact on Darwin was circumscribed, Darwin's impact on caricature was considerable, at least in terms of subject matter. Darwin and Darwinism provided caricaturists and humor writers with an easy target for visual jokes, some rather biting but most genial. Indeed, Darwin's image probably circulated more widely in caricatured form than in the various photographic portraits of him, although photographs were of course the basis for some of the caricatures. Darwin's correspondents often drew his attention to the appearance of such caricatures, and he or his family members saved a number of them, for the Darwin Papers contain more than a dozen, from such venues as *Punch*, *Fun*, *Figaro*, and *The Hornet*.[32]

Two motifs dominate the caricature of Darwin and Darwinism: Darwin as a monkey and representations of species transformations. So common was the former that Linley Sambourne provided one for *Punch* in anticipation of the publication of Darwin's book on *Climbing Plants* (fig. 6.5)! The latter generally depicted or implied the (usually sudden) evolution of an animal into a human or *vice versa*, again with the monkey–man connection prominent. Even when good natured, these cartoons relied for their humor on what was clearly a widespread sense of Darwinism's fundamental absurdities – that species could change abruptly, that such an obviously superior species as humans could have developed from animals, that the great Darwin himself was the descendant of apes. Darwin encountered misrepresentations of how natural selection worked not just in cartoons but even from those who had read his books. Rejlander, for example, having completed his presentation copy of the *Descent*, wrote to Darwin that while the book had enlarged his mind, "my reason cannot believe in the creations of an adult – at any one time – any more than of a plant jumping full grown into existence."[33] To some extent, Darwin had himself to blame for such notions. His notorious imaginary illustration in the *Origin* of the transformation of the black bear into an aquatic mammal akin to whales positively invited caricature:

In North America the black bear was seen by Hearne swimming for hours with widely open mouth, thus catching, like a whale, insects in the water. Even in so extreme a case as this, if the supply of insects were constant, and if better adapted competitors did not already exist in the country, I can see no difficulty in a race of bears being rendered, by natural selection, more and more aquatic in their structure and habits, with larger and larger mouths, till a creature was produced as monstrous as a whale.[34]

Echoing in Darwin's prose, unfortunately for him, is an exchange between Hamlet and Polonius in which the Prince, feigning madness, rapidly alters his description of the shape of a cloud – it is like a camel, then a weasel, then a whale – the fawning Polonius concurring successively with each. Darwin removed the second sentence at the urging of Charles Lyell (no doubt on scientific rather than literary grounds) for the second edition, but the damage was already done: ridiculed by Owen in his review of the *Origin* as more "gross" than "any instance of hypothetical transmutation in Lamarck," this example was invoked by Darwin's critics for many years.[35]

Darwin and his allies could take pleasure in the cleverness of the jokes – the mere existence of such things confirmed the impact of Darwin's ideas – but they understood that these images could also reinforce and extend misunderstandings and oversimplifications of natural selection. The step from even the most playful caricature to Owen's professional ridicule was not that large. "I see some laughable 'skits' upon your theory in the 'Illustrated Times', consisting of a series of absurd (but clever) sketches illustrating the development of a man servant making off with a dish of eatables from a dog stealing some bones [fig. 6.6]," wrote Roland Trimen to Darwin from

Figure 6.6 "The Origin of Species, Dedicated by Natural Selection to Dr. Charles Darwin, No. 3 – Good Dog – (Drawn by C. H. Bennett.)" Wood engraving from a drawing by C. H. Bennett. *Illustrated Times*, 16 May 1863.

Cape Town. But then in his next sentence, Trimen adds: "I was glad to see some remarks of yours in the April 'Athenaeum' showing how different your theory essentially is from that of Lamarck." It is not clear if Trimen sees the *Illustrated Times* cartoons as embodying a Lamarckian misinterpretation of Darwinism – they certainly can be read as depicting examples of the inheritance of acquired characteristics, although Darwin's letter to the *Athenaeum* criticizes Lamarck's version of evolution for its belief in "some necessary law of advancement" of organic life, a belief that the cartoons seem to question. Nonetheless, the juxtaposition of these sentences in Trimen's letter suggests that such humor was neither inconsequential nor separable from more serious public discourse among elite scientists about the validity and meanings of Darwin's theory.[36]

These "skits" for the *Illustrated Times* were drawn by the popular and prolific illustrator Charles Henry Bennett (1829–1867). Bennett worked for a variety of comic publications in the 1850s and 60s, including *Diogenes*, *Comic Times*, *Comic News*, and, for the final two years of his life, *Punch*, but he was also in demand as an illustrator of children's books, and he put out titles for adults and children under his own name.[37] His successful and idiosyncratic edition of Aesop's fables in 1857 represented animals in Victorian dress, the fables rewritten to enact similarly updated situations with appropriately contemporary morals. "The Frog and the Ox,"

Figure 6.7 "Shadow Portraits" of R. B. Brough (a) and C. H. Bennett (b). Wood engravings from drawings by C. H. Bennett from Charles H. Bennett and Robert B. Brough, *Character Sketches, Development Drawings, and Original Pictures of Wit and Humour* (London: Ward, Lock, and Tyler, [1872]), 47 and 48.

for example, pokes fun at lower middle-class swells, while "The Daw in Borrowed Plumes" lampoons the nouveaux riches. In the late 1850s he produced a series of popular books built around drawings in which an individual's shadow reveals his true character, joining forces with the equally prolific comic draftsman and writer Robert B. Brough (1828–1860) on *Shadow and Substance* (1860). In 1872, the same year as the *Expression* appeared, the London publishers Ward, Lock, and Tyler issued a work that brought together *Shadow and Substance* and the *Illustrated Times* "skits" as *Character Sketches, Development Drawings, and Original Pictures of Wit and Humour.* While more likely to have been intended to capitalize on the furor over *The Descent of Man*, this book also meshed powerfully with many of the aspects of visual culture associated with the *Expression*.

The Introduction to *Shadow and Substance* explains that Bennett is the inventor of a special magic lantern christened an "eidolograph." Described as a "novel application of luminous rays to portraiture," the eidolograph "will enable the spectator to judge of a sitter's character by the development of his shadow." The book's first "Shadow-portraits" (fig. 6.7) – taken of Brough and Bennett – reveal, like many of those to follow, unflattering animal shapes. Yet author and artist conspire to deny the obvious, at least in their own cases: Brough's shadow-portrait is proclaimed by Bennett to reveal the outline of Shakespeare's profile, the forehead of Molière, and the chin of Byron, while Bennett's is said by Brough to resemble the silhouette of Hogarth and portraits of Raphael. The two men are most enthusiastic about the eidolograph's commercial potential, however. They launch the London Eidolographic Company, predicting a revolution in visual culture:

If it comes out as it promises, it will . . . have the effect of depriving thousands of their means of a livelihood, by shutting up the Photograph. As a drawing-room table amusement, it will force the Stereoscope itself to give up the Ghost. It will also infallibly prove a death blow to the sciences of Physiognomy, Phrenology, and Graphiology.

And indeed, having already succeeded in wiping out "the now extinct race of profile-cutters [silhouette artists]," they intend to compete with the "not yet suppressed race of photographers" by publishing a serial album of eidolographic portraits of living celebrities that will constitute "a more varied . . . edition of 'Men of the Day' than any yet attempted; a compendious portrait gallery of British Worthies of the Nineteenth Century; a collection of Art Treasures unprecedented; and a most unmistakable Book of Beauties."[38] Later they express the desire to produce eidolographic cartes-de-visite. Bennett and Brough use the eidolograph to lampoon the fascination with, and commercialism of, photography and optical gadgetry; poking fun at their own lowbrow art – Bennett is no Raphael, Brough no Shakespeare – they nonetheless lament art's vulgarization, while physiognomy and phrenology are dismissed by mimicking their language and pretensions.

The section of "Development Drawings" is dedicated to Darwin. Bennett complains, in a mock-grumbling way, that he lived a quiet and lazy life until Darwin's own development led him to publish the *Origin*, after which the world became unsettled, and provided much for the caricaturist to illustrate. Like the illustrations for his Aesop, these drawings have the air of an animal fable, as most offer some sort of moral lesson or social commentary, and a few seem aimed at children. Some make fun of stock targets for Victorian humor: the old maid, the dandy, the philistine. A few provide unflattering portraits of working-class figures as violent or loutish. But the dominant theme of these drawings is the way Victorian society has dressed up the immoral acquisition and exploitation of money and property in the garb of respectability. "Slow and Sure" attacks the man of business whose only goal is the accumulation of wealth, "Vulturine" the swindling entrepreneur. An old money-lender is depicted as a weasel, and the "natural selection of Pigeon by Weasel is in just accord with Mr. Darwin's theory of the Origin of Species; and steady as is the progress of society, may we, in our 'struggle for existence,' be protected from the clutches of any such unsleeping attentions." "All's Fish that Comes" depicts the loan shark who is "an Auditor, a Treasurer, an Agent, a Chairman, a Director, a Tax Collector, a Philanthropist, a Political Economist, a Churchwarden, an Overseer, a Social Reformer, a

Figure 6.8 "The Origin of Species, Dedicated by Natural Selection to Dr. Charles Darwin, No. 20 – As Thirsty As A Fish – (Drawn by C. H. Bennett.)" Wood engraving from a drawing by C. H. Bennett. *Illustrated Times*, 10 October 1863.

Charity Commissioner, and a general friend of humanity." "Piggish," an otherwise unsurprising condemnation of gluttony, is given an evolutionary and economic gloss: the gluttonous individual is "lineally descended from a Pig, no matter through how much labour he may have raised a Palace where once stood a Stye."[39] Several of the shadow-portraits offer similarly sharp-edged critiques of Victorian getting and spending.

And yet the note on which the series of Development Drawings ends (both in the *Illustrated Times* and in the book), "As Thirsty as a Fish" (fig. 6.8), depicts the British workman as a drunkard who sees business, duty, and friendship merely as impediments to his indulgence. Even amongst the very few illustrations critical of the working classes, this one stands out for rendering not a particular character type but a sweeping and highly unflattering portrayal of all male workers. As if uncomfortable with this turn, the text suddenly shifts back to Darwin, praising his patience and other superior qualities, nervously absolving him of any responsibility for these "Pictorial Theories," and hoping he will not take offence.[40] But what is it that causes Bennett to worry, even if in jest, about Darwin's displeasure? The general use of evolutionary transformations for social satire? The work's overall critique of business and utilitarian, laissez-faire social policy? The specific attack on the British laborer in this final drawing? Whatever the case, these popular cartoons confirm again that various ideological appropriations of Darwin's theories were as possible in Victorian visual culture as they were in its textual one.

In the arena of gender, an evocative caricature in *Fun* of a simian Darwin (see fig. 1.6) exploited Darwin's account in the *Expression* of blushing. What might appear a rather minor example of emotional expression is in fact central to Darwin's treatment of the subject. It is accorded a full chapter of its own, for it is, says Darwin, "the most peculiar and the most human of all expressions" (XXIII:244). Indeed, this chapter on blushing is the book's final one on human expression and closes the main body of the text. In it, Darwin argues that humans have always valued personal appearance, especially facial appearance, and that when our ancestors knew or supposed that another human was assessing their personal appearance, their attention was drawn inward, and they thought about the part or parts of the body under regard. This stimulated the nerves of, and thus blood flow to, the corresponding region(s), with a blush as the result. The reaction became habitual over time, such that no conscious thought about the body was required to produce a blush. Modern humans have inherited that response.

Darwin's discussion of blushing did not occur in a vacuum but in relation to a considerable body of Victorian medical discourse on the blush. Most central is the Edinburgh-trained surgeon Thomas Burgess's *Physiology or Mechanism of Blushing* (1839), to which Darwin repeatedly refers. Darwin relies heavily on Burgess's discussion of the physiology of blushing and shares the latter's view that all human races, not just light-skinned peoples, blush. Despite his admiration for Burgess's researches, however, Darwin disagreed with him almost completely about the significance of blushing. For Burgess, blushing is further evidence of divine design. The Creator provided the blush so that others can recognize when we have transgressed, and our awareness of this bodily confession thus also checks our inclination to sin. Since Burgess insists that the prostitute and the libertine blush as deeply as the pure and virtuous, he must distinguish between a true blush, which has "some good and substantial MORAL CAUSE," and a false blush, which is the result of "an extreme state of morbid sensibility, over which reason and the moral powers seem to have no control." Burgess rejects phrenology but specifically links his theory of blushing with Lavaterian physiognomy, descanting on the wonderful provisions by which the Creator has ensured that from "physical changes in the human countenance . . . we are enabled to judge with mathematical certainty of the internal feelings of our fellow beings!"[41] Bell in *The Anatomy of Expression* agreed with Burgess that blushing was specially provided by the Creator, but its purposes, he argued, were to communicate excitement rather than shame and to add perfection to the beauty of "youthful and . . . effeminate features" (95–96). For Darwin, by contrast, "attention directed to personal appearance, and not to moral conduct, has been the fundamental element in the acquirement of the habit of blushing" (XXIII:256). Even when we feel guilty, it is not our conscience that causes us to blush, but merely the awareness or suspicion that others are judging us. And while a blush can add beauty to a maiden's face, Darwin rejects the possibility that it originally served as a sexual ornament.

Darwin's gendering of the blush also divorces it from immorality and mutes its connection to sexuality. Like Burgess, Darwin accepts that people of all ages and both sexes blush, and while he does not emphasize the male blush as strongly as Burgess does, he does not focus on the cultural archetype of the blushing *young* woman. He acknowledges that women and the young blush more readily than older men, and many of his examples involve pretty girls being admired or courted. But others include children of both sexes, a shy man at a dinner party, a young man being teased by a girl, a wealthy duke paying his physician, and a lady giving money to a beggar. Darwin's women, moreover, blush not out of shame, as Burgess's do, but out of shyness and modesty: "Many a woman blushes from [shyness], a hundred, perhaps a thousand times, to once that she blushes from having done anything deserving blame, and of which she is truly ashamed" (XXIII:258). When Darwin describes courtship situations they often include shy, awkward young men, and when he asserts that "women are much more sensitive about their personal appearance than men are," he says this is especially true with *elderly* women (XXIII:256). While this of course reinforces and perhaps draws on cultural notions of the general moral purity of women, what I wish to call attention to is the fact that Darwin is attempting simultaneously to resist associating the blush with morality or beauty, both of which were deeply inscribed in understandings of the blush's divinely ordained purposes. If he wishes to challenge Burgess's natural theological account of the blush as a marker of conscience, he also denies Bell's natural theological account of the blush as a marker of ornament and excitement. It's striking, in fact, that Darwin's blushing women are *not* coy and that he insists sexual selection has nothing to do with blushing – despite the fact that women of all races blush.

The cartoon in *Fun*, however, respects almost none of these distinctions, trading instead on much that Darwin mutes or downplays. Intriguingly, Darwin's chapter on blushing in the *Expression* is the only one on humans *without* an illustration. While the technical problems of capturing and representing a blush photographically are obvious, Darwin could certainly have obtained from Rejlander the same kind of staged representation of the gestures accompanying the blush that Rejlander provided him of indignation, disgust, and surprise. Into this visual gap stepped *Fun*. Unlike Darwin, the cartoon focuses on the pretty young woman. She is fashionably, even elegantly, dressed. Covered up and turned away, we see only her profile and one of her hands. (In his discussion of body blushes in the *Expression*, Darwin relied almost exclusively on accounts of women and girls provided by doctors.) But her bustle accentuates her hips and buttocks, and the much older, simian Darwin squats in close proximity to her breasts and loins, his fingers on her pulse. His long, sinuous, phallic tail curls up from between his legs to her eye level in a manner perhaps suggestive of representations of Eve and the serpent. The cartoon is much concerned with human evolution – the caption describes the woman as a "Female descendant of Marine Ascidian" – and her statement to Darwin that he may "say what [he] like[s] about man" clearly references the *Descent*'s account of human origins; but the woman's request that Darwin "leave my emotions alone" creates the impression that the *Expression*'s concern is with the blushing female. Darwin's physiological and evolutionary account of the blush is simultaneously presented as prurient and obtuse, both intimately concerned with and oblivious to the beauty and aesthetic charm of the young woman.

Ruskin saw Darwin's account of the blush in much the same way as the *Fun* cartoonist did. Six years later, in his attack in *Proserpina* on the "unclean stupidity" of scientific materialism, Ruskin chose Darwin's blushing girl as one of his objects of ridicule. Material explanations of natural phenomena may be correct, Ruskin complained, but they miss the higher and more important aesthetic, moral, and spiritual truths. "The blush of a girl," he wrote, "when she first perceives the faltering in her lover's step as he draws near, is related essentially to the existing state of her stomach; and to the state of it through all the years of her previous existence. Nevertheless, neither love, nor chastity, nor blushing, are merely exponents of digestion" (xxv:263). Darwin's reduction of love, chastity, and blushing to a function of digestion is for Ruskin fundamentally the result of his aesthetic inadequacies. As we've seen in previous examinations of other parts of this particular attack, Ruskin concludes that Darwin is ignorant about art, knows nothing about color, and cannot draw. If Ruskin thought Bell was often wrong in his evaluation of expression in painting and sculpture, his sympathies nonetheless lay with Bell's approach to the subject rather than Darwin's.

Unlike the *Fun* cartoon, however, Ruskin's verbal caricature, for all its characteristic outrageousness, had, as usual, a basis in Darwin's text – Darwin's theory of the blush depended on the notion that thinking about a part of the body would cause increased blood flow to it, and he included in his catalog of supporting examples cases involving the digestive tract. Recovering that textual basis reveals Ruskin to have been more familiar with Darwin's work and its details than is usually supposed, but more important, it suggests that Ruskin saw how various pieces of Darwin's post-*Origin* work could be fit together to form a fairly broad-ranging if unsystematic alternative to his own aesthetic theories. His attack in *Proserpina* on sexual selection, Darwin's botanical works, and *The Expression of the Emotions* lashes out at the three major components of that evolutionary alternative. For Ruskin, the danger of Darwin – like the danger of Tyndall and his emphasis on the scientific imagination – lay in the fact that his scientific materialism did not seek to ignore or diminish the aesthetic, but to absorb it.

CHAPTER 7

Darwin's worms

In late April of 1881, his strength failing, Darwin again took up the autobiographical "Recollections of the development of my mind and character" he had written out for his children and grandchildren five years earlier. To that document's survey of "My Several Publications" he added brief accounts of the works he had published since 1876, including the one just completed, which would be his final book: "I have now (May 1, 1881) sent to the printers the MS. of a little book on *The Formation of Vegetable Mould through the Action of Worms*," he wrote. "This is a subject of but small importance; and I know not whether it will interest any readers, but it has interested me. It is the completion of a short paper read before the Geological Society more than forty years ago, and has revived old geological thoughts" (XXIX:156). When *Worms* appeared in October, the sales of this little book surprised both author and publisher. "3500 Worms!!!" wrote Murray's Robert Cooke on 5 November. Inundated with letters and awash in laudatory reviews, Darwin stood amazed at the chord his "subject of small importance" had struck.[1]

The subject and its treatment were vintage Darwin. As they move through the soil, earthworms ingest large quantities of earth, extracting from it the nutrients contained in vegetable matter, passing whatever is undigested as "castings." Although small and seemingly weak, worms produce prodigious results through their large numbers and incessant activity: Darwin estimated that in many parts of England worms process ten tons of earth per acre in a single year. Their actions, moreover, seemed to Darwin to exhibit some level of intelligence rather than mere instinct. They do not approach in the same way the objects of different shapes and sizes they wish to drag into their burrows, but instead appear to inspect them and then to decide on the most efficient way to seize and drag them. And worms are of considerable human and geological significance. The rich layer of surface soil, Darwin argued, is created, turned over, and continually replenished by worms. Castings, blown by wind and washed by rain, are a major component of erosion and thus of geological denudation. Even archaeologists have reason to be grateful to worms, for artifacts and ancient ruins are gradually buried in castings, which protect and preserve them. Closing the book with yet another variation on the ending of the *Origin*, a "wide, turf-covered expanse" doing duty for the "entangled bank," Darwin offered a paean to the lowly worm:

When we behold a wide, turf-covered expanse, we should remember that its smoothness, on which so much of its beauty depends, is mainly due to all the inequalities having been slowly levelled by worms. It is a marvellous reflection that the whole of the superficial mould over any such expanse has passed, and will again pass, every few years through the bodies of worms. The plough is one of the most ancient and most valuable of man's inventions; but long before he existed the land was in fact regularly ploughed, and still continues to be thus ploughed, by earth-worms. It may be doubted whether there are many other animals which have played so great a part in the history of the world, as have these lowly organised creatures. Some other animals, however, still more lowly organised, namely corals, have done far more conspicuous work in having constructed innumerable reefs and islands in the great oceans; but these are almost confined to the tropical zones. (XXVIII:139)

The earthworm was for Darwin a global agriculturalist of greater antiquity than human beings, as industrious a worker as the even more lowly coral, its accomplishments less obvious only because it does not build reefs but rather "level[s]" topographical "inequalities." Characteristically for Darwin, this "levelling" was accomplished not through revolution but the slow, inexorable rhythms of pastoral activity and geological change. Some thirty years earlier, Alfred Tennyson, in his elegy for his beloved friend, Arthur Henry Hallam, had struggled to retain the hope that "not a worm is cloven in vain" even in the face of geological evidence suggesting that humanity's fate, like that of countless other species, was merely to be "blown about the desert dust" (*In Memoriam* 54:9, 56:19). For Darwin, however, the worm was an earlier and more significant plowman, its role in geological processes a cause for marvel and celebration rather than despair.[2]

Compared to most of Darwin's other books, *Worms* was not copiously illustrated, containing just fifteen wood engravings. Surprisingly, in light of the book's subject, only one was actually of a worm – the opening figure was a diagram of a worm's alimentary canal, copied from an article by Ray Lankester in the *Quarterly Journal of the Microscopical Society* (fig. 7.1). This diagram functioned more like the diagrams of facial musculature in the *Expression* than the archetypal crustacean and barnacle in the *Cirripedia* monograph or the opening figure of *Orchis mascula* in *Orchids*.

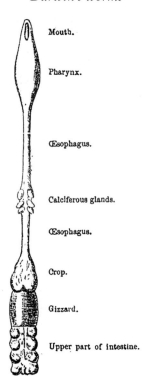

Figure 7.1 "Diagram of the alimentary canal of an earthworm." Wood engraving. Figure 1 from Charles Darwin, *The Formation of Vegetable Mould through the Action of Worms* (London: Murray, 1881), 18.

Its purpose was descriptive rather than theoretical, providing readers with a visual reference for the terminology of earthworm anatomy. But in reducing the worm to its digestive tract, Darwin also pointed to the fact that his specific subject was not the worm *per se* but its role in the formation of vegetable mould. It was what entered and exited that alimentary canal, and what happened to the castings, that mattered. And so of the fourteen other illustrations, three were of the castings themselves, while eleven contained stones and buildings buried by the action of worms. The former depicted piles of excrement in full naturalistic detail. Copied from photographs and reproduced in their actual size, these "tower-like" castings were themselves depicted almost as architectural monuments. Darwin had long been fascinated by nature's oddities, yet here was, arguably, the apex of the Darwinian grotesque: worm shit, lovingly rendered as an object of wonder. (This wonder is perhaps tinged with envy, as Darwin was obsessed throughout his adult life by the frustrating and often debilitating inefficiencies of his own digestive tract.) The larger group of illustrations, that of stones and build-ings, offered a Darwinian version of the picturesque. Darwin took one of the staples of the picturesque – monuments and ruins – and rendered them schematically as geological sections. While Darwin's aesthetic response to natural scenery had long been intimately connected to his geological vision, to see worms as the movers behind a pleasing landscape was to take this inter-twining of the aesthetic and the geological to a greater extreme.[3] Archaeolog-ical and antiquarian illustrations often retained picturesque conventions – landscapes containing realistic renderings of ruins, with human figures to provide a sense of scale – but Darwin subtracted both the landscape and the people, adapting the visual language of geology to sites rarely depicted in such a fashion.

And so it is that with *Worms* we finally, belatedly, arrive at landscape. But only because it was with *Worms* that Darwin himself finally returned to landscape, and to geology. In saying that *Worms* "revived old geological thoughts" and brought to completion a paper delivered to the Geological Society more than forty years earlier, Darwin signaled the way this final book circled back to the beginning of his career.[4] In those early days, both during the *Beagle* voyage and in the years immediately following his return, Darwin saw himself primarily as a geologist. While he edited the volumes on the zoology of the voyage, he authored the three volumes on its geology himself. Only when his *Journal of Researches into the Geology and Natu-ral History of the Various Countries Visited by HMS Beagle* appeared in a second edition in 1845 was the order of "geology" and "natural history" in the title reversed, with natural history given the place of prominence. In the 1870s, however, with the books that completed the arguments of the *Origin* out of the way, geological thoughts began to revive in earnest for Darwin. New editions of *The Structure and Distribution of Coral Reefs* (1874) and *Geological Observations on South America* (1876) appeared at the same time as his interest in earthworms was increasing. Paradoxically, although the *Origin*, the *Variation*, and the *Descent* had offered a radical new vision of nature and of landscape, they were books that focused mainly on parts and pieces rather than wholes.[5] So, too, with the botany books. Despite the all-encompassing ambitions and implications of Darwin's the-ory, his books mainly offered close-ups of individual organisms and parts of organisms rather than panoramas. Passages about "the face of nature" or "the entangled bank" were the exception, necessary for keeping the wider prospect in view. *Worms*, like his return to coral reefs and South American geology, offered Darwin the chance to lift his physical as well as intellectual gaze.

That gaze was also aesthetic. Cataloguing in his autobiographical recollections his "curious and lamentable loss of the higher aesthetic tastes,"
Darwin partially exempted the appreciation of landscapes. While he no
longer responded with "exquisite delight" to "fine scenery," he retained
"some taste" for it (XXIX:158). And indeed, while he was at work on *Worms*,
Darwin twice visited the Lake District, reveling in its landscape. Every
walk at his "beloved Coniston," his children recalled of their 1879 sojourn,
afforded "fresh delight" that left him "never tired of praising the beauty of
the broken hilly country at the head of the lake." During a return trip two
years later, with *Worms* in proof, Emma reported him as much taken with
the "beauty and views."[6] It is little wonder that the book closed with a landscape vision, a meditation on the beauty of a "wide, turf-covered expanse."

And yet that meditation, as we have seen, focused not on the beauty of
the landscape but on the role of worms in creating it. The imagetext that
was *Worms* had almost nothing to say, at least not directly, about aesthetics
and visual culture. This was not the *Descent*, with its evolutionary account
of beauty, nor the *Expression*, with its discussions of art, nor the books on
plant fertilization, with their explanation of the role of color and ornament in the botanical kingdom. As usual, however, Darwin's treatment of
his subject, both textually and visually, seemed calculated to comment on
both traditional fine art categories and contemporary visual forms. Donald
Ulin has argued suggestively that *Worms* "threaten[ed] the status quo by
linking physical and intellectual activities, effacing a distinction essential to
much nineteenth-century cultural criticism," especially that of Coleridge
and Matthew Arnold.[7] In *Worms*, Ulin sees Darwin as subverting the idealized high-culture landscapes of the sublime and the picturesque with the
material low-culture form of the grotesque, particularly the carnivalesque
that Mikhail Bakhtin associated with Rabelais. While drawing on Ulin's
insights, I want both to read the actual illustrations for *Worms* and to treat
them in relation to that other great nineteenth-century cultural critic –
Ruskin – with his rather different vision of the grotesque and the picturesque. No evidence, direct or circumstantial, suggests that Ruskin read
Darwin's book when it appeared. Yet Ruskin entertained Darwin at his Lake
District home during Darwin's stay at Coniston in 1879, and it is possible
he did so again in 1881.[8] And it is not difficult to guess how Ruskin would
have received the book and its illustrations. In most respects, Darwin's work
aligns itself with Ruskin's ignoble grotesque and low picturesque, and while
these are not without some shreds of virtue and merit, they are decidedly
inferior to their noble counterparts, making *Worms*, like the rest of Darwin's
books, dangerous in its cultural and moral implications.

WORM CASTINGS AND THE GROTESQUE

Much of Darwin's work, and many of his illustrations, can be characterized as grotesque: the bizarre sexual arrangements of barnacles and orchids;
the outré forms of fancy pigeons; the extravagant plumage, ornament, and
weaponry of male birds; the hideous facial expressions of Duchenne's galvanized old man; the elaborate traps of insectivorous plants.[9] Indeed, Darwinism as a whole is informed by many aspects commonly associated with the
grotesque. The term itself was originally applied to the designs in the fres-
coes discovered during the fourteenth century in the underground ruins (the
grottoes) of the Baths of Titus in Rome.[10] These designs featured fanciful
depictions of plant, animal, and human forms, often playfully combined. In
the centuries that followed, however, the grotesque took on different meanings, depending on which aspects of the original subjects were emphasized,
with some of these meanings connected to style as much as or more than
subject matter. The imaginative, fanciful elements could link the grotesque
broadly to the comic. The blending of forms could be used to connect the
grotesque to the deliberate combination of disparate styles and subjects,
while the blended forms themselves could be viewed positively, as a celebration of life in its dynamic, fecund glory, or negatively, as monstrous
and terrifying, evidence of the horrors that result from failing to respect
boundaries and accept restraints. In the grotesque realism of Rabelais were
to be found highly exaggerated situations and characters, frequent variation
and mixing of styles, a delight in jokes and wordplay, and a naturalistic view
of life focused in representations of the body as a site of earthly excess – of
eating and drinking, defecation and urination, copulation, pregnancy, and
birth. Although the grotesque continued to thrive in popular taste during
the Enlightenment, neoclassical aestheticians regarded with disdain its violations of decorum and its vulgar humor. Darwinism, with its blurring of
boundaries and blending of categories, its focus on variation, eccentricity,
and irregularity, and its interest in bodies and their functions, especially
sexual reproduction, digestion, defecation, and death, thus had many of the
hallmarks of the grotesque. While Darwin and his allies clearly reveled in
nature's grotesqueries, and took delight in their celebration of them, those
who regarded nature as complete, ordered, stable, and hierarchical looked
upon Darwin's vision with horror.

Darwin's treatment of worms and his illustrations of worm castings fall
squarely within the tradition of grotesque realism. Bakhtin argues that
grotesque realism is not only relentlessly material but also relentlessly positive about that materiality. Its "essential principle" is degradation – "a transfer

to the material level, to the sphere of earth and body," of "all that is high, spiritual, ideal, abstract." "The artistic logic of the grotesque image," says Bakhtin, "ignores the closed, smooth, and impenetrable surface of the body and retains only its excrescences and orifices." The essential parts of the grotesque body are thus those in which "the confines between bodies and between the body and the world are overcome": the bowels, the phallus, the anus, and especially the mouth. In grotesque realism, "the body swallows the world and is itself swallowed by the world." Grotesque realism is concerned with death and decay, but always in the context of the bringing forth of new life. Its world is fertile, abundant, and festive.[11] Darwin's opening illustration (see fig. 7.1) treats earthworms in precisely this way, presenting them as a giant digestive tract, from mouth to intestine. His fundamental concern throughout the book is with worms' "excrescences and orifices": the way worms ingest soil and organic material, process it in their alimentary canals, and expel what they do not absorb as castings. So thoroughly do worms break down the division between their bodies and the world that the world almost literally passes through their bodies, over and over again. This fact, in Darwin's view, is cause for wonder and celebration, for worms thus help to create and aerate the soil, converting the products of death and decay into a source of regeneration and life.

The burden of the book's early chapters is thus to establish that worms are indeed capable of passing large quantities of castings. This is the point that the three illustrations of castings serve, and in style as well as subject matter they conform to the conventions of grotesque realism. Each is marked by irregularity and complexity, a mass of convolutions. Each is highly naturalistic – engraved from a photograph, and presented at its actual size. And size not only matters but is stressed. The first is from a species whose castings typically "rise like towers" (XXVIII:47) to a height of two and a half inches, and sometimes to three inches or more. The second is similar but even taller, and the bits of vegetation sprouting out of it testify to the fertility of the castings (see fig. 7.2). The third, produced by a species over a foot in length and "as thick as a man's little finger," is remarkable for the diameter of its convolutions and its mass (the largest member of the group from which this specimen came, notes the astonished Darwin, had convolutions "rather more than one inch in diameter" and weighed "above a quarter of a pound!" [XXVIII:56]). Such massive castings, moreover, are neither isolated nor present only where decaying vegetable matter is copious. The first specimen was obtained from a location where worms subsist on soil only, yet five or six large castings could often be found in a square foot. The second came from the Botanic Gardens in Calcutta, where

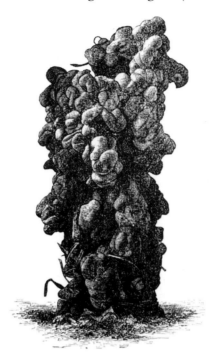

Figure 7.2 "A tower-like casting, probably ejected by a species of Perichaeta, from the Botanic Garden, Calcutta." Engraving from a photograph. Figure 3 from Charles Darwin, *The Formation of Vegetable Mould through the Action of Worms* (London: Murray, 1881), 124.

castings were so large and numerous that the lawns had to be rolled daily to preserve their appearance. The third was found at a high elevation in an arid climate.

To marvel at worms and worm castings can be regarded as a fundamentally comic act, subversive of political and cultural elites. Grotesque realism was informed by the humor of folk culture, the degradation of the high and the mighty and the elevation of the low and the powerless, a carnivalesque inversion of the social hierarchy. In Darwin's day, this aspect of the grotesque lived on for contemporaries particularly in the novels of Dickens and the caricature of *Punch* – where, however, it was generally advancing the aims of bourgeois more than working-class culture. As the title of the prolific antiquarian Thomas Wright's important *History of Caricature and Grotesque in Literature and Art* (1865) suggests, caricature and the grotesque could be used virtually as synonyms, although for Wright the grotesque was limited to depictions of the fantastic or the extremely ugly or comic, and only became caricature when used for purposes of ridicule.[12] Whether one embraced or lamented the social functions of the grotesque depended on ideology as well as aesthetics. In their survey of the Victorian grotesque, Colin Trodd, Paul Barlow, and David Amigoni argue that in the hands of writers like Dickens and Wright, the grotesque was associated with a liberal society and a humanist ethic, "seek[ing] in deviations and eccentricities a means to destabilize the rationalizing and systematizing functions of the bureaucratic systems of knowledge." For critics like Matthew Arnold, G. H. Lewes, and Walter Bagehot, however, the grotesque "was a sign of the ruination of authentic culture by a sentimental, democratic popular realism – a realism which seeks experiential plenitude through the swarming of expressive detail."[13]

As usual, Darwin's work did not enact the direct "ruination of authentic culture" but the subtle undermining of it, principally through alignment with, and celebration of, the "deviations and eccentricities" that defenders of authentic culture looked upon with disdain. Certainly aware of how easily he and his theories could be caricatured for purposes playful or cruel, Darwin was perhaps content to glorify his grotesque worms, leaving any caricature of elite culture at best implied. He gave his worm castings the same visual treatment accorded to architectural monuments and antiquarian or archaeological artifacts, while the monuments and artifacts discussed and pictured later in the book were significant textually and visually not for their own sake but for the evidence they provided of the activity of worms. And indeed, as I noted above, these monuments and artifacts would not exist, or not exist as they do, were it not for worm castings. The remains of Roman towns and fallen monoliths at Stonehenge have been buried in worm castings, yet this is not presented as degradation and ruination but as preservation. The burial is not the literal bringing down to earth of ancient cultures and their civic and religious ideals but the building-up of earth by worms, which are themselves elevated not as grave diggers but as builders. Worms have played an important part in the natural and human history of the world, in a sense making human culture possible. Yet their preservation of ancient monuments is as inadvertent as their creation and aeration of the soil. Darwin does not ridicule human high culture here – his laughter at the role of worms in human history is a backstage chuckle – but his delight in worms and their achievements is palpable. They display rudimentary intelligence, and, although omnivorous, exhibit a certain degree of discrimination and taste when confronted with a choice of food. They level by building out of their own castings "tower-like" monuments as marvelous as a Celtic monolith, a Roman villa, or a medieval abbey.

GEOLOGY, ARCHAEOLOGY, AND THE PICTURESQUE

Darwin's use of architectural and geological language to describe worms' castings – in addition to being "tower-like" they are sometimes measured from "base" to "summit" and often treated like miniature volcanoes, the soft combination of earth and undigested matter being thrown up suddenly and then, lava-like, hardening – is not merely in keeping with his use of ancient structures to measure worm activity and his geological approach to the problem. It connects *Worms* to the picturesque, the contemporary landscape form in which architecture and geology came most intimately together. Yet if Darwin's treatment of worm castings seemed to indulge in grotesque realism, his handling of ruins virtually amounted to a massive revision or even rejection of the picturesque.

In the late eighteenth and early nineteenth centuries, the reaction against neoclassicism brought the grotesque back into favor in elite artistic and literary circles, although with its serious rather than its carnivalesque associations emphasized. Edmund Burke, in his influential *Philosophical Inquiry into the Origin of our Ideas of the Sublime and the Beautiful* (1756), had associated the grotesque with the trivial and the comic in contrast to the seriousness of the sublime, with the ugly in contrast with the beautiful. Subsequent theorists, however, developed the category of the picturesque for those scenes that induced serious reflection and feelings of pleasure even though they lacked the subject matter and stylistic features of the sublime and the beautiful. Picturesque scenes contained elements of beauty, despite lacking the curved lines, gentle chiaroscuro, and smooth surfaces associated by Burke with the beautiful, and elements of the sublime, even though they depicted tranquil, rustic landscapes rather than the majesty and violence of towering peaks, resounding cataracts, and stormy skies. As Frances Barasch has shown, the picturesque essentially acknowledged that grotesque elements could contribute to solemn or pleasurable responses to landscapes whose comparatively ignoble subjects – blasted trees, crumbling ruins, and ragged peasants – were characterized by irregular lines, strong contrasts of light and shade, and rough or rugged textures.[14] Ruins in particular lent themselves to such treatment and thus were a common feature of picturesque landscapes. In fact, discussing the picturesque in the third volume of *Modern Painters* in 1856, Ruskin made "a delight in ruin" the characteristic feature of the picturesque (VI:9).

By Darwin's youth, the conventions of the picturesque had been firmly established, and the "exquisite delight" he then took in "fine scenery" was often couched in the language of the period's aesthetic terminology. Darwin

Figure 7.3 "Remains of the Cathedral at Concepcion." Engraving from a sketch by John
Wickham from Robert Fitzroy, ed., *Narrative of the Surveying Voyages of His Majesty's Ships
Adventure and Beagle . . .* , 3 vols. (London: Colburn, 1839) II: facing p. 405. A picturesque
rendering of the massive Chilean earthquake experienced by Darwin and his shipmates
on the *Beagle*.

owned and annotated an 1823 edition of Burke's essay on the sublime and
the beautiful.[15] His *Journal of Researches* employs "picturesque" and "sublime" liberally, particularly for South American landscapes, and he explicitly describes the ruins of Concepcion, Chile, as "picturesque" following a
massive earthquake. First Lieutenant John Wickham's sketch of the scene
(fig. 7.3), reproduced in Fitzroy's official *Narrative* of the voyage, captures Concepcion in precisely this manner. Aboard the *Beagle*, Darwin was
friendly with ship's artist Augustus Earle and then with his replacement,
Conrad Martens. Martens, who had studied under watercolorist Copley
Fielding, later the teacher and friend of Ruskin as well, produced topographical drawings as well as a variety of sublime and picturesque sketches
(fig. 7.4). When Darwin saw Martens again in Australia in 1836, he purchased two watercolors, one of the Santa Cruz River expedition and one
of the *Beagle* in Tierra del Fuego.[16] In 1862, Martens sent Darwin another
watercolor from the *Beagle* voyage via Wickham.

Figure 7.4 "Britannia or Tower Rock, Port Desire," "Anchorage and Spanish Ruins, Port
Desire," "Upper Part of Port Desire Inlet," and "Bivouac at the Head of Port Desire
Inlet." Engravings from watercolor sketches by Conrad Martens from Robert Fitzroy, ed.,
Narrative of the Surveying Voyages of His Majesty's Ships Adventure and Beagle . . . , 3 vols.
(London: Colburn, 1839) II: facing p. 316. Martens's sketches deploy picturesque
conventions, particularly in the illustration of the Spanish ruins. Darwin owned three of
Martens's watercolors from the voyage.

BRITANNIA OR TOWER ROCK, PORT DESIRE.

ANCHORAGE, AND SPANISH RUINS, PORT DESIRE.

UPPER PART OF PORT DESIRE INLET.

BIVOUAC AT THE HEAD OF PORT DESIRE INLET.

Roman Walls of Caerwent.

Figure 7.5 "Roman Walls of Caerwent." Wood engraving from Thomas Wright,
*Uriconium; A Historical Account of the Ancient Roman City, and of the Excavations made
upon its Site at Wroxeter, in Shropshire* (London: Longmans, 1872), 92. Picturesque
conventions in an illustration for an antiquarian/archaeological text by Thomas Wright,
the most famous antiquarian of Darwin's day.

The depiction of ruins in a picturesque fashion remained common in a
variety of contexts throughout the century. Thomas Wright's popular and
copiously illustrated *The Celt, The Roman, and The Saxon: A History of the
Early Inhabitants of Britain* (originally published in 1852) almost invariably
depicted ruins in the picturesque tradition, as did his *Wanderings of an
Antiquary* (1854). Edgar Barclay's *Stonehenge and Its Earth-Works* (1895) contained numerous picturesque illustrations of the famous stone circle; while
published fourteen years after *Worms*, its survey of the history of theories
about the monument included many illustrations from earlier works, and
thus provided a sort of visual history as well.[17] Wright's book on the Roman
excavations at Wroxeter, to which Darwin refers in *Worms* (xxviii:98), contained fewer picturesque engravings, and the most finished of these were
not of the Wroxeter ruins themselves, but the presence of such illustrations
in a fairly technical antiquarian/archaeological work indicates just how natural the picturesque had become for illustrating ruins even outside of fine
art contexts (fig. 7.5). During the 1870s and early 80s, Darwin's friend and
neighbor, John Lubbock, was active in efforts to preserve Britain's ancient
monuments, purchasing land on which endangered monuments, including
the large stone circle at Avebury, stood, introducing in Parliament a National
Monuments Protection Bill starting in 1873 (finally passed, in watered-down
form, a decade later), and penning the introduction for Charles Philip
Kains-Jackson's *Our Ancient Monuments and the Land Around Them* (1880),

this latter containing loosely picturesque illustrations.[18] By 1880 a thriving photographic tourist industry was producing picturesque cartes-de-visite of the countryside, and middle-class tourists, armed with their own cameras, were capturing picturesque subjects, including the remains of Celtic monuments, Roman towns, and medieval abbeys.[19] Darwin himself owned three cartes of the Roman ruins at Chedworth – two of an essentially documentary variety depicting mosaic tile floors, but one a picturesque view of the excavations.[20]

Long familiar with the terminology and iconography of the picturesque and aware of the precedents for employing it in archaeological and antiquarian works, Darwin could not have failed to be aware that his readers, encountering discussions of ancient monuments and ruins, would at some level associate *Worms* with these other works. And Darwin was not discussing just any monuments and ruins, but iconic ones representative of major eras and events in Britain's past – Celtic Stonehenge, Roman Silchester (among the largest and most complete Roman remains in Britain), Beaulieu Abbey (partially destroyed during Henry VIII's dissolution of the monasteries). Given Darwin's focus on the role of worms in the burial of such sites, it made sense not to treat them picturesquely. But this treatment did not simply remove Darwin's illustrations from aesthetic and cultural contexts, especially since the illustrations for *Worms* could seem almost militantly anti-picturesque, because Darwin treated these picturesque archaeological sites as geological sections.

While Darwin's book was very much a work of natural history – a bit more than half was devoted to the habits of worms and their processing of soil – it was almost equally concerned with geology and archaeology. Two of its six body chapters dealt with "the action of worms in the denudation of the land," while a third discussed "the part which worms have played in the burial of ancient buildings." This geological and archeological component to Darwin's investigations, which might appear rather odd at first sight, had its roots in his initial curiosity about worms. In the early fall of 1837, the proofs of his *Journal of Researches* just sent off, Darwin visited his Uncle Josiah Wedgwood's home in Staffordshire. During one of their walks, Uncle Jos pointed out several meadows in which a layer of small fragments of cinders and lime, strewn on the surface some years before, was now buried to a depth of several inches. The cause, Uncle Jos hypothesized, was earthworms – it was not that the layer of detritus had sunk, but that worms had covered it with their castings. Intrigued, Darwin investigated further. Within six weeks, back in London, he presented a paper entitled "On the Formation of Mould" to the Geological Society.[21] Having spoken to the same body earlier in the year on corals, and already planning the separate book on them that would form part of the *Geology* of the *Beagle* voyage, Darwin was primed to see worms through a geological as much as a zoological eye.

Thus began Darwin's distinctive lifelong fascination with the actions of these insignificant creatures. In 1844, he reported again on his Uncle Jos's fields, this time to the *Gardeners' Chronicle*, updating and correcting his earlier account.[22] Over the years he continued to collect observations and data while he worked on other projects, as usual enlisting family members and foreign correspondents to assist him. Sons Horace, Francis, and William, nieces Sophy and Lucy Wedgwood, and cousin Francis Galton were all recruited. His friend Asa Gray, the Harvard botanist; Scottish geologist Archibald Geikie; John Scott of the Royal Botanic Garden in Calcutta; the Director of the Geological Survey, A. C. Ramsay; J. L. G. Krefft of the Australian Museum in Sydney; the civil servant and amateur botanist T. H. Farrer (whose second wife was one of Darwin's nieces, and whose daughter married Horace Darwin in 1880) – all provided information, measurements, and observations. From examining the burial of discarded cinders it was also, of course, not a long step to examining the burial of boulders and human structures, and Darwin's desire to write about worms resurfaced in the 1870s as he obtained more and more evidence of their actions from archaeological sites and ancient monuments. Ramsay sent Darwin a sketch of the pavement of his home's eighteenth-century courtyard, sunk because of the action of worms, in late 1871. William was dispatched to Beaulieu Abbey in Hampshire to collect worm castings in January of 1872. In the summer of 1877, Darwin traveled on a series of worm excursions. On 19 June he was at Stonehenge with George; "I'm afraid it will 1/2 kill F[ather]," Emma wrote to their daughter, Henrietta, "but he is bent on going, chiefly for the worms." Fortunately, the old soldier guarding the monument "was quite agreeable to any amount of digging." Three days later Darwin was himself at Beaulieu Abbey; in August he was present at the beginning of the excavations of a Roman villa recently discovered by Farrer on his property at Abinger, Surrey. That fall, Francis and Horace were sent to Chedworth, Gloucestershire, and Silchester in Hampshire to look for signs of worm activity at Roman ruins, in the company at the latter of J. G. Joyce, the superintendent of the excavations, who also provided Darwin with extensive notes and elaborate drawings of the site. In 1880–81, as he worked on the book in earnest at home, Darwin solicited additional archaeological evidence in a final intense round of source-pumping. William scouted yet another recently unearthed Roman villa at Brading on the Isle of Wight. Farrer answered queries about both his Abinger villa and the Silchester excavations, Joyce having died. Dr. Henry Johnson, superintendent of the Wroxeter excavations, twice

(a)

A. Cinders.   B. Burnt Marl.   C. Quartz Pebbles.

(b)   NO. 16.—SECTION OF THE LOWEST PLAIN AT PORT S. JULIAN.

A A. Superficial bed of reddish earth, with the remains of the Macrauchenia, and with recent sea-shells on the surface.
B. Gravel of porphyritic rocks.
C and D. Pumiceous mudstone.
E and F. Sandstone and argillaceous beds. } Ancient tertiary formation.

Figure 7.6 (a) "Section of Field." Wood engraving. Figure 1 from Charles Darwin, "On the Formation of Mould," *Transactions of the Geological Society of London*, 2nd series, pt. 3, vol. 5 (1840): 506. From the very beginning, Darwin illustrated his earthworm researches with the visual language of geological sections. (b) "Section of the lowest plain at Port S. Julian." Wood engraving. Figure 16 from Charles Darwin, *Geological Observations on Coral Reefs, Volcanic Islands, and on South America*, 3 vols. (London: Smith, Elder, 1851) III:95.

visited the ruins to make observations and take measurements in response to Darwin's questions.[23]

Darwin's geological view of earthworm activity was present from the point of his initial fascination. His original paper for the Geological Society in 1837 was illustrated with a woodcut depicting a columnar cross-section of the soil from Uncle Jos's field, with grass at the top and several layers of soil beneath it (fig. 7.6a). Thinking of himself at the time primarily

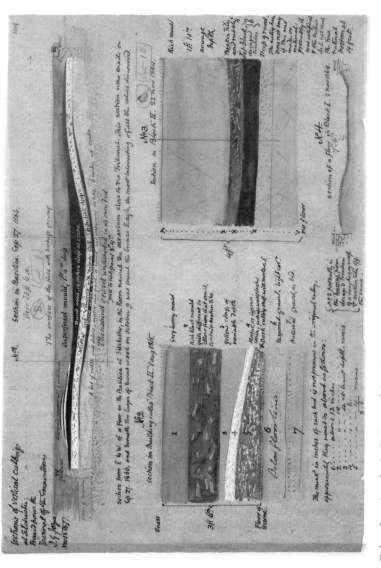

Figure 7.8 Colored tracings by J. G. Joyce of the Silchester excavations. "No. 1" has a pencil and a blue wax crayon mark apparently in Darwin's hand, and "No. 3" also has a crayon mark. Darwin used No. 1 as the basis for figure 7.7b on p. 263. Figure 10 in *The Formation of Vegetable Mould through the Action of Worms*. Darwin Papers, Cambridge University Library, DAR 65.104.

colored tracings – "of too great length to be here introduced entire," wrote Darwin (XXVIII:90) – are heavily annotated with Darwin's instructions to the engraver (as are all the extant drawings and proof engravings of the illustrations for *Worms*), which indicate what parts are to be reproduced and seek consistency in the representation of various layers and the objects within them from illustration to illustration (fig. 7.8). By reproducing only "the most characteristic portions" of Joyce's drawings (XXVIII:90), Darwin essentially converted traverse sections – that other staple of geology's visual language – into columnar ones. Yet traverse sections are not absent: several of Darwin's illustrations of the site depict a more extended horizontal view and directional orientation, the remnants of walls analogous to geological beds, "subsided" tile floors analogous to surface topography (fig. 7.9a). Again, a comparison with Darwin's simple (fig. 7.9b) and more elaborate (fig. 7.9c) traverse sections in *Geological Observations on South America* underscores the fundamentally geological nature of the illustrations for *Worms*.[25]

The fact that Darwin copied or borrowed from others' archaeological drawings indicates that he appropriated rather than invented the application of geology's visual conventions to archaeological sites. Nonetheless, his geological approach to the burial of objects by earthworms was present from the outset of his investigations in 1837. As a geological problem – a question of elevation, stratification, subsidence, and denudation – it merited a geological solution and geological illustration. Darwin was, after all, originally more interested in processes and product than in the agent, in "the formation of vegetable mould" more than in worms themselves. While he grew increasingly fascinated with worms, "observations on their habits" only rose to the level of an appendage, both in the book's full title and in its text. And yet the buried object – whether cinders spread on a field, a fallen monolith from Stonehenge, or a Roman villa – was also not the focus of Darwin's attention, but rather a convenient measuring device. It was earthworms, not archaeological curiosity, that took him to Salisbury and Abinger.

His sections, and especially the prominence of them in his text, thus cut against the visual grain. Such illustrations were at best infrequent in archaeological, anthropological, and antiquarian works and were virtually absent from the visitors' guides and books devoted to these same sites. Wright's *The Celt, The Roman, and The Saxon*, for example, contained no sectional representations among its numerous illustrations of ruins. His book on the Wroxeter excavations included three sectional-type drawings, but none was really like Darwin's. The case is similar with Barclay's *Stonehenge*. Thomas Buckman's *Notes on the Roman Villa at Chedworth*, cited by Darwin in *Worms*, contains only a plan of the excavations, maps and ground plans

South.   North.

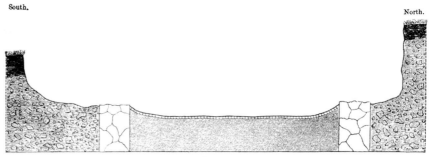

Fig. 14.

A north and south section through the subsided floor of a corridor, paved with tesseræ. Outside the broken-down bounding walls, the excavated ground on each side is shown for a short space. Nature of the ground beneath the tesseræ unknown. Silchester. Scale $\frac{1}{36}$.

Figure 7.9 (a) "A north and south section through the subsided floor of a corridor, paved with tesserae . . ." Wood engraving. Figure 14 from Charles Darwin, *The Formation of Vegetable Mould through the Action of Worms* (London: Murray, 1881), 214. Darwin's "north and south section" is strikingly similar to the traverse sections he had used to illustrate his work on South American geology.

No. 21.—SECTION OF THE TERTIARY FORMATION AT COQUIMBO.

Surface of plain, 252 feet above sea.

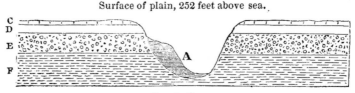

Level of sea.

F—Lower sandstone, with concretions and silicified bones, ⎫ with fossil shells, all, or nearly
E—Upper ferruginous sandstone, with numerous Balani, ⎬ all, extinct.
C and D—Calcareous beds with recent shells. A—Stratified sand in a ravine, also with recent shells.

Figure 7.9 (b) "Section of the tertiary formation at Coquimbo." Wood engraving. Figure 21 from Charles Darwin, *Geological Observations on Coral Reefs, Volcanic Islands, and on South America* (London: Smith, Elder, 1851), III:128.

being of course the most common way to represent such sites for both visitors and readers. Wright's book on Wroxeter contained a number of such plans, including two large foldout ones. Darwin had similar plans for several of the other locations he discusses in *Worms* – including one by Farrer of Abinger and one by Joyce of Silchester – but did not utilize them.[26] As we've seen so often with Darwin, the types of illustration he does *not* use are often as revealing as those he does. In this case, the rejection of maps and ground

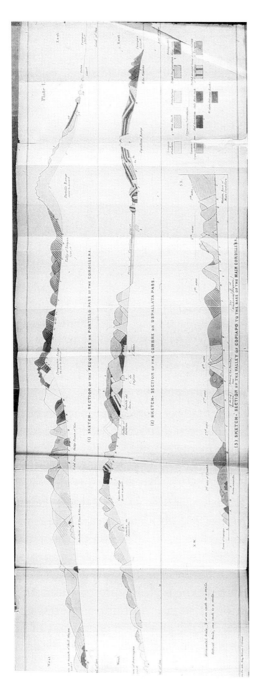

Figure 7.9 (c) Top: "Sketch – Section of the Peuquenes or Portillo Pass of the Cordillera," Middle: "Sketch – Section of the Cumbre or Uspallata Pass," and bottom: "Sketch – Section up the Valley of Copiapo to the Base of the Main Cordillera." Colored lithograph. Plate 1 from Charles Darwin, *Geological Observations on Coral Reefs, Volcanic Islands, and on South America* (London: Smith, Elder, 1851).

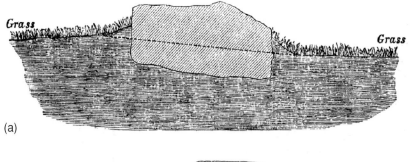

(a)

(b)

Figure 7.10 (a) "Section through one of the fallen Druidical stones at Stonehenge, showing how much it had sunk into the ground" and (b) "Traverse section across a large stone, which had lain on a grass field for 35 years." Wood engravings. Figures 7 and 6 from Charles Darwin, *The Formation of Vegetable Mould through the Action of Worms* (London: Murray, 1881), 156, 151. University of Michigan Libraries.

plans reinforces his fundamentally geological approach. A bird's-eye view of the whole is unnecessary and even distracting when the focus is on surface topography and what exists below ground.

To convert Roman ruins into geological sections was thus to reject the picturesque vision of tourist or traveler. Such was the case as well with Darwin's depiction of Stonehenge (fig. 7.10a): a single, fallen stone, again regarded in geological terms, its subsidence measured against the uneven building up of the turf adjacent to it, much like the pieces of marl and cinders in his Uncle Jos's field, indistinguishable from its companion illustration (fig. 7.10b) of a stone from a Surrey lime kiln pulled down a mere forty years earlier. Here was no gesture to the typical representations of Stonehenge – no reference to the rest of its stones, no human figures, no sense of the surrounding plain. Neither of the two wood engravings of Stonehenge in Wright's *Wanderings of an Antiquary*, the second of which (fig. 7.11) includes one of the fallen outer stones that Darwin pictures, focuses on a single mono-lith, and both include human figures, one of whom in the second illustration carries a shepherd's crook. Another pair of engravings, this one from Barclay's

Figure 7.11 "Stonehenge, From the North." Wood engraving from Thomas Wright, *Wanderings of an Antiquary* (London: Nichols, 1854), facing pages 293–94. This picturesque illustration for Wright's popular antiquarian book includes one of the fallen stones depicted by Darwin in figure 7.10a.

Stonehenge, demonstrates the introduction of the rustic (fig. 7.12). The first, reproduced from Inigo Jones's 1620 work on the monument, contains a pair of seventeenth-century gentlemen and their dog in the foreground, with another pair, one of them sketching, seated on the turf in the left background; the second, taken from the same point by Barclay, replaces the gentleman with sheep and their shepherd. In Turner's dramatic rendering of Stonehenge for his *Picturesque Views in England and Wales* in 1838 (fig. 7.13), the lightning strike has killed or knocked out the shepherd, who lies prostrate in the right foreground, his dog howling, his flock stunned, dead, or scattered.[27] For Ruskin in *Modern Painters*, this work, which set "the standard of storm-drawing" (III:413), represented the divine judgment of the Christian God upon the religion of the Druids (VII:189–91; XXI:223). Darwin's illustration obviously carries no such meaning, but it stands in contrast even to the representations of Jones, Wright, and Barclay. Darwin's view is not panoramic but close up, a geological cross-section in which the horizon is at ground level, and humans are absent. The magnificent monument of the Salisbury plain is put on the same visual level in Darwin's book as the modern detritus of the industrial age. Typically for Darwin, this leveling was accomplished not so much by lowering Stonehenge as by elevating industrial detritus. Lubbock could lament the "modern barbarism" that, for the sake of paving stones and the unimpeded passage of the plow,

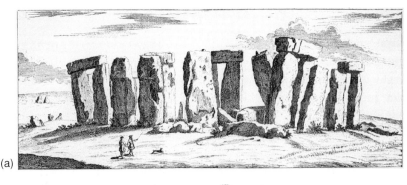

(a)

(b)

Figure 7.12 (a) View of Stonehenge made in 1620 by Inigo Jones and (b) in the late nineteenth century from the same vantage point. Engravings from Edgar Barclay, *Stonehenge and Its Earth-Works* (London: Nutt, 1895), between pages 16 and 17, and between pages 6 and 7. The cultivated gentlemen in Jones's illustration are replaced by sheep and a shepherd in the later one, a reflection of the picturesque introduction of an idealized rusticity.

Figure 7.13 *Stone Henge*. Engraving by R. Wallis from a watercolor by J. M. W. Turner for *Picturesque Views in England and Wales* (London: Longman, 1838). Turner's rendering also contains sheep and shepherd, but it departs dramatically from the tranquility of the picturesque. Ruskin interpreted the work as depicting the Christian God's judgment upon the Druids. Darwin's renderings of Stonehenge stand in stark contrast both to Turner's and to those of the picturesque tradition.

was "destroy[ing] such interesting, I might almost say sacred, monuments of the past," but for Darwin, stones were stones.[28] Glacial boulders, Celtic monuments, Roman pavements, abbey floors, wrecked lime kilns – all afforded the opportunity to study and measure the activity of worms.

Worms was one of Darwin's most favorably reviewed books. Virtually every reader praised Darwin's careful, detailed experiments and his patient collection of evidence. His claims about the significance of worms were almost uniformly accepted. Few so much as mentioned his illustrations, and none saw in them, as they had in the illustrations to the *Expression*, a threat to the fine arts. Contributing to this was undoubtedly the fact, noted by many reviewers, that Darwin's arguments in this work did not invoke natural selection, and his explanations were not dependent on its truth. It was not necessary on this occasion, as it had been in particular with the botany books and the *Expression*, to separate description and theory, endorsing the one while rejecting, or at least withholding acceptance of, the other. But Darwin made clear in his Introduction that skepticism about the stupendous cumulative effects of the lowly earthworm was the same prejudice against which Lyellian geology and natural selection had struggled. Citing a critic of his earlier claims about the activity of worms, Darwin wrote that "Here we have an instance of that inability to sum up the effects of a continually recurrent cause, which has often retarded the progress of science, as formerly in the case of geology, and more recently in that of the principle of evolution" (xxviii: 3). This passage caught the eye of many reviewers, the supporters of Darwinism quoting it as evidence of the book's place in the master's campaign on behalf of natural selection, the skeptics and opponents using it to distinguish between sound, empirically grounded inference and premature speculation, and even to advance a diametrically different reading. An early, anonymous reviewer in the *Spectator* argued that Darwin's demonstration of the earthworm's place in the natural economy, and of its central importance to humans, further bolstered the argument from design, a position echoed in the *Quarterly Review* by Henry Wace, divine and ecclesiastical historian, and future Dean of Canterbury. The anonymous *London Quarterly* reviewer went further. He not only saw the book as providing "the clearest evidences of design," but also suggested that Darwin had written it to show "how much he has been misunderstood" by atheists and agnostics. Indeed, "Mr. Darwin deserves a share of the credit bestowed on the Duke [*sic*] of Bridgewater's treatise-writers, in spite of his having declined to push his inferences to their just conclusions."[29] The cultural threat posed by Darwin's work was rarely forgotten, even when his imagetext's subversive qualities were understated or even unintended.

RUSKIN AND THE GROTESQUE

Ruskin may or may not have read Darwin's *Worms*, but he had certainly
had much to say about the grotesque and the picturesque. From the late
1840s through the following decade, Ruskin theorized extensively about
them in his two major architectural writings, *The Seven Lamps of Architecture* (1849) and *The Stones of Venice* (1851–53), and in the third and fourth
volumes of *Modern Painters* (1856). For Ruskin, as Elizabeth Helsinger has
argued, the noble forms of the grotesque and the picturesque were versions
of, even alternatives to, the conventional sublime of Burke.[30] They were
indices of healthy minds and healthy societies. The ignoble grotesque and
low picturesque, on the other hand, were often markers of the sensuality
and irreverence of both individuals and nations. Darwin's versions of the
grotesque and the picturesque in *Worms* come much closer to the latter than
the former, a fact which would not have surprised Ruskin, given his view
of Darwin's mind and his assessment of Victorian society.

Ruskin's most extensive discussion of the grotesque appeared in the final
volume of *The Stones of Venice*, his main purpose to distinguish between the
noble grotesque of the northern medieval Gothic and the ignoble grotesque
of the late Renaissance. Charting the decline of Venice through the changes
in its architecture, and especially through its architectural ornament, Ruskin
made the grotesque a measure of the mental and moral health of both artist
and nation:

Wherever the human mind is healthy and vigorous in all its proportions, great in
imagination and emotion no less than in intellect, and not overborne by a hardened
and undue pre-eminence of the mere reasoning faculties, there the grotesque will
exist in full energy. And, accordingly, I believe that there is no test of greatness
in periods, nations, or men, more sure than the development, among them or in
them, of a noble grotesque; and no test of comparative smallness or limitation,
of one kind or another, more sure than the absence of grotesque invention, or
incapability of understanding it. (XI:187)

The ability to create and understand the noble grotesque – and noble
architecture as a whole – was for Ruskin centrally and famously connected
throughout *Stones* to a nation's attitude towards work and labor.[31] The workmen of modern England, Ruskin argued, like those of ancient Greece, are
slavish and servile, their imaginations repressed in the repetitious production of the same object or form. The medieval stone-carver at work on the
great Gothic cathedrals, on the other hand, though guided and supervised,
was free to express his imagination.

Refusing to reduce the grotesque to either its comic or serious forms, Ruskin argued that the grotesque always contained "ludicrous" and "fearful" elements, with the former predominating in what he termed the "sportive" grotesque and the latter predominating in the "terrible" or sublime grotesque. The sportive grotesque he associated with play, its noble forms produced by those who play wisely, understanding that life cannot be all solemn and serious, but who also never lose a "deep love of truth, of God, and of humanity" (XI:153) even in recreation, and those who play of necessity, because their work is tiring and irksome. Those who play wisely rarely produce the grotesque in art, and when they do, it is more likely to be serious and of the terrible variety. The noble grotesque produced by those who play of necessity is the grotesquerie of the northern Gothic – the cathedral ornaments of the medieval stone-carvers, whose work was imperfect but joyful and good. When united with the noble form of the picturesque, this form, too, can rise in grandeur and approach the terrible grotesque. The ignoble form of the sportive grotesque, on the other hand, is produced by those who play inordinately. It is the grotesque of the late Renaissance, the work of aristocrats and sensualists, those who make play their life, and in so doing, increase the misery of others. Such men "delight in the contemplation of bestial vice, and the expression of low sarcasm" (XI:145). They are "more sensible to what is ludicrous and accidental, than to what is grave and essential, in any subject . . . Very generally minds of this character are active and able; and many of them are so far conscientious, that they believe their jesting forwards their work. But it is difficult to calculate the harm they do by destroying the reverence which is our best guide into all truth" (XI:155).

Ruskin's terrible grotesque expresses the human fear of sin and death, but it does so in "peculiar temper" and without entering fully into the depth of that fear. The producer of the terrible grotesque approaches his subject in a spirit of apathy, mockery, or unhealthy, uncontrolled imaginativeness. Each of these attitudes is capable of generating noble or ignoble forms of the grotesque, with the distinction lying in the fact that the master of the noble grotesque knows the depth of what he mocks, but the master of the ignoble grotesque does not – his, says Ruskin, is "the laughter of the idiot and the cretin" (XI:167).

Like other Victorian commentators, Ruskin saw Dickens and the caricaturists of *Punch* as the most prominent contemporary exemplars of the grotesque, although modern England, like Venice of the late Renaissance, was a nation of moral, intellectual, and economic disease, and thus a place where the noble grotesque did not thrive. The Dickensian grotesque was for Ruskin a form of the terrible grotesque, that in which fear of sin and death is approached in a spirit of mockery or satire, a special province of the lower classes:

Nothing is so refreshing to the vulgar mind as some exercise of [mockery], more especially on the failings of their superiors; and . . . wherever the lower orders are allowed to express themselves freely, we shall find humour, more or less caustic, becoming a principal feature in their work. The classical and Renaissance manufacturers of modern times having silenced the independent language of the operative, his humour and satire pass away in the word-wit which has of late become the especial study of the group of authors headed by Charles Dickens; all this power was formerly thrown into noble art, and became permanently expressed in the sculptures of the cathedral. (xi:172–73)

The noble terrible grotesque of the Gothic workman is spoken in his own voice, the horrors of sin and death mocked but understood. He is free to lampoon his superiors' failings, but his superiors, themselves noble, allow and encourage this expression, for the good of the workman, and of themselves, and of their society. Modern factory owners, by contrast, have silenced the expressive voices of their workers both politically and artistically. The noble grotesque once given permanent form in cathedrals is now, Ruskin complains, ventriloquized in the "word-wit" of Dickens's novels.

Contemporary caricature, too, even in its highest forms, could not for Ruskin approach the "great imaginative grotesque" (vi:469) of the northern Gothic. When he extended his account of the grotesque to painting and drawing in *Modern Painters*, Ruskin, despite his great respect for the work of such caricaturists as George Cruikshank, John Leech, John Tenniel, and George du Maurier, relegated them to an appendix on "Modern Grotesque" rather than discussing their work in his chapter on the grotesque ideal. Such men have peculiar powers in the observation of character, but they "catch at faults and strangenesses" and have no eye for beauty (vi:469). Their influence over the popular mind is great, and at their best they provide "thorough moral teaching" through their "stern understanding of the nature of evil, and tender human sympathy" (vi:471). As Linley Sambourne's two *Worms*-inspired 1881 caricatures of Darwin for *Punch* demonstrate, however, the work of popular caricaturists was often not thoroughly and unambiguously moral. Sambourne's caricatures added the earthworm to the evolutionary genealogy of humans – the one textually, the other visually – and both suggested Darwinism's disruptive religious and political implications. In the first (fig. 7.14), Darwin's cultural role as skeptic and questioner is figured through his posture (he sits thinking, hand on chin, finger to mouth), the

Figure 7.14 "Punch's Fancy Portraits.–No. 54. Charles Robert Darwin, LL.D., F.R.S."
Wood engraving by Linley Sambourne for *Punch* 81 (22 October 1881): 190.

large question mark formed by the worm that rises out of the grave at which
he has been digging, and the book entitled "Diet of Worms" lying at his
side (a reference to the 1521 Diet at which Luther refused to recant, defying
both the Holy Roman Emperor, Charles V, and the Pope). In the second
(fig. 7.15), the Biblical creation story is represented in evolutionary terms,
the worm that slithers out of the word "Chaos" at the lower left spiraling
through a series of life forms that leads to apes, primitive humans, and finally
to a Victorian gentleman, who doffs his hat to a God-like Darwin seated
on a throne. The first caricature alludes to Job 25:6 in its title, making
literal the Biblical text's metaphorical statement of human insignificance
and unworthiness, while the second's reference to Hamlet's "politic worm"
offers a reminder of another leveling power of worms – that a beggar may
fish with a worm that has eaten of a dead king, and eat of a fish that has
fed on that worm. But is Darwin's status as a scientific Luther and a secular

Figure 7.15 "Man is But a Worm." Wood engraving by Linley Sambourne for *Punch's Almanack for 1882* (6 Dec. 1881).

god being hailed, denounced, or simply noted? Is Darwin like Hamlet in being the scourge of tyrant and regicide, or in being a murderer of the foolish and the innocent? Sambourne's caricatures catch at the strangeness of Darwinism, but their moral ambiguity leaves unclear the depth of their understanding of its potential for evil.

As themselves specimens of the grotesque, neither Darwin's book nor his illustrations of worm castings would have risen for Ruskin to the level of nobility. Viewed with a Ruskinian eye, *Worms* indeed combines the sportive and the terrible. Darwin's playfulness, while not that of the sensualist, was nonetheless that of the person who places value only in the evidence of the senses, and who thus has an eye for what is accidental rather than essential, the ludicrous rather than the grave. His eye for worms and worm castings, like his eye for orchids and sundews, for the blue noses of mandrills and the red faces of blushing girls, is inappropriate and misplaced. While Darwin's mind was clearly active and able and conscientious, Ruskin, as we have seen, had often expressed the view that its influence was pernicious, its focus on material causes destroying, like that of the producer of the ignoble grotesque, "the reverence which is our best guide into all truth." Darwin took up death but refused to fear it, or to see it as the product of sin. His laughter was not that of the idiot and the cretin, and he knew the depth of what he satirized, but he questioned his culture's view of that depth. Confronting his own death, Darwin celebrated the worms that would devour him. All of this made him both contributor to and symptom of the national disease. In studying and illustrating worm castings, Darwin did what Ruskin many years earlier had specifically pronounced against: "I thought it unnecessary to warn the reader," Ruskin wrote of architectural ornament in the first volume of *The Stones of Venice*, "that he was not to copy forms of refuse or corruption; and that, while he might legitimately take the worm or the reptile for a subject of imitation, he was not to study the worm cast" (IX:350). That some of England's modern architects had adorned the walls of their buildings with carvings of organic forms so poorly conceived and executed as to resemble worm castings was for Ruskin a visible sign of aesthetic and national degradation. That Darwin had adorned his book with carefully executed engravings of worm castings would have further confirmed that sense of degradation.

RUSKIN AND THE PICTURESQUE

Ruskin's noble picturesque, like his noble grotesque, was also linked to the sublime. In "The Lamp of Memory" for *The Seven Lamps of Architecture* (1849), Ruskin ascribed the distinctive character of the picturesque to what he called "parasitical sublimity." That is, the picturesque can achieve sublime effects, but it does so indirectly, by depicting objects or forms not in themselves sublime, but suggestive of other objects or forms that are. The parasitical sublimity of the picturesque was "a sublimity dependent on the accidents, or on the least essential characters, of the objects to which it belongs" (VIII:236), as the ruggedness of a cottage roof may suggest a sublime mountain aspect even though the cottage itself is not a sublime object. This view of the picturesque's inferiority to the sublime reflected Ruskin's recently developed ambivalence towards the picturesque after a period of youthful infatuation.[32] On the one hand, he was drawn to the picturesque's emphasis on nature and the potential in its use of ruins to imply a moral thematics of decay – the downfall of tyranny and corrupt empire in medieval castles and Roman monuments, the end of Catholic superstition in moldering abbeys.

On the other, he was troubled by the picturesque's tendency to aestheticize natural forms, ruined buildings, and human figures – to convert a grove of trees or a formation of rock, an ancient monument or a crumbling castle, a solitary peasant or a group of rustics, into a mere compositional element, without regard for the individual detail of the first, without understanding of the world of the second, and without sympathy for the impoverishment of the third. Ruskin, in other words, understood what recent scholars of the picturesque have demonstrated so vividly: that the picturesque of the late eighteenth and early nineteenth centuries aestheticized poverty and ruin, idealizing a landscape that had been rapidly disappearing as commons were enclosed and converted into farmland, and as the factories of the industrial revolution sprang up in the countryside and then migrated to new manufacturing towns, boons to landowners and industrialists but economically devastating to the rural poor.[33]

In the years that followed, Ruskin set out to expose the picturesque's sentimentalizing of poverty and to restore the moral meaning of ruins. The latter mission was spectacularly instantiated in *The Stones of Venice*, while the former was taken up in the fourth volume of *Modern Painters*. The problem he addressed in *Modern Painters* was, as usual, one largely of his own making. For Ruskin, the rise of the picturesque in the seventeenth century was part of the larger decline of art begun in the Renaissance. The "delight in ruin" that he argued was the characteristic feature of the picturesque was "perhaps the most suspicious and questionable of all the characters distinctively belonging to our temper, and art" (VI:9). Yet his beloved Turner was without question a picturesque painter. Thus Ruskin endeavored to distinguish between the "noble" or "Turnerian" picturesque and its "low" or "surface" form, seeing in Turner's work a refusal to take pleasure in the depiction of poverty and decay.

As so often in Ruskin's work, his discussion melded aesthetics, morality, science, and political economy. Ruskin's analysis of the picturesque and its "delight in ruin" opened volume IV of *Modern Painters*, which was devoted to "Mountain Beauty" and expanded on the first volume's demonstration of Turner's superiority over all other landscapists as a painter of geological truths. The low and noble picturesque lay for Ruskin on a continuum, the precise position depending on the level of the artist's sympathy for his subject. In the low picturesque, the artist is essentially "heartless," feeling only delight, not regret, at the sight of ruin and disorder (VI:19). He takes pleasure in the mere outward appearance, the variety of color and form, of the objects he depicts. The sublimity of the low picturesque, then, is not merely parasitical but unintended – the artist is unaware of the cottage roof's mountain aspect. The sublimity of the noble picturesque, on the other hand, lies beneath the surface features and is consciously sought there by the artist. The noble picturesque expresses not outward form but inner character, and that inner character is one "of *suffering*, of *poverty*, or *decay*, nobly endured by unpretending strength of heart. Nor only unpretending, but unconscious. If there be visible pensiveness in the building, as in a ruined abbey, it becomes, or claims to become, beautiful; but the picturesqueness is in the unconscious suffering" (VI:14–15, original emphasis). The epitome for Ruskin of a nobly picturesque building was the tower of the church at Calais – weather-beaten but strong, old but still useful, expressive of "that agedness in the midst of active life which binds the old and new into harmony" (VI:11). Turner was the modern artist who refused to aestheticize poverty and ruin and was most able to capture this inner character of unconscious suffering. In England, and in the low picturesque, by contrast, the past was treated as past and dead. Ruins were specimens of the past, objects of nostalgia, "useless and piteous, feebly or fondly garrulous of better days," part of the "entire denial of all human calamity and care" (VI:11, 15). Yet the painter or lover of the low picturesque is not a moral monster, says Ruskin. Simple-minded and of limited sympathy, he is nonetheless kind-hearted and humble, and he understands that there is often as much happiness in a peasant's cottage as a king's palace. Thus the low picturesque should be cultivated, for it can lead to "a truer sympathy with the poor, and a better understanding of the right ways of helping them," and this in turn would cause the English to stop "destroy[ing] so many ancient monuments, in order to erect 'handsome' streets and shops instead" (VI:22). It was sentiments such as these that made it possible for Lubbock to invoke Ruskin in his campaign to protect Britain's ruins from destruction by modern barbarians.

Ruskin could only have seen the illustrations of monuments and ruins in *Worms* as a case of the low picturesque, another example of the good-hearted Darwin's limited and misguided vision. Inviting Lubbock to Brantwood in 1887, apologizing for "all the ill-tempered things I've said about insects and evolution," Ruskin wrote that "you will see the Lake Country first from my terrace – where . . . Darwin has walked also" (XXXVII:590). When Darwin walked that terrace eight years earlier, looking out across Coniston Water, Ruskin must have heard his guest's expressions of picturesque pleasure. From their meetings over the years, Ruskin appreciated Darwin's simplicity and humility, especially towards nature (XIX:xliv–xlv), but he much lamented the dangerous tendencies to which these traits led in Darwin's published works, as he explained in a letter to Darwin's son-in-law, R. B. Litchfield, just after that 1879 visit:

It has indeed been a great pleasure to me to be brought into some nearer and kinder relations with Mr. Darwin; but you must not think I did not before recognize in him all that you speak of so affectionately. There is no word in any of my books of disrespect towards *him*, though I profoundly regret that the very simplicity and humility of his character prevents his separating what of accurately observed truth he has taught us from the wild and impious foolishness of the popular views of our day. (xxxviii:334; original emphasis)

Like the painter and lover of the low picturesque, Darwin was no moral monster. But his understanding and sympathies had not been adequately cultivated, and as a result he failed to appreciate the moral meanings in the peacock's tail, the orchid's form, the maiden's blush, or the landscape's aspect. If he did not aestheticize poverty or take delight in ruins, his conversion of picturesque scenes into geological sections did not allow for the expression of unconscious suffering. Darwin's was not a noble, Turnerian picturesque. When he looked at a beautiful turf-covered expanse, he saw the leveling action of worms. When he visited Stonehenge, he did so not to marvel at its vastness or interpret its lessons but to dig at the base of its monoliths for evidence of worm castings. When he stood in the trenches of the Roman villa at Abinger, he examined not the ruins but the soil. Litchfield, like Ruskin an ardent supporter of the Working Men's College, knew the right ways to help the poor, but Darwin's work contributed to the "wild and impious foolishness" – the irreverent materialism – of the present day.

GEOLOGY AND LANDSCAPE: SCIENTIFIC NATURALISM AND THE SCIENTIFIC IMAGINATION

Closing his first "literary child," his *Journal of Researches* of the *Beagle* voyage, some forty years earlier, Darwin had surveyed "the advantages and disadvantages, the pains and pleasures" of such a journey. "Pleasure derived from beholding the scenery and the general aspect of the various countries," he wrote, "has decidedly been the most constant and highest source of enjoyment." But for Darwin, landscape could become monotonous without scientific understanding of its different features. Pleasure in landscape, he went on to say, "depends chiefly on an acquaintance with the individual parts of each view; I am strongly induced to believe that as in music, the person who understands every note will, if he also possesses a proper taste, more thoroughly enjoy the whole, so he who examines each part of a fine view may also thoroughly comprehend the full and combined effect." A traveler who also understands botany and geology is thus at an aesthetic advantage over one who does not. With this, the author of *Modern*

Painters would certainly have agreed. But when Ruskin showed Darwin his Turners, Darwin withheld out of politeness what he later confessed: "that he could make out absolutely nothing of what Mr. Ruskin saw in them."[34] Ruskin would not have been surprised. He knew of Darwin's ignorance of good art and had lamented Darwin's inability to draw. In his elementary treatise on drawing and painting, *The Laws of Fésole* (1877–78), two parts of which he sent to Darwin after Darwin's 1879 visit to Brantwood, Ruskin wrote that "Anatomy is necessary in the education of surgeons; botany in that of apothecaries; and geology in that of miners. But none of the three will enable you to draw a man, a flower, or a mountain" (xv:360). That a man who could not appreciate Turner converted picturesque ruins into geological sections, and illustrated his book with engravings made from photographs of worm castings, was to be bewailed rather than wondered at.

In his youth, Ruskin, like Darwin, was drawn most strongly to geology. When in London he attended Geological Society meetings, hearing Darwin's debut paper early in 1837 on the elevation of the coast of Chile; when the two young men met in Oxford a few months later, at the home of Ruskin's mentor William Buckland, the famous geologist and Bridgewater author, they talked all evening.[35] Elected a Fellow of the Geological Society in 1840, Ruskin later punningly recalled that it had then been "the summit of my earthly ambition" to become its President (xxvi:97). At the Oxford meeting of the British Association for the Advancement of Science in 1847, he served as one of the secretaries to the Geological section (viii:xxv). The first and fourth volumes of *Modern Painters* were as much geological as artistic treatises, devoted to the proposition that Turner was a geologist without knowing it. Writing in reference to the fourth volume's geological discussions, John James Ruskin declared of his son in 1858 that "from Boyhood he has been an artist, but he has been a geologist from Infancy."[36] Nor did his interest wane with the completion of *Modern Painters*. In the 1860s came a number of geological talks and articles, many for the *Geological Magazine*. From 1875 to 1883 Ruskin issued his current geological lectures – most originally delivered at Oxford or the London Institution – under the title *Deucalion: Collected Studies of the Lapse of Waves, and Life of Stones*.

In matters geological, Darwin was not Ruskin's whipping boy. That honor, of course, was reserved for Darwin's friend and ally, John Tyndall. Ruskin's hostility towards Tyndall had both personal and intellectual causes. Ruskin attacked Tyndall for what he regarded as Tyndall's ill-treatment of J. D. Forbes, whom Ruskin had met in the Alps in 1844, in a controversy over glacier theory that flared intermittently from the 1850s well into the 1870s. Tyndall was also one of scientific naturalism's chief publicists, championing

effects of undulatory geological forces – but that very tenuousness suggests the extent to which Ruskin saw the work of the scientific naturalists, their accounts of rocks and birds and fish and flowers, as interconnected, and not merely at a general level.

Three years later still, with Darwin lying dead in Westminster Abbey, Ruskin returned again to *Deucalion*, and in doing so, to its purpose. The installments of the work issued thus far, Ruskin admits, contain his most recent geological work rather than collecting and arranging his earlier, scattered writings. The previous installment on snakes, moreover, seems to have strayed even further from the volume's ostensible purpose. And so it is necessary, he says, to explain his "modes of thought and reasoning" in "matters of higher science than geology" if he is to bring order to the volume. Such an explanation would not have been needed twenty years ago, but since the early 1860s – the time frame is surely significant – "the laws of decent thought and rational question have been so far transgressed (even in our universities, where the moral philosophy they once taught is now only remembered as an obscure tradition, and the natural science in which they are proud, presented only as an impious conjecture)" that it cannot now be taken for granted (xxvi:333–34). Natural science sundered from moral philosophy, confident in its ability to account even for the immaterial by reference only to the material, is for Ruskin a social and political calamity as well as an individual and moral one: "the discoverers of modern science have, almost without exception, provoked new furies of avarice, and new tyrannies of individual interest; or else have directly contributed to the means of violent and sudden destruction, already incalculably too potent in the hands of the idle and the wicked" (xxvi:339). The link between scientific naturalism and laissez-faire political economy could not be more forcefully asserted: the "discoverers of modern science" are fueling the greed and self-interest that oppress the hard-working poor and destroy the natural environment. To rest pridefully satisfied in the demonstration that a snake is a lizard with its legs dropped off, is to be without the most important wisdom – for good and ill – we may learn of serpents. From the hubris of scientific naturalism it is in Ruskin's eyes a short and inexorable step to the destruction of the nature it studies – living and nonliving, human and nonhuman, alike.

His alternative genealogies for the snake, Ruskin admits, are virtually impossible to demonstrate empirically. And so his lecture must itself appear "superficially comic, or at least grotesque," a "piece of badinage" rather than a serious riposte to Huxley (xxvi:343). But like the practitioner of the noble grotesque, Ruskin knows the depth of that which he mocks. He playfully figures the serpent in forms more marvelous than Huxley's, yet his subject – sin and death – is more terrible, and his love of truth extends, as it does for all those who play wisely, to God and humanity. His lecture, Ruskin says, must be understood as an illustration "of the harmonies and intervals in the being of the existent animal creation – whether it be developed or undeveloped." By 1883 Ruskin is willing to concede the possibility that natural selection is no occult power, no mere phantasm of Darwin's brain. He refuses to accept, however, that such a theory, even if true, is adequate, and he denies that its application to metaphysical issues is either revealing or valid:

The lower conditions of intellect which are concerned in the pursuit of natural science . . . are . . . dependent for their perfection on the lower feelings of admiration and affection which can be attached to material things: these also – the curiosity and ingenuity of man – live by admiration and love; but they differ from the imaginative powers in that they are concerned with things seen – not with the evidences of things unseen – and it would be well for them if the understanding of this restriction prevented them in the present day as severely from speculation as it does from devotion. (XXVI:338)

The curiosity and ingenuity of men such as Darwin, Ruskin acknowledges, is rooted in admiration and love. But admiration and love for material things is a lower form of intellectual exercise, and metaphysical speculation based on material things is impious. The truths of landscape were to be found in Turner, not Tyndall. The morality of aesthetics was to be found in nature, not in natural selection.

Darwin, of course, had seen things differently.

Notes

1 SEEING THINGS: CHARLES DARWIN AND VICTORIAN VISUAL CULTURE

1. W. J. T. Mitchell, *Picture Theory: Essays on Verbal and Visual Representation* (Chicago: University of Chicago Press, 1994), 5.
2. Providing a full list of sources for this point would be tantamount to launching a bibliography of virtually the entire Darwin industry. Some of the works I have in mind, however, are Stephen G. Alter, *Darwinism and the Linguistic Image: Language, Race, and Natural Theology in the Nineteenth Century* (Baltimore: Johns Hopkins University Press, 1999); Gillian Beer, *Darwin's Plots: Evolutionary Narrative in Darwin, George Eliot and Nineteenth-Century Fiction* (London: Routledge, 1983; 2nd edn. Cambridge: Cambridge University Press, 2000); Michael Ghiselin, *The Triumph of the Darwinian Method* (Berkeley: University of California Press, 1969); James Krasner, *The Entangled Eye: Visual Perception and the Representation of Nature in Post-Darwinian Narrative* (New York: Oxford University Press, 1992); George Levine, *Darwin and the Novelists: Patterns of Science in Victorian Fiction* (Cambridge: Harvard University Press, 1988); Dov Ospovat, *The Development of Darwin's Theory: Natural History, Natural Theology, and Natural Selection, 1838–1859* (Cambridge: Cambridge University Press, 1981); Robert Young, *Darwin's Metaphor: Nature's Place in Victorian Culture* (Cambridge: Cambridge University Press, 1985); various publications by Peter Bowler, Janet Browne, Sandra Herbert, M. J. S. Hodge, James Moore, Michael Ruse, and S. S. Schweber; and of course the ongoing Darwin Correspondence Project.
3. Martin J. S. Rudwick, "The Emergence of a Visual Language for Geological Science, 1760–1840," *History of Science* 14 (1976): 149–95, with the quotation from 184n10, original emphasis.
4. The bibliographic information cited here is taken from R. B. Freeman, *The Works of Charles Darwin: An Annotated Bibliographic Handlist*, 2nd edn. (Folkestone: Dawson, 1977); Phillip Prodger, *An Annotated Catalogue of the Illustrations of Human and Animal Expression from the Collection of Charles Darwin* (Lewiston, NY: Mellen, 1998); Prodger, "Concordance of Illustrations," in Charles Darwin, *The Expression of the Emotions in Man and Animals*, ed. Paul Ekman (New York: Oxford University Press, 1998), 417–23.

5. Darwin to Murray, 23 Apr. 1845, 31 May 1845, and 4 June 1845; *The Correspondence of Charles Darwin*, ed. Frederick Burkhardt et al., 14 vols. to date (Cambridge: Cambridge University Press, 1985–) III:180, 196, 203.

6. Darwin to Murray, 25 Jan. 1860, *Correspondence* VIII:51.

7. In addition to the work cited above, see Phillip Prodger, "Illustration as Strategy in Charles Darwin's *The Expression of the Emotions in Man and Animals*," *Inscribing Science: Scientific Texts and the Materiality of Communication*, ed. Timothy Lenoir (Stanford: Stanford University Press, 1998), 140–81; and "Photography and *The Expression of the Emotions*," in Darwin, *Expression of the Emotions*, ed. Ekman, 399–410.

8. 31 May 1859; *Correspondence* VII:300, original emphasis. Darwin continued to remind Murray of the importance of the diagram during the preparation of subsequent editions of the *Origin*, even of the last one in 1872. See Darwin to Murray, 2 Apr. 1859, 14 May 1859, 26 Dec. 1859, 5 Dec. 1860, 8 Jan. 1872; *Correspondence* VII:277, 298, 455; VIII:515; and letter 8152 in *A Calendar of the Correspondence of Charles Darwin, 1821–1882*, 2nd edn. (Cambridge: Cambridge University Press, 1994).

9. *The Origin of Species By Charles Darwin: A Variorum Text*, ed. Morse Peckham (Philadelphia: University of Pennsylvania Press, 1959), 273–74. The wording is that of the first edition, although subsequent revisions to the passage were minor.

10. Beer, *Darwin's Plots*, 38. For Beer's comments on the diagram, see 92–94. See Alter, *Darwinism and the Linguistic Image*, 28–34, 108–45 for an extended discussion of the relation of Darwin's diagram to similar tree-like representations of the development of languages. For a rhetorical reading of the diagram, see John Angus Campbell, "Why Was Darwin Believed? Darwin's *Origin* and the Problem of Intellectual Evolution," *Configurations* 11 (2003): 211–15.

11. The diagram originally appeared at Darwin's insistence in fold-out format and oriented as I have displayed it. This enhanced the diagram's visual similarity both to taxonomic trees and to geological sections. Modern editions of the *Origin*, however, while retaining the diagram's original location in the text, tend to print it on its own page and rotate it counter-clockwise by 90°, thereby reducing these similarities. My reading draws on Rudwick, "Emergence of a Visual Language."

12. Ann Shelby Blum, *Picturing Nature: American Nineteenth-Century Zoological Illustration* (Princeton: Princeton University Press, 1993), 122, 199, 142.

13. Blum, *Picturing Nature*, 14–15.

14. See Wilfrid Blunt and William T. Stearn, *The Art of Botanical Illustration*, new edn. (London: Antique Collectors Club/Royal Botanic Gardens, 1994), and Gill Saunders, *Picturing Plants: An Analytical History of Botanical Illustration* (Berkeley: University of California Press, 1995).

15. Blunt and Stearn, *Botanical Illustration*, 236–43 and Charlotte Klonk, *Science and the Perception of Nature: British Landscape Art in the Late Eighteenth and Early Nineteenth Centuries* (New Haven: Yale University Press, 1996), 37.

16. Lorraine Daston and Peter Galison, "The Image of Objectivity," *Representations* 40 (1992): 81–128. Three recent major studies on the importance of objectivity and distance for Victorian science and culture are Amanda Anderson, *The Powers of Distance: Cosmopolitanism and the Cultivation of Detachment* (Princeton: Princeton University Press, 2001), George Levine, *Dying to Know: Scientific Epistemology and Narrative in Victorian England* (Chicago: University of Chicago Press, 2002), and David Wayne Thomas, *Cultivating Victorians: Liberal Culture and the Aesthetic* (Philadelphia: University of Pennsylvania Press, 2004). *Gentlemen of Science* is the title of Jack Morrell and Arnold Thackeray's study of the early years of the British Association for the Advancement of Science (Oxford: Oxford University Press, 1981). The importance of gentlemanly values in the formation of British science during the seventeenth century is demonstrated in Steven Shapin and Simon Schaffer, *Leviathan and the Air Pump: Hobbes, Boyle, and the Experimental Life* (Princeton: Princeton University Press, 1985) and Steven Shapin, *A Social History of Truth* (Chicago: University of Chicago Press, 1994).

17. [8th Duke of Argyll, George Douglas Campbell], "The Supernatural," *Edinburgh Review* 116 (1862): 392.

18. Balfour Stewart and P. G. Tait, *The Unseen Universe, or, Physical Speculations on a Future State*, 3rd edn. (New York: Macmillan, 1875), 128–39.

19. [T. S. Baynes], "Darwin on Expression," *Edinburgh Review* 137 (1873): 492–93, 497.

20. "Science and Superstition," *Punch* 64 (18 Jan. 1873): 21.

21. For a collection of essays by art historians on specific cases of Darwin's influence on nineteenth-century visual culture in America, France, and Germany, see Linda Nochlin and Martha Lucy, eds., *The Darwin Effect: Evolution and Nineteenth-Century Visual Culture*, special issue of *Nineteenth-Century Art Worldwide* 2.2 (2003), accessed 28 Oct. 2005. http://19thc-artworldwide.org/spring_03. For a study of the relationship between words and images in discussions of cloud phenomena in Victorian scientific and visual culture, see Katharine Anderson, "Looking at the Sky: The Visual Context of Victorian Meteorology," *British Journal for the History of Science* 36 (2003): 301–32. For Gould's work on the visual representation of evolution as progressive and linear, see *Wonderful Life: The Burgess Shale and the Nature of History* (New York: Norton, 1989), 23–52. Adrian Desmond and James Moore's *Darwin* (New York: Warner, 1992) contains numerous reproductions of such caricatures and cartoons, as does Janet Browne's two-volume biography, *Charles Darwin: Voyaging* (New York: Knopf, 1995) and *Charles Darwin: The Power of Place* (New York: Knopf, 2002).

22. *Fun* 16 n.s. (1872): 203, 209, 261, and 17 n.s. (1873): 44, 68, 73–74.

23. In his biography of Rejlander, *Father of Art Photography: O. G. Rejlander, 1813–1875* (Greenwich, CT: New York Graphic Society, 1973), Edgar Yoxall Jones claims that 60,000 24×30 cm prints and 250,000 cartes-de-visite were produced (38). Philip Prodger regards these numbers as exaggerated but agrees that "Ginx's Baby" was one of the most widely reproduced photographs of the period. See

"Rejlander, Darwin, and the Evolution of 'Ginx's Baby,'" *History of Photography* 23 (1999): 260–68.

24. [Baynes], "Darwin on Expression," 516.

25. *Art Journal* n.s. 12 (1873): 31.

26. C. Stephen Finley, in *Nature's Covenant: Figures of Landscape in Ruskin* (University Park: Penn State University Press, 1992), has argued that the theory of beauty developed in the *Modern Painters II* is consistent with comments in the later volumes and in the rest of Ruskin's work. This challenges the prevailing characterization of Ruskin's aesthetics most influentially articulated by George P. Landow in *The Aesthetic and Critical Theories of John Ruskin* (Princeton: Princeton University Press, 1971), but even Landow sees Ruskin as remaining committed to his fundamental positions. I would add that the public, while sometimes puzzled by seemingly contradictory individual judgments, did not regard Ruskin's general principles as contradictory. On the Ruskin-inspired moral language of English art criticism in the latter part of the century, see Kate Flint, "Moral Judgement and the Language of English Art Criticism 1870–1910," *Oxford Art Journal* 6.2 (1983): 58–66.

27. John Ruskin, *Modern Painters*, vol. II, *The Works of John Ruskin*, Library Edition, ed. E. T. Cooke and Alexander Wedderburn, 39 vols. (London: George Allen, 1903–1912), IV:35. Subsequent references to Ruskin's work are from this edition and are noted parenthetically in the text.

28. Elizabeth K. Helsinger, *Ruskin and the Art of the Beholder* (Cambridge: Harvard University Press, 1982). On Ruskin's approaches to science and art, see also Finley, *Nature's Covenant*; Patricia Ball, *The Science of Aspects: The Changing Role of Fact in the Work of Coleridge, Ruskin, and Hopkins* (London: Athlone, 1971); Paul L. Sawyer, *Ruskin's Poetic Argument, The Design of the Major Works* (Ithaca: Cornell University Press, 1985), chs. 6, 11; and Jonathan Smith, *Fact and Feeling: Baconian Science and the Nineteenth-Century Literary Imagination* (Madison: University of Wisconsin Press, 1994), ch. 5.

29. Stephen Finley, "Ruskin, Darwin, and the Crisis of Natural Form," *Cahiers Victoriens et Edouardiens* 25 (1987): 7–24; Robert Hewison, *John Ruskin: The Argument of the Eye* (Princeton: Princeton University Press, 1976); Frederick Kirchoff, "A Science Against Sciences: Ruskin's Floral Mythology," *Nature and the Victorian Imagination*, ed. U. C. Knoepflmacher and G. B. Tennyson (Berkeley: University of California Press, 1977), 246–58; Raymond E. Fitch, *The Poison Sky: Myth and Apocalypse in Ruskin* (Athens: Ohio University Press, 1982); Francis O'Gorman, "The Eagle and the Whale: John Ruskin's Argument with John Tyndall," *Time and Tide: Ruskin and Science*, ed. Michael Wheeler (London: Pilkington, 1996), 45–64; Beverly Seaton, "Considering the Lilies: Ruskin's 'Proserpina' and Other Victorian Flower Books," *Victorian Studies* 28 (1984–85): 255–82; Paul Sawyer, "Ruskin and Tyndall: The Poetry of Matter and the Poetry of Spirit," *Victorian Science and Victorian Values: Literary Perspectives*, ed. James Paradis and Thomas Postlewait (New Brunswick, NJ: Rutgers University Press, 1985), 217–46; Sawyer, *Ruskin's Poetic Argument*, ch. 11; Dinah Birch, "Ruskin and the Science of *Proserpina*," *New Approaches to Ruskin*, ed. Robert

Hewison (London: Routledge, 1982), 142–56; Birch, *Ruskin's Myths* (Oxford: Clarendon, 1988), 172–94; Anthony Lacy Gully, "Sermons in Stone: Ruskin and Geology," *John Ruskin and the Victorian Eye* (New York: Abrams, 1993), 158–83.

30. Ed Block, Jr., "Evolutionist Psychology and Aesthetics: *The Cornhill Magazine, 1875–1880,*" *Journal of the History of Ideas* 45 (1984): 465–75; Kate Flint, *The Victorians and the Visual Imagination* (Cambridge: Cambridge University Press, 2000), 38, 244–51; Regenia Gagnier, *The Insatiability of Human Wants: Economics and Aesthetics in Market Society* (Chicago: University of Chicago Press, 2000) and "Production, Reproduction, and Pleasure in Victorian Aesthetics and Economics," *Victorian Sexual Dissidence*, ed. Richard Dellamora (Chicago: University of Chicago Press, 1999), 127–46; Timothy Lenoir, "The Eye as Mathematician: Clinical Practice, Instrumentation, and Helmholtz's Construction of an Empiricist Theory of Vision," *Hermann von Helmholtz and the Foundations of Nineteenth-Century Science*, ed. David Cahan (Berkeley: University of California Press, 1994), 109–53; Jonathan Smith, "Grant Allen, Physiological Aesthetics, and the Dissemination of Darwin's Botany," *Science Serialized: Representations of the Sciences in Nineteenth-Century Periodicals*, ed. Geoffrey Cantor and Sally Shuttleworth (Cambridge: MIT Press, 2004), 285–306; R. Steven Turner, *In the Eye's Mind: Vision and the Helmholtz–Hering Controversy* (Princeton: Princeton University Press, 1994).

31. Darwin to Erasmus, 21 Dec. 1828, and Darwin to Whitley, 23 July 1834; *Correspondence* 1:70–71, 397.

32. Darwin to W. D. Fox, 3 Nov. 1829, and Darwin to Whitley, 23 July 1834; *Correspondence* 1:95, 397.

33. William Ivins, *Prints and Visual Communications* (London: Routledge, 1953), 93.

34. Jonathan Crary, *Techniques of the Observer: On Vision and Modernity in the Nineteenth Century* (Cambridge: MIT Press, 1990). Recent studies on Victorian visual culture include Patricia Anderson, *The Printed Image and the Transformation of Popular Culture 1790–1860* (Oxford: Clarendon, 1991); Carol Armstrong, *Scenes in a Library: Reading the Photograph in the Book* (Cambridge: MIT Press, 1998); Carol T. Christ and John O. Jordan, eds., *Victorian Literature and the Victorian Visual Imagination* (Berkeley: University of California Press, 1995); Flint, *The Victorians and the Visual Imagination*; Jennifer Green-Lewis, *Framing the Victorians: Photography and the Culture of Realism* (Ithaca: Cornell University Press, 1996); B. E. Maidment, *Reading Popular Prints, 1790–1870* (Manchester: Manchester University Press, 1996); Martin Meisel, *Realizations: Narrative, Pictorial, and Theatrical Arts in Nineteenth-Century England* (Princeton: Princeton University Press, 1983); Stephen Oettermann, *The Panorama: History of a Mass Medium*, trans. Deborah Lucas Schneider (New York: Zone, 1997); Peter W. Sinnema, *Dynamics of the Pictured Page: Representing the Nation in the Illustrated London News* (Aldershot: Ashgate, 1998); Christopher Wood, *Victorian Panorama: Paintings of Victorian Life* (London: Faber and Faber, 1976). Studies

of the book trade and visual media on which I have relied are Patricia Anderson, "Illustration," *Victorian Periodicals and Victorian Society*, ed. J. Don Vann and Rosemary T. VanArsdel (Toronto: University of Toronto Press, 1994), 127–42; M. Susan Barger and William B. White, *The Daguerreotype: Nineteenth-Century Technology and Modern Science* (Washington, DC: Smithsonian Institution Press, 1991); Eric De Maré, *The Victorian Woodblock Illustrators* (London: Gordon Fraser, 1980); Paul Goldman, *Victorian Illustrated Books 1850–1870: The Heyday of Wood Engraving* (London: British Museum Press, 1994); Basil Hunnisett, *Steel-Engraved Book Illustration in England* (London: Scolar Press, 1980); Estelle Jussim, *Visual Communications and the Graphic Arts: Photographic Technologies in the Nineteenth Century* (New York: Bowker, 1974); Kenneth Lindley, *The Woodblock Engravers* (Newton Abbot: David and Charles, 1970); Percy Muir, *Victorian Illustrated Books* (London: Batsford, 1971); Michael Twyman, *Lithography 1800–1850* (London: Oxford University Press, 1970); Geoffrey Wakeman, *Victorian Book Illustration: The Technical Revolution* (Newton Abbot: David and Charles, 1973).

35. Brian S. Baigrie, ed., *Picturing Knowledge: Historical and Philosophical Problems Concerning the Use of Art in Science* (Toronto: University of Toronto Press, 1996).

36. Jean Anker, *Bird Books and Bird Art: An Outline of the Literary History and Iconography of Descriptive Ornithology* (Copenhagen: Levin and Munksgaard, 1938). Blunt's book first appeared in 1950.

37. Christine Jackson, *Bird Illustrators: Some Artists in Early Lithography* (London: Witherby, 1975); *Wood Engravings of Birds* (London: Witherby, 1978); *Bird Etchings: The Illustrators and Their Books, 1655–1855* (Ithaca: Cornell University Press, 1985); Maureen Lambourne, *The Art of Bird Illustration* (London: Wellfleet, 1990).

38. Martin J. S. Rudwick, *The Great Devonian Controversy* (Chicago: University of Chicago Press, 1985); Rudwick, *Scenes From Deep Time: Early Pictorial Representations of the Prehistoric World* (Chicago: University of Chicago Press, 1992), 1. For Shapin and Schaffer's original articulation of "literary technology," see *Leviathan and the Air Pump*. In *Picturing Nature*, Blum explicitly locates her study of nineteenth-century American zoological illustration in relation to Rudwick's work.

39. Ivins, *Prints and Visual Communications*, especially ch. 3; Jussim, *Visual Communications and the Graphic Arts*. The stimulating and idiosyncratic work of Edward R. Tufte also focuses on the need for clarity and economy in the visual communication of information, but Tufte uses only historical examples to analyze how to achieve these ends. See his *The Visual Display of Quantitative Information* (Cheshire, CT: Graphics Press, 1983); *Envisioning Information* (Cheshire, CT: Graphics Press, 1990); and *Visual Explanations: Images and Quantities, Evidence and Narrative* (Cheshire, CT: Graphics Press, 1997).

40. Rudwick, "Visual Language," 152, 182 (original emphasis). The other historian of nineteenth-century science to stress the importance of illustration as early

as the 1970s, David Knight, has conceptualized the image–text relationship in similar terms. See *Zoological Illustration: An Essay Towards a History of Printed Zoological Pictures* (Folkestone, Kent: Dawson, 1977) and "Scientific Theory and Visual Language," *The Natural Science and the Arts: Aspects of Interaction from the Renaissance to the Twentieth Century*, Uppsala Studies in the History of Art 22, ed. Allan Ellenius (Uppsala: Almqvist, 1985), 106–24.

41. Rudwick, *Scenes*, 255n.

42. Blum, *Picturing Nature*, 6–7.

43. Bruno Latour, "Drawing Things Together," *Representation in Scientific Practice*, ed. Michael Lynch and Steve Woolgar (Cambridge, MA: MIT Press, 1990), 39. This essay is a reprint with minor changes of Latour's "Visualization and Cognition: Thinking With Eyes and Hands," *Knowledge and Society* 6 (1986): 1–40. For inscription and inscription devices, see Bruno Latour and Steve Woolgar, *Laboratory Life: The Social Construction of Scientific Facts* (London: Sage, 1979), ch. 2. In response to criticism, Latour has recently offered the term "in-formation" as a synonym for inscription to emphasize the material process of transformation, and he has argued that immutable mobiles are immutable only in certain key features rather than in toto, and that the immutability of these features is not unproblematic. See "How to Be Iconophilic in Art, Science, and Religion?" *Picturing Science, Producing Art*, ed. Caroline A. Jones and Peter Galison (New York: Routledge, 1998), 418–40, especially 425–26.

44. Lynch and Woolgar, *Representation in Scientific Practice*, viii (original emphasis).

45. Latour, "Drawing Things Together," 42, 46.

46. Barbara Maria Stafford, *Body Criticism: Imaging the Unseen in Enlightenment Art and Medicine* (Cambridge: MIT Press, 1991); Ludmilla Jordanova, *Sexual Visions: Images of Gender in Science and Medicine between the Eighteenth and Twentieth Centuries* (Madison: University of Wisconsin Press, 1989); Sander L. Gilman, *Seeing the Insane* (New York: Wiley, 1982); Gilman, *Disease and Representation: Images of Illness from Madness to AIDS* (Ithaca: Cornell University Press, 1988); Gilman, *Picturing Health and Illness: Images of Identity and Illness* (Baltimore: Johns Hopkins University Press, 1995); W. J. T. Mitchell, *The Last Dinosaur Book* (Chicago: University of Chicago Press, 1998).

47. Timothy Lenoir, ed. *Inscribing Science: Scientific Texts and the Materiality of Communication* (Stanford: Stanford University Press, 1998); Jones and Galison, eds., *Picturing Science, Producing Art*. Galison's *Image and Logic: A Material Culture of Microphysics* (Chicago: University of Chicago Press, 1997) also treats visual images in science as material objects and offers a rich and nuanced analysis of the relationship between what he calls "image devices" and "logic devices."

48. Lenoir, "Inscription Practices and the Materiality of Communication," *Inscribing Science*, 4.

49. Simon Schaffer, "The Leviathan of Parsonstown: Literary Technology and Scientific Representation," *Inscribing Science*, ed. Lenoir, 184.

50. Mitchell, *Picture Theory*, 5.

2 DARWIN'S BARNACLES

1. For accounts of Darwin's barnacle work and its significance, see Rebecca Stott, *Darwin and the Barnacle* (New York: Norton, 2003); Browne, *Charles Darwin: Voyaging*, chs. 19–21 passim; *Correspondence* IV:388–409; Desmond and Moore, *Darwin*, chs. 22–24, 27 passim; Ghiselin, *Triumph of the Darwinian Method*, ch. 5; Neal C. Gillespie, "Preparing for Darwin: Conchology and Natural Theology in Anglo-American Natural History," *Studies in the History of Biology* 7 (1984): 93–145; A. E. Gunther, "J. E. Gray, Charles Darwin, and the *Cirripedes*, 1846–1851," *Notes and Records of the Royal Society of London* 34 (1979): 53–63; William A. Newman, "Darwin and Cirripedology," *Crustacean Issues* 8 (1993):349–434; Mary P. Winsor, "Barnacle Larvae in the Nineteenth Century: A Case Study in Taxonomic Theory," *Journal of the History of Medicine and Allied Sciences* 24 (1969): 294–309.

2. James A. Secord, *Victorian Sensation: The Extraordinary Publication, Reception, and Secret Authorship of Vestiges of the Natural History of Creation* (Chicago: University of Chicago Press, 2000).

3. On transcendental anatomy and its relation to the science of both Owen and Darwin, see Toby A. Appel, *The Cuvier–Geoffroy Debate: French Biology in the Decades Before Darwin* (Oxford: Oxford University Press, 1987); Peter J. Bowler, "Darwinism and the Argument from Design: Suggestions for a Reevaluation," *Journal of the History of Biology* 10 (1977): 29–43; Adrian Desmond, *Archetypes and Ancestors: Paleontology in Victorian London, 1850–1875* (London: Blond & Briggs, 1982); Desmond, *The Politics of Evolution: Morphology, Medicine, and Reform in Radical London* (Chicago: University of Chicago Press, 1989); Ospovat, *The Development of Darwin's Theory*; and Nicolaas A. Rupke, *Richard Owen: Victorian Naturalist* (New Haven: Yale University Press, 1994).

4. Richard Owen, *Lectures on the Comparative Anatomy and Physiology of the Invertebrate Animals*, 2nd edn. (London: Longman, 1855), 292.

5. Blum, *Picturing Nature*, 199.

6. Rebecca Stott, "'Through a Glass Darkly': Aquarium Colonies and Nineteenth-Century Narratives of Marine Monstrosity," *Gothic Studies* 2 (2000): 305–27; Stott, "Darwin's Barnacles: Mid-Century Victorian Natural History and the Marine Grotesque," *Transactions and Encounters: Science and Culture in the Nineteenth Century*, ed. Roger Luckhurst and Josephine McDonagh (Manchester: Manchester University Press, 2001), 151–81; and Stott, *Darwin and the Barnacle*.

7. On Darwin as a geologist, see Sandra Herbert, *Charles Darwin: Geologist* (Ithaca: Cornell University Press, 2005).

8. Edward Heron-Allen, *Barnacles in Nature and in Myth* (London: Oxford University Press, 1928).

9. Lorraine Daston and Katharine Park, *Wonders and the Order of Nature, 1150–1750* (New York: Zone, 1998), 18–19, 49–52, 330–31, 359.

10. John V. Thompson, *Zoological Researches and Illustrations, 1828–1834* (London: Society for the Bibliography of Natural History, 1968), 73.

11. Thompson, *Zoological Researches*, 70.
12. For information about Thompson and the bibliographic details of the *Zoological Researches*, see Alwyne Wheeler's introduction to the Society for the Bibliography of Natural History's facsimile reprint and the *DNB* entry on Thompson.
13. Thomas H. Huxley, "Lectures on General Natural History. Lecture XII," *Medical Times and Gazette* 15 (1857): 238.
14. Beer, *Darwin's Plots*, 111.
15. Thompson, *Zoological Researches*, 73, 71.
16. Darwin to Lyell, 2 Sept. 1849; *Correspondence* IV:252–53 (original emphasis).
17. Browne, *Charles Darwin: Voyaging*, 479.
18. See David Elliston Allen, *The Naturalist in Britain: A Social History*, 2nd edn. (Princeton: Princeton University Press, 1994), 111–22; Lynn Barber, *The Heyday of Natural History, 1820–1870* (Garden City, NY: Doubleday, 1980); William H. Brock, "*Glaucus*: Kingsley and the Seaside Naturalists," *Cahiers Victoriens et Edouardiens* 3 (1976): 25–36, rpt. in *Science for All: Studies in the History of Victorian Science and Education* (Brookfield, VT: Variorum, 1996); Barbara T. Gates, *Kindred Nature: Victorian and Edwardian Women Embrace the Living World* (Chicago: University of Chicago Press, 1998); Lynn L. Merrill, *The Romance of Victorian Natural History* (Oxford: Oxford University Press, 1989), ch. 8.
19. See John F. Travis, *The Rise of the Devon Seaside Resorts, 1750–1900* (Exeter: University of Exeter Press, 1993) and John K. Walton, *The English Seaside Resort: A Social History, 1750–1914* (New York: St. Martin's, 1983).
20. Philip F. Rehbock, "The Victorian Aquarium in Ecological and Social Perspective," *Oceanography: The Past*, ed. Mary Sears and Daniel Merriman (New York: Springer-Verlag, 1980), 522–39.
21. "Gosse's Sea-side Holiday," *British Quarterly Review* 24 (1856): 34.
22. On the narrative of natural theology, see Barbara T. Gates and Ann B. Shteir, eds, *Natural Eloquence: Women Reinscribe Science* (Madison: University of Wisconsin Press, 1997), 11–12, and Gates, *Kindred Nature*, 38–40. Drawing on the distinction in modern science writing articulated by Greg Myers in *Writing Biology: Texts in the Social Construction of Scientific Knowledge* (Madison: University of Wisconsin Press, 1990) between the "narrative of science" (the professional discourse of scientists) and the "narrative of nature" (the more informal, less technical discourse aimed at popular audiences), Gates and Shteir propose that in the nineteenth century the narrative of natural theology played the role of the "narrative of nature" until about 1850, when it was displaced among popularizers by a "narrative of natural history" – personal, anecdotal, nontheoretical accounts of nature that focused on the encounter with nature in largely secular terms, without a specific natural theological gloss. Bernard Lightman, while adopting Gates and Shteir's terms, has argued that the narrative of natural theology continued much later, although in modified forms, a position with which Gates has concurred in *Kindred Nature*. See Bernard Lightman,

"'The Voices of Nature': Popularizing Victorian Science," *Victorian Science in Context*, ed. Bernard Lightman (Chicago: University of Chicago Press, 1997), 187–211, and "The Story of Nature: Victorian Popularizers and Scientific Narrative," *Victorian Review* 25 (2000): 1–29. I would argue that Gosse's books blended the narratives of natural theology, natural history, and science in varying proportions from title to title depending on his aims and audience, and that the popularity of his books was perhaps due in part to his ability to work simultaneously in all three of these narrative registers.

23. Philip Henry Gosse, *Tenby: A Sea-Side Holiday* (London: Van Voorst, 1856), 120.

24. Peter Bailey, *Leisure and Class in Victorian England: Rational Recreation and the Contest for Control* (London: Routledge, 1978); Philip Henry Gosse, *A Naturalist's Rambles on the Devonshire Coast* (London: Van Voorst, 1853), v.

25. "Gosse's Sea-side Holiday," 53.

26. *Illustrated London News* 29 (2 Aug. 1856): 127.

27. [Samuel Warren,] "An Old Contributor at the Sea-Side," *Blackwood's Edinburgh Magazine* 78 (1855): 482, 488.

28. "Gosse's Sea-side Holiday," 48.

29. Charles Kingsley, *Glaucus; Or, The Wonders of the Shore* (London: Macmillan, 1855) 39, 44–45. Subsequent references appear in the text. All the passages cited here originally appeared in Kingsley's lengthy 1854 review article for the *North British Review* on the seaside books of Gosse, Landsborough, Harvey, and Pratt that formed the basis for *Glaucus*. For discussions of the conception of the body in Kingsley's muscular Christianity and its relation to Victorian social and cultural issues, see James Eli Adams, *Dandies and Desert Saints: Styles of Victorian Masculinity* (Ithaca: Cornell University Press, 1995), ch. 3, and the essays by David Rosen, Donald Hall, and Laura Fasick in Donald E. Hall, ed., *Muscular Christianity: Embodying the Victorian Age* (Cambridge: Cambridge University Press, 1994). Although this latter volume does not treat the naturalist as muscular Christian in any detail, a reader of *Glaucus* can readily integrate it into Kingsley's program.

30. Huxley also referred to the barnacle larva's eventual need to "settle down in life" in his notice of Darwin's *Monograph* for the *Westminster Review* 61 (1854): 264.

31. Edward Bulwer-Lytton, *What Will He Do With It?*, vols. XXII and XXIII of *The Works of Edward Bulwer-Lytton* (New York: Collier, 1901), XXII:217–19, 221. For Darwin's appreciation in his *Autobiography* of Bulwer-Lytton's joke, see *Works* XXIX:142–43.

32. Charles Dickens, *Little Dorrit*, ed. Harvey Peter Sucksmith (Oxford: Clarendon, 1979), 100; bk. 1 ch. 10. Subsequent references are cited in the text. On the specific contexts of Dickens's attack, see Trey Philpotts, "Trevelyan, Treasury, and Circumlocution," *Dickens Studies Annual* 22 (1993): 283–301.

33. "Sea-Gardens," *Household Words* 14 (1856): 244. Between 1851 and 1854, at least six articles on or related to marine natural history appeared in *Household Words*,

including one on Gosse's *Aquarium*. Another six appeared during the serial run of *Little Dorrit*, and two more were published within three months of the novel's completion, one of the latter referring to Kingsley's *Glaucus*.

34. Ruth Bernard Yeazell, "Do It or Dorrit," *Novel* 25 (1991): 33–49.

35. "Gosse's Sea-side Holiday," 33.

36. [James Fitzjames Stephen,] "The License of Modern Novelists," *Edinburgh Review* 106 (1857): 126–27.

37. [Stephen,] "Modern Novelists," 130. On Stephen's liberalism, see Julia Stapleton, "James Fitzjames Stephen: Liberalism, Patriotism, and English Liberty," *Victorian Studies* 41 (1998): 243–63.

38. Wood, *Victorian Panorama*, 187–90, with quotations on 187. Aubrey Noakes, *William Frith, Extraordinary Victorian Painter* (London: Jupiter, 1978), 51–58, with quotation on 57. The painting did not disappear from public view, for the dealer from whom Victoria purchased the painting retained engraving rights. For John Ruskin, who regarded Frith's panoramas as technically proficient but morally debasing, the public demand for engravings of them, especially *Ramsgate Sands* and *The Railway Station*, was a significant contributor to the deterioration in engraving in England (see *Works* XXII:388–89).

39. Mary Cowling, whose study of the influence of physiognomy on Victorian art demonstrates the class stereotypes and class frictions generally displayed in images of seaside life, draws attention to the large number of women and children in *Ramsgate Sands* and argues that the painting is essentially a domestic genre scene moved outdoors. *The Artist as Anthropologist: The Representation of Type and Character in Victorian Art* (Cambridge: Cambridge University Press, 1989), 216–31.

40. *Athenaeum* (6 May 1854): 560; *Times* (29 Apr. 1854): 12.

41. *Illustrated London News* 29 (2 Aug. 1856): 131.

42. Marcia Pointon, *William Dyce, 1806–1864: A Critical Biography* (Oxford: Clarendon, 1979), 173. See also Pointon's "The Representation of Time in Painting: A Study of William Dyce's *Pegwell Bay: A Recollection of October 5th, 1858*," *Art History* 1 (1978): 99–103, and Leslie Parris, *The Pre-Raphaelites* (London: Tate Gallery, 1984), 182–83. Malcolm Warner largely echoes the views of Pointon and Parris in his catalogue entry on *Pegwell Bay* for the 1997 exhibition at the National Gallery of Art, Washington, D. C., *The Victorians: British Painting, 1837–1901* (New York: Abrams, 1996), 107–08.

43. Herbert Sussman, *Fact Into Figure: Typology in Carlyle, Ruskin, and the Pre-Raphaelite Brotherhood* (Columbus: Ohio State University Press, 1979), 4–5.

44. Edmund Gosse, *The Life of Philip Henry Gosse* (London: Kegan Paul, 1890), 340.

45. Edmund Gosse, *Father and Son* (Harmondsworth: Penguin, 1983), 192. On Hunt's Evangelical symbolism, see George P. Landow, *William Holman Hunt and Typological Symbolism* (New Haven: Yale University Press, 1979).

46. For Edmund's framing of his father's intellectual life around his disastrous encounter with Darwinism and Lyellian geology, see *Father and Son*, 35,

102–06. While this reading of Gosse's intellectual life contains elements of truth, it seriously oversimplifies, as Frederic Ross has shown, both Gosse's science and his reaction to Darwin. Ann Thwaite's biography of Edmund similarly questions the accuracy of *Father and Son*'s representation of Gosse's childhood relationship with his father. Frederic R. Ross, "Philip Gosse's *Omphalos*, Edmund Gosse's *Father and Son*, and Darwin's Theory of Natural Selection," *Isis* 68 (1977): 85–96; Ann Thwaite, *Edmund Gosse: A Literary Landscape, 1849–1928* (London: Secker and Warburg, 1984).

47. *The Aquarium*, 2nd edn. (London: Van Voorst, 1856), 38; *A Naturalist's Rambles*, 54.

48. For discussions of Gosse as a natural theologian see Merrill, *Victorian Natural History* and Barber, *Heyday of Natural History*. On Paley and the influence of his natural theology in nineteenth-century Britain, see Aileen Fyfe, "The Reception of William Paley's *Natural Theology* in the University of Cambridge," *British Journal for the History of Science* 30 (1997): 321–35; Neil C. Gillespie, "Divine Design and the Industrial Revolution: William Paley's Abortive Reform of Natural Theology," *Isis* 81 (1990): 214–29; and D. L. LeMahieu, *The Mind of William Paley: A Philosopher and His Age* (Lincoln, NE: University of Nebraska Press, 1976). On the natural theology of the Bridgewater Treatises, see Charles Coulton Gillispie, *Genesis and Geology: A Study in the Relations of Scientific Thought, Natural Theology, and Social Opinion in Great Britain, 1790–1850* (New York: Harper & Row, 1959); John M. Robson, "The Fiat and Finger of God: The Bridgewater Treatises," *Victorian Faith in Crisis: Essays on Continuity and Change in Nineteenth-Century Religious Belief*, ed. Richard J. Helmstadter and Bernard Lightman (Stanford: Stanford University Press, 1990), 71–125; Jonathan R. Topham, "Beyond the 'Common Context': The Production and Reading of the Bridgewater Treatises," *Isis* 89 (1998): 233–62; and Young, "Natural Theology, Victorian Periodicals and the Fragmentation of a Common Context," 126–63. Formerly viewed in the aggregate as an updated version of Paley and a final assertion of the design argument before its demolition by Darwin, the Bridgewater Treatises are now regarded as providing different versions of natural theology that went beyond merely extending Paley and that continued to be influential even after 1859.

49. *A Naturalist's Rambles*, 20, 354; *Evenings at the Microscope* (London: SPCK, 1859), 248.

50. Frank M. Turner, "The Secularization of the Social Vision in British Natural Theology," *Contesting Cultural Authority: Essays in Victorian Intellectual Life* (Cambridge: Cambridge University Press, 1993), 101–27.

51. *The Aquarium*, 199–200; *A Year at the Shore* (London: Isbister, 1873), 325–26.

52. John Hedley Brooke, "Natural Theology and the Plurality of Worlds: Observations on the Brewster–Whewell Debate," *Annals of Science* 34 (1977): 221–86; Brooke, "The Natural Theology of the Geologists: Some Theological Strata," *Images of the Earth: Essays in the History of the Environmental Sciences*, ed. L. J. Jordanova and Roy S. Porter (Chalfont St. Giles: British Society for the History

of Science, 1979), 39–64; and Brooke, "The Fortunes and Functions of Natural Theology," *Science and Religion: Some Historical Perspectives* (Cambridge:
Cambridge University Press, 1991), 192–225.

53. James Patrick Callahan, *Primitivist Piety: The Ecclesiology of the Early Plymouth
Brethren* (Lanham, MD: Scarecrow, 1996); F. Roy Coad, *A History of the Brethren
Movement* (Exeter: Paternoster, 1968).

54. On typology in Victorian culture, see George P. Landow, *Victorian Types,
Victorian Shadows: Biblical Typology in Victorian Literature, Art, and Thought*
(Boston: Routledge, 1980), and Sussman, *Fact into Figure*.

55. *The Aquarium*, 117, 208. Sussman notes Gosse's reliance on typology but does
not attempt to read his illustrations typologically, as I do here.

56. *The Aquarium*, 93, 43.

57. *Tenby*, 23; *A Naturalist's Rambles*, 55.

58. *A Naturalist's Rambles*, 207–08; *The Aquarium*, 118–19. See also Richard R. Yeo,
"The Principle of Plenitude and Natural Theology in Nineteenth-Century
Britain," *British Journal for the History of Science* 19 (1986): 263–82.

59. *The Aquarium*, vii.

60. Rudwick, *Scenes from Deep Time*, 98, 179–80, 233.

61. *Manual of Marine Zoology for the British Isles* (London: Van Voorst, 1855),
170; *Tenby*, 118, 120; *A Year at the Shore*, 145. Gosse from the outset rejected
Darwin's classification of barnacles within the *Crustacea*, instead putting them
in a separate class of their own.

62. Philip Henry Gosse, *The Romance of Natural History*, 2nd series (London:
Nisbet, 1861), 343.

63. *A Year at the Shore*, 62–63.

64. Philip Gosse, "British Sea-Anemones and Corals: Original Sketches and Drawings in Colour by Philip Henry Gosse and his Correspondents, 1839–1861,"
Horniman Museum (London), items 44, 56, 28, and 55, on folio pages 25, 34,
15, and 33, respectively.

65. Christopher Hamlin, "Robert Warington and the Moral Economy of the
Aquarium," *Journal of the History of Biology* 19 (1986): 134–35, 147.

66. Philip Henry Gosse, *Actinologia Britannica: A History of the British Sea-
Anemones and Corals* (London: Van Voorst, 1860), 39.

67. *A Year at the Shore*, 78.

3   DARWIN'S BIRDS

1. Audubon to John Bachman, 20 Apr. 1835, *John James Audubon: Writings and
Drawings*, ed. Christoph Irmscher (New York: Library of America, 1999), 832
(original emphasis).

2. On the history of ornithological illustration see especially the works of Christine
Jackson: *Bird Illustrators*; *Wood Engravings of Birds*; *Bird Etchings*; and *Prideaux
John Selby: A Gentleman Naturalist* (Northumberland: Spredden, 1992). Works
such as Loudon's *Entertaining Naturalist* (1843), Wood's *Illustrated Natural*

History (1853), Morris's *History of British Birds* (1851–57), and Johns's *Birds of the Wood and Field* (1859–62) went through multiple editions and were frequently reprinted through the century. On these and other popularizers, see Gates, *Kindred Nature*; Lightman, "'The Voices of Nature'" and "The Story of Nature."

3. Gordon C. Sauer, *John Gould, The Bird Man: Associates and Subscribers* (Mansfield Centre, CT: Martino, 1995).

4. *John James Audubon: Writings and Drawings*, 834.

5. Quoted in Isabella Tree, *The Ruling Passion of John Gould* (New York: Grove Weidenfeld, 1991), 61.

6. For information on Gould's life and works, in addition to Tree, *Ruling Passion of John Gould* see Maureen Lambourne, *John Gould – Bird Man* (Milton Keynes: Royal Society for Nature Conservation, 1987); Gordon C. Sauer, *John Gould, The Bird Man: A Chronology and Bibliography* (London: Sotheran, 1982); Sauer, *John Gould, The Bird Man: Bibliography 2* (Mansfield Centre, CT: Martino, 1996); Ann Datta, *John Gould in Australia* (Carlton South, Victoria: Miegunyah, 1997); Ann Datta and Gordon C. Sauer, *John Gould, The Bird Man: Correspondence*, 4 vols. to date (Mansfield Centre, CT: Martino, 1998–); Christine E. Jackson and Maureen Lambourne, "Bayfield – John Gould's Unknown Colourer," *Archives of Natural History* 17 (1990): 189–200; Allan McEvey, *John Gould's Contribution to British Art: A Note on its Authenticity* (Sydney: Australian Academy of the Humanities, 1973).

7. Frank Sulloway, "Darwin and His Finches: The Evolution of a Legend," *Journal of the History of Biology* 15 (1982): 1–53; "Darwin's Conversion: The *Beagle* Voyage and its Aftermath," *Journal of the History of Biology* 15 (1982): 325–96; "The *Beagle* Collection of Darwin's Finches (Geospizinae)," *Bulletin of the British Museum (Natural History) Zoology Series* 43 (1982): 361–90.

8. Tree, *Ruling Passion of John Gould*, 170–76.

9. John Gould, *An Introduction to the Trochilidae, or Family of Humming-birds* (London, 1861), 5.

10. In the absence of direct comments by Gould, Gould scholars have tended to take his claims to be agnostic about natural selection at face value. Gordon C. Sauer, for example, states that Gould "never commented on Darwin's theory of evolution" (*John Gould, The Bird Man: A Chronology and Bibliography*, xviii). Maureen Lambourne echoes this, declaring that "in spite of violent Darwinian controversy which raged in the 1860s, no comment was made, even in letters, either to support or oppose the new theories" (*John Gould – Bird Man*, 21). Such statements, while technically true, miss the larger point that Gould's books were presented in non- or even anti-Darwinian terms.

11. Gould, *Introduction to the Trochilidae*, 25.

12. C. R. W[eld]., "Humming-Birds," *Fraser's* 65 (1862): 458.

13. Owen to Gould, 15 Oct. 1861, Gould Papers, Natural History Museum (London) Zoology Library, MSS GOU A, no.31 in Gould–Owen correspondence. Quoted by permission of the Trustees of the Natural History Museum.

14. Gould, *Introduction to the Trochilidae*, 18.
15. Duke of Argyll [George Douglas Campbell]. *The Reign of Law*, 5th edn. (New York: Routledge, n.d.), 232. The Preface to this edition is dated January 1868.
16. Argyll, *Reign of Law*, 230.
17. Darwin to Gould, 6 Oct. 1861; *Correspondence* IX:295.
18. Darwin's copy of Gould's *Introduction* is part of the Darwin Papers at the Cambridge University Library. Darwin marks many of the same passages quoted here and utilized by the Duke of Argyll. These annotations may also be found in *Charles Darwin's Marginalia*, ed. Mario A. DiGregorio, vol. I (New York: Garland, 1990).
19. John Gould, *An Introduction to the Birds of Great Britain* (London, 1873), iii.
20. Thomas Bewick, *History of British Birds*, 2 vols. (Newcastle, 1797–1804), I:vii.
21. Blum, *Picturing Nature*, 13–18.
22. *Introduction to the Birds of Great Britain*, 3.
23. A "Gould plate," while typically based on a sketch by Gould, was not executed by him: unlike Bewick and Audubon, Gould relied on other artists to work up his sketches. Elizabeth Gould, the artist of fig. 3.2, was still new to bird illustration and lithography when she assisted with *The Birds of Europe*, but the basic characteristics of the early Gould plates were equally evident in the work of the more artistically accomplished Edward Lear. On Gould's place in the history of ornithological illustration, see Anker, *Bird Books and Bird Art*; Blum, *Picturing Nature*; S. Peter Dance, *The Art of Natural History* (New York: Arch Cape Press, 1990); Knight, *Zoological Illustration*; Lambourne, *The Art of Bird Illustration*; Lambourne, *John Gould's Birds of Great Britain* (London: Book Club Associates, 1980); Sacheverell Sitwell, *Fine Bird Books 1700–1900* (New York: Atlantic Monthly, 1990).
24. *An Introduction to the Birds of Great Britain*, iii.
25. See, for example, John Gould, *The Birds of Great Britain*, vol. I, pl. 2 (golden eagle); vol. I, pl. 6 (common buzzard); vol. I, pl. 19 (merlin); vol. I, pl. 28 (barn-owl); vol. IV, pl. 7 (red grouse); and vol. V, pl. 44 (black-throated diver). On the Acclimatisation Society, which had disbanded by 1868, see Warwick Anderson, "Climates of Opinion: Acclimatization in Nineteenth-Century France and England," *Victorian Studies* 35 (1992): 135–57; Christopher Lever, *They Dined on Eland: The Story of the Acclimatisation Societies* (London: Quiller, 1992); Harriet Ritvo, *The Animal Estate: The English and Other Creatures in the Victorian Age* (Cambridge: Harvard University Press, 1987), 237–41. Although Gould's name appears (along with Owen's) among the list of the Society's Patrons in its first annual report in 1861, he clearly changed his mind, for in his discussion of the black-throated diver he laments the "inconsistency" of those noblemen "who establish societies for the introduction and acclimatisation of birds from other countries, and yet totally neglect the many fine species worthy of preservation at home!"
26. *The Birds of Great Britain*, vol. II, pl. 66 (chiff-chaff).
27. *The Birds of Great Britain*, vol. III, pl. 46 (parrot crossbill; emphasis added).

28. *The Variorum Origin*, 146.
29. *Birds of Great Britain*, vol. II, pl. 15.
30. The collection of Gould drawings at the University of Kansas's Spencer Library contains seven sketches (Gould 262, 265, 266, 383, 396, 501, and 560). Two are devoted to the water lily, three are studies of the chicks, one is of the adults, and one is a rough sketch of the entire scene. 262 and 266 are heavily annotated by Gould.
31. *Birds of Great Britain*, vol. IV, pl. 85.
32. *The Poetical Works of William Wordsworth*, ed. Ernest de Selincourt and Helen Darbishire, 2nd edn., 5 vols. (Oxford: Clarendon, 1949–54), II:207.
33. *The Birds of Great Britain*, vol. III, pl. 67.
34. Robert Fairley, ed., *Jemima: The Paintings and Memoirs of a Victorian Lady* (Edinburgh: Canongate, 1988) 54–55, 68. See also Gates, *Kindred Nature*, 79–83.
35. *An Introduction to the Birds of Great Britain*, 91–92.
36. J. B., "Cuckoo and Pipit," *Nature* 5 (1872): 383; J. H. B., "Cuckoos," *Nature* 9 (1873): 123. Blackburn had also published a finished version of her sketch in her children's book about *The Pipits* (1871), so the various versions of the image circulated quite widely. A friend of Ruskin and deeply committed to his injunction to draw what one sees, Blackburn objected to Gould's alterations, although not on the grounds of their natural theological implications, with which she concurred.
37. For debates about the cuckoo's behavior and its significance, see my "The Cuckoo's Contested History," *Trends in Ecology and Evolution* 14 (1999): 415.
38. *The Variorum Origin*, 394–95.
39. Gillian Beer, "Descent and Sexual Selection: Women in Narrative," *Darwin's Plots*, ch. 7; Jennifer E. Gerstel, "Sexual Selection and Mate Choice in Darwin, Eliot, Gaskell, and Hardy," Ph.D dissertation, University of Toronto, 2002; Rosemary Jann, "Darwin and the Anthropologists: Sexual Selection and its Discontents," *Victorian Studies* 37 (1994): 287–306; Evelleen Richards, "Darwin and the Descent of Woman," *The Wider Domain of Evolutionary Thought*, ed. David Oldroyd and Ian Langham (Dordrecht: Reidel, 1983), 57–111; Cynthia Eagle Russett, *Sexual Science: The Victorian Construction of Womanhood* (Cambridge: Harvard University Press, 1989); Ruth Bernard Yeazell, *Fictions of Modesty: Women and Courtship in the English Novel* (Chicago: University of Chicago Press, 1991); Yeazell, "Nature's Courtship Plot in Darwin and Ellis," *Yale Journal of Criticism* 2 (1989): 33–53. On sexual selection and American literature, see Bert Bender, *The Descent of Love: Darwin and the Theory of Sexual Selection in American Fiction, 1871–1926* (Philadelphia: University of Pennsylvania Press, 1996) and *Evolution and "The Sex Problem": American Narratives During the Eclipse of Darwinism* (Kent, OH: Kent State University Press, 2004).
40. Helena Cronin, *The Ant and the Peacock: Altruism and Sexual Selection from Darwin to Today* (Cambridge: Cambridge University Press, 1991). For a discussion of the limitations of modern feminist discussions of sexual selection, see

Richard Kaye, *The Flirt's Tragedy: Desire Without End in Victorian and Edwardian Fiction* (Charlottesville: University Press of Virginia, 2002), ch. 2; and George Levine, "'And If It Be a Pretty Woman All the Better': Darwin and Sexual Selection," *Literature, Science, Psychoanalysis, 1830–1970: Essays in Honour of Gillian Beer*, ed. Helen Small and Trudi Tate (Oxford: Oxford University Press, 2003).

41. Alfred R. Wallace, "Humming-Birds," *Fraser's* 28 o.s./22 n.s. (1877): 784.

42. G. N. Douglass and Karl Groos quoted in Cronin, *The Ant and the Peacock*, 143, 157.

43. Both Darwin and his brother, Erasmus, were members of the Athenaeum, and on at least one occasion Erasmus consulted its copy of *The Birds of Great Britain* on Charles's behalf. Erasmus to Darwin, 1873–1881(?); *Calendar*, letter 13790.

44. Darwin to V. O. Kovalevsky, 3 June and 24 June [1867]; Darwin to [Bibliogr. Inst. Hildburghausen?], 8 June 1868; *Calendar*, letters 5562, 5575, and 6235; Darwin to [Bibliogr. Inst. Hildburghausen?], [Aug.–Dec. 1868] (draft), Darwin Papers, University of Cambridge, DAR 96:52. (All quotations from unpublished material in the Darwin Papers are by permission of the Syndics of Cambridge University Library. Subsequent references to items in the Darwin Papers will be cited by DAR classmark.) In a letter to Darwin, Brehm's German publishers ascribe the success of the *Thierleben*, which was quickly translated into several languages, to its Darwinian point of view, and they seek Darwin's recommendation to a publisher for an English translation. (H. J. Meyer to Darwin, 30 July 1867, DAR 171.2:169.) Darwin immediately sought to induce his own publisher, John Murray, to commission a translation, ultimately without success. See Darwin to Murray, 4 Aug. 1867, 6 Aug. 1867, and 9 Jan. 1868, and Murray to Darwin, 5 Aug. 1867, Letters 5594, 5597, 5599, and 5781 in *Calendar*.

45. Both Brehm and his father, C. L. Brehm (1787–1864), also a famous ornithologist, were subscribers of Gould, but the bower-bird is the only one of Brehm's illustrations used by Darwin to be taken from Gould. See Sauer, *John Gould the Bird Man: Associates and Subscribers*.

46. Strickland to Gould, 9 Nov. 1841; Gould, *Correspondence* II:359 (original emphasis). "Gould's Birds of Australia," *Annals and Magazine of Natural History* 9 (1842):338.

47. On the paintings, see Gould to Jardine, 2 July 1841; Gould, *Correspondence* II:316. Loudon obtained Gould's permission to reproduce his illustrations and descriptions of the satin bower bird for a new edition of her *Entertaining Naturalist*, a work that went through many editions and was widely used in schools. Wood's *New Illustrated Natural History* (1855), another frequently reprinted work, included extended extracts from Gould on the satin bower-bird, with illustrations based on, if not copied from, *The Birds of Australia*. Loudon to Gould, 9 Nov. 1842; Gould, *Correspondence* III:127. See Loudon's *Entertaining Naturalist*, 242–44, 274–77, and Wood's *The New Illustrated Natural History* (London: Routledge, 1855), 326–28, 370–72. Gould's friend the physician and ornithologist C. R. Bree later told Gould that his illustrations had been copied

in popular publications without acknowledgment not only in Britain but "all over Europe" (9 Apr. 1858; quoted in Datta, *John Gould in Australia*, 180).

48. Gould, *Supplement* to *The Birds of Australia* (London: 1851–69), pl. 36 (fawn-breasted bower-bird).

49. *Proceedings of the Zoological Society of London* 7 (1840): 94.

50. *The Birds of Australia*, 7 vols. (London, 1840–48), vol. IV, pl. 10.

51. Gould, *Handbook* to *The Birds of Australia*, 2 vols. (London, 1865) 1: 444.

52. Darwin to Sclater, 4 Jan. [1871], Zoological Society of London.

53. Murray to Darwin, 10 May 1871, DAR 171.398; Darwin to Robert Cooke, 8 Apr. 1874, DAR 143.290; Wood to Darwin, 24 Apr. 1871, DAR 89.22–23. Wood, who worked extensively for *The Field*, took a particular interest in the courtship of birds and had published articles and illustrations on the same spectacular instances of male display relied upon by Darwin. He had already initiated a correspondence with Darwin on the subject while Darwin was still at work on the *Descent*. T. W. Wood, "Plumage of the Argus Pheasant and Bird of Paradise," *The Field* 34 (26 June 1869): 538; "The 'Eyes' of the Argus Pheasant," *The Field* 35 (28 May 1870): 457; "The Courtship of Birds," *The Student and Intellectual Observer* 5 (1870–71): 113–25.

54. Wood to Darwin, 14 June 1870, DAR 181.147; Argyll, *Reign of Law* 234.

55. Letter 51 (March 1875), *Works* XXXIV:291. On Ruskin and Gould, see also Maureen Lambourne, "John Ruskin, John Gould and Ornithological Art," *Apollo* 126 n.s. (1987): 185–89.

56. Ruskin's complex response to Gould continued well into the 1880s. He explained in donating *The Birds of New Guinea* to Whitelands College that the installments were "in my way" at his Brantwood home and that he had subscribed merely "to please the old man" (XXXVII:381). Yet a few years later, commenting on Millais's *The Ruling Passion*, a painting of an old ornithologist surrounded by birds and children supposedly based on a visit by Millais to Gould and exhibited at the Royal Academy in 1885, Ruskin was moved to declare what a happy life Gould must have lived, and how he wished he himself had devoted himself to birds (XXXIV:670).

57. "Introductory Notice" (1872) to the Catalogue of the Rudimentary Series compiled by Ruskin for the Oxford drawing schools (XXI:165).

58. This is consistent with Ruskin's more extended assessment of Bewick the previous year in his lectures on engraving, *Ariadne Florentina* (*Works* XXII).

59. Both Joseph Wolf, the great animal painter who drew many birds for Gould, and Alfred Newton accused Gould of overcoloring. See A. H. Palmer, *The Life of Joseph Wolf, Animal Painter* (London: Longmans, 1895), 72–73.

60. Gould makes this specific comment of the long-eared owl (*Birds of Great Britain*, vol. I, pl. 31) but he repeats variations of it throughout the work.

61. *Works* XXV:36. Ruskin on some occasions spoke respectfully of Darwin's researches, and the two men met several times in these years and expressed admiration for each other. They first encountered each other at the home of William Buckland, Oxford geologist and Dean of Westminster, in 1837, shortly

after Darwin's return from the *Beagle*. In 1868, Ruskin's American friend Charles Eliot Norton, staying at the time in Kent, arranged a meeting at Darwin's house; Darwin paid a return visit the next day. While Ruskin disagreed strenuously with Darwin's theories, he enjoyed Darwin's open personality and sympathized with Darwin's patient, detailed investigations of nature. At some point Darwin visited Ruskin's family home at Denmark Hill, and in 1879 he called on Ruskin at his Lake District home. See *Works* XIX:xliv–xiv, 358n, and *The Ruskin Family Letters*, ed. Van Akin Burd, 2 vols. (Ithaca: Cornell University Press, 1973) 415, 463.

62. Ruskin's text reads: "The extremity of these breast plumes [in the robin] parts slightly into two, as you see in the peacock's, and many other such decorative ones" (xxv:39). The robin lecture was delivered in March 1873, and the drawing is dated to that year by Christopher Newall, "Ruskin and the Art of Drawing," *John Ruskin and the Victorian Eye* (New York: Abrams, 1993), 112, fig. 82.

63. Charles Darwin, *The Descent of Man, and Selection in Relation to Sex* (1871; Princeton: Princeton University Press, 1981), II:91.

64. Ruskin to R. B. Litchfield (Darwin's son-in-law), August 1879, *Works* XXXVIII:334. Ruskin also sent at this same time to Litchfield's wife, Henrietta, Darwin's daughter, "a minute, exquisitely finished painting of one barb of a peacock's feather."

4 DARWIN'S PLANTS

1. Darwin, *Autobiography*, *Works* XXIX:76, 102, 104–06, 148–56; Mea Allen, *Darwin and His Flowers* (New York: Taplinger, 1977); *The Variorum Origin*, 186. Stanley Edgar Hyman was perhaps the first literary critic to appreciate Darwin's botanical work; see *The Tangled Bank: Darwin, Marx, Frazer and Freud as Imaginative Writers* (New York: Atheneum, 1962), 63–75.

2. Joseph Dalton Hooker, *Flora Tasmaniae*, vol. III of *The Botany of the Antarctic Voyage of H. M. Discovery Ships Erebus and Terror, in the Years 1839–1843* (London: Reeve, 1847–60), x; William Ogle, "Editor's Preface" to Anton Kerner, *Flowers and Their Unbidden Guests*, trans. and ed. by Ogle (London: Kegan Paul, 1878), vii; Hermann Müller, *The Fertilisation of Flowers*, trans. and ed. D'Arcy W. Thompson (London: Macmillan, 1883), with a preface by Darwin dated 1882. Hooker used the occasion of his Presidential Address to the British Association for the Advancement of Science in 1868 to publicize Darwin's fertilization studies, calling them "the greatest botanical discoveries made during the last ten years" (*Report of the 38th Meeting of the BAAS* [London: Murray, 1869], lxvi). On various biogeographical aspects of Darwin's relation to nineteenth-century British and Continental botany, see Janet Browne, *The Secular Ark: Studies in the History of Biogeography* (New Haven: Yale University Press, 1983). For a contemporary sense of the unusual positioning of Darwin's botanical work, see the review of Darwin's *Power of Movement in Plants* in *The Athenaeum*, 18 Dec. 1880, 817.

3. T. H. Huxley, "On the Border Territory Between the Animal and the Vegetable Kingdoms," *Macmillan's Magazine* 33 (1876): 373–84; A[ndrew] W[ilson], "Can we Separate Animals from Plants?" *Cornhill* 37 (1878): 336–50; [R. J. Mann], "Darwin on the Movements of Plants," *Edinburgh Review* 153 (1881): 497–514, with the quotation on 506.

4. Darwin to Murray, 21 Sept. [1861]; *Correspondence* IX:273. See also Michael T. Ghiselin's Foreword to the University of Chicago Press's 1984 reprint edition of *Orchids*, xi–xix.

5. Darwin to Murray, 24 Sept. [1861]; *Correspondence* IX:279.

6. Blunt and Stearn, *The Art of Botanical Illustration*; Jack Goody, *The Culture of Flowers* (Cambridge: Cambridge University Press, 1993); Hans-Michael Herzog, ed., *The Art of the Flower: The Floral Still Life from the 17th to the 20th Century* (Zurich: Edition Stemmle, 1996); Peter Mitchell, *Themes in Art: Flowers* (London: Scala, 1992); Nicolette Scourse, *The Victorians and Their Flowers* (London: Croom Helm, 1983); Pamela Gerrish Nunn, *Problem Pictures: Women and Men in Victorian Painting* (Aldershot: Scolar, 1995), ch. 2; Beverly Seaton, *The Language of Flowers: A History* (Charlottesville: University Press of Virginia, 1995); Ann B. Shteir, *Cultivating Women, Cultivating Science: Flora's Daughters and Botany in England, 1760–1860* (Baltimore: Johns Hopkins University Press, 1996); Vibeke Woldbye, ed., *Flowers Into Art: Floral Motifs in European Painting and Decorative Arts* (The Hague: SDU, 1991).

7. Winifred Baer, "Botanical Decorations on Porcelain," *Flowers into Art*, ed. Woldbye, 82–92. See also Una des Fontaines, "The Darwin Service and the First Printed Floral Patterns at Etruria," *Proceedings of the Wedgwood Society* 6 (1966): 69–90.

8. On seventeenth-century Dutch art and natural science, see Svetlana Alpers, *The Art of Describing: Dutch Art in the Seventeenth Century* (Chicago: University of Chicago Press, 1983); on the Dutch still life specifically, see Norman Bryson, *Looking at the Overlooked: Four Essays on Still Life Painting* (Cambridge: Harvard University Press, 1990), 96–135, and Norbert Schneider, "The Early Floral Still Life," *The Art of the Flower*, ed. Herzog, 15–21. On Darwin's pigeons, see James A. Secord, "Nature's Fancy: Charles Darwin and the Breeding of Pigeons," *Isis* 72 (1981): 162–86. Darwin owned Bernard P. Brent's *The Pigeon Book* (London: Cottage Gardener, n.d.) and Edmund Saul Dixon's *Ornamental and Domestic Poultry: Their History and Management* (London: Gardeners' Chronicle, 1848) and *The Dovecote and the Aviary* (London: Murray, 1851). Tegetmeier to Darwin, 27 Mar. 1865 and 4 July 1866, *Correspondence* XIII:93–94 and DAR 178.72. Tegetmeier secured Wells's services and oversaw his work for Darwin (he also drew three heads of poultry breeds for the *Variation*), who was as usual extremely precise about these illustrations. See Tegetmeier to Darwin, 13 Mar. 1865, 27 Mar. 1865, 10 Apr. 1865, 22 Jan. 1866, 23 Sept. 1866, 15 Oct. 1866; *Correspondence* XIII:81, 93–94, 119–20 and DAR 178.71, 75–76; Darwin to Tegetmeier, 14 Mar. 1865, 28 Mar. 1865, 6 Apr. 1865, 7 Apr. 1865, 5 Jan. 1866, 4 Aug. 1866, 14 Sept. 1866; *Correspondence* XIII:82–83, 98–99, 112–13 and

DAR 148.37, 38, 70. Darwin knew Weir's work and originally suggested him to Tegetmeier, for he felt Weir could draw the fancy breeds accurately and without exaggeration, but he concurred with Tegetmeier's recommendation of Wells after comparing one of Weir's pigeons for *The Field* with Wells's. On the gendering of the floral still life and of flower painting, see Bryson, "Still Life and 'Feminine' Space," *Looking at the Overlooked*, 136–78, and Nunn, *Problem Pictures*. On the gendering of scientific botany as masculine in the early Victorian period, see Shteir, *Cultivating Women*. For Darwin's comments about his early zeal for hunting, see *Works* XXIX:97–98.

9. Stuart Durant, *Christopher Dresser* (London: Academy, 1993); Widar Halén, *Christopher Dresser* (London: Phaidon, 1990); Michael Whiteway, *Christopher Dresser 1834–1904* (Milan: Skira, 2001).
10. 24 Sept. [1861]; *Correspondence* 9:277.
11. Darwin to W. E. Darwin, 12 Oct. [1861]; Darwin to Murray, 21 Oct. [1861]; *Correspondence* IX:302, 310.
12. [13 Apr. 1850]; *Correspondence* IV:332. On the emerging association of art with an unscientific subjectivity at mid-century, see Lorraine Daston, "Scientific Objectivity With and Without Words," *Little Tools of Knowledge: Historical Essays on Academic and Bureaucratic Practices*, ed. Peter Becker and William Clark (Ann Arbor: University of Michigan Press, 2001), 259–84.
13. Merle A. Reinikka, *A History of the Orchid* (Coral Gables, FL: University of Miami Press, 1972).
14. Darwin to Daniel Oliver, 23 Mar. [1861]; Darwin to Hooker, 24 Sept. [1861]; *Correspondence* IX:65, 277.
15. Darwin's original version of the diagram is reproduced in *Correspondence* IX:333. Lindley (1799–1865), the prolific Professor of Botany at University College, was an orchid expert and key figure in the increased popular interest in orchid growing in the 1830s and 40s. Darwin consulted with Lindley on *Orchids*, owned the second (1836) edition of Lindley's *A Natural System of Botany*, borrowed Lindley's *The Genera and Species of Orchidaceous Plants* (London: Ridgways, 1830–40) from Hooker, and consulted (see XVIII:14) the third edition of Lindley's *The Vegetable Kingdom* (London: Bradbury and Evans, 1853). Darwin's annotations to Lindley's *Natural System* indicate he took special notice of Lindley's several homological diagrams, one of which is for orchids and appears on p. x. Another homological diagram of orchids similar to Darwin's appears in Lindley's *Vegetable Kingdom* on p. 183. On Darwin's annotations of Lindley, see *Charles Darwin's Marginalia*, 501.
16. [Duke of Argyll], "The Supernatural," 394–95; this material appears verbatim in the opening chapter of *The Reign of Law* (1866).
17. John Lubbock, *British Wild Flowers Considered in Relation to Insects* (London: Macmillan, 1882), 96; J. E. Taylor, *Flowers: Their Origin, Shapes, Perfumes, and Colours*, 3rd edn. (London: Bogue, 1885), with the quotation from the Preface to the 1st (1878) edition on p. viii and the *Lythrum* diagram on p. 241.

18. Taylor, *Flowers*, 3; *The Sagacity and Morality of Plants* (London: Chatto & Windus, 1884), 303.

19. M. C. Cooke, *Freaks and Marvels of Plant Life* (London: SPCK, 1882), 21.

20. On Allen see Peter Morton, "*The Busiest Man in England*": *Grant Allen and the Writing Trade, 1875–1900* (New York: Palgrave Macmillan, 2005), Edward Clodd, *Grant Allen: A Memoir* (London: Grant Richards, 1900), and David Cowie, "The Evolutionist at Large: Grant Allen, Scientific Naturalism, and Victorian Culture," Ph.D dissertation, University of Kent at Canterbury, 2000.

21. Lightman, "The Story of Nature."

22. "Pleased With a Feather," *Cornhill* 39 (1879): 712–22 and "An English Weed," *Cornhill* 45 (1882): 542–54 are two overt examples of Allen's lay sermons. On Huxley's use of religious language for secular ends, see James Paradis, *T. H. Huxley: Man's Place in Nature* (Lincoln: University of Nebraska Press, 1978).

23. Grant Allen, *The Evolutionist at Large* (New York: Fitzgerald, 1881), 36–37, 46–47.

24. Grant Allen, "Our Debt to Insects," *Gentleman's Magazine* 256 (1884): 452, 465.

25. On popularization as a process of knowledge-making rather than the passive diffusion of specialist research, see Roger Cooter and Stephen Pumphrey, "Separate Spheres and Public Places: Reflections on the History of Science Popularization and Science in Popular Culture," *History of Science* 32 (1994): 237–67; Stephen Hilgartner, "The Dominant View of Popularization: Conceptual Problems, Political Uses," *Social Studies of Science* 20 (1990): 519–39; Richard Whitley, "Knowledge Producers and Knowledge Acquirers: Popularisation as a Relation between Scientific Fields and Their Publics," *Expository Science: Forms and Functions of Popularisation*, ed. Terry Shinn and Richard Whitley (Dordrecht: Reidel, 1985), 3–28. For an extended examination of Allen as a popularizer of Darwin's botanical writings, see my "Grant Allen, Physiological Aesthetics, and the Dissemination of Darwin's Botany," 285–306.

26. Alfred R. Wallace, review of *Vignettes from Nature*, by Grant Allen, *Nature* 25 (1882): 38; Darwin to Allen, 17 Feb. 1881, quoted in Clodd, *Grant Allen*, 111. For a somewhat different assessment of Allen's science, see Morton, "Busiest Man," 95–110.

27. *The Variorum Origin*, 367, 737. The wording about beauty as a source of delight for the Creator as well as for man was added by Darwin in the final and heavily revised 6th edition in 1872, very probably in response to arguments such as those advanced by Argyll in *The Reign of Law* and those attacking sexual selection after the appearance of the *Descent*.

28. W. Proudfoot Begg, *The Development of Taste* (Glasgow: Maclehose, 1887), 171.

29. Bernard Bosanquet, *A History of Aesthetic* (London: Swan Sonnenschein, 1892), 441–47; Vernon Lee [Violet Paget] and Clementina Anstruther-Thomson, "Beauty and Ugliness," *Contemporary Review* 72 (1897): 544–69, 669–88; *"Beauty and Ugliness" and Other Studies in Physiological Aesthetics* (London: John Lane, 1912). On Lee's aesthetics see Vineta Colby, *Vernon Lee:*

A Literary Biography (Charlottesville: University Press of Virginia, 2003), 152–72, and Gates, *Kindred Nature*, 181–87.

30. Alfred C. Haddon, *Evolution in Art: As Illustrated by the Life-Histories of Designs* (London: Scott; New York: Scribner's, 1902), 2, 306.

31. For recent assessments of Ruskin's relationship to contemporary art movements, see Linda Dowling, *The Vulgarization of Art: The Victorians and Aesthetic Democracy* (Charlottesville: University Press of Virginia, 1996); Christine Ferguson, "Decadence and Scientific Fulfillment," *PMLA* 117 (2002): 465–78; Adam Parkes, "A Sense of Justice: Whistler, Ruskin, James, Impressionism," *Victorian Studies* 42 (2000): 593–629; Nicholas Shrimpton, "Ruskin and the Aesthetes," *Ruskin and the Dawn of the Modern*, ed. Dinah Birch (Oxford: Oxford University Press, 1999), 131–51. For discussions of physiological aesthetics, see Block, "Evolutionist Psychology and Aesthetics"; Flint, *The Victorians and the Visual Imagination*; Gagnier, *The Insatiability of Human Wants* and "Production, Reproduction, and Pleasure in Victorian Aesthetics and Economics." For the emerging scholarship on the relationship between Darwinism and Aestheticism, see Gowan Dawson, "Walter Pater, Aestheticism, and Victorian Science," Ph.D dissertation, University of Sheffield, 1998; Dawson, "Intrinsic Earthliness: Science, Materialism, and the Fleshly School of Poetry," *Victorian Poetry* 41 (2003): 113–29; and Kaye, *The Flirt's Tragedy*, ch. 2.

32. Frederick Kirchhoff argues that Ruskin "discards" this earlier distinction to indicate "his growing dissatisfaction with [professional scientists'] notion of the relationship between the observer and the natural world" ("A Science Against Sciences: Ruskin's Floral Mythology," 250). I agree with Kirchhoff that Ruskin's science in *Proserpina* "does not radically differ from that in *Modern Painters*," but I believe Ruskin in effect seeks to articulate an appropriate science of essences that incorporates the science of aspects, and that this was fueled by the realization that the new Darwinian botany was being presented as a truer science of aspects as well as of essences. See also Ball, *The Science of Aspects*.

33. On Ruskin and art education, see Robert Hewison, *Ruskin and Oxford: The Art of Education* (Oxford: Clarendon, 1996). On Ruskin's science as part of his educational views and practice, and its role in contemporary debates on education, see Francis O'Gorman, "Ruskin's Science of the 1870s: Science, Education, and the Nation," *Ruskin and the Dawn of the Modern*, ed. Birch, 35–56.

34. Kirchhoff, "A Science Against Sciences" 250–54; Birch, "Ruskin and the Science of *Proserpina*," 143, 145; Birch, *Ruskin's Myths*, 172–94; Tim Hilton, *John Ruskin: The Later Years* (New Haven: Yale University Press, 2000), 310–11. See also Finley, "Ruskin, Darwin, and the Crisis of Natural Form," 7–24.

35. A joking reference in a letter (22 Aug. 1868) from Ruskin to his good friend Charles Eliot Norton, who arranged a meeting between Ruskin and Darwin that same summer, suggests Ruskin was familiar with Darwin's Linnean papers on primroses and cowslips well before their publication in book form. Sending some fossils to Norton, Ruskin wrote "the first time Darwin takes them in hand they will become *Prim*-Stones to you (I am glad to escape writing the other

word after "Prim"), and *Stones*-Lips, instead of Cows . . . When is he going to write – ask him – the "Retrogression" of Species, or the Origin of Nothing?" (*Works* XXXVI:553; original emphasis).

36. *Works* XXV:220–21, 309, 390–91, 414, 484–85, 541; John Lubbock, "Common Wild Flowers Considered in Relation to Insects," *Nature* 10 (1874): 402–06, 422–26; Asa Gray, "The Relations of Insects to Flowers," *Contemporary Review* 41 (1882): 598–609. Lubbock's articles were the basis of his popular book of the same title; for Ruskin's comment about being made "miserable" by them, see *Works* XXXVII:165.

37. In many cases Ruskin's plates and figures serve an explicit educative function for art students as "studies" to be examined and copied. Indeed, *Proserpina's* illustrations, Ruskin contends, will be of "permanent value" for precisely this reason: Burgess's wood engravings are "the best exercises in black and white I have yet been able to prepare for my drawing pupils," and Allen's steel engravings "may also be used with advantage as copies for drawings with pen and sepia." Ruskin placed a number of the plates in his Educational Series at Oxford, and all were available for separate purchase at sixpence each until 1890 (XXV:464, 205, liv–lvi).

38. For Ruskin on lithography, see XIX:159. For additional praise of the *Flora Danica*, see XIII:530; XV:482. For his views of wood and metal engraving, see his 1872 Oxford lectures on the subject, issued in print form as *Ariadne Florentina* between 1873 and 1876, in *Works* XXII.

39. Saunders, *Picturing Plants*, 132. Yet Sowerby also drew many of the plates for *Flora Londinensis*.

40. Cowie also discusses Allen's opposition to Ruskin, in "The Evolutionist at Large," but I find his treatment of Ruskin problematic, and my arguments here put greater emphasis on the connections between Allen's aesthetics and Darwinian botany.

41. Grant Allen, *Physiological Aesthetics* (New York: Appleton, 1877), vii–viii.

42. Grant Allen, "Aesthetic Evolution in Man," *Mind* 5 (1880): 446.

43. Grant Allen, "Dissecting a Daisy," *Cornhill* 37 (1878): 75.

44. Grant Allen, "The Origin of Fruits," *Cornhill* 38 (1878): 188.

5   DARWIN'S FACES I

1. Phillip Prodger has done extensive work on the illustrations in the *Expression*. See his *An Annotated Catalogue of the Illustrations of Human and Animal Expression from the Collection of Charles Darwin*; Appendices 3–5 in Paul Ekman's edition of the *Expression*; and "Illustration as Strategy in Charles Darwin's *Expression of the Emotions in Man and Animals*," *Inscribing Science: Scientific Texts and the Materiality of Communication*, ed. Timothy Lenoir (Stanford: Stanford University Press, 1998), 140–81.

2. Prodger ("Photography and *The Expression*," 400) questions Darwin's identification of some of the engravings in which Cooper employed photographic transfer, arguing that "there is little evidence to suggest that this process was

actually used," and that despite Darwin's assertion of this process's fidelity in cases where an original drawing was copied, such plates in the *Expression* "frequently bear little resemblance" to their drawings.

3. John Murray to Darwin, 31 May [1871], DAR 171.400; Robert Cooke [Murray's assistant] to Darwin, 1 Aug. 1872, 6 Aug. 1872, 9 Aug. 1872, 14 Aug. 1872, 16 Aug. 1872, 23 Aug. 1872, 26 Aug. 1872, 2 Oct. 1872, 20 Nov. 1872; DAR 171.411–13, 415–16, 418–19, 421, 431; Cooke to George Darwin, 13 Aug. 1872, DAR 171.414; Darwin to Cooke, 20 Nov. 1872, 7 Dec. 1872, DAR 143.288–89; Darwin to Riviere, 1 Apr. 1872, 4 Apr. 1872, 19 May 1872, 29 May 1872, 2 June 1872 [misdated 1871] DAR 147.317–21; Riviere to Darwin, 3 Apr. 1872, 16 May 1872, 20 May 1872, 22 May 1872, 6 June 1872, DAR 176.175–78, 181.

4. Anthony Hamber, "The Photography of the Visual Arts, 1839–1880," *Visual Resources* 5 (1989): 289–310; 6 (1989): 19–41, 165–79, 219–41. On the use of photography within nineteenth-century literacy movements to disseminate cultural artifacts to the masses, see Mary Warner Marien, *Photography and Its Critics: A Cultural History, 1839–1900* (Cambridge: Cambridge University Press, 1997), 112–40.

5. John Graham, "Lavater's *Physiognomy* in England," *Journal of the History of Ideas* 22 (1961): 562.

6. On the physiognomic tradition in nineteenth-century England, with particular attention to Bell, the Pre-Raphaelites, Spencer, and Darwin, see Lucy Hartley, *Physiognomy and the Meaning of Expression in Nineteenth-Century Culture* (Cambridge: Cambridge University Press, 2001). On Le Brun, see Jennifer Montagu, *The Expression of the Passions: The Origin and Influence of Charles Le Brun's "Conférence sur l'expression générale et particulière"* (New Haven: Yale University Press, 1994). On Camper, see Miriam Claude Meijer, *Race and Aesthetics in the Anthropology of Petrus Camper (1722–1789)* (Amsterdam: Rodopi, 1999). George Combe, *Phrenology Applied to Painting and Sculpture* (London: Simpkin, 1855). Moreau's long essay appears in volume IV of L.-J. Moreau, ed., *L'Art de Connaître les Hommes par la Physionomie* (Paris, 1820). On the passions and art more generally, see Richard Meyer, ed., *Representing the Passions: Histories, Bodies, Visions* (Los Angeles: Getty Research Institute, 2003).

7. G.-B. Duchenne de Boulogne, *The Mechanism of Human Facial Expression*, ed. and trans. R. Andrew Cuthbertson (Cambridge: Cambridge University Press, 1990). Cuthbertson's essay on "The Highly Original Dr. Duchenne" (225–41) includes a discussion of Duchenne's application of his research to aesthetics.

8. Darwin to Robert Cooke, 27 Oct. 1872, DAR 143.287.

9. *Art Journal* 12 n.s. (1873): 31; Henry Holbeach [William Brighty Rands], "Mr. Darwin on Expression in Man and Animals," *Saint Paul's* 12 (1873): 190–211, with quotation from 205; *Athenaeum* 2350 (9 Nov. 1872): 591 and 2351 (16 Nov. 1872): 631–32, with quotation from 632; [Baynes], "Darwin on Expression," 516.

10. Ruskin, *Works* XXV:263–64; IV:381. Ruskin to John James Ruskin, [2 Apr. 1845] and [15 June 1845], *Ruskin in Italy: Letters to His Parents, 1845*, ed. Harold I. Shapiro (Oxford: Clarendon, 1972), I, 115.

11. [Baynes], "Darwin on Expression," 517.
12. Darwin owned the ninth (1874) edition of Bell's Bridgewater Treatise on the hand, read the first edition of Bell's *Essays on the Anatomy of Expression in Painting* in 1840; and owned and heavily annotated the retitled third edition, *Essays on the Anatomy and Philosophy of Expression* (London: Murray, 1844). The quotations are from this third edition, 82–83; subsequent references will be cited in the text. For Darwin and Bell, see Janet Browne, "Darwin and the Face of Madness," *The Anatomy of Madness: Essays in the History of Psychiatry*, ed. W. F. Bynum, Roy Porter, and Michael Shepherd, 3 vols. (London: Tavistock, 1985), 1:151–65.
13. F[rederick]. A[rnold]., "Sir Charles Bell," *Fraser's* 91 (1875): 88.
14. On Darwin's changing opinion of photography's documentary value, see Gilman, *Seeing the Insane*, ch. 15, and *Disease and Representation*, ch. 8; and Prodger, "Illustration as Strategy."
15. A[rnold]., "Sir Charles Bell," 92–93.
16. Graham, "Lavater's *Physiognomy*," 562.
17. On the purposes of Lavater's physiognomy and its connection to his theology and social views, see the essays by Ellis Shookman, Christoph Siegrist, and Carsten Zelle in Shookman, ed., *The Faces of Physiognomy: Interdisciplinary Approaches to Johann Caspar Lavater* (Columbia, SC: Camden House, 1993).
18. On phrenology in nineteenth-century Britain, see Roger Cooter, *The Cultural Meaning of Popular Science: Phrenology and the Organization of Consent in Nineteenth-Century Britain* (Cambridge: Cambridge University Press, 1984); David de Giustino, *Conquest of Mind: Phrenology and Victorian Social Thought* (London: Croom Helm, 1975); John van Wyhe, *Phrenology and the Origins of Victorian Scientific Naturalism* (Aldershot: Ashgate, 2004) and *The History of Phrenology on the Web*, http://pages.britishlibrary.net/phrenology/; G. N. Cantor, "The Edinburgh Phrenology Debate: 1803–1828," *Annals of Science* 32 (1975): 195–212; Steven Shapin, "Phrenological Knowledge and the Social Structure of Early Nineteenth-Century Edinburgh," *Annals of Science* 32 (1975): 219–43; Shapin, "The Politics of Observation: Cerebral Anatomy and Social Interests in the Edinburgh Phrenology Disputes," *On the Margins of Science: The Social Construction of Rejected Knowledge*, ed. Roy Wallis (Keele: University of Keele, 1979), 139–78; Robert M. Young, *Mind, Brain and Adaptation in the Nineteenth Century: Cerebral Localization and its Biological Context from Gall to Ferrier* (Oxford: Clarendon, 1970). On phrenology and *Vestiges*, see Secord, *Victorian Sensation*. On phrenology and mesmerism, see Allison Winter, *Mesmerized: Powers of Mind in Victorian Britain* (Chicago: University of Chicago Press, 1998).
19. Charles Darwin, *Charles Darwin's Notebooks, 1836–1844*, ed. Paul H. Barrett et al. (Ithaca: Cornell University Press, 1987), 565–66, with additional references to Lavater on 322, 385, 556.
20. *Charles Darwin's Notebooks*, 526, 533.
21. William E. Marshall, *A Phrenologist Amongst the Todas* (London: Longmans, 1873). For Darwin's annotations, see *Charles Darwin's Marginalia*, 566–67.

Darwin subsequently incorporated three references to Marshall's work in the second edition of the *Descent*. Marshall's book is discussed briefly by Martin Kemp, "'A Perfect and Faithful Record': Mind and Body in Medical Photography before 1900," *Beauty of Another Order: Photography in Science*, ed. Ann Thomas (New Haven: Yale University Press, 1997), 129–30.

22. On Le Brun's lines, drawn on animal faces as well as human ones, see Montagu, *The Expression of the Passions*, 21–28. On Camper and Lavater, see Meijer, *Race and Aesthetics*, 115–23.

23. Montagu, *The Expression of the Passions*, 20–21. Darwin owned a 1701 English translation of Le Brun, although he did not annotate it. See *Charles Darwin's Marginalia*, 484–85, 487.

24. Cooter, *Cultural Meaning of Popular Science*, 75.

25. Gilman, *Seeing the Insane*, 109.

26. For Haydon's defense of physiognomy and phrenology, see *Lectures on Painting and Design*, 2 vols. (London: Longman, 1844–46), 1:14–15, 56–68. For studies of the influence of physiognomy on nineteenth-century European and American artists, see Cowling, *The Artist as Anthropologist*; Julie F. Codell, "Expression over Beauty: Facial Expression, Body Language, and Circumstantiality in the Paintings of the Pre-Raphaelite Brotherhood," *Victorian Studies* 29 (1986): 255–90; Hartley, *Physiognomy and the Meaning of Expression*; Judith Wechsler, *A Human Comedy: Physiognomy and Caricature in 19th Century Paris* (Chicago: University of Chicago Press, 1982); Katherine Hart, "Physiognomy and the Art of Caricature," in *Faces of Physiognomy*, ed. Shookman, 126–38; Charles Colbert, *A Museum of Perfection: Phrenology and the Fine Arts in America* (Chapel Hill: University of North Carolina Press, 1997).

27. Secord, *Victorian Sensation*, 507–11.

28. Rosemary Jann, "Evolutionary Physiognomy and Darwin's *Expression of the Emotions*," *Victorian Review* 18.2 (1992): 1–27.

29. Prodger, "Illustration as Strategy," 158–61.

30. Darwin to Riviere, 1 Apr. 1872, and 19 May 1872, DAR 147.318, 320 (original emphasis); Riviere to Darwin, 3 Apr. 1872, DAR 176.175.

31. Darwin to Browne, 30 Dec. 1873, DAR 143.346.

32. Darwin notes in one case that the original photograph shows the desired facial features much more clearly than in the reproduction (XXIII:176n9), and in the case of one of the engravings taken from a photograph acknowledges discrepancies between the two (XXIII:232).

33. See volume V, plates 193–207 of Moreau.

34. Review of *The Expression of the Emotions in Man and Animals*, by Charles Darwin, *Athenaeum* 2350 (9 Nov. 1872): 591; Review of *The Expression of the Emotions in Man and Animals*, by Charles Darwin, *The Journal of the Anthropological Institute of Great Britain and Ireland* 2 (1873): 444–46, with the quotation on 445; [Rands], "Mr. Darwin on Expression," 209.

35. Ruskin, *Works* XXXIII:364. "The Fireside – John Leech and John Tenniel" was delivered in Oxford on 7 and 10 November 1883, published separately that same month, and issued as part of *The Art of England* the following year.

36. E. D. Cope, "Evolution of Human Physiognomy," *Knowledge* 4 (1883): 136–37, 168–69. Ruskin refers to this article as "a scientific survey of South America," which it most certainly is not, but the illustrations are indeed those from it. They are preserved in the Ashmolean Museum's collection of Ruskin's teaching materials from his Oxford years, WA.RS.REF.163.b.

6 DARWIN'S FACES II

1. William C. Darrah, *Cartes de Visite in Nineteenth Century Photography* (Gettysburg, PA: Darrah, 1981), especially 4–10. See also Oliver Matthews, *The Album of Carte-de-Visite and Cabinet Portrait Photographs, 1854–1914* (London: Reedminster, 1974) and John Tagg, *The Burden of Representation: Essays on Photographies and Histories* (Amherst: University of Massachusetts Press, 1988), ch. 1.
2. The Darwin family photos are in the Darwin Papers, DAR 225. On photographs of Darwin, see Janet Browne, "I Could Have Retched All Night: Charles Darwin and His Body," *Science Incarnate: Historical Embodiments of Natural Knowledge*, ed. Christopher Lawrence and Steven Shapin (Chicago: University of Chicago Press, 1998), 240–87. Tegetmeier to Darwin, 8 Jan. [1868?], DAR 178.69. For Darwin's collection of photographs, including those of works of art, see Prodger, *An Annotated Catalogue*.
3. Marien, *Photography and Its Critics*, 90.
4. On Rejlander see Jones, *Father of Art Photography*; Stephanie Spencer, *O. G. Rejlander: Photography as Art* (Ann Arbor: UMI Research Press, 1985) and "O. G. Rejlander: Art Studies," *British Photography in the Nineteenth Century: The Fine Art Tradition*, ed. Mike Weaver (Cambridge: Cambridge University Press, 1989), 121–31; Roy Flukinger, *The Formative Decades: Photography in Great Britain, 1839–1920* (Austin: University of Texas Press, 1985), 12, 61, 89; Green-Lewis, *Framing the Victorians*, 54–61.
5. Darwin to James Crichton Browne, 7 Apr. 1871, DAR 143.336.
6. Rejlander to Darwin, 30 Apr. 1871 and 11 Nov. 1871, DAR 176.115–16.
7. DAR 53.1.C.33–37, 65, 92.
8. On medical and psychiatric photography, the history of representations of madness, and the relationship between Browne and Darwin, see Sander Gilman, *The Face of Madness: Hugh W. Diamond and the Origin of Psychiatric Photography* (New York: Brunner/Mazel, 1976), as well as his *Seeing the Insane, Disease and Representation*, and *Picturing Health and Illness*.
9. Prodger, *An Annotated Catalogue*, 101–03, 106.
10. Darwin to Browne, 7 Apr. 1871, DAR 143.336. On photography and the Anthropological Institute, see Roslyn Poignant, "Surveying the Field of View: The Making of the RAI Photographic Collection," *Anthropology and Photography, 1860–1920*, ed. Elizabeth Edwards (New Haven: Yale University Press, 1992), 42–73.
11. Darwin to Browne, 8 June 1869, 8 June 1870, 8 Feb. 1871, 20 Feb. 1871; DAR 143.328, 332–34.

12. Gilman, *Disease and Representation*, 137–39. Prodger argues that Browne's photographs were ultimately of little use to Darwin because they focused on abnormal expressions ("Photography and *The Expression*," 406). I find it hard to reconcile this view with Darwin's statement to Browne that the latter's photos were not expressive *enough* for Darwin's purpose.

13. Green-Lewis, *Framing the Victorians*, 159.

14. Prodger, "Photography and *The Expression*," 409; "Illustration as Strategy," 170.

15. Darwin to Browne, 30 Dec. 1873; DAR 143.346.

16. Prodger, "Illustration as Strategy," 166.

17. Darwin to Browne, 22 May 1869 and 8 June 1869; DAR 143.327–28.

18. Green-Lewis, *Framing the Victorians*, 161.

19. See Lindsay Smith, *The Politics of Focus: Women, Children, and Nineteenth-Century Photography* (Manchester: Manchester University Press, 1998).

20. Phillip Prodger, "Rejlander, Darwin, and the Evolution of 'Ginx's Baby'"; "Illustration as Strategy," 173–76; Jones, *Father of Art Photography*, 38. On Jenkins and his novel, see G. C. Kinnane, "A Popular Victorian Satire: 'Ginx's Baby' and its Reception," *Notes and Queries* 220 (1975): 116–17; Brian Maidment, "What Shall We Do with the Starving Baby? – Edward Jenkins and *Ginx's Baby*," *Literature and History* 6 (1980): 161–73; Jeremy Poynting, "John Edward Jenkins and the Imperial Conscience," *Journal of Commonwealth Literature* 21 (1986): 211–21.

21. Robert Cooke to Darwin, 20 Nov. 1871; Darwin to Cooke, 20 Nov. 1871; DAR 171.431 and 143.288.

22. *Athenaeum* 2351 (16 Nov. 1872): 632; [Baynes,] "Darwin on Expression," 513; "Darwin on the Expression of the Emotions," *Graphic* 6 (1872): 463. On the heliotype process and the *Expression*'s innovative use of it, see Lucien Goldschmidt and Weston J. Naef, *The Truthful Lens: A Survey of the Photographically Illustrated Book* (New York: The Grolier Club, 1980), 39–40.

23. John Ruskin, *Ruskin in Italy*, 225. See also *Works* III:210n.

24. For Ruskin's positioning in the larger cultural debates about photography in this period, see Marien, *Photography and its Critics*, 58–65 and Lindsay Smith, *Victorian Photography, Painting and Poetry: The Enigma of Visibility in Ruskin, Morris and the Pre-Raphaelites* (Cambridge: Cambridge University Press, 1995).

25. *Athenaeum* 2351 (16 Nov. 1872): 632.

26. Such constructions of "miniature melodramatic tales" were common to many Victorian texts, from conduct manuals to medical and sanitary treatises, although Darwin differed in not casting his around a specific moral. See Gesa Stedman, *Stemming the Torrent: Expression and Control in the Victorian Discourses on Emotions, 1830–1872* (Aldershot: Ashgate, 2002), 185–91.

27. Engel's illustrations are reproduced in plates 120 and 121 (in vol. III) and 454 (in vol. VII) of Moreau; Darwin's marginalia confirm that he read through the appearance of the Engel plates in volume III, and while volume VII was one of three volumes (excluding the index volume) that he did not annotate, it is likely, given his attention to the set as a whole, that he at least skimmed it. On

the influence of Siddons's work see Alan S. Downer, "Players and Painted Stage: Nineteenth-Century Acting," *PMLA* 61 (1946): 574–75; George Taylor, *Players and Performances in the Victorian Theatre* (Manchester: Manchester University Press, 1989), 38–40; Shearer West, *The Image of the Actor: Verbal and Visual Representation in the Age of Garrick and Kemble* (London: Pinter, 1991), 78–80.

28. On various representations of actors in the first half of the century, see West, *The Image of the Actor*. On the popularity of cartes-de-visite of actors, see Lou W. McCulloch, *Card Photographs, A Guide to Their History and Value* (Exton, PA: Schiffer, 1981), 50.

29. In addition to Downer, "Players and Printed Stage," Taylor, *Players and Performances*, and West, *Image of the Actor*, see Marc Baer, *Theater and Disorder in Late Georgian England* (New York: Oxford University Press, 1992); Michael R. Booth, *English Melodrama* (London: Jenkins, 1965) and *Theatre in the Victorian Age* (Cambridge: Cambridge University Press, 1991); Peter Brooks, *The Melodramatic Imagination: Balzac, Henry James, Melodrama, and the Mode of Excess* (New Haven: Yale University Press, 1976); Elaine Hadley, *Melodramatic Tactics: Theatricalized Dissent in the English Marketplace, 1800–1885* (Stanford: Stanford University Press, 1995); Joseph R. Roach, *The Player's Passion: Studies in the Science of Acting* (Ann Arbor: University of Michigan Press, 1993). On the sensational content of drama and melodrama during the period, see Richard D. Altick, "The Blood-Stained Stage and Other Entertainments," ch. 4 of *Victorian Studies in Scarlet* (New York: Norton, 1970), and Lynn M. Voskuil, "Feeling Public: Sensation Theater, Commodity Culture, and the Victorian Public Sphere," *Victorian Studies* 44 (2002): 245–74. On the pervasive visual interconnections among Victorian art, fiction, and theater, see Meisel, *Realizations*.

30. Gustave Garcia, *The Actor's Art* (London: Pettitt, 1882); William Archer, *Masks or Faces? A Study in the Psychology of Acting* (London: Longmans, 1888). On Garcia's book, see Michael Baker, *The Rise of the Victorian Actor* (London: Croom Helm, 1978), 157.

31. For an overview of English caricature, see *English Caricature, 1620 to the Present* (London: Victoria and Albert Museum, 1984).

32. DAR 140.4:5–9, 141.6, 225.175–85. On Victorian satire of science, with special attention to *Punch* and scientific naturalism, see James G. Paradis, "Satire and Science in Victorian Culture," *Victorian Science in Context*, ed. Bernard Lightman (Chicago: University of Chicago Press, 1997), 143–75.

33. Rejlander to Darwin, 30 Apr. 1871; DAR 176.115.

34. *The Variorum Origin*, 333.

35. Darwin to Lyell, 25 [Nov. 1865] and [10 Dec. 1859]; *Correspondence* VII:400, 422–23. [Richard Owen], "Darwin on the Origin of Species," *Edinburgh Review* III (1860): 518.

36. Trimen to Darwin, 16 July 1863; *Correspondence* XI:540. Darwin's letter of 18 April 1863 to the *Athenaeum* was published in the 25 April issue and is printed in *Correspondence* XI:324–26, with the quotation from 325.

37. M. H. Spielmann, *The History of "Punch"* (London: Cassell, 1895), 525–26; Joseph Swain, "Charles Henry Bennett," *Good Words* 29 (1888): 589–94.
38. Charles H. Bennett and Robert B. Brough, *Character Sketches, Development Drawings, and Original Pictures of Wit and Humour* (London: Ward, Lock, and Tyler, [1872]), 46, 48, 49. "Shadow-portrait" was an early and, in Darwin's time, still common term in Britain for the silhouette, which had indeed been largely displaced by portrait photography by the time Bennett published his first "Shadow" book. Lavater's use of silhouettes in his *Physiognomy* had increased the popularity of the silhouette both in Britain and on the Continent during the late eighteenth and early nineteenth centuries, so the reading of an individual's character from his eidolograph is a particularly pointed dig at physiognomy. On the silhouette, see Sue McKechnie, *British Silhouette Artists and Their Work, 1760–1860* (London: Sotheby Parke Bernet, 1978), 5–6, 22–23. On the importance of new optical gadgets in Victorian England, see Crary, *Techniques of the Observer*.
39. Bennett and Brough, *Character Sketches*, 17–18, 29–30, 13.
40. Bennett and Brough, *Character Sketches*, 40.
41. Thomas H. Burgess, *The Physiology or Mechanism of Blushing* (London: Churchill, 1839), 48, 178.

7 DARWIN'S WORMS

1. [Robert Cooke] to Darwin, 5 Nov. 1881, DAR 171; Darwin to Francis Darwin, 9 Nov. [1881], DAR 211.
2. For an insightful reading of this passage, and of *Worms* as a whole, see Adam Phillips, *Darwin's Worms: On Life Stories and Death Stories* (New York: Basic Books, 2000).
3. On Darwin's geological landscape vision during the *Beagle* voyage, see my "Seeing Through Lyell's Eyes: The Uniformitarian Imagination and *The Voyage of the Beagle*," ch. 3 of *Fact and Feeling*; for a different view, see James Paradis, "Darwin and Landscape," *Victorian Science and Victorian Values: Literary Perspectives*, ed. James Paradis and Thomas Postlewait (New Brunswick: Rutgers University Press, 1985), 85–110. The earliest, and still one of the only, literary critics to discuss *Worms* is Stanley Edgar Hyman, *The Tangled Bank: Darwin, Marx, Frazer and Freud as Imaginative Writers* (New York: Atheneum, 1962), 75–78.
4. On Darwin as a geologist, see Sandra Herbert, *Charles Darwin: Geologist* (Ithaca: Cornell University Press, 2005).
5. On the Darwinian vision of nature and its role in more abstract, psychologically interior landscape perception, see Krasner, *The Entangled Eye*.
6. *The Life and Letters of Charles Darwin*, ed. Francis Darwin, 2 vols. (New York: Appleton, 1905), 1:107. Emma Darwin to Henrietta Darwin, [4 July 1881], DAR 219.9:267.

7. Donald Ulin, "A Clerisy of Worms in Darwin's Inverted World," *Victorian Studies* 35 (1992): 296.

8. Cook and Wedderburn state that Darwin visited Ruskin at Brantwood in early 1881 (*Works* xxv:xlvi), but this cannot be correct, as Darwin was not in the Lake District until that June. The "Mr. Darwin" with whom Ruskin dined was probably one of Darwin's sons.

9. On Darwin's barnacle monograph and the grotesque, see Stott, "Darwin's Barnacles."

10. Major studies of the grotesque include Wolfgang Kayser, *The Grotesque in Art and Literature*, trans. Ulrich Weisstein (Bloomington: Indiana University Press, 1963); Mikhail Bakhtin, *Rabelais and His World*, trans. Helene Iswolsky (Cambridge: MIT Press, 1968); and Frances K. Barasch, *The Grotesque: A Study in Meanings* (The Hague: Mouton, 1971). Unlike Kayser and Bakhtin, Barasch focuses on England. For the Victorian period, the most important work is *Victorian Culture and the Idea of the Grotesque*, ed. Colin Trodd, Paul Barlow, and David Amigoni (Aldershot: Ashgate, 1999).

11. Bakhtin, *Rabelais and His World*, 19, 317–18, 370.

12. Frances K. Barasch, "Introduction: The Meaning of the Grotesque," *A History of Caricature and Grotesque*, by Thomas Wright (1865; New York: Ungar, 1968), lvii. Parts of Wright's book, which was issued in a second edition in 1875, had also appeared in the *Art Journal* in 1863–64.

13. Trodd, Barlow, and Amigoni, ed., "Introduction: Uncovering the Grotesque in Victorian Culture," *Victorian Culture and the Idea of the Grotesque*, 7, 10.

14. Barasch, *History of Caricature and Grotesque*, 115–17.

15. *Charles Darwin's Marginalia*, 103–04. For the importance of these aesthetic categories to Darwin's view of nature, see David Kohn, "The Aesthetic Construction of Darwin's Theory," *The Elusive Synthesis: Aesthetics and Science*, ed. Alfred I. Tauber (Dordrecht: Kluwer, 1996), 13–48.

16. Two of Martens's sketchbooks, one from his time with the *Beagle*, as well as biographical information, are available online: "Conrad Martens Sketchbooks I and III," Cambridge University Library, 2003, http://www.lib.cam.ac.uk/ConradMarten/. See also Browne, *Charles Darwin: Voyaging* 265–70, 283, 315. Ruskin discusses his training with Fielding in *Praeterita* (*Works* xxxv: 213–18).

17. Wright's *The Celt, The Roman, and The Saxon: A History of the Early Inhabitants of Britain* appeared in updated second (1861) and third (1875) editions; after his death in 1877, it was issued in revised fourth (1885), fifth (1892), and sixth (1902) editions. Thomas Wright, *Wanderings of an Antiquary; Chiefly Upon the Traces of the Romans in Britain* (London: Nichols, 1854); Edgar Barclay, *Stonehenge and Its Earth-Works* (London: Nutt, 1895).

18. Gill Chitty, "'A Great Entail': The Historic Environment," *Ruskin and Environment: The Storm-Cloud of the Nineteenth Century*, ed. Michael Wheeler (Manchester University Press, 1995), 114–15. John Lubbock, "On the Preservation of Our Ancient National Monuments," *The Nineteenth Century* 1 (1877): 256–69, reprinted in *Addresses, Political and Educational* (London: Macmillan,

1879), 154–71. Charles Philip Kains-Jackson, *Our Ancient Monuments and the Land Around Them* (London: Elliot Stock, 1880).

19. John Taylor, *A Dream of England: Landscape, Photography and the Tourist's Imagination* (Manchester: Manchester University Press, 1994), 24, 59–60. On the continuing power of the picturesque in tourism and travel from 1825 to 1875, see James Buzard, *The Beaten Track: European Tourism, Literature, and the Ways to Culture, 1800–1918* (Oxford: Clarendon, 1993), 187–215.

20. DAR 64.2.74–76.

21. Charles Darwin, "On the Formation of Mould," *Transactions of the Geological Society of London* 5 (1840): 505–09; reprinted in *The Collected Papers of Charles Darwin*, ed. Paul H. Barrett, 2 vols. (Chicago: University of Chicago Press, 1977), 1:49–53.

22. *Gardeners' Chronicle* (1844): 218; *Collected Papers* 1:195. Darwin annotated one of the offprints of his Geological Society paper with observations from this 1844 visit. See DAR 139.7.

23. *Works* XXVIII:80, 87–90, 99. A. C. Ramsay to Darwin, 27 Dec. 1871, 3 Jan. 1872, 18 June 1881, DAR 176.17–19. Emma Darwin to Henrietta Litchfield, [18 and 20 June 1877], DAR 219.9:149, 153. Darwin to William Darwin, 18 June 1880, DAR 210.6. T. H. Farrer to Darwin, 6 Oct. 1880, DAR 164(1)F.100.

24. Ramsay to Darwin, 27 Dec. 1871, DAR 176.17.

25. Annotated proofs of the illustrations for *Worms* are DAR 64.2.83 and 65.94, 96–101, 105, 107. Joyce's annotated tracings and Darwin's engraving instructions for them are DAR 65.102–08. A lengthy "Memorandum on Silchester" copied from Joyce's journal of the excavations and containing a sketch that is the basis for Darwin's figure 13 is DAR 64.2.63; Francis and Horace Darwin's "Notes on Mr. Joyce's Report," DAR 64.2.67 and 69, contains annotated sketches that are the bases for Darwin's figures 14 and 15; DAR 65.109–11 are the annotated sketches of figures 13, 14, and 15.

26. Section-type illustrations appear on pages 42, 96, and 137 of Wright's *Uriconium: A Historical Account of the Ancient Roman City, and of the Excavations made upon its Site at Wroxeter, in Shropshire* (London: Longmans, Green, 1872). Thomas Buckman and Robert W. Hall, *Notes on the Roman Villa, at Chedworth* (Cirencester: Savory, 1872); Darwin owned the 2nd edition (1873) of this 6d pamphlet, although the plan is missing from his copy (see DAR 64.2.77). In addition to the ground plans of Abinger by Farrer and Silchester by Joyce (DAR 64.2.41 and 65) are untitled pencil and pen sketches of a site that could be Chedworth (DAR 64.2.38 and 62).

27. For the development of Turner's book and the early exhibition history of his original watercolors and the engravings based on them, see both Andrew Wilton's introduction and Eric Shanes's discussion in *Turner's Picturesque Views in England and Wales, 1825–1838* (New York: Harper and Row, 1979).

28. Lubbock, Preface to Kains-Jackson, *Our Ancient Monuments*, vi.

29. "The Plough of the Animal World," *Spectator* 54 (22 Oct. 1881): 1334–36; [Henry Wace], "Darwin on Earth-Worms," *Quarterly Review* 153 (1882): 179–202; "The

Latest Development of Darwinism," *London Quarterly Review* 57 (1882): 387, 389.

30. Helsinger, *Ruskin and the Art of the Beholder*, 111–39. See also Raimonda Modiano, "The Legacy of the Picturesque: Landscape, Property, and the Ruin," *The Politics of the Picturesque: Literature, Landscape and Aesthetics since 1770*, ed. Stephen Copley and Peter Garside (Cambridge: Cambridge University Press, 1994), 196–219.

31. On the importance of Ruskin's emphasis on labor to the Victorian grotesque, see Isobel Armstrong, *Victorian Poetry: Poetry, Poetics and Politics* (London: Routledge, 1993), 232–51.

32. Michael Wheeler, "Ruskin Among the Ruins: Tradition and the Temple," *The Lamp of Memory: Ruskin, Tradition and Architecture*, ed. Michael Wheeler and Nigel Whiteley (Manchester: Manchester University Press, 1992), 77–97.

33. Ann Bermingham, *Landscape and Ideology: The English Rustic Tradition, 1740–1860* (Berkeley: University of California Press, 1986), 68–85; Stephen Daniels, "The Political Iconography of Woodland in Later Georgian England," *The Iconography of Landscape: Essays on the Symbolic Representation, Design and Use of Past Environments*, ed. Denis Cosgrove and Stephen Daniels (Cambridge: Cambridge University Press, 1988), 43–82; Elizabeth K. Helsinger, *Rural Scenes and National Representations: Britain, 1815–1850* (Princeton: Princeton University Press, 1997); Anne Janowitz, *England's Ruins: Poetic Purpose and the National Landscape* (Cambridge: Blackwell, 1990). On the cultural role of ruins in eighteenth-century Britain, see Malcolm Andrews, *The Search for the Picturesque: Landscape Aesthetics and Tourism in Britain, 1760–1800* (Aldershot: Scolar, 1989), 41–50; on Roman ruins see Janowitz, *England's Ruins*, 20–53; on the abbey see Michael Charlesworth, "The Ruined Abbey: Picturesque and Gothic Values," in *The Politics of the Picturesque*, ed. Copley and Garside, 62–80. On Ruskin's view of the picturesque in relation to other commentators, see Modiano, "The Legacy of the Picturesque" and Malcolm Andrews, "The Metropolitan Picturesque," in *The Politics of the Picturesque*, ed. Copley and Garside, 196–219, 282–98.

34. *Life and Letters of Charles Darwin*, 1:103.

35. Ruskin to John James Ruskin, 10 Jan. and 22 Apr. 1837, *Works* xxxvi:9, 14.

36. John James Ruskin to Jane Simon, 19 Feb. 1858, *Works* xxvi:xxvi.

37. The story of the Forbes–Tyndall dispute is told by J. S. Rowlinson, "The Theory of Glaciers," *Notes and Records of the Royal Society of London* 26 (1971): 189–204 and Rowlinson, "Tyndall's Work on Glaciology and Geology," *John Tyndall: Essays on a Natural Philosopher*, ed. W. H. Brock, N. D. McMillan, and R. C. Mollan (Dublin: Royal Dublin Society, 1981), 113–28; Ruskin's role is described by Cook and Wedderburn in *Works* xxvi:xxxiii–xli and analyzed by Sawyer in "Ruskin and Tyndall," and O'Gorman in "The Eagle and the Whale."

38. On the cultural status of Tyndall's "scientific use of the imagination" and Ruskin's response to it, see my *Fact and Feeling*, 34–35, 168–78. For a more

general discussion of Tyndall's notion of the scientific imagination, see Anna Therese Cosslett, "Science and Value: The Writings of John Tyndall," in *John Tyndall*, ed. Brock, McMillan, and Mollan, 181–92, and Stephen S. Kim, *John Tyndall's Transcendental Materialism and the Conflict Between Religion and Science in Victorian England* (Lewiston, NY: Mellen, 1996), 60–71.

39. [Wace], "Darwin on Earthworms," 184–85.

Bibliography

ARCHIVAL SOURCES

Darwin, Charles, Darwin Papers, Cambridge University Library
    Letters, Dittrick Medical History Center, Case Western Reserve University, Cleveland, OH
Gosse, Philip, Aquarium MS, Brotherton Collection, Brotherton Special Collections Library, University of Leeds
    "British Sea-Anemones and Corals: Original Sketches and Drawings in Colour by Philip Henry Gosse and his Correspondents, 1839–1861," Horniman Museum, London
    Orchids and their Culture, Natural History Museum Botany Library, London
P. H. Gosse MSS, Cambridge University Library
Gould, John, Gould Correspondence, Natural History Museum Zoology Library, London
    Drawings, Ellis Collection, Kenneth Spencer Research Library, University of Kansas

PRINT AND ONLINE SOURCES

Adams, James Eli, *Dandies and Desert Saints: Styles of Victorian Masculinity* (Ithaca: Cornell University Press, 1995)
Allen, David Elliston, *The Naturalist in Britain: A Social History*, 2nd edn. (Princeton: Princeton University Press, 1994)
Allen, Grant, "Aesthetic Evolution in Man," *Mind* 5 (1880): 430–64
    The Colour-Sense: Its Origin and Development (Boston: Houghton, 1879)
    "Dissecting a Daisy," *Cornhill* 37 (1878): 61–75
    "An English Weed," *Cornhill* 45 (1882): 542–54
    The Evolutionist at Large (New York: Fitzgerald, 1881)
    "The Origin of Fruits," *Cornhill* 38 (1878): 174–88
    "Our Debt to Insects," *Gentleman's Magazine* 256 (1884): 452–69
    Physiological Aesthetics (New York: Appleton, 1877)
    "Pleased With a Feather," *Cornhill* 39 (1879): 712–22
Allen, Mea, *Darwin and His Flowers* (New York: Taplinger, 1977)

Alpers, Svetlana, *The Art of Describing: Dutch Art in the Seventeenth Century* (Chicago: University of Chicago Press, 1983)

Alter, Stephen G., *Darwinism and the Linguistic Image: Language, Race, and Natural Theology in the Nineteenth Century* (Baltimore: Johns Hopkins University Press, 1999)

Altick, Richard D., *Punch: The Lively Youth of a British Institution, 1841–1851* (Columbus: Ohio State University Press, 1997)

    Victorian Studies in Scarlet (New York: Norton, 1970)

Anderson, Amanda, *The Powers of Distance: Cosmopolitanism and the Cultivation of Detachment* (Princeton: Princeton University Press, 2001)

Anderson, Katharine, "Looking at the Sky: The Visual Context of Victorian Meteorology," *British Journal for the History of Science 36* (2003): 301–32

Anderson, Patricia, "Illustration," *Victorian Periodicals and Victorian Society*, ed. J. Don Vann and Rosemary T. VanArsdel (Toronto: University of Toronto Press, 1994), 127–42

    The Printed Image and the Transformation of Popular Culture 1790–1860 (Oxford: Clarendon, 1991)

Anderson, Warwick, "Climates of Opinion: Acclimatization in Nineteenth-Century France and England," *Victorian Studies 35* (1992): 135–57

Andrews, Malcolm, "The Metropolitan Picturesque," *The Politics of the Picturesque: Literature, Landscape and Aesthetics since 1770*, ed. Stephen Copley and Peter Garside (Cambridge: Cambridge University Press, 1994), 282–98

    The Search for the Picturesque: Landscape Aesthetics and Tourism in Britain, 1760–1800 (Aldershot: Scolar, 1989)

Anker, Jean, *Bird Books and Bird Art: An Outline of the Literary History and Iconography of Descriptive Ornithology* (Copenhagen: Levin and Munksgaard, 1938)

Anonymous, Review of *The Expression of the Emotions in Man and Animals*, by Charles Darwin, *Art Journal* n.s. 12 (1873): 31

Appel, Toby A., *The Cuvier–Geoffroy Debate: French Biology in the Decades Before Darwin* (Oxford: Oxford University Press, 1987)

Archer, William, *Masks or Faces? A Study in the Psychology of Acting* (London: Longmans, 1888)

Argyll, Duke of [George Douglas Campbell], *The Reign of Law*, 5th edn. (New York: Routledge, n.d.)

    "The Supernatural," *Edinburgh Review* 116 (1862): 378–97

Armstrong, Carol, *Scenes in a Library: Reading the Photograph in the Book* (Cambridge: MIT Press, 1998)

Armstrong, Isobel, *Victorian Poetry: Poetry, Poetics and Politics* (London: Routledge, 1993)

A[rnold]., F[rederick]., "Sir Charles Bell," *Fraser's* 91 (1875): 88–99

Audubon, John James, *The Birds of America* [1827–38] (New York, 1840–44)

    John James Audubon: Writings and Drawings, ed. Christoph Irmscher (New York: Library of America, 1999)

Baer, Marc, *Theater and Disorder in Late Georgian England* (New York: Oxford University Press, 1992)

Baer, Winifred, "Botanical Decorations on Porcelain," *Flowers Into Art: Floral Motifs in European Painting and Decorative Arts*, ed. Vibeke Woldbye (The Hague: SDU, 1991), 82–92

Baigrie, Brian S., ed., *Picturing Knowledge: Historical and Philosophical Problems Concerning the Use of Art in Science* (Toronto: University of Toronto Press, 1996)

Bailey, Peter, *Leisure and Class in Victorian England: Rational Recreation and the Contest for Control* (London: Routledge, 1978)

Baker, Michael, *The Rise of the Victorian Actor* (London: Croom Helm, 1978)

Bakhtin, Mikhail, *Rabelais and His World*, trans. Helene Iswolsky (Cambridge: MIT Press, 1968)

Ball, Patricia, *The Science of Aspects: The Changing Role of Fact in the Work of Coleridge, Ruskin, and Hopkins* (London: Athlone, 1971)

Barasch, Frances K., *The Grotesque: A Study in Meanings* (The Hague: Mouton, 1971)

   "Introduction: The Meaning of the Grotesque," *A History of Caricature and Grotesque*, by Thomas Wright (1865; New York: Ungar, 1968)

Barber, Lynn, *The Heyday of Natural History, 1820–1870* (Garden City, NY: Doubleday, 1980)

Barclay, Edgar, *Stonehenge and Its Earth-Works* (London: Nutt, 1895)

Barger, M. Susan, and William B. White, *The Daguerreotype: Nineteenth-Century Technology and Modern Science* (Washington, DC: Smithsonian Institution Press, 1991)

[Baynes, T. S.,] "Darwin on Expression," *Edinburgh Review* 137 (1873): 492–528

Beer, Gillian, *Darwin's Plots: Evolutionary Narrative in Darwin, George Eliot and Nineteenth-Century Fiction* (London: Routledge, 1983)

Begg, W. Proudfoot, *The Development of Taste* (Glasgow: Maclehose, 1887)

Bell, Charles, *Essays on the Anatomy and Philosophy of Expression*, 3rd edn. (London: Murray, 1844)

Bender, Bert, *The Descent of Love: Darwin and the Theory of Sexual Selection in American Fiction, 1871–1926* (Philadelphia: University of Pennsylvania Press, 1996)

   Evolution and "The Sex Problem": American Narratives During the Eclipse of Darwinism (Kent, OH: Kent State University Press, 2004)

Bennett, Charles H. and Robert B. Brough, *Character Sketches, Development Drawings, and Original Pictures of Wit and Humour* (London: Ward, Lock, and Tyler, [1872])

Bermingham, Ann, *Landscape and Ideology: The English Rustic Tradition, 1740–1860* (Berkeley: University of California Press, 1986)

Bewick, Thomas, *History of British Birds*, 2 vols. (Newcastle: Beilby & Bewick, 1797, 1804)

Birch, Dinah, "Ruskin and the Science of *Proserpina*," *New Approaches to Ruskin*, ed. Robert Hewison (London: Routledge, 1982), 142–56
    Ruskin's Myths (Oxford: Clarendon, 1988)
B.[lackburn], J. [emima], "Cuckoo and Pipit," *Nature* 5 (1872): 383
    "Cuckoos," *Nature* 9 (1873): 123
Block, Ed, Jr., "Evolutionist Psychology and Aesthetics: *The Cornhill Magazine*, 1875–1880," *Journal of the History of Ideas* 45 (1984): 465–75
Blum, Ann Shelby, *Picturing Nature: American Nineteenth-Century Zoological Illustration* (Princeton: Princeton University Press, 1993)
Blunt, Wilfrid, and William T. Stearn, *The Art of Botanical Illustration*, new edn. (London: Antique Collectors Club/Royal Botanic Gardens, 1994)
Booth, Michael R., *English Melodrama* (London: Jenkins, 1965)
    Theatre in the Victorian Age (Cambridge: Cambridge University Press, 1991)
Bosanquet, Bernard, *A History of Aesthetic* (London: Swan Sonnenschein, 1892)
Bowler, Peter J., "Darwinism and the Argument from Design: Suggestions for a Reevaluation," *Journal of the History of Biology* 10 (1977): 29–43
Brent, Bernard P., *The Pigeon Book* (London: Cottage Gardener, n.d.)
Brock, William H., "*Glaucus*: Kingsley and the Seaside Naturalists," *Cahiers Victoriens et Edouardiens* 3 (1976): 25–36
Brooke, John Hedley, "Natural Theology and the Plurality of Worlds: Observations on the Brewster–Whewell Debate," *Annals of Science* 34 (1977): 221–86
    "The Natural Theology of the Geologists: Some Theological Strata," *Images of the Earth: Essays in the History of the Environmental Sciences*, ed. L. J. Jordanova and Roy S. Porter (Chalfont St. Giles: British Society for the History of Science, 1979), 39–64
    Science and Religion: Some Historical Perspectives (Cambridge: Cambridge University Press, 1991)
Brooks, Peter, *The Melodramatic Imagination: Balzac, Henry James, Melodrama, and the Mode of Excess* (New Haven: Yale University Press, 1976)
Browne, Janet, *Charles Darwin: The Power of Place* (New York: Knopf, 2002)
    Charles Darwin: Voyaging (New York: Knopf, 1995)
    "Darwin and the Face of Madness," *The Anatomy of Madness: Essays in the History of Psychiatry*, ed. W. F. Bynum, Roy Porter, and Michael Shepherd, 3 vols. (London: Tavistock, 1985), 1:151–65
    "I Could Have Retched All Night: Charles Darwin and His Body," *Science Incarnate: Historical Embodiments of Natural Knowledge*, ed. Christopher Lawrence and Steven Shapin (Chicago: University of Chicago Press, 1998), 240–87
    The Secular Ark: Studies in the History of Biogeography (New Haven: Yale University Press, 1983)
Bryson, Norman, *Looking at the Overlooked: Four Essays on Still Life Painting* (Cambridge: Harvard University Press, 1990)
Buckman, Thomas and Robert W. Hall, *Notes on the Roman Villa, at Chedworth* (Cirencester: Savory, 1872)

Bulwer-Lytton, Edward, *What Will He Do With It?* (New York: Collier, 1901). *The Works of Edward Bulwer-Lytton*, 30 vols., vols. XXII and XXIII

Burgess, Thomas H., *The Physiology or Mechanism of Blushing* (London: Churchill, 1839)

Buzard, James, *The Beaten Track: European Tourism, Literature, and the Ways to Culture, 1800–1918* (Oxford: Clarendon, 1993)

Callahan, James Patrick, *Primitivist Piety: The Ecclesiology of the Early Plymouth Brethren* (Lanham, MD: Scarecrow, 1996)

Campbell, John Angus, "Why Was Darwin Believed? Darwin's *Origin* and the Problem of Intellectual Evolution," *Configurations* 11 (2003): 203–37

Cantor, G. N., "The Edinburgh Phrenology Debate: 1803–1828," *Annals of Science* 32 (1975): 195–212

Charlesworth, Michael, "The Ruined Abbey: Picturesque and Gothic Values," *The Politics of the Picturesque: Literature, Landscape and Aesthetics since 1770*, ed. Stephen Copley and Peter Garside (Cambridge: Cambridge University Press, 1994), 62–80

Chitty, Gill, "'A Great Entail': The Historic Environment," *Ruskin and Environment: The Storm-Cloud of the Nineteenth Century*, ed. Michael Wheeler (Manchester University Press, 1995), 102–22

Christ, Carol T. and John O. Jordan, eds., *Victorian Literature and the Victorian Visual Imagination* (Berkeley: University of California Press, 1995)

Clodd, Edward, *Grant Allen: A Memoir* (London: Grant Richards, 1900)

Coad, F. Roy, *A History of the Brethren Movement* (Exeter: Paternoster, 1968)

Codell, Julie F., "Expression over Beauty: Facial Expression, Body Language, and Circumstantiality in the Paintings of the Pre-Raphaelite Brotherhood," *Victorian Studies* 29 (1986): 255–90

Colbert, Charles, *A Museum of Perfection: Phrenology and the Fine Arts in America* (Chapel Hill: University of North Carolina Press, 1997)

Colby, Vineta, *Vernon Lee: A Literary Biography* (Charlottesville: University Press of Virginia, 2003)

Combe, George, *Phrenology Applied to Painting and Sculpture* (London: Simpkin, 1855)

"Conrad Martens Sketchbooks I and III," Cambridge University Library, 2003, 8 July 2003 http://www.lib.cam.ac.uk/ConradMarten/

Cook, Theodore Andrea, *The Curves of Life: Being an Account of Spiral Formations and Their Application to Growth in Nature, to Science and to Art* (London: Constable, 1914)

  Spirals in Nature and Art (London: Murray, 1903)

Cooke, M. C., *Freaks and Marvels of Plant Life* (London: SPCK, 1882)

Cooter, Roger, *The Cultural Meaning of Popular Science: Phrenology and the Organization of Consent in Nineteenth-Century Britain* (Cambridge: Cambridge University Press, 1984)

Cooter, Roger and Stephen Pumphrey, "Separate Spheres and Public Places: Reflections on the History of Science Popularization and Science in Popular Culture," *History of Science* 32 (1994): 237–67

Cope, E. D., "Evolution of Human Physiognomy," *Knowledge* 4 (1883): 136–37, 168–69

Cosslett, Anna Therese, "Science and Value: The Writings of John Tyndall," *John Tyndall: Essays on a Natural Philosopher*, ed. W. H. Brock, N. D. McMillan, and R. C. Mollan (Dublin: Royal Dublin Society, 1981), 181–92

Cowie, David, "The Evolutionist at Large: Grant Allen, Scientific Naturalism, and Victorian Culture," Ph.D dissertation, University of Kent at Canterbury, 2000

Cowling, Mary, *The Artist as Anthropologist: The Representation of Type and Character in Victorian Art* (Cambridge: Cambridge University Press, 1989)

Crary, Jonathan, *Techniques of the Observer: On Vision and Modernity in the Nineteenth Century* (Cambridge: MIT Press, 1990)

Cronin, Helena, *The Ant and the Peacock: Altruism and Sexual Selection from Darwin to Today* (Cambridge: Cambridge University Press, 1991)

Cuthbertson, R. Andrew, "The Highly Original Dr. Duchenne," *The Mechanism of Human Facial Expression*, ed. and trans. R. Andrew Cuthbertson (Cambridge: Cambridge University Press, 1990), 225–41

Dance, S. Peter, *The Art of Natural History* (New York: Arch Cape Press, 1990)

Daniels, Stephen, "The Political Iconography of Woodland in Later Georgian England," *The Iconography of Landscape: Essays on the Symbolic Representation, Design and Use of Past Environments*, ed. Denis Cosgrove and Stephen Daniels (Cambridge: Cambridge University Press, 1988), 43–82

Darrah, William C., *Cartes de Visite in Nineteenth Century Photography* (Gettysburg, PA: Darrah, 1981)

Darwin, Charles, *A Calendar of the Correspondence of Charles Darwin, 1821–1882*, 2nd edn., ed. Frederick Burkhardt and Sydney Smith (Cambridge: Cambridge University Press, 1994)

  Charles Darwin's Marginalia, ed. Mario A. DiGregorio, vol. 1 (New York: Garland, 1990)

  Charles Darwin's Notebooks, 1836–1844, ed. Paul H. Barrett et al. (Ithaca: Cornell University Press, 1987)

  The Collected Papers of Charles Darwin, ed. Paul H. Barrett, 2 vols. (Chicago: University of Chicago Press, 1977)

  The Correspondence of Charles Darwin, ed. Frederick Burkhardt et al., 14 vols. to date (Cambridge: Cambridge University Press, 1985–)

  The Descent of Man, and Selection in Relation to Sex (1871; Princeton: Princeton University Press, 1981)

  The Life and Letters of Charles Darwin, ed. Francis Darwin, 2 vols. (New York: Appleton, 1905)

  The Origin of Species By Charles Darwin: A Variorum Text, ed. Morse Peckham (Philadelphia: University of Pennsylvania Press, 1959)

  The Works of Charles Darwin, ed. Paul H. Barrett and R. B. Freeman, 29 vols. (New York: NYU Press, 1986–89)

Daston, Lorraine, "Scientific Objectivity With and Without Words," *Little Tools of Knowledge: Historical Essays on Academic and Bureaucratic Practices*, ed. Peter Becker and William Clark (Ann Arbor: University of Michigan Press, 2001), 259–84

Daston, Lorraine and Peter Galison, "The Image of Objectivity," *Representations* 40 (1992): 81–128

Daston, Lorraine and Katharine Park, *Wonders and the Order of Nature, 1150–1750* (New York: Zone, 1998)

Datta, Ann, *John Gould in Australia* (Carlton South, Victoria: Miegunyah, 1997)

Datta, Ann and Gordon C. Sauer, eds., *John Gould, The Bird Man: Correspondence*, 4 vols. to date (Mansfield Centre, CT: Martino, 1998–)

Dawson, Gowan, "Intrinsic Earthliness: Science, Materialism, and the Fleshly School of Poetry," *Victorian Poetry* 41 (2003): 113–29

"Walter Pater, Aestheticism, and Victorian Science," Ph.D dissertation, University of Sheffield, 1998

de Giustino, David, *Conquest of Mind: Phrenology and Victorian Social Thought* (London: Croom Helm, 1975)

De Maré, Eric, *The Victorian Woodblock Illustrators* (London: Gordon Fraser, 1980)

des Fontaines, Una, "The Darwin Service and the First Printed Floral Patterns at Etruria," *Proceedings of the Wedgwood Society* 6 (1966): 69–90

Desmond, Adrian, *Archetypes and Ancestors: Paleontology in Victorian London, 1850–1875* (London: Blond & Briggs, 1982)

The Politics of Evolution: Morphology, Medicine, and Reform in Radical London (Chicago: University of Chicago Press, 1989)

Desmond, Adrian and James Moore, *Darwin* (New York: Warner, 1992)

Dickens, Charles, *Little Dorrit*, ed. Harvey Peter Sucksmith (Oxford: Clarendon, 1979)

Dixon, Edmund Saul, *The Dovecote and the Aviary* (London: Murray, 1851)

Ornamental and Domestic Poultry: Their History and Management (London: Gardeners' Chronicle, 1848)

Dowling, Linda, *The Vulgarization of Art: The Victorians and Aesthetic Democracy* (Charlottesville: University Press of Virginia, 1996)

Downer, Alan S., "Players and Painted Stage: Nineteenth-Century Acting," *PMLA* 61 (1946): 522–76

Duchenne de Boulogne, G.-B., *The Mechanism of Human Facial Expression*, ed. and trans. R. Andrew Cuthbertson (Cambridge: Cambridge University Press, 1990)

Durant, Stuart, *Christopher Dresser* (London: Academy, 1993)

English Caricature, 1620 to the Present (London: Victoria and Albert Museum, 1984)

Fairley, Robert, ed., *Jemima: The Paintings and Memoirs of a Victorian Lady* (Edinburgh: Canongate, 1988)

Ferguson, Christine, "Decadence and Scientific Fulfillment," *PMLA* 117 (2002): 465–78

Finley, C. Stephen, *Nature's Covenant: Figures of Landscape in Ruskin* (University Park: Penn State University Press, 1992)
  "Ruskin, Darwin, and the Crisis of Natural Form," *Cahiers Victoriens et Edouardiens* 25 (1987): 7–24
Fitch, Raymond E., *The Poison Sky: Myth and Apocalypse in Ruskin* (Athens: Ohio University Press, 1982)
Flint, Kate, "Moral Judgement and the Language of English Art Criticism 1870–1910," *Oxford Art Journal* 6.2 (1983): 58–66
  The Victorians and the Visual Imagination (Cambridge: Cambridge University Press, 2000)
Flukinger, Roy, *The Formative Decades: Photography in Great Britain, 1839–1920* (Austin: University of Texas Press, 1985)
Freeman, R. B., *The Works of Charles Darwin: An Annotated Bibliographic Handlist*, 2nd edn. (Folkestone: Dawson, 1977)
Fyfe, Aileen, "The Reception of William Paley's *Natural Theology* in the University of Cambridge," *British Journal for the History of Science* 30 (1997): 321–35
Gagnier, Regenia, *The Insatiability of Human Wants: Economics and Aesthetics in Market Society* (Chicago: University of Chicago Press, 2000)
  "Production, Reproduction, and Pleasure in Victorian Aesthetics and Economics," *Victorian Sexual Dissidence*, ed. Richard Dellamora (Chicago: University of Chicago Press, 1999), 127–46
Galison, Peter, *Image and Logic: A Material Culture of Microphysics* (Chicago: University of Chicago Press, 1997)
Garcia, Gustave, *The Actor's Art* (London: Pettitt, 1882)
Gates, Barbara T., *Kindred Nature: Victorian and Edwardian Women Embrace the Living World* (Chicago: University of Chicago Press, 1998)
Gates, Barbara T. and Ann B. Shteir, eds., *Natural Eloquence: Women Reinscribe Science* (Madison: University of Wisconsin Press, 1997)
Gerstel, Jennifer E., "Sexual Selection and Mate Choice in Darwin, Eliot, Gaskell, and Hardy," Ph.D dissertation, University of Toronto, 2002
Ghiselin, Michael, Foreword, *The Various Contrivances by which Orchids are Fertilised by Insects*, by Charles Darwin, 2nd edn. (Chicago: University of Chicago Press, 1984), xi–xix
  The Triumph of the Darwinian Method (Berkeley: University of California Press, 1969)
Gillespie, Neal C., "Divine Design and the Industrial Revolution: William Paley's Abortive Reform of Natural Theology," *Isis* 81 (1990): 214–29
  "Preparing for Darwin: Conchology and Natural Theology in Anglo-American Natural History," *Studies in the History of Biology* 7 (1984): 93–145
Gillispie, Charles Coulton, *Genesis and Geology: A Study in the Relations of Scientific Thought, Natural Theology, and Social Opinion in Great Britain, 1790–1850* (New York: Harper & Row, 1959)
Gilman, Sander L., *Disease and Representation: Images of Illness from Madness to AIDS* (Ithaca: Cornell University Press, 1988)

The Face of Madness: Hugh W. Diamond and the Origin of Psychiatric Photography (New York: Brunner/Mazel, 1976)

Picturing Health and Illness: Images of Identity and Illness (Baltimore: Johns Hopkins University Press, 1995)

Seeing the Insane (New York: Wiley, 1982)

Goldman, Paul, *Victorian Illustrated Books 1850–1870: The Heyday of Wood Engraving* (London: British Museum Press, 1994)

Goldschmidt, Lucien and Weston J. Naef, *The Truthful Lens: A Survey of the Photographically Illustrated Book* (New York: The Grolier Club, 1980)

Goody, Jack, *The Culture of Flowers* (Cambridge: Cambridge University Press, 1993)

Gosse, Edmund, *Father and Son* (Harmondsworth: Penguin, 1983)

The Life of Philip Henry Gosse (London: Kegan Paul, 1890)

Gosse, Philip Henry, *Actinologia Britannica: A History of the British Sea-Anemones and Corals* (London: Van Voorst, 1860)

The Aquarium, 2nd edn. (London: Van Voorst, 1856)

Evenings at the Microscope (London: SPCK, 1859)

Manual of Marine Zoology for the British Isles (London: Van Voorst, 1855–6)

A Naturalist's Rambles on the Devonshire Coast (London: Van Voorst, 1853)

The Romance of Natural History, 2nd series (London: Nisbet, 1861)

Tenby: A Sea-Side Holiday (London: Van Voorst, 1856)

A Year at the Shore (London: Isbister, 1873)

"Gosse's Sea-side Holiday," *British Quarterly Review* 24 (1856): 32–54

Gould, John, *The Birds of Australia*, 7 vols. (London, 1840–48)

The Birds of Great Britain, 5 vols. (London, 1862–73)

An Introduction to the Birds of Great Britain (London, 1873)

An Introduction to the Trochilidae, or Family of Humming-birds (London, 1861)

Gould, Stephen Jay, *Wonderful Life: The Burgess Shale and the Nature of History* (New York: Norton, 1989)

"Gould's Birds of Australia," *Annals and Magazine of Natural History* 9 (1842): 338

Graham, John, "Lavater's *Physiognomy* in England," *Journal of the History of Ideas* 22 (1961): 561–72

Gray, Asa, "The Relations of Insects to Flowers," *Contemporary Review* 41 (1882): 598–609

Green-Lewis, Jennifer, *Framing the Victorians: Photography and the Culture of Realism* (Ithaca: Cornell University Press, 1996)

Gully, Anthony Lacy, "Sermons in Stone: Ruskin and Geology," *John Ruskin and the Victorian Eye* (New York: Abrams, 1993), 158–83

Gunther, A. E., "J. E. Gray, Charles Darwin, and the *Cirripedes*, 1846–1851," *Notes and Records of the Royal Society of London* 34 (1979): 53–63

Haddon, Alfred C., *Evolution in Art: As Illustrated by the Life-Histories of Designs* (London: Scott; New York: Scribner's, 1902)

Hadley, Elaine, *Melodramatic Tactics: Theatricalized Dissent in the English Marketplace, 1800–1885* (Stanford: Stanford University Press, 1995)

Halén, Widar, *Christopher Dresser* (London: Phaidon, 1990)

Hall, Donald E., ed., *Muscular Christianity: Embodying the Victorian Age* (Cambridge: Cambridge University Press, 1994)

Hamber, Anthony, "The Photography of the Visual Arts, 1839–1880," *Visual Resources* 5 (1989): 289–310; 6 (1989): 19–41, 165–79, 219–41

Hamlin, Christopher, "Robert Warington and the Moral Economy of the Aquarium," *Journal of the History of Biology* 19 (1986): 131–53

Hart, Katherine, "Physiognomy and the Art of Caricature," *The Faces of Physiognomy: Interdisciplinary Approaches to Johann Caspar Lavater*, ed. Ellis Shookman (Columbia, SC: Camden House, 1993), 126–38

Hartley, Lucy, *Physiognomy and the Meaning of Expression in Nineteenth-Century Culture* (Cambridge: Cambridge University Press, 2001)

Haydon, Benjamin, *Lectures on Painting and Design*, 2 vols. (London: Longman, 1844–46)

Helsinger, Elizabeth K., *Rural Scenes and National Representations: Britain, 1815–1850* (Princeton: Princeton University Press, 1997)

Ruskin and the Art of the Beholder (Cambridge: Harvard University Press, 1982)

Herbert, Sandra, *Charles Darwin: Geologist* (Ithaca: Cornell University Press, 2005)

Heron-Allen, Edward, *Barnacles in Nature and in Myth* (London: Oxford University Press, 1928)

Herzog, Hans-Michael, ed., *The Art of the Flower: The Floral Still Life from the 17th to the 20th Century* (Zurich: Edition Stemmle, 1996)

Hewison, Robert, *John Ruskin: The Argument of the Eye* (Princeton: Princeton University Press, 1976)

Ruskin and Oxford: The Art of Education (Oxford: Clarendon, 1996)

Hilgartner, Stephen, "The Dominant View of Popularization: Conceptual Problems, Political Uses," *Social Studies of Science* 20 (1990): 519–39

Hilton, Tim, *John Ruskin: The Early Years* (New Haven: Yale University Press, 1985)

John Ruskin: The Later Years (New Haven: Yale University Press, 2000)

Holbeach, Henry [William Brighty Rands], "Mr. Darwin on Expression in Man and Animals," *Saint Paul's* 12 (1873): 190–211

Hooker, Joseph Dalton, *Flora Tasmaniae* (London: Reeve, 1860). Vol. III of *The Botany of the Antarctic Voyage of HM Discovery Ships Erebus and Terror, in the Years 1839–1843*, 3 vols., 1847–60

Hughes, Linda and Michael Lund, *The Victorian Serial* (Charlottesville: University Press of Virginia, 1991)

Hunnisett, Basil, *Steel-Engraved Book Illustration in England* (London: Scolar Press, 1980)

Hunt, John Dixon, *The Wider Sea: A Life of John Ruskin* (London: Dent, 1982)

Huxley, Thomas H., "Lectures on General Natural History. Lecture XII," *Medical Times and Gazette* 15 (1857): 238–41

"On the Border Territory Between the Animal and the Vegetable Kingdoms," *Macmillan's Magazine* 33 (1876): 373–84

Hyman, Stanley Edgar, *The Tangled Bank: Darwin, Marx, Frazer and Freud as Imaginative Writers* (New York: Atheneum, 1962)

Ivins, William, *Prints and Visual Communications* (London: Routledge, 1953)

Jackson, Christine, *Bird Etchings: The Illustrators and Their Books, 1655–1855* (Ithaca: Cornell University Press, 1985)

　Bird Illustrators: Some Artists in Early Lithography (London: Witherby, 1975)

　Prideaux John Selby: A Gentleman Naturalist (Northumberland: Spredden, 1992)

　Wood Engravings of Birds (London: Witherby, 1978)

Jackson, Christine E. and Maureen Lambourne, "Bayfield – John Gould's Unknown Colourer," *Archives of Natural History* 17 (1990): 189–200

Jann, Rosemary, "Darwin and the Anthropologists: Sexual Selection and its Discontents," *Victorian Studies* 37 (1994): 287–306

　"Evolutionary Physiognomy and Darwin's *Expression of the Emotions*," *Victorian Review* 18.2 (1992): 1–27

Janowitz, Anne, *England's Ruins: Poetic Purpose and the National Landscape* (Cambridge: Blackwell, 1990)

Jones, Caroline A. and Peter Galison, eds., *Picturing Science, Producing Art* (New York: Routledge, 1998)

Jones, Edgar Yoxall, *Father of Art Photography: O. G. Rejlander, 1813–1875* (Greenwich, CT: New York Graphic Society, 1973)

Jordanova, Ludmilla, *Sexual Visions: Images of Gender in Science and Medicine between the Eighteenth and Twentieth Centuries* (Madison: University of Wisconsin Press, 1989)

Jussim, Estelle, *Visual Communications and the Graphic Arts: Photographic Technologies in the Nineteenth Century* (New York: Bowker, 1974)

Kains-Jackson, Charles Philip, *Our Ancient Monuments and the Land Around Them* (London: Elliot Stock, 1880)

Kaye, Richard, *The Flirt's Tragedy: Desire Without End in Victorian and Edwardian Fiction* (Charlottesville: University Press of Virginia, 2002)

Kayser, Wolfgang, *The Grotesque in Art and Literature*, trans. Ulrich Weisstein (Bloomington: Indiana University Press, 1963)

Kemp, Martin, "'A Perfect and Faithful Record': Mind and Body in Medical Photography before 1900," *Beauty of Another Order: Photography in Science*, ed. Ann Thomas (New Haven: Yale University Press, 1997), 129–30

　The Science of Art: Optical Themes in Western Art from Brunelleschi to Seurat (New Haven: Yale University Press, 1990)

　Visualizations: The Nature Book of Art and Science (Berkeley: University of California Press, 2000)

Kim, Stephen S., *John Tyndall's Transcendental Materialism and the Conflict Between Religion and Science in Victorian England* (Lewiston, NY: Mellen, 1996)

Kingsley, Charles, *Glaucus; Or, The Wonders of the Shore* (London: Macmillan, 1855)

Kinnane, G. C., "A Popular Victorian Satire: 'Ginx's Baby' and its Reception," *Notes and Queries* 220 (1975): 116–17

Kirchoff, Frederick, "A Science Against Sciences: Ruskin's Floral Mythology," *Nature and the Victorian Imagination*, ed. U. C. Knoepflmacher and G. B. Tennyson (Berkeley: University of California Press, 1977), 246–58

Klonk, Charlotte, *Science and the Perception of Nature: British Landscape Art in the Late Eighteenth and Early Nineteenth Centuries* (New Haven: Yale University Press, 1996)

Knight, David, "Scientific Theory and Visual Language," *The Natural Science and the Arts: Aspects of Interaction from the Renaissance to the Twentieth Century*, Uppsala Studies in the History of Art 22, ed. Allan Ellenius (Uppsala: Almqvist, 1985), 106–24

    Zoological Illustration: An Essay Towards a History of Printed Zoological Pictures (Folkestone, Kent: Dawson, 1977)

Kohn, David, "The Aesthetic Construction of Darwin's Theory," *The Elusive Synthesis: Aesthetics and Science*, ed. Alfred I. Tauber (Dordrecht: Kluwer, 1996), 13–48

Krasner, James, *The Entangled Eye: Visual Perception and the Representation of Nature in Post-Darwinian Narrative* (New York: Oxford University Press, 1992)

Lambourne, Maureen, *The Art of Bird Illustration* (London: Wellfleet, 1990)

    John Gould – Bird Man (Milton Keynes: Royal Society for Nature Conservation, 1987)

    John Gould's Birds of Great Britain (London: Book Club Associates, 1980)

    "John Ruskin, John Gould and Ornithological Art," *Apollo* 126 n.s. (1987): 185–89

Landow, George P., *The Aesthetic and Critical Theories of John Ruskin* (Princeton: Princeton University Press, 1971)

    Victorian Types, Victorian Shadows: Biblical Typology in Victorian Literature, Art, and Thought (Boston: Routledge, 1980)

    William Holman Hunt and Typological Symbolism (New Haven: Yale University Press, 1979)

"The Latest Development of Darwinism," *London Quarterly Review* 57 (1882): 371–91

Latour, Bruno, "Drawing Things Together," *Representation in Scientific Practice*, ed. Michael Lynch and Steve Woolgar (Cambridge, MA: MIT Press, 1990), 19–68

    "How to Be Iconophilic in Art, Science, and Religion?" *Picturing Science, Producing Art*, ed. Caroline A. Jones and Peter Galison (New York: Routledge, 1998), 418–40

    "Visualization and Cognition: Thinking With Eyes and Hands," *Knowledge and Society* 6 (1986): 1–40

Latour, Bruno and Steve Woolgar, *Laboratory Life: The Social Construction of Scientific Facts* (London: Sage, 1979)

Lee, Vernon [Violet Paget] and Clementina Anstruther-Thomson, "Beauty and Ugliness," *Contemporary Review* 72 (1897): 544–69, 669–88

"Beauty and Ugliness" and Other Studies in Physiological Aesthetics (London: John Lane, 1912)

LeMahieu, D. L., *The Mind of William Paley: A Philosopher and His Age* (Lincoln, NE: University of Nebraska Press, 1976)

Lenoir, Timothy, "The Eye as Mathematician: Clinical Practice, Instrumentation, and Helmholtz's Construction of an Empiricist Theory of Vision," *Hermann von Helmholtz and the Foundations of Nineteenth-Century Science*, ed. David Cahan (Berkeley: University of California Press, 1994), 109–53

"Inscription Practices and the Materiality of Communication," *Inscribing Science: Scientific Texts and the Materiality of Communication* (Stanford: Stanford University Press, 1998), 1–19

Lenoir, Timothy, ed., *Inscribing Science: Scientific Texts and the Materiality of Communication* (Stanford: Stanford University Press, 1998)

Lever, Christopher, *They Dined on Eland: The Story of the Acclimatisation Societies* (London: Quiller, 1992)

Levine, George, "'And If It Be a Pretty Woman All the Better': Darwin and Sexual Selection," *Literature, Science, Psychoanalysis, 1830–1970: Essays in Honour of Gillian Beer*, ed. Helen Small and Trudi Tate (Oxford: Oxford University Press, 2003), 37–51

Darwin and the Novelists: Patterns of Science in Victorian Fiction (Cambridge: Harvard University Press, 1988)

Dying to Know: Scientific Epistemology and Narrative in Victorian England (Chicago: University of Chicago Press, 2002)

Levine, George, ed., *Aesthetics and Ideology* (New Brunswick: Rutgers University Press, 1994)

Lightman, Bernard, "The Story of Nature: Victorian Popularizers and Scientific Narrative," *Victorian Review* 25 (2000): 1–29

"'The Voices of Nature': Popularizing Victorian Science," *Victorian Science in Context*, ed. Bernard Lightman (Chicago: University of Chicago Press, 1997), 187–211

Lindley, John, *The Genera and Species of Orchidaceous Plants* (London: Ridgways, 1830–40)

The Vegetable Kingdom, 3rd edn. (London: Bradbury and Evans, 1853)

Lindley, Kenneth, *The Woodblock Engravers* (Newton Abbot: David and Charles, 1970)

Loudon, Jane, *The Entertaining Naturalist* [1843] (London: Bohn, 1850)

Lubbock, John, *British Wild Flowers Considered in Relation to Insects* (London: Macmillan, 1882)

"Common Wild Flowers Considered in Relation to Insects," *Nature* 10 (1874): 402–06, 422–26

"On the Preservation of Our Ancient National Monuments," *The Nineteenth Century* 1 (1877): 256–69

Lynch, Michael, and Steve Woolgar, eds., *Representation in Scientific Practice* (Cambridge: MIT Press, 1990)

Maidment, B. E., *Reading Popular Prints, 1790–1870* (Manchester: Manchester University Press, 1996)

"What Shall We Do with the Starving Baby? – Edward Jenkins and *Ginx's Baby*," *Literature and History* 6 (1980): 161–73

[Mann, R. J.], "Darwin on the Movements of Plants," *Edinburgh Review* 153(1881): 497–514

Marien, Mary Warner, *Photography and Its Critics: A Cultural History, 1839–1900* (Cambridge: Cambridge University Press, 1997)

Marshall, William E., *A Phrenologist Amongst the Todas* (London: Longmans, 1873)

Matthews, Oliver, *The Album of Carte-de-Visite and Cabinet Portrait Photographs, 1854–1914* (London: Reedminster, 1974)

McCulloch, Lou W., *Card Photographs, A Guide to Their History and Value* (Exton, PA: Schiffer, 1981)

McEvey, Allan, *John Gould's Contribution to British Art: A Note on its Authenticity* (Sydney: Australian Academy of the Humanities, 1973)

McKechnie, Sue, *British Silhouette Artists and Their Work, 1760–1860* (London: Sotheby Parke Bernet, 1978)

Meijer, Miriam Claude, *Race and Aesthetics in the Anthropology of Petrus Camper (1722–1789)* (Amsterdam: Rodopi, 1999)

Meisel, Martin, *Realizations: Narrative, Pictorial, and Theatrical Arts in Nineteenth-Century England* (Princeton: Princeton University Press, 1983)

Merrill, Lynn L., *The Romance of Victorian Natural History* (Oxford: Oxford University Press, 1989)

Meyer, Richard, ed., *Representing the Passions: Histories, Bodies, Visions* (Los Angeles: Getty Research Institute, 2003)

Miller, J. Hillis, *Illustration* (Cambridge: Harvard University Press, 1992)

Mitchell, Peter, *Themes in Art: Flowers* (London: Scala, 1992)

Mitchell, W. J. T., *The Last Dinosaur Book* (Chicago: University of Chicago Press, 1998)

Picture Theory: Essays on Verbal and Visual Representation (Chicago: University of Chicago Press, 1994)

Modiano, Raimonda, "The Legacy of the Picturesque: Landscape, Property, and the Ruin," *The Politics of the Picturesque: Literature, Landscape and Aesthetics since 1770*, ed. Stephen Copley and Peter Garside (Cambridge: Cambridge University Press, 1994), 196–219

Montagu, Jennifer, *The Expression of the Passions: The Origin and Influence of Charles Le Brun's "Conférence sur l'expression générale et particulière"* (New Haven: Yale University Press, 1994)

Moreau, L.-J., ed., *L'Art de Connaître les Hommes par la Physionomie* (Paris, 1820)

Morrell, Jack and Arnold Thackeray, *Gentlemen of Science* (Oxford: Oxford University Press, 1981)

Morton, Peter, *"The Busiest Man in England": Grant Allen and the Writing Trade, 1875–1900* (New York: Palgrave Macmillan, 2005)

Muir, Percy, *Victorian Illustrated Books* (London: Batsford, 1971)

Müller, Hermann, *The Fertilisation of Flowers*, trans. and ed. D'Arcy W. Thompson (London: Macmillan, 1883)

Myers, Greg, *Writing Biology: Texts in the Social Construction of Scientific Knowledge* (Madison: University of Wisconsin Press, 1990)

Newall, Christopher, "Ruskin and the Art of Drawing," *John Ruskin and the Victorian Eye* (New York: Abrams, 1993)

Newman, William A., "Darwin and Cirripedology," *Crustacean Issues* 8 (1993): 349–434

Noakes, Aubrey, *William Frith, Extraordinary Victorian Painter* (London: Jupiter, 1978)

Nochlin, Linda, and Martha Lucy, eds., *The Darwin Effect: Evolution and Nineteenth-Century Visual Culture*, spec. issue of *Nineteenth-Century Art Worldwide* 2.2 (2003), http://19thc-artworldwide.org/spring_03, accessed 28 Oct. 2005

Nunn, Pamela Gerrish, *Problem Pictures: Women and Men in Victorian Painting* (Aldershot: Scolar, 1995)

Oettermann, Stephen, *The Panorama: History of a Mass Medium*, trans. Deborah Lucas Schneider (New York: Zone, 1997)

Ogle, William, "Editor's Preface," to *Flowers and Their Unbidden Guests*, by Anton Kerner, trans. and ed. by William Ogle (London: Kegan Paul, 1878)

O'Gorman, Francis, "The Eagle and the Whale: John Ruskin's Argument with John Tyndall," *Time and Tide: Ruskin and Science*, ed. Michael Wheeler (London: Pilkington, 1996), 45–64

"Ruskin's Science of the 1870s: Science, Education, and the Nation," *Ruskin and the Dawn of the Modern*, ed. Dinah Birch (Oxford: Oxford University Press, 1999), 35–56

Ospovat, Dov, *The Development of Darwin's Theory: Natural History, Natural Theology, and Natural Selection, 1838–1859* (Cambridge: Cambridge University Press, 1981)

[Owen, Richard,] "Darwin on the Origin of Species," *Edinburgh Review* 111 (1860): 487–532

Lectures on the Comparative Anatomy and Physiology of the Invertebrate Animals, 2nd edn. (London: Longman, 1855)

Palmer, A. H., *The Life of Joseph Wolf, Animal Painter* (London: Longmans, 1895)

Paradis, James, "Darwin and Landscape," *Victorian Science and Victorian Values: Literary Perspectives*, ed. James Paradis and Thomas Postlewait (New Brunswick: Rutgers University Press, 1985), 85–110

"Satire and Science in Victorian Culture," *Victorian Science in Context*, ed. Bernard Lightman (Chicago: University of Chicago Press, 1997), 143–75

T. H. Huxley: Man's Place in Nature (Lincoln: University of Nebraska Press, 1978)

Parkes, Adam, "A Sense of Justice: Whistler, Ruskin, James, Impressionism," *Victorian Studies* 42 (2000): 593–629

Parris, Leslie, *The Pre-Raphaelites* (London: Tate Gallery, 1984)

Petherbridge, Deanna and Ludmilla Jordanova, *The Quick and the Dead: Artists and Anatomy* (Berkeley: University of California Press, 1997)

Pettigrew, J. Bell, *Design in Nature*, 3 vols. (London: Longmans, 1908)

Pevsner, Nikolaus, "Frith and the Irregular," *Architectural Review* 120 (1956): 191

Phillips, Adam, *Darwin's Worms: On Life Stories and Death Stories* (New York: Basic Books, 2000)

Philpotts, Trey, "Trevelyan, Treasury, and Circumlocution," *Dickens Studies Annual* 22 (1993): 283–301

"The Plough of the Animal World," *Spectator* 54 (22 Oct. 1881): 1334–36

Poignant, Roslyn, "Surveying the Field of View: The Making of the RAI Photographic Collection," *Anthropology and Photography, 1860–1920*, ed. Elizabeth Edwards (New Haven: Yale University Press, 1992), 42–73

Pointon, Marcia, "The Representation of Time in Painting: A Study of William Dyce's *Pegwell Bay: A Recollection of October 5th, 1858*," *Art History* 1 (1978): 99–103

  William Dyce, 1806–1864: A Critical Biography (Oxford: Clarendon, 1979)

Poynting, Jeremy, "John Edward Jenkins and the Imperial Conscience," *Journal of Commonwealth Literature* 21 (1986): 211–21

Prodger, Phillip, *An Annotated Catalogue of the Illustrations of Human and Animal Expression from the Collection of Charles Darwin* (Lewiston, NY: Mellen, 1998)

  "Concordance of Illustrations," *The Expression of the Emotions in Man and Animals*, ed. Paul Ekman (New York: Oxford University Press, 1998), 417–23

  "Illustration as Strategy in Charles Darwin's *The Expression of the Emotions in Man and Animals*," *Inscribing Science: Scientific Texts and the Materiality of Communication*, ed. Timothy Lenoir (Stanford: Stanford University Press, 1998), 140–81

  "Photography and *The Expression of the Emotions*," *The Expression of the Emotions in Man and Animals*, ed. Paul Ekman (New York: Oxford University Press, 1998), 399–410

  "Rejlander, Darwin, and the Evolution of 'Ginx's Baby,'" *History of Photography* 23 (1999): 260–68

Rehbock, Philip F., "The Victorian Aquarium in Ecological and Social Perspective," *Oceanography: The Past*, ed. Mary Sears and Daniel Merriman (New York: Springer-Verlag, 1980), 522–39

Reinikka, Merle A., *A History of the Orchid* (Coral Gables, FL: University of Miami Press, 1972)

Richards, Evelleen, "Darwin and the Descent of Woman," *The Wider Domain of Evolutionary Thought*, ed. David Oldroyd and Ian Langham (Dordrecht: Reidel, 1983), 57–111

Ritvo, Harriet, *The Animal Estate: The English and Other Creatures in the Victorian Age* (Cambridge: Harvard University Press, 1987)

Roach, Joseph R., *The Player's Passion: Studies in the Science of Acting* (Ann Arbor: University of Michigan Press, 1993)

Robson, John M., "The Fiat and Finger of God: The Bridgewater Treatises," *Victorian Faith in Crisis: Essays on Continuity and Change in Nineteenth-Century Religious Belief*, ed. Richard J. Helmstadter and Bernard Lightman (Stanford: Stanford University Press, 1990), 71–125

Ross, Frederic R., "Philip Gosse's *Omphalos*, Edmund Gosse's *Father and Son*, and Darwin's Theory of Natural Selection," *Isis* 68 (1977): 85–96

Rowlinson, J. S., "The Theory of Glaciers," *Notes and Records of the Royal Society of London* 26 (1971): 189–204

"Tyndall's Work on Glaciology and Geology," *John Tyndall: Essays on a Natural Philosopher*, ed. W. H. Brock, N. D. McMillan, and R. C. Mollan (Dublin: Royal Dublin Society, 1981), 113–28

Rudwick, Martin J. S., "The Emergence of a Visual Language for Geological Science, 1760–1840," *History of Science* 14 (1976): 149–95

The Great Devonian Controversy (Chicago: University of Chicago Press, 1985)

Scenes From Deep Time: Early Pictorial Representations of the Prehistoric World (Chicago: University of Chicago Press, 1992)

Rupke, Nicolaas A., *Richard Owen: Victorian Naturalist* (New Haven: Yale University Press, 1994)

Ruskin, John, *The Ruskin Family Letters*, ed. Van Akin Burd, 2 vols. (Ithaca: Cornell University Press, 1973)

Ruskin in Italy: Letters to His Parents, 1845, ed. Harold I. Shapiro (Oxford: Clarendon, 1972)

The Works of John Ruskin, Library Edition, ed. E. T. Cook and Alexander Wedderburn, 39 vols. (London: George Allen, 1903–1912)

Russett, Cynthia Eagle, *Sexual Science: The Victorian Construction of Womanhood* (Cambridge: Harvard University Press, 1989)

Sauer, Gordon C., *John Gould, The Bird Man: Associates and Subscribers* (Mansfield Centre, CT: Martino, 1995)

John Gould, The Bird Man: Bibliography 2 (Mansfield Centre, CT: Martino, 1996)

John Gould, The Bird Man: A Chronology and Bibliography (London: Sotheran, 1982)

Saunders, Gill, *Picturing Plants: An Analytical History of Botanical Illustration* (Berkeley: University of California Press, 1995)

Sawyer, Paul L., "Ruskin and Tyndall: The Poetry of Matter and the Poetry of Spirit," *Victorian Science and Victorian Values: Literary Perspectives*, ed. James Paradis and Thomas Postlewait (1981; New Brunswick, NJ: Rutgers University Press, 1985), 217–46

Ruskin's Poetic Argument: The Design of the Major Works (Ithaca: Cornell University Press, 1985)

Schaffer, Simon, "The Leviathan of Parsonstown: Literary Technology and Scientific Representation," *Inscribing Science: Scientific Texts and the Materiality of Communication*, ed. Timothy Lenoir (Stanford: Stanford University Press, 1998), 182–222

Schneider, Norbert, "The Early Floral Still Life," *The Art of the Flower: The Floral Still Life from the 17th to the 20th Century*, ed. Hans-Michael Herzog (Zurich: Edition Stemmle, 1996), 15–21

"Science and Superstition," *Punch* 64 (18 Jan. 1873): 21

Scourse, Nicolette, *The Victorians and Their Flowers* (London: Croom Helm, 1983)

"Sea-Gardens," *Household Words* 14 (1856): 241–45

Seaton, Beverly, "Considering the Lilies: Ruskin's 'Proserpina' and Other Victorian Flower Books," *Victorian Studies* 28 (1984–85): 255–82

   The Language of Flowers: A History (Charlottesville: University Press of Virginia, 1995)

Secord, James A., "Nature's Fancy: Charles Darwin and the Breeding of Pigeons," *Isis* 72 (1981): 162–86

   Victorian Sensation: The Extraordinary Publication, Reception, and Secret Authorship of Vestiges of the Natural History of Creation (Chicago: University of Chicago Press, 2000)

Shanes, Eric, *Turner's Picturesque Views in England and Wales, 1825–1838* (New York: Harper and Row, 1979)

Shapin, Steven, "Phrenological Knowledge and the Social Structure of Early Nineteenth-Century Edinburgh," *Annals of Science* 32 (1975): 219–43

   "The Politics of Observation: Cerebral Anatomy and Social Interests in the Edinburgh Phrenology Disputes," *On the Margins of Science: The Social Construction of Rejected Knowledge*, ed. Roy Wallis (Keele: University of Keele, 1979), 139–78

   A Social History of Truth (Chicago: University of Chicago Press, 1994)

Shapin, Steven, and Simon Schaffer, *Leviathan and the Air Pump: Hobbes, Boyle, and the Experimental Life* (Princeton: Princeton University Press, 1985)

Shookman, Ellis, ed., *The Faces of Physiognomy: Interdisciplinary Approaches to Johann Caspar Lavater* (Columbia, SC: Camden House, 1993)

Shrimpton, Nicholas, "Ruskin and the Aesthetes," *Ruskin and the Dawn of the Modern*, ed. Dinah Birch (Oxford: Oxford University Press, 1999), 131–51

Shteir, Ann B., *Cultivating Women, Cultivating Science: Flora's Daughters and Botany in England, 1760–1860* (Baltimore: Johns Hopkins University Press, 1996)

Sinnema, Peter W., *Dynamics of the Pictured Page: Representing the Nation in the Illustrated London News* (Aldershot: Ashgate, 1998)

Sitwell, Sacheverell, *Fine Bird Books 1700–1900* (New York: Atlantic Monthly, 1990)

Smith, Jonathan, "The Cuckoo's Contested History," *Trends in Ecology and Evolution* 14 (1999): 415

   "Darwin's Barnacles, Dickens's *Little Dorrit*, and the Social Uses of Victorian Seaside Studies," *LIT: Literature, Interpretation, Theory* 10 (2000): 327–47

   Fact and Feeling: Baconian Science and the Nineteenth-Century Literary Imagination (Madison: University of Wisconsin Press, 1994)

   "Grant Allen, Physiological Aesthetics, and the Dissemination of Darwin's Botany," *Science Serialized: Representations of the Sciences in Nineteenth-Century Periodicals*, ed. Geoffrey Cantor and Sally Shuttleworth (Cambridge: MIT Press, 2004), 285–306

"John Gould, Charles Darwin, and the Picturing of Natural Selection," *The Book Collector* 50 (2001): 51–76

"Philip Gosse and the Varieties of Natural Theology," *Reshaping Christianity: Innovation and Pluralization in the Nineteenth Century*, ed. Linda Woodhead (Aldershot: Ashgate, 2001), 251–62

Smith, Lindsay, *The Politics of Focus: Women, Children, and Nineteenth-Century Photography* (Manchester: Manchester University Press, 1998)

Victorian Photography, Painting and Poetry: The Enigma of Visibility in Ruskin, Morris and the Pre-Raphaelites (Cambridge: Cambridge University Press, 1995)

Spencer, Stephanie, "O. G. Rejlander: Art Studies," *British Photography in the Nineteenth Century: The Fine Art Tradition*, ed. Mike Weaver (Cambridge: Cambridge University Press, 1989), 121–31

O. G. Rejlander: Photography as Art (Ann Arbor: UMI Research Press, 1985)

Spielmann, M. H., *The History of "Punch"* (London: Cassell, 1895)

Stafford, Barbara Maria, *Body Criticism: Imaging the Unseen in Enlightenment Art and Medicine* (Cambridge: MIT Press, 1991)

Voyage Into Substance: Art, Science, Nature and the Illustrated Travel Account, 1760–1840 (Cambridge: MIT Press, 1984)

Stapleton, Julia, "James Fitzjames Stephen: Liberalism, Patriotism, and English Liberty," *Victorian Studies* 41 (1998): 243–63

Stedman, Gesa, *Stemming the Torrent: Expression and Control in the Victorian Discourses on Emotions, 1830–1872* (Aldershot: Ashgate, 2002)

Stein, Roger B., *John Ruskin and Aesthetic Thought in America, 1840–1900* (Cambridge: Harvard University Press, 1967)

[Stephen, James Fitzjames,] "The License of Modern Novelists," *Edinburgh Review* 106 (1857): 124–56

Stewart, Balfour and P. G. Tait, *The Unseen Universe, or, Physical Speculations on a Future State*, 3rd edn. (New York: Macmillan, 1875)

Stott, Rebecca, *Darwin and the Barnacle* (New York: Norton, 2003)

"Darwin's Barnacles: Mid-Century Victorian Natural History and the Marine Grotesque," *Transactions and Encounters: Science and Culture in the Nineteenth Century*, ed. Roger Luckhurst and Josephine McDonagh (Manchester: Manchester University Press, 2001), 151–81.

"'Through a Glass Darkly': Aquarium Colonies and Nineteenth-Century Narratives of Marine Monstrosity," *Gothic Studies* 2 (2000): 305–27

Sulloway, Frank, "The *Beagle* Collection of Darwin's Finches (Geospizinae)," *Bulletin of the British Museum (Natural History) Zoology Series* 43 (1982): 361–90

"Darwin and His Finches: The Evolution of a Legend," *Journal of the History of Biology* 15 (1982): 1–53

"Darwin's Conversion: The *Beagle* Voyage and its Aftermath," *Journal of the History of Biology* 15 (1982): 325–96

Sussman, Herbert, *Fact Into Figure: Typology in Carlyle, Ruskin, and the Pre-Raphaelite Brotherhood* (Columbus: Ohio State University Press, 1979)

Swain, Joseph, "Charles Henry Bennett," *Good Words* 29 (1888): 589–94

Tagg, John, *The Burden of Representation: Essays on Photographies and Histories* (Amherst: University of Massachusetts Press, 1988)

Taylor, George, *Players and Performances in the Victorian Theatre* (Manchester: Manchester University Press, 1989)

Taylor, J. E., *Flowers: Their Origin, Shapes, Perfumes, and Colours*, 3rd edn. (London: Bogue, 1885)

The Sagacity and Morality of Plants (London: Chatto & Windus, 1884)

Taylor, John, *A Dream of England: Landscape, Photography and the Tourist's Imagination* (Manchester: Manchester University Press, 1994)

Thomas, David Wayne, *Cultivating Victorians: Liberal Culture and the Aesthetic*. (Philadelphia: University of Pennsylvania Press, 2004)

Thompson, D'Arcy Wentworth, *On Growth and Form* (Cambridge: Cambridge University Press, 1917)

Thompson, John V., *Zoological Researches and Illustrations, 1828–1834* (London: Society for the Bibliography of Natural History, 1968)

Thwaite, Ann, *Edmund Gosse: A Literary Landscape, 1849–1928* (London: Secker and Warburg, 1984)

Topham, Jonathan R., "Beyond the 'Common Context': The Production and Reading of the Bridgewater Treatises," *Isis* 89 (1998): 233–62

Travis, John F., *The Rise of the Devon Seaside Resorts, 1750–1900* (Exeter: University of Exeter Press, 1993)

Tree, Isabella, *The Ruling Passion of John Gould* (New York: Grove Weidenfeld, 1991)

Trodd, Colin, Paul Barlow and David Amigoni, eds., *Victorian Culture and the Idea of the Grotesque* (Aldershot: Ashgate, 1999)

Tufte, Edward R., *Envisioning Information* (Cheshire, CT: Graphics Press, 1990)

The Visual Display of Quantitative Information (Cheshire, CT: Graphics Press, 1983)

Visual Explanations: Images and Quantities, Evidence and Narrative (Cheshire, CT: Graphics Press, 1997)

Turner, Frank M., *Contesting Cultural Authority: Essays in Victorian Intellectual Life* (Cambridge: Cambridge University Press, 1993)

Turner, R. Steven, *In the Eye's Mind: Vision and the Helmholtz–Hering Controversy* (Princeton: Princeton University Press, 1994)

Twyman, Michael, *Lithography 1800–1850* (London: Oxford University Press, 1970)

Ulin, Donald, "A Clerisy of Worms in Darwin's Inverted World," *Victorian Studies* 35 (1992): 295–308

van Wyhe, John, *The History of Phrenology on the Web*, 18 Feb. 2005 http://pages.britishlibrary.net/phrenology/

Phrenology and the Origins of Victorian Scientific Naturalism (Aldershot: Ashgate, 2004)

Voskuil, Lynn M., "Feeling Public: Sensation Theater, Commodity Culture, and the Victorian Public Sphere," *Victorian Studies* 44 (2002): 245–74

[Wace, Henry,] "Darwin on Earth-Worms," *Quarterly Review* 153 (1882): 179–202

Wakeman, Geoffrey, *Victorian Book Illustration: The Technical Revolution* (Newton Abbot: David and Charles, 1973)

Wallace, Alfred R., "Humming-Birds," *Fraser's* 28 o.s./22 n.s. (1877): 773–91
Review of *Vignettes from Nature*, by Grant Allen, *Nature* 25 (1882): 38

Walton, John K., *The English Seaside Resort: A Social History, 1750–1914* (New York: St. Martin's, 1983)

Warner, Malcolm, *The Victorians: British Painting, 1837–1901* (New York: Abrams, 1996)

[Warren, Samuel,] "An Old Contributor at the Sea-Side," *Blackwood's Edinburgh Magazine* 78 (1855): 478–97, 562–85

Wechsler, Judith, *A Human Comedy: Physiognomy and Caricature in 19th Century Paris* (Chicago: University of Chicago Press, 1982)

W[eld]., C. R., "Humming-Birds," *Fraser's* 65 (1862): 457–68

West, Shearer, *The Image of the Actor: Verbal and Visual Representation in the Age of Garrick and Kemble* (London: Pinter, 1991)

Wheeler, Michael, "Ruskin Among the Ruins: Tradition and the Temple," *The Lamp of Memory: Ruskin, Tradition and Architecture*, ed. Michael Wheeler and Nigel Whiteley (Manchester: Manchester University Press, 1992), 77–97

Wheeler, Michael, ed., *Ruskin and Environment: The Storm-Cloud of the Nineteenth Century* (Manchester University Press, 1995)
Time and Tide: Ruskin and Science (London: Pilkington, 1996)

Whiteway, Michael, *Christopher Dresser 1834–1904* (Milan: Skira, 2001)

Whitley, Richard, "Knowledge Producers and Knowledge Acquirers: Popularisation as a Relation between Scientific Fields and Their Publics," *Expository Science: Forms and Functions of Popularisation*, ed. Terry Shinn and Richard Whitley (Dordrecht: Reidel, 1985), 3–28

W[ilson], A[ndrew], "Can we Separate Animals from Plants?" *Cornhill* 37 (1878): 336–50

Wilton, Andrew, Introduction, *Turner's Picturesque Views in England and Wales, 1825–1838*, ed. Eric Shanes (New York: Harper and Row, 1979)

Winsor, Mary P., "Barnacle Larvae in the Nineteenth Century: A Case Study in Taxonomic Theory," *Journal of the History of Medicine and Allied Sciences* 24 (1969): 294–309

Winter, Allison, *Mesmerized: Powers of Mind in Victorian Britain* (Chicago: University of Chicago Press, 1998)

Woldbye, Vibeke, ed., *Flowers Into Art: Floral Motifs in European Painting and Decorative Arts* (The Hague: SDU, 1991)

Wood, Christopher, *Victorian Panorama: Paintings of Victorian Life* (London: Faber and Faber, 1976)

Wood, J. G., *The New Illustrated Natural History* [1853] (London: Routledge, 1855)

Wood, T. W., "The Courtship of Birds," *The Student and Intellectual Observer* 5 (1870–71): 113–25
"The 'Eyes' of the Argus Pheasant," *The Field* 35 (28 May 1870): 457

"Plumage of the Argus Pheasant and Bird of Paradise," *The Field* 34 (26 June 1869): 538

Wright, Thomas, *The Celt, The Roman, and The Saxon: A History of the Early Inhabitants of Britain*, 2nd edn. (London: Hall, 1861)

Uriconium: A Historical Account of the Ancient Roman City, and of the Excavations made upon its Site at Wroxeter, in Shropshire (London: Longmans, Green, 1872)

Wanderings of an Antiquary; Chiefly Upon the Traces of the Romans in Britain (London: Nichols, 1854)

Yeazell, Ruth Bernard, "Do It or Dorrit," *Novel* 25 (1991): 33–49

Fictions of Modesty: Women and Courtship in the English Novel (Chicago: University of Chicago Press, 1991)

"Nature's Courtship Plot in Darwin and Ellis," *Yale Journal of Criticism* 2 (1989): 33–53

Yeo, Richard R., "The Principle of Plenitude and Natural Theology in Nineteenth-Century Britain," *British Journal for the History of Science* 19 (1986): 263–82

Young, Robert, *Darwin's Metaphor: Nature's Place in Victorian Culture* (Cambridge: Cambridge University Press, 1985)

Mind, Brain and Adaptation in the Nineteenth Century: Cerebral Localization and its Biological Context from Gall to Ferrier (Oxford: Clarendon, 1970)

Index

Page numbers in italics indicate illustrations.

CAMBRIDGE STUDIES IN NINETEENTH-CENTURY
LITERATURE AND CULTURE

General editor
Gillian Beer, *University of Cambridge*

Titles published

1. The Sickroom in Victorian Fiction: The Art of Being Ill
Miriam Bailin, *Washington University*

2. Muscular Christianity: Embodying the Victorian Age
edited by Donald E. Hall, *California State University, Northridge*

3. Victorian Masculinities: Manhood and Masculine Poetics in Early Victorian
Literature and Art
Herbert Sussman, *Northeastern University, Boston*

4. Byron and the Victorians
Andrew Elfenbein, *University of Minnesota*

5. Literature in the Marketplace: Nineteenth-Century British Publishing
and the Circulation of Books
edited by John O. Jordan, *University of California, Santa Cruz*
and Robert L. Patten, *Rice University, Houston*

6. Victorian Photography, Painting and Poetry
Lindsay Smith, *University of Sussex*

7. Charlotte Brontë and Victorian Psychology
Sally Shuttleworth, *University of Sheffield*

8. The Gothic Body:
Sexuality, Materialism and Degeneration at the *Fin de Siècle*
Kelly Hurley, *University of Colorado at Boulder*

9. Rereading Walter Pater
William F. Shuter, *Eastern Michigan University*

10. Remaking Queen Victoria
edited by Margaret Homans, *Yale University*
and Adrienne Munich, *State University of New York, Stony Brook*

11. Disease, Desire, and the Body in Victorian Women's Popular Novels
Pamela K. Gilbert, *University of Florida*

12. Realism, Representation, and the Arts in Nineteenth-Century Literature
Alison Byerly, *Middlebury College, Vermont*

13. Literary Culture and the Pacific
Vanessa Smith, *University of Sydney*

14. Professional Domesticity in the Victorian Novel: Women, Work and Home
Monica F. Cohen